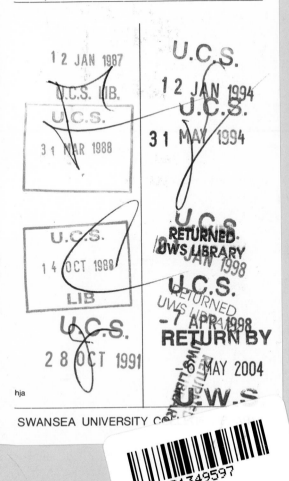

The Foundations of
Macroeconomic and
Monetary Theory

The Foundations of
Macroeconomic and
Monetary Theory

P. J. N. SINCLAIR

OXFORD UNIVERSITY PRESS

1983

Oxford University Press, Walton Street, Oxford OX2 6DP

London Glasgow New York Toronto
Delhi Bombay Calcutta Madras Karachi
Kuala Lumpur Singapore Hong Kong Tokyo
Nairobi Dar es Salaam Cape Town
Melbourne Auckland
and associated companies in
Beirut Berlin Ibadan Mexico City Nicosia

Oxford is a trade mark of Oxford University Press

Published in the United States
by Oxford University Press, New York

British Library Cataloguing in Publication Data

Sinclair, P. J. N.
 The foundations of macroeconomic and monetary
 theory.
 I. Macroeconomics
 I. Title
 339   HB172.5

ISBN 0-19-877189-4
ISBN 0-19-877190-8 Pbk

Library of Congress Cataloging in Publication Data

Sinclair, P. J. N.
 The foundations of macroeconomic and monetary theory.

 Bibliography: p.
 Includes index.
 1. Macroeconomics.   2. Money.   3. Keynesian economics.
I. Title.
HB172.5.S55   1983   339.5   83-2351
ISBN 0-19-877189-4
ISBN 0-19-877190-8 (pbk.)

Typeset by Joshua Associates, Oxford
and printed by Thomson Litho Ltd., East Kilbride

Acknowledgements

I am most grateful for valued advice and comments to, among others, David Begg, David Currie, Nicholas Dimsdale, Walter Eltis, Richard Smethurst, and unnamed readers for Oxford University Press. I owe an especial debt of gratitude to John Flemming, who went through a draft of the text with minute care. He rescued me from error or obscurity at numerous points. Although I claim full responsibility for any surviving or new errors, the reader may be consoled by the fact that the criticisms of John Flemming and others have led to great improvements. Andrew Schuller of Oxford University Press has been unfailingly generous and patient.

I should also like to thank Max Corden, Max Hartwell, Sir John Hicks, and Francis Seton. I was very privileged to be taught economics by them. Whatever merits this book has are due in no small part to their example. Many colleagues have helped to frame my thoughts, in both discussions and their written work. Such a list would be enormous; to name just a few, in addition to those already mentioned, I am particularly grateful to Tony Courakis, Avinash Dixit, James Mirrlees, Keizo Nagatani, Thomas Sargent, and Joseph Stiglitz. This book began as a course of first-year graduate lectures at Oxford on Macroeconomic and Monetary Theory. I wish to thank my many graduate and undergraduate pupils over the years. They have deepened my enthusiasm for the subject, and helped me to sharpen my perceptions of it. My thanks are due, also, to the Principal and Fellows of Brasenose College, Oxford, for a generous contribution towards the cost of typing.

My greatest debt is to Shelagh Hefferman. Her help has been absolutely invaluable. She has checked and corrected the typescript, the algebra, and the diagrams; she has queried the subject matter and the exposition at countless points where it was faulty; she has brought order to my chaotic notation; and she has constructed the bibliography. I dare not think how much longer the book would have taken to appear but for her unstinting help.

Contents

List of Figures

List of Tables

Introduction

Macroeconomics is the study of economic aggregates. Its existence as a distinct and unified subject begins with the publication in 1936 of *The General Theory of Interest, Employment and Money* by John Maynard Keynes. Its origins can be traced back much earlier, to the separate topics which it combines: the theories of interest, general equilibrium, money, distribution, growth, and economic fluctuations. Yet it is Keynes who offers us the grand perspective on these issues. Keynes in fact provoked more questions than he answered. Since 1936, there have been six major programmes of research in macroeconomic theory. These are:

(1) to provide a choice-theoretic basis for the various macroeconomic relations postulated by Keynes and developed by later writers;
(2) to integrate the monetary and real elements of macroeconomic theory;
(3) to integrate the elements of aggregate supply with those of aggregate demand;
(4) to reconcile Keynesian macroeconomic theory as closely as possible with general equilibrium theory, and to identify the points at which the two diverge;
(5) to endogenize the stock of capital, which for Keynes had been a parameter; and
(6) to endogenize expectations, which Keynes had again treated as a parameter.

Much of the early progress in this great enterprise was made by Hicks (162, 166), particularly in programmes 2 and 4. It was Harrod who first tackled 5 (147). Among many scholars who developed macroeconomic theory in the 1950s, four names stand out: Friedman, for work on 1 and 6 (121, 125); Patinkin, 2, 3, and 4 (247); Solow, 5 (304); and Tobin, especially on 1 and 2 (319, 320). The 1960s saw the sowing of the seeds of two ideas that were to dominate macroeconomic theory in the 1970s; Clower's concept of quantity rationing constraints in disequilibrium (60), and Muth's concept of rational expectations (228). This book has two overriding objectives. One is to report the central findings of research in these six programmes to date, in an analytical and coherent fashion. The early chapters of the book, particularly chapters 1 and 2, provide the choice-theoretic foundations that underlie the macroeconomic behaviour of households and producers. Chapter 7 sets out to integrate aggregate supply with aggregate demand, and the real and monetary aspects of macroeconomic theory. It also builds upon the analysis of earlier chapters to provide an integrated framework for studying rationing models of disequilibrium. It is chapter 10 that explores the consequences of endogenizing the capital stock, in the setting of growth theory; and adaptive and rational expectations, the fruit of programme 6, are examined in numerous contexts (above all, chapters 1 and 8).

The book's second overriding objective is to present a systematic account of major topics in both macroeconomic theory and monetary theory. Chapters 1–4, 7, and 9 constitute a book on macroeconomic theory; chapters 5 to 8 inclusive comprise a self-contained book on the theory of money. Chapter 7, entitled 'The

Aggregate Economy', is the core of the whole book, which these two parts have in common. It is final-year undergraduates for whom the book is primarily designed; they might be undertaking courses in either macroeconomic theory, or money, or both. But it is also intended to be of use to graduates studying these subjects, and to fellow economists. Furthermore, the fact that ideas and models are explained and assembled step by step, with little use of formal mathematics, should make the book accessible to second-year undergraduates. At the end of each chapter, the reader will find a summary of the frequently-used notation.

	Real elements	*Common elements*	*Monetary elements*
Foundations	ch. 1 (personal sector) ch. 2 (corporate sector) ch. 3 (government sector) ch. 4 (overseas sector)		ch. 5 (demand for money) ch. 6 (supply of money)
Aggregate economy: short run		ch. 7 (aggregate economy)	
Long-run analysis	ch. 9 (growth theory)		ch. 8 (optimal monetary policy in the long run)

FIG. I. The structure of the book

The structure of the book may be illustrated as in Figure I. There are nine chapters in all. The first four are concerned with the four major sectors of the economy. The personal sector is covered in chapter 1, while chapter 2 deals with the corporate sector and chapter 3 with the government. The overseas sector is the subject of chapter 4. These four chapters concentrate on the elements that together constitute total aggregate demand. In a sense therefore, chapters 1-4 start from the Keynesian social accounting identity $Y = C + I + G + X - M$. They examine each of the variables that appear on the right-hand side of that equation in turn.

The economic role of the personal and corporate sectors is not limited, however, to demand. Households supply labour and other factors of production. Producers supply goods. Consequently, chapter 1 analyses the personal sector's supply of factors, in addition to its demand for goods. In chapter 2, producers' demand for new capital goods is studied alongside their demand for labour and their output of goods. This approach has the virtue of giving a neater classification in sociological terms. Far more important, there is a powerful economic logic to it. It has been conventional for supply and demand decisions to be studied in isolation from each other. The unfortunate consequence of this is that the student learns to treat these subjects quite separately. He ignores the crucial links between, for example, the household's labour supply, portfolio and consumption decisions. This leads him into inconsistency and error. The proper starting point for *all* household decisions is the maximization of expected lifetime utility subject to an intertemporal budget restraint. Consumption spending, labour supply and portfolio behaviour all emerge from this common basis of optimization. What distinguishes the various theories of consumption is simply the variation in the set of assumptions about the consumer's objectives or environment that govern the optimization decision. Similarly, the theories of investment, employment, production and pricing—for inputs and outputs alike—descend from the *producer's* optimization decision. This is illustrated in chapter 2. There is a supply aspect in chapters 3 and 4 as well. Chapter 3 examines why governments supply the goods they do, and explores the motives for and the effects of redistributive taxation. International factor movements form part of the subject-matter of chapter 4.

The first four chapters deal primarily with *real* rather than *monetary* issues. Chapter 1 provides a skeletal account of the demand of money, as a by-product of the integrated approach to household behaviour; chapter 2 touches at several points upon the impact that financial variables have on the corporate sector; and in chapter 4, money is seen to play a critical role influencing payments and the exchange rate. But it is the real side of the macroeconomy which is the primary focus of these four chapters. Monetary analysis is, on the whole, incidental and peripheral. By contrast, in chapter 5 money is the centrepiece of attention. Chapter 5 examines the demand for money, and chapter 6 its supply. Chapter 5 contains a detailed analysis of transaction costs and asset-price uncertainty, and how each of these helps to determine the demand for money. Chapter 6 presents a simple theory of bank behaviour, based once again on the principles of optimization, and then proceeds to explore the role played by the Central Bank in the determination of the money supply. Taken together, chapters 5 and 6 form the basic elements for the theory of money.

Chapter 7 is both real *and* monetary. The real and monetary elements of previous chapters are brought together to provide an aggregate short-run model of the macroeconomy. The chapter starts with equilibrium. The effects of parameter disturbances, such as changes in tastes, technology, government spending and taxation, and the money supply, are subjected to scrutiny. Real balance effects on factor supply and commodity demand are considered; the classical neutrality propositions about money are demonstrated; and the rational expectations analysis of behaviour by individual economic agents, considered in earlier chapters, is extended.

After this point is reached in chapter 7, equilibrium gives way to disequilibrium. Chapters 1 and 2 had already examined the effects of quantity rationing upon households and producers separately. Various types of interactive spillover effects of disequilibrium are now considered in a simple aggregate model. When the consequences of price rigidities are explored, the traditional Keynesian model emerges as one of several possible disequilibrium regimes. The chapter continues with an analysis of unemployment, inflation, and the links (or absence of links) between the two. In the last two chapters, discussion moves from the short run to the long run. Chapter 8 addresses the issue of optimum monetary policy in the long run, while chapter 9 presents the central aspects of the theory of economic growth. Chapter 8 is monetary and chapter 9 is real.

Many economic textbooks, above all books on macroeconomic and monetary topics, are inclined to present arguments in a pre-digested form. The details of models are sacrificed for ease of reading; assumptions are often implicit or unstated. This book departs from tradition in this respect. The reader, particularly the undergraduate reader, is asked kindly if he will bear with what may be a rather unfamiliar style of writing. But there is a purpose behind it. Every chapter contains a basic model; some contain more than one. The models consist of sets of assumptions. The assumptions provide a convenient starting point for answering questions on each subject. But the answers are often no more general than the assumptions that imply them. In economics, everything is likely to depend on everything else. The answer to most questions is 'It all depends'. Prudence and intellectual honesty both require one to state the assumptions that underlie economic reasoning. Far from asserting anything about what the world is like (where they would often fail lamentably), the assumptions act as an admission of the narrowness of the results established, and as an invitation—a challenge—to widen them. So they are an excellent way of organizing one's thoughts on each subject. In later sections of each chapter, the assumptions of the basic models are relaxed. What follows from the removal or alteration of assumptions may vary from minor qualifications to the results, to complete breakdown of the analysis.

Lastly, a word of apology to anyone hoping to find a detailed treatment of empirical work on the subjects embraced in this book. He will, I fear, be disappointed. The book does contain some references to empirical findings, but space prevents anything but an exiguous treatment, and on the great majority of topics covered, the focus of the book is exclusively theoretical. Even on theoretical material, moreover, it would be wrong to suggest that this book is fully comprehensive. Several topics in macroeconomic theory are covered only briefly, and several others (such as the role of natural resources, or the technical aspects of the aggregation problem) hardly appear at all. It would be impossible to do full justice to every aspect of macroeconomic and monetary theory in ten volumes, let alone one.

Chapter 1

The Personal Sector

The first macroeconomic relationship that the student learns is, as we have observed already, probably the equation $Y = C + I + G + X - M$. A society's aggregate income equals the sum of: consumption spending; investment spending; government spending; and the surplus of exports over imports. Consumption is the first term he encounters. It is not just the first. It is the largest, too. Consumers' expenditure accounts for between three-fifths and three-quarters of national income in most economies.

In Keynesian models, consumption plays a major role in determining the level of income. It does this in two ways. First, how consumption varies with income—the marginal propensity to consume—governs, or helps to govern, the size of the multiplier. Second, 'autonomous consumption', which is the level consumption would fall to if income were zero, is a part of total autonomous spending on home-produced goods (call this TAS). In the simplest linear systems, aggregate income equals the product of TAS and the multiplier. Short-run Keynesian models of the aggregate economy that develop from this idea, as well as non-Keynesian models which do not, form the subject matter of much of chapter 7.

In models which differ from the Keynesian account by assuming that markets clear, it is saving rather than consumption that helps to sustain an economy's output. The more consumed, the less invested. The less invested, the smaller next period's stocks of capital, and the lower the economy's capacity to supply output. The long-run effects of saving in such models are among the topics considered in chapter 9. In equilibrium models of this kind, the level of output is influenced by the aggregate supply of labour. For a given population, this in turn depends upon households' willingness to supply labour, in time and effort. Finally, the demand for assets in general, and for money in particular, is a major element in most macroeconomic models. It often helps to set the price level of goods, for a given supply of money. It may also influence interest rates, output and employment.

Consumption, saving, labour supply, the demand for money: each of these is central to macroeconomic analysis. Each is a different aspect of the economic behaviour of households. This gives them a common sociological basis. More than this, *they have a common foundation in economic theory*. They can be, and really should be, treated as distinct but related outcomes of the process of optimization by households. Households' freedom to make choices may of course be circumscribed in various ways, as we shall see. But what such restrictions mean is best understood in contrast to what happens when they are absent.

The natural place to start our analysis of the macroeconomy is with the behaviour of society's personal sector. Attention is accordingly directed in this chapter to the economic decisions undertaken by individuals and households. We start with an integrated analysis of spending, working, saving, and lending decisions over an individual's lifetime. Initially, in section I, the framework is restricted to a simplifying set of assumptions. The purpose of this is not to describe reality but to form a simple basis for subsequent analysis and discussion, when these assumptions are relaxed. This is done in section II. We are then enabled to establish the logical foundations of the various macroeconomic theories of household behaviour. We can see clearly what these theories have in common, and also where and why they differ. These macroeconomic theories themselves are the focus of section III, with which the chapter concludes.

I: The Utility-maximizing Approach

I: 1 *Introduction*

Consumption spending, labour supply, and portfolio behaviour are all inter-dependent. This is seen most easily in the traditional utility-maximizing approach. This shows the individual determining an optimal lifetime programme of working, spending, money holding, lending, and bequests. Lifetime utility, U, is held to depend upon consumption, leisure, money holdings and bequests enjoyed or undertaken throughout life. U is maximized subject to a lifetime budget restraint which states that the present value of all purchases and bequests planned in each period does not exceed the present value of lifetime resources. These resources comprise the initial value of property of all kinds, plus the discounted present value of all wage income and any receipts of capital, net of tax payments.

I: 2 *The Lifetime Budget Restraint*

Let A_0 denote the present value of property held now (at date 0). Suppose, for simplicity's sake, that A can be held in just two kinds of asset: money, M, bearing a nominal rate of return $R_m \geq 0$, and bonds, B, bearing a nominal rate of return $R > R_m$. Let L_j denote a legacy, or transfer of capital, received (if $L_j > 0$) or made (if $L_j < 0$) at date j. Let w_j denote the hourly wage rate at date j, h_j the individual's endowment of time, measured in hours, at date j, and l_j his hours of work devoted to earning wages. Suppose all wage income at date j is liable to tax at the rate t_j, and that the individual may also pay lump-sum taxes of ψ_j (ψ_j could be negative, as under a government programme of income-maintenance). Assume that R is a unique number, the rate at which one individual can borrow or lend in unlimited amounts, and a rate which is independent of the length of loan. Under these assumptions, we may write the individual's lifetime budget restraint in discrete time as:

$$A_0 + \sum_{j=0}^{T} v_j(L_j - \psi_j) + \sum_{j=0}^{T} v_j w_j l_j (1 - t_j) \geq (R - R_m) \sum_{j=0}^{T} v_j M_j + \sum_{j=0}^{T} \sum_{i=0}^{m} v_j P_{ij} X_{ij}. \quad (1.1)$$

Here, v_j is the 'discount factor' for date j, equal to $\{1/(1 + R)\}^j$. This converts values at the future date j into present values: the present time is indicated by $j = 0$. We assume that the individual knows his life will end at date T, and that in any period j until then he will buy X_{ij} units of good i at a price of P_{ij}. There are m goods in all which may be bought at each date. Denoting discounted present value by 'DPV', we may express (1.1) in words as (initial wealth + DPV of net receipts of capital and lump-sum transfers from the state + DPV of after-tax wage income) cannot be less than (interest foregone on DPV of money holdings + DPV of all consumption spending). The fourth term in (1.1),

$$(R - R_m) \sum_{j=0}^{T} v_j M_j,$$

gives the discounted present value of all lifetime money holdings, multiplied by their opportunity cost. This is the interest differential $R - R_m$, the gap between the interest yield on bonds, and that on money. If money is taken to consist only of notes and coins, the simplest and narrowest definition, R_m, will, of course, be zero. Note that M_j, A_0, L_j and ψ_j are all defined in *nominal* terms. The nominal value of a variable at a given date is its 'money price', or the sum of money for which it may be traded then.

I: 3   *The Homogeneity Property*

Our first important result follows directly from (1.1). If M_j, A_0, L_j, ψ_j and all prices and wage rates (for each date j) are multiplied by any positive number, inequality (1.1) will remain unaffected—provided, that is, that it is the *same* positive number and that *all* of these variables are multiplied by it. Inequality (1.1) is, therefore, said to be *homogeneous of degree zero in all nominal magnitudes*. If, in addition, the utility function U is homogeneous of degree zero in nominal magnitudes—this means that U depends only upon the 'real' variables, X_{ij}, $h_j - l_j$, and real money holdings (M_j/P_j) and real bequests—we derive the result that the optimal programme of real money holding, real bequests, purchases of goods and labour supply is unaffected by an equiproportionate change in all nominal magnitudes. A doubling of all nominal money holdings, nominal wealth, nominal capital transfers and all prices and wage rates for every period will have no *real* effects upon our individual's behaviour. If the behaviour of producers as well as households is independent of nominal magnitudes, and all markets always clear, money is found to be *neutral*. Equilibrium values of real variables such as quantities and relative prices, are independent of the level of the money supply, provided that the ratios of the A_0, M_j, L_j and ψ_j to each other are given.

I: 4   *The Model's Assumptions*

In order to proceed further, and investigate how particular changes in the individual's economic environment affect his behaviour, we need to examine how his optimal programme is determined. His utility function, U, is maximized subject to his lifetime budget restraint (1.1). From this emerges a set of first-order conditions for utility maximization. The optimal programme is the solution to this set of simultaneous equations, provided that (i) it satisfies the second-order test and generates a maximum, not a minimum, for utility; and (ii), in the case of non-uniqueness, it gives the highest value for utility of all solutions.

To be specific, it helps to fix ideas by stating formally a list of assumptions. These assumptions are a convenient and simplifying starting point. They should not be thought of as an approximate description of reality. They merely provide assistance in the first steps of the argument. They remind us of the conditions sufficient or necessary to establish the results obtained, and they point the ways forward in any attempt to generalize these results. We assume:

(A1) perfect divisibility of labour and all commodities;

(A2) given prices for all commodities and labour, which the individual cannot alter;

(A3) storage costs are prohibitive;

(A4) there are no adjustment costs or delivery lags;

(A5) externalities are confined to the motive to bequeathe Z_T/P_T, in real terms, at date T;

(A6) taxation is confined to a wage tax at rate t_j, and a lump-sum tax of ψ_j, in period j;

(A7) there is a unique rate of interest R per period, which is common to all lenders and borrowers in the bond market, and which does not vary with the duration of the loan;

(A8) the individual has complete knowledge of all prices for all dates, and of the dates of death (T) and retirement from work $(S < T)$, and also a complete set of preferences relating to both future and present goods;

(A9) total utility increases with X_{ij}; leisure $(h_j - l_j)$; real balances[1] of money (M_j/P_j) (here, P_j is an index of P_{ij} for date j); and with the terminal bequest (Z_T/P_T). Indifference curves between any pair of goods are strictly convex.

Making utility depend on real balances of money is best explained by reference to the transactions costs that they allow one to save. Money may be thought to yield a stream of convenience. It saves time and trouble, as well as explicit transactions costs that would be incurred if cash reserves

---

[1] There are two subtle difficulties here. One is the dependence of utility on prices, as well as on quantities. The other is the construction of the index of prices. The first is due to the fact that it is *real*, not nominal money balances that contribute to utility (for example by saving transactions costs). As we shall see below, and again in chapter 5 when we return to the demand for money in more detail, the demand for real balances should be homogeneous of degree zero in all prices. Yet the price deflator by which money balances are to be divided is a subjective matter, and, worse still, an endogenous variable: for it depends on how expenditure is to be distributed between goods. That is the second difficulty.

The inelegant dependence of utility on both prices and quantities, and the index-number problem, can both be removed by using a fully *indirect* utility function. Utility would then be made to depend upon (i) the nominal value of all endowments, including money, time that could be used for remunerated work, and other assets; and (ii) all prices (including wage rates, interest rates, etc.). This indirect utility function could then be maximized, subject to the budget restraint, with respect to *prices* rather than quantities. The index-number problem also vanishes, of course, if the model is confined to just one good (for each date considered). When simplified versions of (1.1) are set to work in chapter 7, this one-good restriction is in force. In retaining the direct utility function approach (which makes utility depend explicitly upon real balances, and on quantities of other goods) chapter 7 is following a well-trodden path. This is how Patinkin presented the real-balance effect (247), and Malinvaud's analysis of macroeconomic disequilibria (204) does the same. Benassy (38), however, uses the indirect utility function, on the mechanics of which the interested reader may wish to consult Varian (327).

kept being converted in and out of other assets. Exactly how transactions costs of various kinds are saved by holding money is examined in detail in chapter 5. Another possible advantage of money is that it may provide a safe refuge from riskier alternatives. This motive for an 'asset' demand for money is again considered in chapter 5; it is in any case inconsistent with the certainty assumed, provisionally, in A8. It is worth stressing that money may not be desirable 'for its own sake'. It is the characteristics it provides that really explain why it is wanted. This may be no less true of other goods acquired or held, as argued by Becker (34). Finally, money enters the utility function in some models as a vehicle—often the only vehicle—for transmitting purchasing power from one period to the next. The disequilibrium models of Benassy (38) and Malinvaud (204) are examples.

Total utility is to be maximized subject to the budget restraint (1.1). We write

$$U = U\left(X_{ij}, h_j - l_j, \frac{M_j}{P_j}, \frac{Z_T}{P_T}\right) \text{ with all marginal utilities positive; } (1.2)$$

(A10) holdings of money, acquisitions of goods and retentions of leisure are non-negative:

$$M_j, X_{ij}, h_j - l_j \geqslant 0. \tag{1.3}$$

I: 5 *The Model's Results*

The maximization of (1.2) subject to (1.1) and (1.3) gives rise to numerous first-order conditions. There are $(2 + N)(T + 1) + S + 1$ of these in all, in addition to the restraints (1.1) and (1.3). For each date j we have

$$\partial U/\partial(h_j - l_j) \leqslant \lambda v_j w_j (1 - t_j), \qquad s \geqslant j \geqslant 0, \tag{1.4}$$

$$\partial U/\partial X_{ij} \leqslant \lambda v_j P_{ij} \qquad\qquad T \geqslant j \geqslant 0, N \geqslant i \geqslant 0, \tag{1.5}$$

$$\partial U/\partial(M_j/P_j) \leqslant \lambda(R - R_m)v_j, \qquad T \geqslant j \geqslant 0, \tag{1.6}$$

$$\partial U/\partial(Z_T/P_T) \leqslant \lambda v_T. \tag{1.7}$$

In words, (1.4) states that the marginal utility of wealth, λ cannot be less than the ratio of the marginal utility of leisure at date j to the DPV of the after-tax wage rate at j; (1.5), that the ratio of the marginal utility of good i at date j to the DPV of its price at j must not exceed λ; (1.6), that the ratio of the marginal utility of real money holdings at j to the DPV of their opportunity cost must not exceed λ; and, lastly, (1.7) that the DPV of λ cannot be less than the marginal utility of the terminal bequest. Let us see why this is so. If (1.4) failed, our individual's utility would increase if he planned to cut back his time at work, and increase his leisure, at date j. If (1.5) did not hold, he would benefit from increasing his planned purchases of good i at date j, and by raising his money holdings then if (1.6) were broken. Lastly, failure of (1.7) would mean that he would be made happier by deciding to leave more to his heirs.

The optimal programme for consumption (X_{ij}), labour supply (l_j), money hold-ing (M_j/P_j) and bequests (Z_T/P_T) emerges as the solution to the set of simultaneous inequalities (1.1), and (1.3) to (1.7). Uniqueness and optimality are guaranteed by assumption A9: strict convexity of the indifference curves precludes multiple solutions, and the combination of strict convexity and positive marginal utilities ensures that the solution is optimal, not pessimal. If the solution satisfies (1.3) as strict inequalities (so that every good, including leisure and money, is 'bought' at each date, and a terminal bequest is made) then (1.4)–(1.7) are equations. The assumption of positive marginal utilities (A9) precludes satiation, so that the budget restraint (1.1) is satisfied as an equation. When (1.4)–(1.7) are equations, the opti-mum programme may be stated simply: total wealth and earnings should be allocated between every good (commodities, leisure and money) at every date so that the marginal utility derived from it should be *equiproportional to its present* (i.e. DPV) *price.* The price of leisure is the wage rate since this is its opportunity cost. Similarly, the price of holding money is $R - R_m$.

Commodities X_{00} to X_{N0} will be purchased now. But commodities to be con-sumed in the future cannot be acquired until when they are wanted: prohibitive storage costs (A3) preclude acquisitions in advance. But they may be pre-empted. Our individual will be indifferent between paying P_{ij} at the date of acquisition (date j), and paying $P_{ij}v_j$ now (or, for that matter, $P_{ij}(1 + R)^{k-j}$ at any date k). When he actually pays the bill for his purchase makes no difference, since interest is added to bills due and deducted from pre-purchases, at the same rate as he can borrow or lend. Assumption A7 ensures this. The same is true of wage contracts: the actual timing of payments makes no difference.

Total spending at date zero, and hence if date zero is defined to be 'now', total *current consumption* spending, will equal

$$\sum_{i=0}^{N} P_{i0}X_{i0}.$$

Total *current income*, as it would normally be measured, will equal $R(A_0 - M_0 + L_0 - \psi_0) + R_mM_0 + w_0(1 - t_0)l_0 - \psi_0$. This equals disposable, or after-tax income. To taxed wage income are added the interest yield from bonds and money holdings, minus this period's lump sum tax payment (or receipt, if ψ_0 is negative). Definitional difficulties emerge if the price of bonds can change, or if inflation expectations are introduced. The former raises the question of whether capital gains on asset holdings should be treated as income; the latter leads to the distinction between real and nominal rates of interest (the latter including either actual or expected inflation, the former not). If income is defined as the rate at which you can spend if you keep the real value of your wealth intact, it should be taken to include (i) the amount by which nominal capital gains exceed the rate of inflation, and (ii) real, as opposed to nominal, interest receipts. By this definition, income will differ somewhat from the formula given above. *Current savings* are the excess of current income over

$$\sum_{i=0}^{N} P_{i0}X_{i0}.$$

Current nominal bondholdings equal $A_0 - M_0 + L_0 - \psi_0$.

The optimal programme prescribes a particular plan for labour supply, for the portfolio, and for consumption spending and saving or dissaving throughout life. All these aspects of behaviour are interdependent, and jointly determined. It is generally not possible to assign a single variable as the exclusive or even dominant variable affecting one aspect of behaviour. Statements like 'Savings depend on income', 'The demand for bananas depends upon the price of bananas' or 'The demand for money is governed by wealth' are misleading oversimplifications.

I: 6   *The Motives for Saving*

None the less, five important motives can be identified for saving. First, there is the desire to defer some consumption expenditure until after retirement, when wage income will no longer be earned. The longer the period of retirement relative to the working life, the more the individual is likely to save while he is in work. In aggregate, the faster the growth rate of population, the higher the ratio of those in work to the retired, and the higher the community's savings are likely to be. Second, there is the desire to bequeathe; the level of savings will be positively related to the size of the planned value of (Z_T/P_T) in the optimal programme. Third, there is the role of pure time-preference or impatience, as reflected in the rate at which future utility is discounted by the individual. For example, suppose (1.2) takes the 'additively separable' form of a weighted sum of each period's utility function U_j:

$$U = \sum_{j=0}^{T} (1 + \rho)^{-j} U_j\left(X_{ij}, h_j - l_j, \frac{M_j}{P_j}\right). \tag{1.8}$$

Here, ρ measures the rate of time preference, or subjective rate of discount. The smaller this subjective discount rate, the greater the emphasis on sacrificing present leisure and present consumption for future leisure and future consumption, and hence the greater the incentive to save. The fourth motive is the wish to transfer purchasing power away from periods of abnormally high income or abnormally low consumption needs towards those with the opposite characteristics. Lastly there is the desire to accumulate money balances. All these motives can be discerned within the present framework. A sixth, springing from uncertainties about the future, is considered later (section II. 9).

We turn now to consider the effects of changes in certain variables upon consumption spending, saving, labour supply and portfolio behaviour. The complete effects can be found by totally differentiating the first-order conditions (1.1) and (1.3)-(1.7). As this is a laborious and intricate exercise, what follows will give a simplified account of the major results.

I: 7   *The Effects of a Rise in Endowments*

A change in the level of wealth may take the form of a rise (or fall: we shall consider only a rise) in the initial holdings of assets, A_0. The demand for all goods with a positive wealth-elasticity of demand will rise. Indeed, if the utility function (1.2) is homothetic (i.e., if the ratio of marginal utilities of any pair of goods is independent of wealth), the demand for all good, including leisure, will rise equiproportionately. This implies a fall in the planned supply of labour for the current period and every future period, and a rise in money holdings planned at each date. With a general utility function, only inferior goods will register a fall in demand. Labour supply rises only in the distinctly unlikely case where leisure is inferior. If all goods are normal, the planned purchases of all goods at all dates go up, labour supply planned for each date drops, and money holdings planned at each date increase.

The savings ratio may rise or fall. There are two factors that will normally tend to reduce it. Present consumption expenditure will go up (barring inferiority), squeezing savings. The increased demand for leisure will tend to cut wage earnings, assuming that this period's leisure is normal, again reducing savings. Against these effects, one factor will work to increase savings. This is the increase in property income, $R\Delta A_0$. The higher the rate of interest, the stronger this effect on measured income and savings will be, and the greater the chance that the savings ratio goes up. Another factor which governs whether the individual saves more or less is his life expectation. The longer he expects to live, the less he will tend to raise consumption, or lower labour supply, in any period, so the likelier it becomes that he will save more.

A fall in the present lump-sum tax payment—or an increase in current lump-sum receipts—will have identical effects to those of a rise in A_0. Increased expectations of legacies, or transfer receipts, or reduced expectations of net lump-sum tax payments in future periods, will also raise the demand for all normal goods. Labour supply, commodity demand and money holdings will be affected in just the same way as a rise in wealth. The current savings ratio is certain to fall this time, barring inferior goods, because the $R\Delta A_0$ effect does not apply.

Thus far we have considered the effects of a rise in pecuniary endowments. What happens if the individual's endowment of time in period j, h_j, increases? One may think of certain activities (for instance, commuting, dishwashing, illness, or sleep) as neither leisure nor labour supplied for remunerative work. A time-saving domestic innovation, or a medical improvement, may therefore increase h_j. This would raise

$$\sum_{j=0}^{S} v_j w_j h_j (1 - t_j),$$

which is the DPV of maximum possible earnings from work. A rise in this would act much like an increase in pecuniary endowments: the demand for all but inferior goods would increase. There would, however, be one important difference: labour supply would increase *in addition* to leisure.

An increase in life expectation, on the other hand, would raise labour supply and reduce the demand for commodities, and money holdings, in each period, given an exogenous retirement date. Expectation of later retirement tends to have the opposite effects.

Finally, an important qualification. The demands for different commodities rarely behave alike. Some commodities are more complementary with leisure, for example, than others. A rise in wealth that tends to raise the demand for all goods, including leisure, will certainly succeed in raising the demand for golf balls. But the demand for calculator batteries and overalls, which are complementary with work, is liable to fall.

I: 8 *The Effects of a Change in Wage Rates*

Consider, first, a rise in w_k. This exerts two effects: a wealth effect and a substitution effect. The wealth effect arises because of an increase in the DPV of maximum possible labour earnings,

$$\sum_{j=0}^{S} v_j w_j h_j (1 - t_j),$$

by

$$h_k \frac{1 - t_k}{(1 + R)}.$$

As before, this must raise the demand for all but inferior goods, be they leisure, real money balances or commodities. The substitution effect is undirectional, unless it happens to be zero because the indifference surface has a corner at the relevant point. If substitution does occur, it must be away from leisure at date k (the opportunity cost of which has risen), and into all other goods, *en bloc*. The substitution effect taken by itself cannot therefore reduce labour supply for date k. Labour supply at a date other than k will tend to fall for two reasons: the effect of substitution between leisure in the two periods, and the wealth effect (assuming that the second period's leisure is a normal good). The same reasoning points to a likely increase in the demand for money balances, and commodities, at any period. Only if a particular commodity is complementary with leisure at date k, or suffers from a sufficiently powerful negative wealth effect, will the demand for it fall.

Labour supply at date k is in all probability subject to two contrary influences. There is a wealth effect which must lower it, unless leisure at k is inferior, and also a substitution effect which must increase it (or at least leave it unchanged, in a limiting case). Unless the elasticities of substitution between leisure at k, and other goods including leisure at other dates, are low, the substitution effect will predominate, and the supply of labour at this date will increase. In the case of a Cobb-Douglas utility function, for instance, where the substitution elasticity between every pair of goods is constant, uniform and unitary, we find

$$\frac{\partial (h_k - l_k)}{\partial w_k / w_k} = \frac{\gamma_k [E - v_k w_k (1 - t_k) h_k]}{v_k w_k (1 - t_k)}, \tag{1.9}$$

where E equals the DPV of total endowments,

$$A_0 + \sum_{j=0}^{T} v_j (L_j - \psi_j) + \sum_{j=0}^{S} v_j w_j h_j (1 - t_j),$$

and γ_k is the ratio of the elasticity of U to leisure at date k, to the sum of the elasticities of U to all goods. Since E includes much more than merely the DPV of maximum labour earnings at date k, $v_k w_k h_k (1 - t_k)$, (1.9) will be negative. In general, period k's leisure must either be inferior, or be rather strongly complementary with other goods, for l_k to fall when w_k rises. The reason for this, and for the fact that (1.9) is unambiguously negative, is that in a multi-period framework substitution occurs not just between leisure and consumption goods at the same date, but also between leisure at different dates: and also that the endowment of maximum possible labour earnings at date k contributes only a very small part to E. (E stands for the individual's total wealth endowment, both human wealth (earning capacity) and non-human.) This makes for a weaker wealth effect, in contrast to a multi-dimensional substitution effect.

To sum up, a rise in w_k is very likely to raise the demands for money and commodities in all periods, and to lower labour supply in all other periods; the labour supply in period k is quite likely, but not certain, to rise. There should be a large increase in savings in period k. What, now, of a rise in the wage rate for *every* period? Consider an equiproportionate rise in every w_j.

In this case, the demand for money and for commodities will increase for every period, except for any good which happens to be inferior. Labour supply will rise in each period if there is powerful substitution between leisure and other goods. This will be observed in the Cobb–Douglas case, provided only that the non-human wealth elements in E,

$$A_0 + \sum_{j=0}^{T} v_j(L_j - \psi_j),$$

are positive. But substitution effects are in general *less* likely to overcome the wealth effect now that the wage rate has risen for every period, and not just for date k. In contrast to the latter case, there is now no substitution between leisure at one date and leisure at others: marginal rates of substitution between them will not have changed, since w_j/w_k is unchanged. Since planned post-retirement consumption spending will increase, the savings ratio should increase following a uniform rise in all wage rates. A rise in w_k alone could lead to a large rise in period k's savings ratio, and probably to a small fall in the savings ratio for other periods.

I: 9   *The Effects of a Change in Prices*

A uniform, equiproportionate rise in all commodity prices at all dates will affect the optimal programme in much the same way as an equiproportionate fall in all periods' wage rates. Real wage rates are reduced, encouraging substitution. This time, substitution will occur away from commodities into leisure. Also, there is a wealth effect arising from a reduction in the *purchasing power* of the DPV of maximum labour earnings. The wealth effect to which this gives rise will lower the demand for all but inferior goods; the wealth effect, therefore, tends to stimulate labour supply, and to reduce the demands for money and commodities.

There is, however, one major difference between a rise in all prices and a fall in all wage rates. The former reduces the real value of bonds and money holdings, while the latter leaves it unchanged. The former also lowers the real value of the planned bequest, Z_T. Consequently, we may infer that consumption spending will be squeezed more strongly by the uniform rise in prices than by an equiproportionate cut in all wage rates. Our individual will be driven to rebuild his real holdings of money and other assets. This will also make a rise in his labour supply a likelier response to an across-the-board rise in prices than to an equiproportionate fall in all wage rates.

Now consider a uniform increase in all prices at date k only. The pattern of substitution is different. Since it is only period k's goods which have risen in price, there will be a tendency to substitute into commodities in other periods, as well as into leisure. The demand for nominal money holdings at date k should increase, although that for real money balances at that date will probably fall. If it is only commodity i at date k which experiences the rise in price, substitution between commodities at date k needs to be added to intertemporal consumption substitution and leisure–consumption substitution; and the wealth effects become still weaker. The demand for commodity i at date k will fall, unless (most improbably) it is a Giffen good; the demand for commodities with which it is complementary in consumption will also fall, while the demand for its substitutes will increase.

I: 10 *The Effects of a Change in Wage Tax Rates*

In our model, a rise in the rate of wage tax acts exactly like a fall in the wage rate for the period(s) in question. Consequently, an increase in t_k *only* will tend to raise labour supply at other dates, and reduced planned consumption spending and money holdings for all dates; and it will be rather likely to reduce labour supply for date k itself. An increase in the rate of wage tax expected in all periods will have a more drastic adverse effect on planned consumption spending and money holdings in all periods; what effect it has on labour supply is unclear.

There is one qualification that we need to recognize here. A change in the expected rates of wage tax may well be accompanied by a revision in expected levels of lump-sum taxation, whether positive or negative. If our individual thinks that wage tax rates are being raised in order to finance higher negative lump-sum taxes, he is likelier to respond by reducing his planned labour supply than if he expects the additional tax proceeds to be devoted to providing public goods. The only exception to this is if the additional government expenditure were to provide goods that were complementary with leisure. A wage tax surcharge to defray the costs of expanding the provision of national parks or public broadcasting could be highly adverse to the supply of labour, however attractive the measure might be for other reasons.

I: 11 *Changes Over Time in Endowment, Wage Rates, Prices and Wage Tax Rates*

So far we have considered 'comparative static' changes in several variables which combine to determine the individual's optimal programme. We have posed the counterfactual question, 'How would the programme have differed, had a particular variable been higher or lower?' This question differs from, 'How will the programme change as a result of an actual change in a particular variable between two dates?' The answer to the second question is 'Not at all', if this change had been anticipated. Assumption A8 of the model states that the individual has perfect knowledge of the future variables of all exogenous variables. This rules out the possibility of unanticipated events. Our individual has perfect foresight.

Perfect foresight is a highly restrictive assumption. The implications of relaxing it will be discussed below. But one point can be made now. The analysis and results of the model are not changed in any respect if the individual holds *single-valued* expectations for all the future values of variables. If expectations of future wage rates, price levels, tax rates, tax transfers and bequests, as well as of dates of retirement and death, and of his own future preferences, are held with complete confidence, all the results carry through. As far as this period's determination of the optimal programme is concerned, it is not necessary that these expectations be subsequently fulfilled. Any later revisions of expectations will cause revisions of the optimal programme; and how the optimal programme changes in the light of altered forecasts by the individual about his economic environment is precisely what the previous three sections have analysed. Actual and planned behaviour changes at the point when news arrives to cause expectations of a future variable to be revised, and not at the date when the forecast event itself occurs. Announcements of future changes in wage tax rates will have immediate effects on planned behaviour, if they have not been expected. It will be at this stage that consumer spending registers its initial charge, and not when the new tax rate starts to be applied.

I: 12 *A Change in the Rate of Interest on Bonds*

A rise in the rate of interest, R, will have far-reaching effects on the optimal programme. We return now to the counterfactual approach adopted in sections 8, 9, and 10, and ask how the optimal programme *would have differed* if the interest rate had taken a different value.

A rise in the rate of interest, R, has the following effects:

(i) The *yield on holdings of bonds* increases. If the bonds have a fixed capital value, either because they have a floating 'coupon' of interest attached to them, like an interest-bearing bank deposit, or because they have a very brief term to maturity, like a three-month bill, this increase in yield will be translated into an increase in actual *income*. At least, income will increase for an individual whose holdings of such bonds are positive; for those with negative holdings, actual income will fall.

A rise (fall) in actual income will by itself tend to raise (lower) the measured level of savings,

$$\text{income minus} \sum_{i=0}^{N} P_{i0}X_{i0},$$

and also the measured savings ratio,

$$1 - \sum_{i=0}^{N} P_{i0}X_{i0}/\text{income}.$$

(ii) The *capital value of holdings of bonds* tends to decline. This must happen if the bonds have a fixed coupon and anything but a very short term to maturity. To this extent, the rise in R acts like a fall in A_0, since this is exactly what it will induce.

    A fall in A_0, we saw in section (8), will lower the demand for all but inferior goods. Labour supply will tend to rise, and the demand for money and commodities will tend to fall, in each period. The level of savings and the savings ratio should increase. The opposite will occur if holdings of fixed-interest financial instruments are negative.

(iii) There is a decline in the *DPV of human wealth*, expected receipts of capital from legacies or transfers, and of expected lump-sum tax payments or receipts. Since the aggregate of these assets is almost certainly positive, effects on spending, labour supply and portfolio behaviour will resemble those of a fall in A_0. The sensitivity of the DPV of an expected future receipt to R increases directly with the length of time concerned: the DPV of maximum possible labour earnings in period j (call this g) is $w_j h_j (1 - t_j)(1 + R)^{-j}$ so that

$$\frac{1 + R}{R} \frac{\partial \log g}{\partial \log R},$$

the interest-elasticity of g multiplied by $(1 + R/R)$, equals simply $-j$.

(iv) There is a decline in the *DPV of planned future consumption spending*, and of the opportunity costs of future money holdings and future leisure. This is tantamount to an *increase* in wealth, with effects opposite to those observed in (ii) and (iii). By itself, effect (iv) will imply higher planned consumption spending, higher money balances and lower labour supply—barring inferior goods. The magnitude of the effect varies with the length of time considered: as was seen in (iii), the DPV of planned consumption spending twenty years hence falls much more than that of just one year ahead.

(v) The *opportunity cost of money holdings* rises. This will induce portfolio substitution out of money into bonds. What this effect implies for consumption expenditures is less clear. The sharper incentive to economize on money holdings will affect the demand for particular commodities differently. The demand for wallets should fall, while that for shoe leather and car tyres should rise with an increase in the frequency of shopping. The rise in the opportunity cost of money holdings will also exert a small, negative wealth effect on the demand for all but inferior goods. The supply of labour will probably rise very slightly.

(vi) The *relative prices* of present, or near future goods, to goods in the more distant future, increase. Present leisure rises in opportunity cost in terms of future leisure. Similarly, with money holdings, and above all with commodities. This change in relative prices will induce substitution which can, as always, only be unidirectional. Unless there is complete complementarity between goods at different dates, present and near future consumption spending will decline in favour of far future consumption; there will be substitution out of money balances in the present and near future into money balances further periods ahead; and planned labour supply will tend to fall in the far future and increase in the present and near future.

(vii)   The DPV of the expected real *terminal bequests*, (Z_T/P_T), will fall. This will induce a favourable wealth effect upon the demand for all but inferior goods, and a substitution effect towards the terminal bequest.

Balancing these effects against each other, we note that (ii) and (iii) run counter to (iv) and the wealth effect in (vii). Which pair predominates depends upon the relative timing of the income (or income opportunities) and the outlays. There must be some presumption that with the typical individual, effects (iv) and (vii) will overcome (ii) and (iii). This is chiefly because expected consumption expenditures outlast earnings opportunities. On average, earnings tend to come earlier than consumption outlays. In work, one both earns and consumes; the retired only consume. Furthermore, if the individual's bonds are in a floating-interest, capital-secure form, and they may well be, effect (ii) is nullified. There is also the fact that bequests in our model, and also in practice, (almost) invariably follow rather than precede any legacies received.

But before concluding that the wealth effect of a rise in R is positive on average, we must take note of one or two qualifications. Earnings often rise with age, sometimes very steeply. This is particularly marked in many of the professions, and also for the fortunate few who reach senior positions in private industry or the public sector. It may be suspected that entry into certain careers has been held down by the device of enforcing low pay and unpleasant conditions on those in their early years. Then there is the phenomenon of learning by doing, of productivity rising with experience. If a worker's skills do mature with practice, and if these skills are transferable and visible to other potential employers, wage will rise with age. By contrast, consumption needs may exhibit a rather flatter time-profile. Calorific requirements from food in fact decline by about 1 per cent per annum after the age of 25. Sedentary and usually relatively inexpensive leisure activities appeal less to the young than the old. The expenses of child-rearing will be heaviest in early middle life. Finally, even if the youthful members of society do experience an unambiguously positive wealth effect from a rise in R—because their consumption spending on average follows their income in time—we cannot infer that society will on average do so, too. For the retired, or those nearing retirement, who will have accumulated a large share of the national assets, a rise in R will probably exert a powerful negative wealth effect. This is especially likely if their assets are held in a predominantly fixed-interest form. Even if retirement incomes are provided and guaranteed by insurance and pension companies, the balance sheet effects of a fall in their holdings of fixed-interest securities may lead on to increased premiums for those in work, and also to a reduction in wealth for shareholders in the companies concerned.

The wealth effect of a rise in R is, therefore, ambiguous. But the substitution effects are not. What is in doubt with the substitution effect are not their sign but their magnitude. That there must be some tendency for current labour supply, incomes, and savings to rise, and current consumption spending to fall, is incontestable. But the size of these intertemporal substitutions may be modest. The most clear-cut effect is (v), that upon the demand for money: this looks almost certain to fall.

I: 13 *A Change in the Rate of Interest on Money*

A rise in R_m, the rate of interest paid on money, reduces the opportunity cost of holding money. The effects will be opposite to those described in section (12), effect (v). The demand for money will increase, at the expense of bonds. There will also be a modest favourable wealth effect on the demand for all save inferior goods, and some reshuffling, in most cases very small, of the demand for leisure and for particular commodities.

I: 14 *A Change in Anticipated Inflation Reflected in Wages, Prices, and Nominal Interest Rates*

Let us now suppose that the rate of inflation expected in each period is increased (again, counterfactually) and that inflation affects wage rates and all commodity prices neutrally. The anticipated rate of inflation is fully reflected, let us assume, in both R and R_m.

These circumstances remove effects (iv), (v), (vi), and (vii) in the analysis of a change in R. Effect (iv) vanishes because the DPV of future consumption spending, and of the opportunity costs of future leisure and money holdings are unchanged. Negative pressure from a higher value of R is balanced by positive pressure from higher P_j. The same reasoning explains the removal of effects (vi) and (vii). Effect (v) disappears because we have assumed that R_m rises in parallel with R.

Effect (iii) is largely, perhaps wholly, removed as well. The DPV of future earnings opportunities,

$$\sum_{j=0}^{S} w_j h_j (1 - t_j)(1 + R)^{-j},$$

is unaffected because the forecast of higher rate of increase in future nominal wage rates is offset by a higher nominal rate of interest. If the DPV of forecasts of future legacies and tax transfers is also unaffected, effect (iii) disappears completely. This leaves us with effects (i) and (ii) which, however, do not vanish. Either measured income increases (effect (i)), or real wealth goes down (effect (ii)). In all probability, both effects will occur. It is interesting to see that *both* will tend to raise the current value of the measured savings ratio.

If the higher expected inflation rate is fully reflected in R, but not reflected at all in R_m, effect (v) of section (12) reappears. The opportunity cost of holding money rises, and the demand for it should fall. There will be a modest adverse wealth effect on the demand for all expect inferior goods; some substitution effects will occur *vis à vis* leisure and commodities, most of trivial size. Any change in labour supply should probably be upward, reinforcing the likelihood of a rise in the current savings ratio as conventionally measured.

One reason for studying the effects of inflation expectations on savings seriously is provided by the following curious fact. Since the Second World War when trust-worthy national income statistics start to become available, there has been a very close statistical link between the UK's personal sector savings ratio and long-term nominal interest rates (such as Consol rates). The two variables are not just highly correlated—their numerical values are extremely close. In the USA, however, there is almost no relationship discernible between the two. But in Britain the measured savings ratio appears to be highly sensitive to actual or expected inflation.[2]

II: Generalizing the Utility-maximizing Model

II: 1 *Introduction*

The time has now come to extend our utility-maximizing model by relaxing the assumptions of the model presented in I: 4. Repealing the assumptions introduces many new factors that affect household behaviour. It will also permit us to identify those features that unite, and those that distinguish, the various hypotheses about household behaviour that economists have advanced in the past.

II: 2 *Relaxing the Assumption of Perfect Divisibility of Labour and All Commodities*

Imperfect divisibility of goods makes the budget restraint discontinuous. Choices are confined to limited sections of the budget plane. Such confinements are exemplified by dwellings, motor-cars, and, above all, jobs.

A job is usually a binary activity. Either you have it or you do not. 'Part-time' jobs account for barely one-third of all jobs in Great Britain. Overtime working, rather common in manufacturing industry in the UK and much rarer in the USA and elsewhere in Western Europe, is normally involuntary.

Administrative difficulties facing the employer go far to explain the inflexibility of working hours and the rarity of part-time jobs. Variety in workers' contracts governing wage rates, working hours and other conditions would make negotiations protracted and complex. Furthermore, the output of organizations is usually the product of teamwork, and not simply the sum of the fruits of each worker's separate input. The team needs to be co-ordinated to function efficiently, and, at the very least, its members must synchronize their work. But the worker's preferences also enter the story. The length of the working week is subject to revision in regular negotiations over pay and working conditions between the employer and the employee's representatives (who often take the form of trade-union officials).

---

[2] See, for example, Davidson, *et al.* (78). This effect is to be distinguished from the impact of *unexpected* inflation upon savings, which Deaton (79) finds to have been positive in the UK. Deaton argues that a sudden, unexpected jump in inflation may not be fully detected by consumers for a while, since they are likely to have only limited information about current prices. If they see that the current prices of apples and raincoats are unexpectedly high, they may react by buying less now in the belief that oranges and umbrellas have now become relatively cheaper; and it takes time for them to realize that they have not. We might call Deaton's concept the 'Surprise Demand Function' by analogy with the Lucas Surprise Supply Function (196), discussed below (chapter 7, section VI).

Any marked preference for longer or shorter hours (or merely *different* hours) on the part of a large group of workers would sooner or later be reflected in pressure to negotiate them. The worker can also vote with his feet, accepting the offer of another job with a more attractive package of pay and working conditions. If there were a large unsatisfied demand for such jobs, it would pay some employers to meet it by offering them. The similarity of working hours across different firms and industries in an economy suggests similarity in workers' preferences. It could also testify, of course, to the strength of the desire to conform.

Some of the discontinuity of labour offers may be 'bridged' in various ways. The worker who would prefer to work shorter hours than the norm may change jobs quite often and take long vacations of his own choosing between them. He may also opt for early retirement. The incentive to do this will be strong if he can receive generous unemployment benefit when he is not working, and also if his income in the 'vacation' period is sustained by the repayment of income tax paid in earlier periods during the fiscal year when the annualized rate of weekly or monthly pay was much higher. On the other hand, a record of frequent job changes with long intermissions is not at all likely to appeal to prospective employers; people who behave like this may seriously damage their lifetime earnings prospects. If the worker wishes to work longer hours, there may be opportunities for second, part-time jobs; he can also pay himself a higher imputed wage, by selecting a cheaper but lengthier mode of travel to work, by refusing to buy or rent time-saving domestic gadgets, and by other types of 'do-it-yourself'. Since the imputed wage for self-employment of this kind is untaxed, the marginal rate of income tax will be an important influence on such choices. To the extent that an individual is encouraged to forsake his comparative advantage in employment, there is also an efficiency loss to consider.

If the discontinuity of labour is entirely unbridgeable, the individual must choose between leisure of $h_j - \bar{l}_j$ and h_j. In the first case, he has a job; in the second, he is unemployed. He will maximize U hypothetically in the two cases, subject in the first to

$$A_0 + \sum_{j=0}^{T} v_j(L_j - T_j) + \sum_{j=0}^{S} v_j w_j \bar{l}_j(1 - t_j) - \sum_{j=0}^{T} \sum_{i=0}^{N} v_j P_{ij} X_{ij} -$$

$$- (R - R_m) \sum_{j=0}^{T} v_j M_j - v_T Z_T \geq 0, \tag{1.10}$$

and in the second to

$$A_0 + \sum_{j=0}^{T} v_j(L_j - T_j) + \sum_{j=0}^{S} v_j b_j - \sum_{j=0}^{T} \sum_{i=0}^{N} v_j P_{ij} X_{ij} -$$

$$- (R - R_m) \sum_{j=0}^{T} v_j M_j - v_T Z_T \geq 0, \tag{1.11}$$

with respect to the X_{ij}, Z_T and M_j. The l_j are, of course, no longer choice variables. Here, $\bar{l}_j$ represents the constrained hours of work at date j, and b_j the unemployment benefit (net of any tax) at j. He will select the option that promises the higher utility. Which option he accepts will certainly depend on the relative magnitudes of $w_j \bar{l}_j$ and b_j.

Whichever of the options he accepts, labour supply has ceased to be a variable within his own control. His decision on whether or not to work now fixes his income, with only minor qualifications. He will still have the opportunity to split his current wealth as he likes between bonds and money; and he can choose how much to save, thereby giving him some degree of control now over his future income. Traditional macroeconomic theories of consumer behaviour vary in several respects, as we shall soon see; but they share one characteristic: the individual's current income is exogenous to him. This implicit assumption that they share may be attributed to indivisibility in labour. Alternatively, it may be justified by the hypothesis of 'rationing' in the labour market, which prevents workers from choosing as many hours of work as they would wish. The rationing explanation we shall consider below, in section (3). When labour income is exogenized, the concept of human wealth takes on a precise form: it is

$$\sum_{j=0}^{S} v_j w_j (1 - t) \bar{l}_j.$$

Total lifetime resources, E, are now

$$A_0 + \sum_{j=0}^{T} v_j (L_j - \psi_j) + \sum_{j=0}^{S} v_j w_j (1 - t_j) \bar{l}_j.$$

Once he has decided whether or not to work, these are completely exogenous to the individual.

The loss of choice of *hours* of work does not, however, imply that the worker exercises no freedom of action in employment. He can take leisure 'on the job'. His punctuality, assiduity, and rapidity of work are variables to some degree within his own control. It is costly for his employer to monitor his activity. There is a limit to what the supervisor can observe. The difficulty confronting the employer is known as the 'Principal-Agent Problem'.[3] The employer is the Principal, the employee his Agent; the former's task is to devise a system embracing wage and conditions contract, monitoring, and rewards and penalties that maximizes his objective (most simply, profits)—but he must accept that the latter has a will of his own, and inevitably some discretion.

The cynic will argue that the worker dislikes effort. If the employer believes this, he will attempt to connect the worker's pay and conditions prospects as closely as he can afford to the quality of his work, and to the effort he puts into it. In this he (the employer) may be assisted by a trade union, or obstructed by it, if the union is

[3] See for example Ross (265) and Shavell (293). Some of the ideas go back to Coase (62). See also Calvo and Wellisz (54), and Grossman and Hart (352).

motivated by 'majoritarian tyranny' or a Rawlsian concern for the 'marginal' worker.[4] In any event, the quality of the individual's work is very likely to vary positively with the following variables: (i) the ease and frequency of dismissals from employment; (ii) the expected loss of earnings prospects consequent upon dismissal; (iii) the extent of opportunities for promotion, and the rewards from promotion; (iv) the strength of the connection between effort at work and current pay. When the nature of the productive process makes 'payment by results' impossible on an individual worker basis, and requires large teams, (iv) will be extremely weak. If, in addition, dismissals are infrequent, costly for the employer, and cushioned by reasonable prospects of re-employment or unemployment pay, and promotion appears highly improbable, the worker will have very little incentive to work hard.

This is easily formalized. Let lifetime utility, U, depend on the vector of commodities consumed at each date j (x_j), real money holdings at j, the real terminal bequest, and (negatively in this case) effort at work at date j, e_j:

$$U = U\left(f_j\left(X_j, \frac{M_j}{P_j}, e_j\right), \frac{Z_T}{P_T}\right). \tag{1.12}$$

Let (12) be maximized subject to a lifetime budget condition

$$A_0 + \sum_{j=0}^{T} v_j(L_j - \psi_j) + H_0 - \sum_{j=0}^{T} \sum_{i=0}^{N} v_j P_{ij} X_{ij} - (R - R_m) \sum_{j=0}^{T} v_j M_j - v_T Z_T \geq 0. \tag{1.13}$$

H denotes the DPV of lifetime earnings,

$$\sum_{j=0}^{S} v_j w_j (1 - t_j) \bar{l}_j.$$

H is an increasing function of e_j: higher effort is to some extent rewarded by a higher after-tax wage rate per period ($w_k(1 - t_k)\bar{l}_k$), at the time or later.

First-order conditions for optimum commodity purchases, money holdings and bequests are as in the standard model (equations (5)–(7) respectively, in section I: 5). But there is a new optimum 'work' condition. Instead of (1.4), we have

$$-\partial U / \partial e_j \leq \lambda \partial \left[\sum_{k=j}^{S} v_k w_k (1 - t_k) \bar{l}_k\right] / \partial e_j. \tag{1.14}$$

(1.14) states that the marginal disutility of effort at each date j should just balance (or at least not exceed) the marginal effect of effort at that date on prospective lifetime earnings, multiplied by the marginal utility of wealth. The smaller, the more delayed, or the more heavily taxed the reward for effort, and also the closer he is to retiral, the less the effort that the individual will choose to expend. A very

---

[4] Rawls (261) holds that a society should seek to maximize the welfare of its least advantaged member, as a primary objective. See especially chapter 3.

weak connection between effort and reward has a further important effect. It turns wage income into a largely *unconditional* income stream, upon which his own effort has next to no effect. H then acts like non-human wealth, A_0. A weakening in the effort-reward link is equivalent *partly* to a rise in the relative price of commodities and other goods (which will cause substitution out of effort) and *partly* to a rise in wealth. The latter effect will raise the demand for all except inferior goods. If 'diseffort' is a normal good, wealth and substitution effects will reinforce each other in reducing the quality of the individual's work.

Indivisibilities in commodities are not as acute a problem as those in jobs. None the less they do carry important implications. Again, they make the budget restraint discontinuous. Indivisible goods can be bought only in multiples of one. Formally, the individual's optimization becomes a task in *integer programming*; the central idea of this has already been seen at work for the case of job indivisibility, when utility in the two states was maximized hypothetically subject to the different budget restraints (1.10) and (1.11), and the individual selected the option that gave the higher utility. As with jobs, the discontinuities introduced by indivisibilities may be bridged to some degree over time by *dynamic* discontinuities in purchasing commodities; you buy a motor car every three or five years; you shop for foodstuffs at discrete intervals. This way of tackling the problem of indivisibilities is greatly facilitated by storage. Section (4) considers the effects of relaxing the assumption of prohibitive storage costs. Purchases of durable goods are discussed in detail at that point.

Indivisibilities in goods pose more difficulties for single-member households than multi-member ones. Until now, we have made the individual synonymous with the household. Indivisibilities in the provision of certain goods, and collective consumability of certain other goods ('public goods')—particularly when exclusion from them is impossible or difficult—are instrumental in shaping the many layers of institution which lie between the individual and the society in which he lives: the nuclear family, the extended family, the club, the tribe, and the city.[5] Darwinian mechanisms of natural selection are also powerful influences. We shall return to issues raised by the multi-member household in section II: 6.

II: 3 *Relaxing the Assumption that All Prices and Wage Rates are Parametric*

The assumption of the standard utility-maximizing model that is repealed in this section is A2. Indivisibilities interrupt the continuity of the budget restraint; non-parametric prices introduce *non-linearity*. If the price of one good is given, and the other rises (falls) with the amount bought, the budget restraint becomes concave (convex). The price of a good may rise or fall with the amount required; it tends to rise when the buyer is a monopsonist, and fall if there are fixed costs in making transactions, which give rise to 'bulk-discounts'. If the price of each commodity is a differentiable function of the amount bought, the first-order condition (1.5) for utility-maximization in the standard model, $\partial U/\partial X_{ij} \leqslant \lambda v_j P_{ij}$, becomes

---

[5] For further discussion of the social implications of public goods, see chapter 3, section I.

$$\partial U/\partial X_{ij} \leqslant \lambda v_j P_{ij}\left(1 + \frac{1}{\text{elasticity of } P_{ij} \text{ to } X_{ij}}\right). \qquad (1.15)$$

If these elasticities are non-negative, the primary consequence of non-parametric prices will be to diversify consumption expenditure widely: the individual will avoid large purchases of any good with a large elasticity. Negative elasticities have the opposite effect: expenditure tends to concentrate upon particular goods. There is also a threat to the second-order condition for utility maximization, which is fulfilled if and only if the highest attainable indifference (hyper-)surface touches the budget (hyper-)plane from *outside*, not inside. Convexity of the indifference surface is no longer sufficient for this if the budget restraint is also convex. In the two-goods case, if both the indifference curve and the budget restraint are convex to the origin at the point of tangency, the former must be convex to the latter for the maximization condition to be met.

A much more serious issue arises when the prices are not differentiable functions of the volume of the good bought. In this case, the budget restraint is kinked. A concave kink arises when the individual is *rationed in disequilibrium*. Suppose there is excess demand for carrots at the ruling price, $\bar{P}_c$. At least one buyer of carrots will be unable to buy all the carrots he wishes. For him, the *marginal* price of carrots will exceed $\bar{P}_c$. It is simplest to assume that he views the marginal price as infinite. Figure 1.1, panel (*a*) illustrates the case where good y_2 is rationed, so that purchases of y_2 may not exceed $\bar{y}_2$; panel (*b*) depicts the case without rationing.

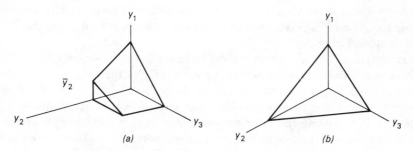

FIG. 1.1. The budget restraint with and without rationing.
(*a*) With y_2 rationed at $\bar{y}_2$. (*b*) Without rationing.

If the rationing constraint binds upon a consumer in a particular product market, he will react by diverting his resources towards other goods. Expenditure on other commodities, and holdings of money, will tend to rise, and labour supply will tend to fall. Particular commodities which are complementary with the rationed good will, however, register a lower level of demand than in the unrationed case. The effects of rationing upon consumer behaviour were first studied by Tobin and Houthakker (323); they have recently received an excellent, exhaustive treatment by Neary and Roberts (233).[6] In a dynamic setting, the individual determining

---

[6] See also chapter 2 (footnote 11 in section III: 3) and chapter 7 (section V) for other applications and for an analysis of their concept of the 'virtual price'.

his optimal programme must consider not just the extent of any rationing he faces in markets today, but also rationing in future periods. Predicting the price of strawberries and the availability of strawberries are *separate* exercises. When markets can be relied upon to clear, only the price forecasts need be made. If not, both are needed. They may well be interdependent. In most economies, there is regrettably an appreciable chance that some state agency will impose a price on a particular commodity below its equilibrium level. The lower the price imposed, the likelier this becomes; and also, if there is already excess demand, the lower the availability of the good to many, perhaps all, of its purchasers.[7] To repeat, the central result is that the individual will divert resources into all goods (including leisure and money) except any really close complements, when the availability of a particular commodity in excess demand is reduced. This holds for forecasts of reduced availability of commodities in future no less than to discoveries of reduced availability now.

Rationing in the labour market is an even more serious possibility. Unemployment is often treated as an excess supply of labour. This is quite correct unless the unemployment is voluntary. In the last section, unemployment was seen to be explicable in terms of job indivisibilities and a high ratio of unemployment benefit to wages; this is an example of voluntary unemployment, to which we may add others.[8] But if a worker cannot sell all the hours of labour that he wishes at the given wage rate, he is involuntarily unemployed. He faces a marginal wage rate of zero. Once again, his labour income is exogenous. In a simple one-period model he will be forced to curtail his total outlays. The demand for most, possibly all commodities will be lower than if the rationing in the labour market had not occurred. Close complements to leisure will be an exception to this: the demand for fishing rods could be higher.

In a dynamic model, labour market rationing in the one period will tend to stimulate additional planned labour supply in others. There are only two cases when this will not happen: first, if a particular period's leisure is strongly complementary with present leisure—our individual might decide to devote his enforced idle time to a training course or lengthy holiday, which also impinged on future work time; second, if the other periods are *also* expected to display rationing in the labour market. Forecasts of future rationing of work opportunities will exert powerful effects: the more pessimistic they are, the lower the planned demand for all goods in all periods (with the two exceptions of inferior goods, and goods which are strongly complementary with leisure in the future periods when rationing is forecast). If a household anticipates rationing in the labour market in *all* periods, his labour income becomes fully exogenous, as with job-indivisibility. The worst that could befall an individual is the loss of livelihood throughout his working life. The sudden onset of grave physical infirmity, for example, or the permanent and effective imposition of a minimum wage rate which clearly exceeded any employer's estimate of the individual's value to him, would lead to a very severe fall in planned outlays in all periods.

[7] Assuming that the supply of the good is positively related to its price.
[8] See chapter 7, section VII: 5.

A final point which emerges from a consideration of non-parametric prices and wage rates is the significance of transactions costs. Transactions costs introduce kinks into the budget restraint. They are of two kinds: fixed (which are incurred no matter how large or small the transaction) and variable (which vary with the size of the transaction). Fig. 1.2 illustrates fixed costs (panel (a)), linear variable (panel (b)) and increasing variable transactions costs (panel (c)), for the case of two goods, x and y, with which the individual is endowed. Point E represents the endowment vector. In (a), he must surmount the fixed cost of making transactions, equal to

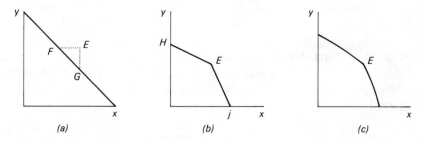

FIG. 1.2. The impact of transactions costs. (a) Fixed costs. (b) Linear variable costs. (c) Increasing variable costs.

FE or EG, before buying or selling any amount of either good. In (b), the budget restraint is also piecewise linear: the gradient of EH (EJ) is minus the ratio of the selling of x (y) to the buying price of y (x). In (c), both arms of the restraint are concave, because the average costs of transactions increase with their size. In each of these cases, transactions costs inhibit transactions in the goods involved. They increase the chance that the individual will not wish to move from his endowment point, E. Transactions costs in the market for bonds have a powerful depressive effect on the demand for bonds. They underlie the demand for money, or at least the inventory approach to the demand for money. In chapter 5 we shall explore this issue in detail.

II: 4 *Relaxing the Assumption of Prohibitive Storage Costs*

So far, the standard model has excluded non-financial durable goods. The assumption of prohibitive storage costs ruled them out. If storage costs are sufficiently modest, there will be circumstances when the individual will wish to acquire commodities before consuming them. A simple example illustrates. Suppose that a particular commodity costs a per period to store, that its price (now P_0) is expected to follow the path $P(t)$, and that the rate of interest is, as before, R. The DPV of the net profit from storing one unit of the good now (0) to τ is

$$\phi = -P_0 - a(1 + (1 + R)^{-1} + \ldots + (1 + R)^{-\tau}) + P(1 + R)^{-\tau}$$

$$= -P_0 - a\frac{1 + R}{R}(1 - (1 + R)^{-\tau - 1}) + P(1 + R)^{-\tau}.$$

Rewriting this in *continuous* time, so that we can choose the optimal storage period

τ^* by maximizing ϕ with respect to τ, we have

$$\phi = -P_0 - \int_0^\tau a e^{-Rt} dt + P(\tau)e^{-R\tau} \qquad (1.16)$$

Maximizing (1.16) with respect to the storage period we find

$$\frac{d\phi}{d\tau} = e^{-R\tau} \cdot \frac{dP(\tau)}{d\tau} - (RP(\tau) + a)e^{-R\tau} = 0 \qquad (1.17)$$

subject to the conditions that ϕ be positive, and the second order test that requires

$$2\frac{dP(\tau)}{d\tau} > a + \frac{1}{R}\frac{d^2 P(\tau)}{d\tau^2}.$$

From (1.17), we infer that the optimum period of storage must satisfy the condition that the proportionate rate at which the good is appreciating at date τ (call this $\hat{P}(\tau)$) equals the rate of interest plus the ratio of the storage cost to the price of the good:

$$\hat{P}(\tau) = R + \frac{a}{P(\tau)}. \qquad (1.18)$$

If the rate of appreciation were faster than this, it would pay to prolong storage; if less, to reduce it. In fact, (1.18) does not just determine when a good that had been acquired at time 0 should be sold. It *also* determines the optimum date for buying. When $\hat{P}(u) > R + a/P(u)$, you should buy before u; when $\hat{P}(u) < R + a/P(u)$, after u. The size of the optimum inventory of commodities stored by households, we may deduce, varies directly with the rate at which their prices are expected to rise, and negatively with both the rate of interest and the level of storage costs. The optimality condition (1.18) is a generalization of the Hotelling rule (167) for equilibrium on the part of owners of depletable natural resources, such as oil. This states that the rate at which the resource is expected to increase in price in nominal (real) terms should equal the nominal (real) rate of interest on alternative assets. In this case, the costs of storage are clearly zero.

Like Hotelling's rule, Condition (1.18) can be expressed in either real or nominal terms. A jump in the anticipated rate of inflation, which affects $\hat{P}$ and R equally and leaves the ratio a/P unchanged, can have no effect. It is only when inflation expectations are not exactly offset by the nominal rate of interest that expectations of inflation affect the incentive to pre-empt goods. This incentive will be sharpened if the nominal interest rate includes only partial allowance for inflation expectations, and reduced if it more than compensates for them.

Some durable goods are acquired at one date and consumed, in their entirety, at a later one. Wine is an example. But most, like clothes, furniture or motor cars, are consumed on numerous occasions over a span of years. The decision to buy a durable is an investment decision. With durable goods of either kind, acquisition and consumption are distinct activities. The assumption of prohibitive storage costs previously allowed us to treat them as one and the same. Non-prohibitive storage costs allow acquisition to precede consumption. The optimum stock of durables that an individual will seek to possess consists of all those with a prospective yield in excess of their opportunity cost. The prospective yield could mean simply the rate of appreciation, if the durable is held simply as an investment for later resale. In most cases it will be held for its own sake, because of the advantages that ownership of the good confers: entertainment, time-saving, comfort, freedom, convenience, or aesthetic pleasure. The owner will derive an imputed rent from the good—the rental payment he avoids by not merely renting it from someone else. The opportunity costs of the good are the interest foregone on the capital sunk in it (or the interest paid on a loan to finance its purchase), plus such other costs as storage, insurance, and maintenance.

The probability that an individual will seek to possess a particular durable good will vary negatively with its purchase price, with the rate of interest, and with any other elements in its opportunity cost as an asset, and positively with his wealth, the strength of his preference for the characteristics it supplies, and the length of time over which these characteristics can be enjoyed. The timing of durables purchases will be strongly influenced by expectation of changes in its price, and also in the rates of tax (if any) applied upon it (see section 7); when capital markets are imperfect (section 8), durable spending will be particularly strong when receipts of current income are high; and even when capital markets are perfect, high values of current income are likely to accompany heavy purchases of durables, since the purchase of durables is really a form of saving. We saw earlier (section I: 8) that a rise in the wage rate expected for one date (k) unaccompanied by increases in wage rates expected at other dates should raise savings at date k substantially. If the current period's wage rate is raised, but expectations of future periods' wage rates are unchanged, current savings will jump. There is therefore every reason to expect that additions to the stock of durables will be positively correlated with 'transitory' income. Friedman defines transitory income as the excess of current over permanent income. Econometric evidence in the USA[9] points to a very high marginal propensity to spend *transitory* income on durables. That on automobiles appears to reach one-third. *Permanent* income, on the other hand, like total wealth from which it is the yield, should be related to the stock of durables possessed—and hence to the rate at which their services are consumed—but not to the rate at which this stock increases.

There is no clear dichotomy between durable and non-durable goods. The costs of storing commodities vary case by case. Storage costs in their full sense include not just the rent on space occupied, but also the rate at which the goods depreciate over time, the cost of insurance against fire and theft, and any cost of ensuring special temperature conditions that may be required. Empirical analysis of consumer behaviour often proceeds on the basis of an essentially arbitrary distinction between durables and non-durables. This buys simplicity and convenience at a price. One clear dichotomy does, however, regularly present itself as a choice confronting the acquirer of a durable good: whether to buy or rent. Under perfectly competitive,

---

[9] Juster and Wachtel (176). Darby (75) claims to find the opposite, but his results fail to confirm his conclusions: see Ferber (108). See also Cragg (70) and Hess (159) for important results on the determinants of durables purchases.

ideal conditions, the purchase price P_D, the rental R_D and the rate of physical depreciation over time, δ, will be related by the equation

$$R_D = P_D(R + \delta - \hat{P}_D^e). \tag{1.19}$$

(1.19) states that the ratio of R_D to P_D will have three components. First, there is the rate of interest, R, that may be earned on an alternative asset: this represents the opportunity cost of the capital tied up in the durable. Then there is the rate of deprecation, δ. Lastly, there is $\hat{P}_D^e$, the *expected* proportionate rate of change of the price of the durable good itself. If (1.19) holds, an agency renting out durables should expect to break even, under ideal conditions. The rental rate should be just high enough to make the agency indifferent between buying the new equipment to rent it out, selling it for what it will fetch after the contracts expire, and merely lending out its capital (or not borrowing) at the rate R. $\hat{P}_D^e$ enters as a negative influence on R_D because any expectation of appreciation in price would make renting out seem more profitable. The leasing rates for computers or calculators, on the other hand, should be very high in relation to their current price, because of the expectation that their price will fall.

The purchase–rental choice is often difficult. Uncertainty plays a large role. We need to trespass on section 9 below, where the perfect knowledge assumption (A8) is relaxed, in order to see this. Renting will seem a better option if the individual is unsure how useful the durable good will be to him; he can choose not to renew a rental contract more easily than selling the thing on a second-hand market. If the quality of the good is variable, and the individual cannot test this beforehand, he will be greatly attracted by a rental contract that allows him to swap it with another, should it malfunction. Rental agencies can pool the risks of defective goods so much more easily than a household can, simply because of the advantage of scale. Renting will also appeal if the individual thinks there is a chance of a large deterioration in his financial circumstances: durable goods are much harder to sell than financial claims.

Why are used durable goods so hard to sell? Transactions costs are part of the explanation, but only part. The real problem is *asymmetry of* information.[10] When a particular new motor car is sold, neither vendor nor purchaser can know how reliable it will be: it may be a good car, or it may be a 'lemon'. But when a used car is offered for sale, the vendor (X) does have some information. X knows how well it has served him. The prospective purchaser (Y) lacks this information. Y asks himself, why is X selling it? Possibly because it is a lemon. If it were not a lemon, X would be keen to hold on to it; if it were a lemon, X would be anxious to sell it as soon as possible. So, Y concludes, used car markets have a much larger share of duds, of defective, low-quality cars, than new car markets. Lemons will change hands quickly, like the proverbial hot potato. Gresham's law operates in the used car markets: the bad drive out the good. The general point is that informational asymmetry leads to adverse selection, and adverse selection in turn to market failure. Other manifestations of the phenomenon include the markets for labour, insurance and credit. Wage rates may be held above equilibrium, because employers

[10] This point was first explored by Akerlof (1).

are anxious to hold on to their good workers; the luckless unemployed worker who tries to offer his services cheaply makes a prospective employer think that the quality of his work would be poor. Insurance against certain risks may be very expensive, or even unavailable, because those who seek cover will seem to be an unrepresentative sample (more risk-prone) of those who do not. This problem is compounded by 'moral hazard': once insured, the individual's own behaviour may change, making the event against which insurance has been given more likely. Adverse selection and moral hazard combine to create a constitutional weakness in credit markets: interest rates tend to be too low, and credit in excess demand. The implications of capital market imperfections for the household are considered in section 8. Returning to the durables markets, we may note that the rental agency may also experience difficulty in selling its used cars. If so, this could make $\hat{P}_D^e$ low in equation (1.19); and this in turn implies a high rental rate, R_D, it will offset some of the disadvantages the household will see in purchasing a new car, rather than renting it.

II: 5 *Relaxing the Assumption of No Adjustment Costs or Delivery Lags*

It was Keynes who first argued that consumers' expenditure displays temporary inertia in the face of changes in variables influencing it.[11] He attributed this to the force of habit. Habits change slowly, not at once. Commitments are entered into, both to buy and to sell. Goods ordered at one date may not be delivered until later; the national income statisticians will observe consumers' expenditure at the second date, when it occurs, and not the earlier date when the decision to incur it was taken. Labour supply and portfolio decisions will also be subject to lags. It may take the accumulation of several pieces of evidence about rates of pay, for example, to induce someone to change his labour supply behaviour. Even then, he may decide to change gradually, to experiment with a small initial rise or reduction in hours of work, postponing the full change until later. Finally, the decision to change *planned* labour supply may not be implemented at once because of con-tractual obligations, or the time taken to find another job. Three separate lags are evident here: the observational lag, the lag due to phased or delayed adjustment of the individual's own choosing, and the lag due to factors outside his control. In the portfolio case, the three lags could take the form of: (i) the time-interval between the first time an individual sees a fall in the rate of interest on bonds, relative to money $(R - R_m)$, and the moment he decides to switch some funds from money into bonds; (ii) the time-interval between making this decision and instruct-ing his bank to carry it out; and (iii) the time taken for the instruction to be executed in full.

It is consumers' expenditure, however, where Keynes's principle of delay has received most attention. Duesenberry (95) built upon it to develop his *relative income hypothesis*. This maintained that an individual's consumption spending would be influenced positively by his current income, negatively by his position in

[11] Keynes (182), p. 97: 'For a man's habitual standard of life usually has the first claim on his income . . . Thus a rising income will often be accompanied by increased saving and a falling income by decreased saving, on a greater scale at first than subsequently'.

the hierarchy of incomes in the society (so that low income earners spent more, all else equal), and positively by his previous peak levels of income or consumption. It is the third element in the hypothesis that draws on the Keynesian principle of delay, while the first reflects Keynes's 'fundamental psychological law'.[12] We shall return to the relative income hypothesis in section III of this chapter; it is to the issue raised by the second element—the externality effect implicit in the relative income position—that we turn next. But two final points are worth noting. Inertia will apply in the face of *unanticipated events*, something for which our perfect knowledge assumption (A8) does not allow. There should be no delays in response to anticipated events: our individual will take what action he needs to in advance. Even phased adjustment in behaviour in response to an event should not imply delay: our individual will start to adjust before it occurs even if he completes the adjustment somewhat after it.

Secondly, inertia on the part of individuals (in the sense of inflexibility, rather than gradual adjustment) does not necessarily imply social inertia. The passing of generations permits social change even if individuals become completely inflexible. An example is habits of work. These are often formed at an early stage of an individual's life. It is then that they may be most open to influence by, for instance, the rewards to effort apparent at the time. Changes in income-tax rates, promotion prospects and rewards, and dismissal regulations may have powerful but very gradual effects upon a nation's working habits.

II: 6 *Relaxing the Assumption of No Externalities*
   (Apart from a Terminal Bequest)

A consumption externality may be defined as a direct dependence, positive or negative, of the utility of one individual upon some activity undertaken by another. Externalities may arise in two ways. First, individuals often join together to form households, and other social organizations, which typically comprise more than one member. Second, activities of one household or individual often affect the utility and behaviour of others.

Multi-member social organizations, such as families, clubs and cities, owe their existence to natural selection mechanisms. Their origins spring from two aspects of certain goods: indivisibility and publicness. We saw in section II: 2 that indivisibilities favour large social units rather than small ones. Public goods (which are collectively consumable, and from which exclusion is impossible)[13] are a limiting case of externalities. Both phenomena encourage groups of individuals to act in unison, and to share. Ease of communication and collective security, for instance, stimulate urbanization. Economic theory usually starts with Robinson Crusoe, but only because this is the natural and simplest place to begin. The actions of the rational independent individual are easier to analyse than the behaviour of groups.

Like marriage partners or monks, members may form or join groups voluntarily.

---

[12] 'That men are disposed, as a rule and on the average, to increase their consumption as their income increases, but not by as much as the increase in their income', Keynes (182), p. 96.

[13] These two characteristics define a *strict* public good. See Samuelson (270) and also chapter 3, section I.

Alternatively, they have little or no choice in the matter, like children joining families or workers joining a trade union that has been granted a closed shop. An individual may be a member of many different kinds of social group. Groups differ in the strength and permanence of the ties that unite their members, and in the range of functions they perform. They differ, too, in the roles their members play. The group may be harmonious or divided, autocratic or democratic. Within the group, members' decisions may be *co-operative* or taken *independently*. This last distinction is fundamental in the analysis of *games*, the theory of which constitutes the major contribution of economic theory to the study of group behaviour.[14] A group whose members act independently will tend to conform, eventually, to a *Cournot–Nash equilibrium*; co-operation leads to a *collusive equilibrium*. Except in the special 'constant-sum' case where the aggregate of members' utilities is independent of the actions they take, the Cournot–Nash equilibrium may well suffer from Pareto inefficiency: all could benefit if each changed his actions. The Prisoner's Dilemma is the most celebrated example of this: optimization by independent invidiauls who treat the behaviour of others as independently given will be inferior *for all* to optimization by the group as a whole. Prisoner's Dilemma poses a grave and recurrent threat to social organizations that allow their members considerable freedom of action. If a group engaged in production distributes its goods or income among its members in a set pattern—for example equally— and permits its members to work as they choose, the reward to individual effort will be weak. The larger the group, the more diluted the incentive to work.[15] If a group allows its members to spend group funds as they wish they will behave as if the prices of commodities were much lower than they are. Furthermore, the smaller the group the stronger the feeling of loyalty towards it. Indivisibilities and public goods foster social groupings and favour larger scale; Prisoner's Dilemma works in the opposite direction. The actual size and character of social institutions reflect the way these contrary forces are resolved. The more the group is able and willing to restrict its members' freedom of action, the less the threat of Prisoner's Dilemma; but coercion can often be costly and miserable.

A group's preferences may be imposed by its leader(s). With often trivial exceptions, it is parents who disburse a family's income and supply its labour. But preferences, or needs, vary with household size and composition. The greater the number of dependants, the greater the outlay on foodstuffs, and perhaps also on clothing and space, and the less spent on entertainment and other luxuries.[16] At the other extreme, decision taking in the group may be highly decentralized. If all goods are divisible, private and parametrically prices, a group's preferences will be uniquely determined when its members' preferences are uniquely given, and when at least

---

[14] The classic treatise is Neumann and Morgenstern (238). See also Bacharach (18), for an excellent recent treatment.

[15] This problem is encountered by communes (see Sen (290)), as well as traditional firms whose output depends on teamwork (see section II: 2 above). A similar phenomenon underlies the Lewis growth model (192). Here, labour market equilibrium equates labour's marginal product in industry with its *average* product in agriculture.

[16] Empirical analysis of this employs adult equivalence scales. See Brown and Deaton (49), and Deaton and Muellbauer (80) ch. 8.

two of the three conditions hold: (i) identical preferences for all members: (ii) homothetic preferences for all members, so that the way spending is distributed between goods is independent of wealth; and (iii) a fixed distribution of wealth between members.

As far as a household is concerned, the labour supply decision now covers more than one individual. Children and aged dependent relatives can contribute to 'household production', performing tasks within the household.[17] More important, female adults can and do contribute to household earnings, by undertaking re-munerated work. A large increase in female participation of the labour force has been a marked feature in all industrial societies in the twentieth century. Child-rearing is apt to interrupt women's careers, however, with the result that working women's incomes may be regarded as less permanent. Children themselves are to a large extent planned; most economic analyses (e.g. (33)) of fertility explore this 'decision' on traditional choice-theoretic lines.

Externalities do not arise merely within groups: the activities of one household may affect the utility and behaviour of others. You are unlikely to want a tele-phone if telephones are rare. If the individual household's or company's demand for telephones is constructed on the assumption of a given stock of telephones distri-buted elsewhere in the economy, it will be less price-elastic than the aggregate social demand for telephones. The urge to emulate or to conform also creates inter-dependencies in demands for many commodities, especially those for which posses-sion or consumption is conspicuous. Saving is, by contrast, a private, unobserved activity. Hence Duesenberry's argument (95) for predicting that the average propensity to consume declines as income rises in cross-sectional comparisons of different households.

II: 7 *Introducing Further Kinds of Taxation*

Assumption A6 of the standard utility-maximizing model allowed for proportional taxes on wage incomes, and also lump-sum taxes which could be positive or negative. In this section, some of the implications of other kinds of taxation for household behaviour are considered briefly.

Taxes are levied on the purchase of commodities. These increase the price paid by the household. The effects of changes in the rates of tax follow those of price changes (section I: 9). If indirect taxation is to be efficient in Ramsey's sense,[18] the rate of tax on a good should be approximately[19] inversely proportional to the elasticity of demand for it. The overall *level* of indirect taxes also affects labour supply, and the demand for money. The demand for money should be related posi-tively to the level of indirect taxes, since transactions balances, at least, will be governed by the price level *inclusive* of indirect taxation at which these transactions

[17] See section II; 10 below.

[18] See Ramsey (259), Dixit (85), and Atkinson and Stiglitz (15). Ramsey-efficiency mini-mizes the utility sacrificed by a representative individual as a result of indirect taxation, for a given total tax yield. It is likely to conflict with income distributional arguments for relating the indirect tax rate on a good positively to the income elasticity of demand for it.

[19] Strictly the inverse proportionality rule works only when cross elasticities of demand can be ignored, utility is separable, and all supply curves are independent and of equal elasticity.

takes place. Labour supply will be affected by indirect taxes in much the same way as by the income-tax rate on earnings: both reduce the opportunity cost of leisure in terms of goods. The similarity is inexact, however, for a number of reasons. Indirect taxes reduce the purchasing power of asset holdings, while the income-tax rate has no direct effect on this; income tax is usually more progressive than indirect taxes; and the fact that income tax is in practice leveied on property income as well as wages introduces an important intertemporal differences between the two—the net of tax interest rate is not the same in the two cases, so that a higher income-tax rate is liable to induce substitution out of future into present leisure. There are two final points that arise with indirect taxation. Expectations of changes in future rates of indirect tax exert a powerful influence on the timing of durable goods purchases; and labour supply will be highly sensitive to the relative tax rates on substitutes for leisure, and complements with leisure.

As already suggested, income tax is levied on interest income and not just on earnings from work. To this extent, a rise in income tax behaves like a fall in the rate of interest: this leads to intertemporal substitution towards present goods (including leisure) at the expense of future goods. There is, in addition, an interesting conflict of effects upon the demand for money. A higher income-tax rate reduces the DPV of future labour earnings. This acts like a fall in wealth, and will tend to lower the demand for money balances. Against this, the opportunity cost of money *also* falls, provoking substitution within the portfolio out of bonds (whose yield will now fall, after tax) into money (whose after-tax yield will fall—if at all— by less). Which effect dominates is unclear. This has important implications. It is even possible that a rise in the rate of income tax will *raise* the level of aggregate demand at a given price level: this can happen if the demand for money falls, and the effect of this outweighs the negative direct impact on spending.[20]

The rate of tax on incomes from both work and property is rarely a single number. The marginal rate varies with income in most countries. Usually, there is a positive association. But the effective marginal rate of income tax can be high on low incomes, too, when the level of transfer payments from the state (such as rebates on rates and rents and school meals charges, and Family Income Supplement in the UK) are subject to means testing. This introduces both concave and convex kinks into the budget restraint between leisure and commodities.[21]

Taxes on inheritance or, when identifiable, on ability to earn[22] have no direct substitution effects in our model. They merely reduce

$$A_0 + \sum_{j=0}^{T} v_j w_j (1 - t_j) h_j,$$

the DPV of maximum lifetime economic resources. By lowering the demand for all save inferior goods, they will tend to stimulate labour supply. Against this, inheritance taxation will lead to substitution if (Z_T/P_T), the real bequest at date T, is

---

[20] See chapter 7, section VI: 3.

[21] The resulting labour supply function has been studied by Hanoch and Honig (146).

[22] See Hammond and Dasgupta (145) for a detailed analysis of ability taxation.

defined to be net of tax. If so, expectations of this tax on bequests may raise or lower saving, since the terminal bequest may or may not be complementary with other goods.

II: 8   *Introducing a Non-unique Rate of Interest*

There are four respects in which rates of interest may not be unique. They may be expressed before or after tax; before or after inflation ('nominal' or 'real'); and as lending or as borrowing rates. Lastly, they may vary with the duration of the loan in question.

The first and second of these differences raise the question of incidence. It is now widely accepted that experience and expectations of inflation lift nominal rates of interest much more than they reduce real rates;[23] indeed, the latter may be largely independent of inflation. There is more to dispute in the case of taxation.[24] The fourth type of non-uniqueness makes the term-structure of interest rates non-horizontal. At the level of the individual, all that changes in our standard model is the lifetime budget restraint (1.1). Here, v_j becomes $(1 + R_{j0})^{-j}$, and the fourth term

$$(R_m - R) \sum_{j=0}^{T} v_j M_j$$

is rewritten

$$\sum_{j=0}^{T} (R_{mj} - R_j) v_j M_j,$$

where R_{j0} is the current annualized rate of interest on a j-period loan, and R_{mj} and R_j denote the annual rates of interest, on money and one period bonds respectively, at date j. These minor changes apply to the first-order conditions (1.4)–(1.7) as well.

This leaves us with the significance of the difference between borrowing and lending rates. These two can differ, principally for two (ultimately related) reasons: transactions costs and uncertainties. The effect of any excess of borrowing rates above lending rates is to create an incentive to synchronize payments and receipts. 'Neither a borrower nor a lender be', as Polonius advised the departing Laertes.[25]

Flemming (112) has shown that this can increase the dependence of current consumption upon current income. He has a simple two-period model where income in each period is exogenous; one consumption good is assumed for each period with known prices for each; tastes are homothetic; and there are two parametric interest rates, $\bar{r}_b$ for borrowers and $\bar{r}_c$ for lenders, with $\bar{r}_b > \bar{r}_c$. The Engel curve showing consumption behaviour when income in period 1 is varied, and

[23] This used not to be the case: see for example, evidence by Sir Roy Harrod and Lord Kaldor to the Radcliffe Committee (258).

[24] Witness the wide variety of estimates of the interest-elasticity of savings (see Atkinson and Stiglitz (15), ch. 3) and of the extent to which corporate income taxes are borne by capital (see, for example, Break (45)).

[25] Shakespeare, *Hamlet*, I. iii. 75.

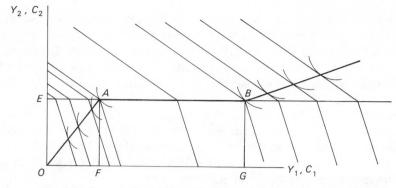

FIG. 1.3. Consumption and income when capital markets are imperfect.

period 2's income is given, becomes piecewise trilinear. This is the thick line in Figure 1.3, with kinks at A and B. In the horizontal section between A and B the marginal propensity to consume current income is unity. Y_2 (period 2 income) is given at E. If Y_1 (period 1 income) is below F, the household borrows at $\bar{r}_b$: the steep lines below EAB have gradient $-(1 + \bar{r}_b)$. If Y_1 exceeds G, it lends, earning the much lower rate $\bar{r}_c$ (all lines above EAB have gradient $-(1 + \bar{r}_c)$). Between A and B, savings are zero. The size of the gap between A and B depends on the difference between $\bar{r}_b$ and $\bar{r}_c$, and also upon the elasticity of substitution between consumption at different dates. If the latter is zero, the indifference curves will be L-shaped, and AB shrivels up to nothing.

II: 9 *Introducing Uncertainty*

The standard model and all its implications carry through if individuals behave *as if* they know the future values of all economic parameters they face (prices, wage rates, tax rates, legacies and interest rates). Individuals in this case have 'single-valued' expectations. Whether or not these expectations prove to be correct has no bearing on their *current* decisions. Their future decisions, however, may well be affected by any revisions in expectations that are made between now and the date at which the decisions are taken. Expectations may be revised in the light of new information, or as a result of errors.

The first attempt to endogenize expectations in the context of individual household decisions was made by M. Friedman.[26] The permanent income hypothesis that he developed is explored in detail below, in section III. Powerful as it is, the permanent income hypothesis focuses attention on only the mean expected values of future periods' incomes. In chapter 5, where the significance of uncertainty for portfolio decisions and the demand for money is studied, we shall see that mean expected values of economic variables are only one part of the story. In this section, we shall explore the effects of uncertainty on savings.

[26] Keynes had dismissed consumers' expectations of their future income as a trivial influence on total expenditure (Keynes (182)). As elsewhere in his work, he also took these expectations to be exogenous. The first of these mistakes was rectified by Hicks (162). Friedman, whose analysis builds upon Hicks's concepts of 'standard income' and 'elasticity of expectations', rectifies the second. See Friedman (121).

There are countless ways in which uncertainty may confront the individual. Future prices of goods; future wage rates, interest rates, tax rates, legacies, prices of assets; future preferences; the availability of jobs at future dates; dates of retirement and demise; future changes in the composition of the household, and other social groups, of which he is a member. We shall analyse just two: uncertainties about future prices and future income.

Consider an individual with a DPV of income, the mean expectation of which is A. He is interested in two goods. These are x_1, which he buys now in the first period, and x_2 which he buys in the second and final period. The price of x_1 is one. The mean expectation of the DPV of the second period price of x_2 is p. With single-valued expectations, our individual maximizes

$$\Phi = U(x_1, x_2) - \lambda [x_1 + px_2 - A] \tag{1.20}$$

with respect to x_1, (the currently planned level of) x_2 and the marginal utility of money, λ. Equivalently, he maximizes

$$U\left(x_1, \frac{A - x_1}{p}\right) \tag{1.21}$$

with respect to x_1. x_1 and x_2 are optimally chosen when $(\partial U/\partial x_2)/(\partial U/\partial x_1)$ equals p. But as soon as multi-valued expectations are introduced, the analysis changes. Suppose, first, that the individual thinks that period 2's price of x_2 (undiscounted) will be either $(p + u)(1 + R)$ or $(p - u)(1 + R)$. Both are, he thinks, equiprobable. His revised maximand is

$$\tfrac{1}{2}U\left(x_1, \frac{A - x_1}{p + u}\right) + \tfrac{1}{2}U\left(x_1, \frac{A - x_1}{p - u}\right). \tag{1.22}$$

(1.22) is rather likely to give different results from (1.21). There is one case where it will not. If $U = x_1^\alpha x_2^\beta$, (1.22) becomes

$$\tfrac{1}{2}x_1^\alpha (A - x_1)^\beta [(p + u)^{-\beta} + (p - u)^{-\beta}], \tag{1.23}$$

the maximization of (1.23) with respect to x_1 yields the result:

$$x_1 = \frac{\alpha}{\alpha + \beta} A,$$

which makes present consumption, x_1, quite independent of u, the uncertain element in future prices. Utility, on the other hand, will fall as $|u|$ increases, given only that $\beta < 1$: this can be seen by differentiating (1.23) with u. The explanation of this paradox lies in the fact that the Cobb–Douglas utility function exhibits zero cross-elasticities of demand: the demand for x_1 does not vary with the price of x_2. The certainty-equivalent discounted price of x_2 is *not* p, but $(\tfrac{1}{2}(p + u)^{-\beta} + \tfrac{1}{2}(p - u)^{-\beta})$, which tends to exceed p when $\beta < 1$. Our individual exhibits risk-aversion when $\beta < 1$, even if $\alpha + \beta > 1$ (i.e. even if there are increasing returns to scale for overall utility in lifetime consumption). He 'plays safe' by assuming a high price of x_2 in period 2, higher than its strict mathematical expectation. But because the demand for x_1 is independent of the price of x_2 in our Cobb–Douglas example, his present consumption is independent of price uncertainty.

Had there been a positive cross-elasticity of demand for x_1 to the price of x_2, x_1 and x_2 would have been substitutes. In this case, risk aversion *vis-à-vis* x_1—which is tantamount to a diminishing marginal utility of x_1—would entail a *positive* relation between present consumption and future price-level uncertainty. The traditional view that future price uncertainty stimulates saving is thus seen to depend in this example upon a *negative* cross-elasticity of demand for current consumption to the 'price' of future goods. If the elasticity of intertemporal substitution in consumption is below unity, and preferences are homothetic, this traditional view will be valid.

Next, income uncertainty. Suppose now that p is known confidently, with single valued expectation, but A is thought to be either $(A + u)$ or $(A - u)$. Again, both events are deemed equally probable. With income rather than price uncertainty and a Cobb–Douglas utility function, the maximand will be

$$\tfrac{1}{2}x_1^\alpha p^{-\beta}[(A + u - x_1)^\beta + (A - u - x_1)^\beta]. \tag{1.24}$$

(1.24) provides only an indirect solution for x_1 unless $\beta = 1$. But differentiating this solution with respect to $|u|$ reveals that x will rise (fall) with an increase in the level of income uncertainty, if $\beta < 1$ ($\beta > 1$). Exactly, the same is true of the effect of $|u|$ on utility. When $\beta < 1$, the certainty-equivalent level of A is less than its mathematical expectation.

The effects of price and income uncertainty are depicted in Figures 1.4 and 1.5. In Figure 1.4, BF represents the budget line in the limiting case with no uncertainty about the price of x_2 in the second period. With price uncertainty, there are two

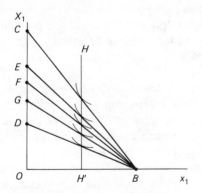

FIG. 1.4. Savings and price uncertainty.

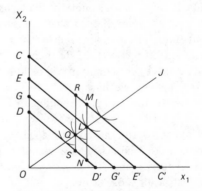

FIG. 1.5. Savings and income uncertainty.

possible budget lines, BC which rules when the price of x_2 will be $(p - u)(1 + R))$ and BD (when it will be $(p + u)(1 + R))$. The mathematical expectation of the consumption of x, if these two states are equiprobable and collectively exhaustive, will be $\{\tfrac{1}{2}(A - x_1)(p - u)\} + \{\tfrac{1}{2}(A - x_1)(p + u)\}$, which is represented by point E. If the marginal utility of y diminishes sufficiently, our individual will behave *as if* the price of x_2 had been known with certainty to lie much closer to $(p + u)(1 + R)$

than to $(p - u)(1 + R)$. For example, he will act as if his budget line had been certain at BG. Fig. 1.4 represents Cobb–Douglas indifference curves, which have the characteristic that the demand for x_1 is independent of the (certainty-equivalent) price of good x_2. Hence the vertical line HH', showing independence of current consumption of (x_1) from the price x_2, from uncertainty about the price of x_2, and from attitudes to such uncertainty. Had x_1 and x_2 been complementary in demand, on the other hand, HH' would have sloped upward from left to right; increased uncertainty about the price of x_2 coupled with diminishing marginal utility of x_2 would then tend to imply *lower* consumption of x_1.

In Figure 1.5, the price of x_2 is known with certainty, but income is uncertain. It may be $(A + u)$, in which case CC' represents the budget restraint: equally probable, however, is the lower income $(A - u)$ which gives a budget restraint of DD'. EE' represents the budget line if u vanishes. But with u positive, our individual will not behave as if his budget line were EE', except in the limiting case of a constant marginal utility of x_2. With diminishing marginal utility of x_2, the utility of point L exceeds the average of the utilities of points M and N. When the individual behaves as if his budget line were GG', the loss in utility in the bad state when income is only $(A - u)$, and the consumption of x_2 is low, is balanced by the gain when income is $(A + u)$ and consumption of x_2 can be high. The loss in utility in the bad state—where consumption will be at S—now offsets the gain in the good state, where consumption will be at R. Our individual is indifferent between certainty of consumption at Q and equal chances of points R and S. Accordingly, he will behave as if he is faced by budget restraint GG'. He will spend less on x_1 current consumption, than he would have if there had been no income uncertainty. Essentially, it is the irreversibility of the consumption decision which leads to this result. It is future consumption which absorbs all the pressure of unforeseen events. You commit yourself to present consumption levels in the light of expectations about future prices and income levels; if you turn out later to be unlucky with your predictions, it will be too late then to undo past consumption decisions, and your final periods of consumption will be miserably low.

The analysis we have conducted provides a sound justification for Keynes's first motive for saving: 'to build up a reserve against unforeseen contingencies' ((182), p. 107). The reason for Friedman's inclusion of the ratio of human to non-human wealth as an influence on the permanent consumption-permanent income ratio, k, also becomes apparent: property income is generally more volatile than labour income. There is much intuitive appeal in the notion of diminishing marginal utility of future periods' consumption levels; and complementarity between consumption levels at different dates seems rather plausible. The availability of insurance, whether private or public, quite probably diminishes savings.[27] It could also reduce labour supply. Comprehensive insurance opportunities against all contingencies form the basis of the Arrow–Debreu model of *contingent commodities*. These are claims which pay their holder if and only if a specified set of events materializes. They are considered in detail in chapter 2, section V. The

---

[27] See Feldstein (105) for an interesting analysis of the effects of social security systems on saving.

concept of contingent commodities is a brilliant device for incorporating uncertainty into a general equilibrium model of the economy. Unfortunately, however, insurance markets are far from complete. Adverse selection and moral hazard combine with transactions costs in confining contingent commodity markets to a tiny fraction of all they might be. We conclude this section with two further points. First, it is highly unlikely that individuals will interest themselves only in the mathematical expectation of future prices and income levels. Consequently, rational certainty-equivalent expectations of the variables will probably be based on their observed variances, skewnesses and other characteristics, as well as on the laws of stochastic motion and economics that are shown to determine their mean levels. This is a major point, with large and as yet unexplored implications. Second, a more consoling observation: for most of us, inflation raises the prices of what we buy and what we sell almost equiproportionately. The only major qualification to this is that we sell labour on average before we buy goods, so that at least unexpected inflation has alarming intergenerational redistributive effects. None the less, if the same factors that raise the price of x_2 in Figure 1.4 *also* raise income in Figure 1.5, their effects on utility, present consumption and present labour supply may be rather smaller than appears at first sight.

II: 10 *Other Approaches*

There are various ways in which the approach can be altered. Lancaster (190) has proposed that household utility depends on the *characteristics* provided by goods, and not directly upon the goods themselves. Becker's theory of the allocation of time (34) also maintains a two-tier approach to household utility: utility depends upon commodities *produced by the household* (meals, entertainment and warmth for example); the commodities are produced by inputs of goods purchased with the rewards from remunerated labour earnings, accompanied by inputs of household time.

Another approach, common in much early macroeconomic theorizing but now somewhat out of favour, is to dispense with the hypothesis of utility maximization entirely. Instead, a positive assertion is made about how households do behave. This is then tested, and rejected or confirmed by the data. Keynes's study of the consumption function belongs to this category. There is no explicit choice-theoretic basis to it. The case for rejecting the utility-maximizing view of the household may be defended on the ground that its behaviour is determined by social and biochemical mechanisms. The notion of optimizing behaviour relies on the freedom to choose, and on the knowledge of the consequences of different courses of action. Neither of these has much descriptive appeal. On the other hand, the utility-maximizing approach may be defended on the ground that it can be made true by definition. Information and decision-taking costs can be incorporated to justify rules of thumb. Observed phenomena such as imitation may be justified with reference to externalities; inertia, by the costs of adjustment or by caution in revising expectations, caution that may be well-founded in past experience. Moreover, imitation and inertia are sometimes offered as explanations of phenomena that *rival* the utility-maximizing approach. This is unreasonable for two reasons. Not merely can inertia and imitation be incorporated within the utility-maximizing approach; they also fail by themselves to give a satisfactory explanation of the phenomenon. We still need to ask what drives the pioneer to act as he does. What is ultimately unappealing about the utility-maximizing approach is not that it is too narrow, but that by itself it is too broad. Its predictive powers descend from the assumptions linked with it. It is perhaps to these that debate should be directed.

III: Aggregate Consumption Functions: A Brief Survey

There are four traditional theories of the consumption function: the *absolute income hypothesis* (AIH), the *relative income hypothesis* (RIH), the *permanent income hypothesis* (PIH) and the *life-cycle hypothesis* (LCH). Of these, the RIH has already received some attention (sections II: 5 and II: 6). What of the others, and how are they related?

The AIH descends from Keynes's 'fundamental psycholgoical law' quoted in footnote 12. In its simplest form, it maintains a linear function between real consumption outlays at one date and current real disposable income

$$C_t = a + bY_t(1 - t_t). \qquad (1.25)$$

Four arguments can be offered in its defence. First, there may be next to no evidence of serial correlation in individuals' actual income receipts. In this case, if income takes a random walk,

$$Y_t - Y_{t-1} = u_t,$$

Y_t will always be the best predictor of any future period's income, as we shall see shortly. Second, we saw in section II: 9 that capital market imperfections may impose a serious penalty on non-synchronized consumption and income paths. If the income path is exogenous to the household, current income will exert a very powerful influence on current consumption, even when current income is taken as a poor proxy for expected future income. Third, there is considerable evidence that the average propensity to consume declines with increases in income in cross-sectional tests. This is quite consistent with (1.25) when a is positive. Lastly, the short-run aggregate consumption function also displays a positive intercept, implying once again a negative association between income and the average propensity to consume.

Unfortunately, however, there is one other 'stylized fact' about consumption with which AIH is inconsistent. This is the long-run constancy of the average propensity to consume identified by Kuznets (187): between 1869 and 1929 income increased fourfold, while the average propensity to save displayed no trend. If (1.25) is valid, a must be zero in the long run. The task of reconciling Kuznets's evidence with the two previous findings (that a is positive in cross-sectional and short-run aggregate time series tests) helped to stimulate the three other hypotheses: PIH, RIH, and LCH. The LCH was propounded by Modigliani and Brumberg (220). They propose that each individual's consumption at date t is a fraction of his lifetime resources, which consist of his current and expected future labour income, and his (non-human) wealth. See Hall (144) and White (332) for tests.

The *Life Cycle Model of consumption* is a simplified version of our standard model. In its simplest form, the model consists of the following assumptions:

(B1) the number of live births grows, and has always grown, at a constant rate $n > 0$;

(B2) everyone enters the labour force at a constant and uniform age, and retires and dies at known, constant and uniform age respectively S and T years after starting work $(S < T)$;

(B3) all income is earned;

(B4) the rate of interest is zero;

(B5) there are no bequests (and hence no inheritances);

(B6) everyone aims to consume at a constant rate, C, between starting work and death, and consumes nothing before starting work;

(B7) the rate of earnings throughout working life, w, is known, uniform and constant;

(B8) there is no taxation and no social security.

From B2-5, B7 and B8, each individual's lifetime income is Sw. B5 tells us that this will equal his or her lifetime consumption spending. From B4, B6 and B8, lifetime consumption equals CT. Hence,

$$C = \frac{S}{T}w \qquad (1.26)$$

for each individual. While he or she works, he saves at the rate $w - C = (T - S/T)w$. Once retired, the individual meets consumption needs by dissaving at the rate $(S/T)w$.

The individual starts work with no wealth. But, saving over the working life leads to steady accumulation. At the point of retirement, his or her wealth peaks at $(S/T)(T - S)w$. It then runs down to zero at death. Turning to aggregate behaviour, we have to add up the population in each age cohort. If z is the number of labour force entrants at date 0, the total working *and* retired population at date 0, N_0, equals

$$N_0 = \int_0^T ze^{-nt}\,dt = \frac{z}{n}(1 - e^{-nT}).$$

Now N_0 is the sum of the working population, N_0^W, and the retired population, N_0^R. These are:

$$N_0^W = \int_0^S ze^{-nt}\,dt = \frac{z}{n}(1 - e^{-nS})$$

and

$$N_0^R = \int_S^T ze^{-nt}\,dt = \frac{z}{n}(e^{-nS} - e^{-nT}).$$

The community's total earnings and consumption are, respectively,

$$\frac{wz}{n}(1 - e^{-nS}) \quad \text{and} \quad c\frac{z}{n}(1 - e^{-nT}) = \frac{wz}{n}\frac{S}{T}(1 - e^{-nT}).$$

From these we may derive the community's average propensity to save, s. This is,

$$s = 1 - \frac{S}{T}\frac{1 - e^{-nT}}{1 - e^{-nS}}. \tag{1.27}$$

From this it may be seen that there are just three influences on the community's average savings propensity: n, the population growth rate; S, the length of the working life; and T, the number of years after starting work that people die. The first and third of these influences on the community's savings are invariably positive in this simple version of the LCM, while the second is always negative. In the special case of $n = 0$, the size of age-cohorts is constant, and the dissaving of the retired exactly balances the saving of those in work; so $s = 0$ as well. The individual's behaviour and aggregate behaviour are illustrated in Figure 1.6. Social net savings are found by multiplying the individual's savings and dissavings path by the social age-distribution curve. When n is positive, each age cohort is more plentiful than the last, and the positive savings of the more numerous workers outweigh the dissavings of the retired.

Naturally, the results alter when the LCM's assumptions are changed. Suppose, for example, that the rate of interest is a positive constant, r, that people aim to increase their consumption by a constant proportion b each year, and that earnings are known to grow at a constant proportion g each year. The faster the growth of earnings, the greater the present value of future earnings in relation to current earnings, and the less the individual worker will save. The larger the desired growth rate of consumption, the greater the wish to postpone consumption, and the more he will save. If b is negative, however, he is impatient, and will save less. For an individual just entering the labour force at date 0, with an initial wage of w_0, the discounted present value of lifetime earnings is

$$\int_0^S w_0 e^{(g-R)t}\,dt = \frac{w_0}{g - R}(e^{(g-R)S} - 1)$$

and the discounted present value of lifetime consumption (where $c_0 =$ initial consumption) is

$$\int_0^T c_0 e^{(b-R)t}\,dt = c_0(e^{(b-R)T} - 1).$$

His initial average propensity to consume, c_0/w_0, therefore equals

$$\frac{e^{(g-R)S} - 1}{e^{(b-R)T} - 1}\left(\frac{b - R}{g - R}\right).$$

His savings at date t will equal the increase in his wealth, ϕ, at date t:

$$\dot{\phi}(t) = w(t) - c(t) + R\int_0^t (w(\tau) - c(\tau))e^{R(t-\tau)}\,d\tau.$$

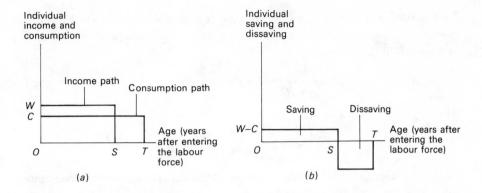

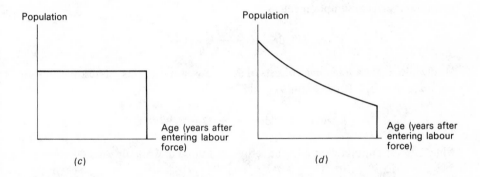

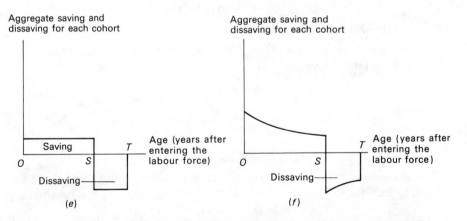

FIG. 1.6. Individual and aggregate saving and dissaving in the simple Life Cycle Model. (a) Income and consumption for the individual. (b) Saving and dissaving for the individual. (c) Social age-distribution of population when $n = 0$. (d) Social age-distribution of population when $n > 0$. (e) Aggregate saving and dissaving cancel out when $n = 0$. (f) Aggregate saving outweighs dissaving when $n > 0$.

Here, savings consist of the amount by which consumption falls short of earnings plus interest on accumulated wealth. Since $c(t) = c_0 e^{bt}$ and given the value of c_0/w_0, we find

$$\dot{\phi}(t) = \frac{w_0}{g - R} (g e^{gt} - R e^{Rt}(1 - \theta) - \theta b e^{bt})$$

where,

$$\theta = \frac{e^{(g-R)S} - 1}{e^{(b-R)T} - 1}.$$

Deriving aggregate consumption requires adding up each age cohort's consumption. Although each person consumes more as he gets older (if $b > 0$), younger generations have higher lifetime earnings than older ones (since $g > 0$). Younger generations are also more numerous (since $n > 0$). Defining $h = g + n - b$, we find that total social consumption equals

$$\int_0^T c_0 z e^{-ht} \, dt = w_0 \frac{b - R}{g - R} \frac{\theta z}{h} (1 - e^{-ht}).$$

Meanwhile, aggregate income consists of aggregate earnings, plus interest receipts on aggregate wealth.[28] Total earnings equal

$$\int_0^S w_0 z e^{-(g+n)t} dt = \frac{w_0 z}{g + n} (1 - e^{-(g+n)S}),$$

while interest on total wealth of the retired and those in work, Φ^R and Φ^W, are:

$$R\Phi^R = \frac{Rzw_0}{g - R} e^{-gS} \left\{ \Psi \frac{1 - e^{-\lambda(T-S)}}{\lambda} + \theta e^{(b-R)S} \left(\frac{1 - e^{-\lambda(T-S)}}{\lambda} + \frac{1 - e^{-h(T-S)}}{h} \right) \right\},$$

$$R\Phi^W = \frac{Rzw_0}{g - R} \left\{ \frac{e^{nS} - 1}{h} - \frac{(1 - \theta)e^{\lambda S} - 1}{\lambda} - \frac{\theta e^{hS} - 1}{h} \right\},$$

where $\lambda = g + n - R$ and $\Psi = e^{gS} - e^{RS}(1 - \theta) - \theta e^{bS}$. The community's average propensity to save is therefore

$$s = 1 - \frac{\dfrac{b - R}{g - R} \dfrac{\theta}{h}(1 - e^{-ht})}{\dfrac{1 - e^{-(g+n)S}}{g + n} + \dfrac{R}{zw_0}(\Phi^R + \Phi^W)}. \tag{1.28}$$

This ratio *increases* with b (if $n > 0$) and varies *negatively* with g (if $n > 0$). It also tends to increase with n, as before, but this may not happen if b is negative or g

---

[28] These are found by cumulating each age cohort's wealth. A worker retires at date t with wealth of

$$\Psi \frac{w_0}{g - R} e^{g(t-S)}.$$

is large. How it varies with R is indeterminate: there are numerous effects, not all in the same direction.

If other assumptions of this simple LCM are relaxed, additional influences on aggregate savings can be identified. State provision of pensions lowers the incentive to save, while expectations of future taxation will raise it. Risk aversion and uncertainty about future earned or unearned income make for higher saving, as does the introduction of a bequest motive. If raising children places large consumption burdens on youthful parents, or if rates of pay increase with seniority, the positive effect of higher population growth—already qualified when b and g are introduced —becomes still less reliable. Although insurance can dispense with the effects of uncertainty about the age of death, unforeseen changes in life expectancy and other demographic variables, such as fertility rates, the extent of female participation in the labour force and the age of child-bearing, will have complex phased effects. Once and for all increases in wage rates cause a temporary jump in the savings ratio, since only the youngest workers can raise their consumption by the same proportion; the retired will consume as before. When S years have elapsed, however, the savings ratio reaches its previous level. By contrast, a rise in wage rates that is known to be temporary produces a much more modest increase in consumption, which will return to its old level after T years or so. In this case, the community's savings ratio rises sharply above trend while wages are higher, and then dips a little below trend for several years thereafter. A temporary jump in births produces a not dissimilar effect. The community's savings ratio goes above trend while the additional people are working, falls below it when they retire, and returns to trend after they die.

The *Permanent Income Hypothesis* relates an individual's consumption to a flow concept, his permanent income. Permanent income is the rate of yield, in real terms, on total lifetime resources, or total wealth. Permanent income satisfies one definition of income: 'the most you can spend without expecting to get poorer'. The concept really originates with Hicks (162), who calls it 'standard income'. It is Friedman (120) who gives it the name 'permanent income'. It can be related to the left-hand side of (1.1) by the definition

$$\text{permanent income} \equiv (R - \hat{P}^e)\left[A_0 + \sum_{j=0}^{T} v_j(L_j - \psi_j) + \sum_{j=0}^{T} v_j w_j l_j(1 - t_j)\right]$$

where $\hat{P}^e$ is the expected rate of inflation, and R, as before, the nominal rate of interest. Permanent income is often treated as exogenously given to the household, however, in which case it can be defined

$$\text{permanent income} \equiv (R - \hat{P}^e)E$$

where E is total lifetime resources, as defined in section II: 2.

Friedman's Permanent Income Hypothesis (PIH) maintains that the systematic component of a household's spending (on non-durable goods, at least)[29] is a

[29] The purchase of a durable good is a portfolio decision, not a consumption decision. Only for non-durable goods can purchase and consumption be regarded as simultaneous.

fraction, k, of its permanent income; and that permanent income can be proxied by a weighted average of present and past observed levels of income.[30]

In its simplest form, Friedman's system consists of two definitions, two equations and an additional assumption. Actual consumption spending, C_t, equals permanent consumption, C_t^P, plus transitory consumption, C_t^T. Similarly actual income, Y_t, consists of permanent and transitory components, $Y_t^P + Y_t^T$. The permanent variables are regular, recurrent magnitudes; the transitory terms reflect non-recurrent, random influences, with no serial correlation. The two equations are

$$C_t^P = k_t Y_t^P, \tag{1.29}$$

$$Y_t^P = (1 - \mu) \sum_{i=0}^{\infty} \mu^i Y_{t-i}, \tag{1.30}$$

where k_t varies with the consumer unit's age and tastes, with interest rates, and also with the ratio of human to non-human wealth; and μ is a parameter lying between 1 and 0 which governs the weighting scheme. The additional assumption makes C_t^T independent of both Y_t^P and Y_t^T, with a mean value of zero.

Equation (1.30) provides a pattern of geometrically declining weights on current and previous income levels. The coefficient $(1 - \mu)$ is required to meet the condition that Y_t^P could not deviate from Y_{t-1} if Y_t were known to have been stationary. If all values of Y_{t-1} were the same up to and including $i = 0$,

$$\sum_{i=0}^{\infty} \mu^i Y_{t-i} = \frac{Y_{t-i}}{1 - \mu}.$$

A high value of μ indicates that only a small weight is placed on current income in forming expectations of future income: consumer spending displays considerable inertia. Indeed, μ is known as the 'inertia coefficient'. The reason for this becomes plain when (1.30) is subjected to the 'Koyck transformation': (1.30) implies

$$Y_{t-1}^P = (1 - \mu) \sum_{i=1}^{\infty} \mu^{i-1} Y_{t-i} \tag{1.31}$$

Subtracting (1.31) from (1.30), and substituting from (1.29), we obtain

$$Y_t^P - \mu Y_{t-1}^P = \frac{C_t^P}{k_t} - \mu \frac{C_{t-1}^P}{k_{t-1}} = (1 - \mu) Y_t$$

or

$$C_t = C_t^T - \mu \frac{k_t C_{t-1}^T}{k_{t-1}} + \mu \frac{k_t C_{t-1}}{k_{t-1}} + k_t (1 - \mu) Y_t. \tag{1.32}$$

---

[30] Some later versions of the PIH take a forward-looking view. The hypothesis here is that an agent's consumption plan is amended only in the light of new information, and that surprises should be random. This implies that consumption will tend to exhibit a random walk. See Hall (144) and Bilson (341), and the critical paper by Muellbauer (358).

If the difference between k_t and k_{t-1} is negligible, and since transitory consumption is a random, serially uncorrelated variable with zero mean, (1.32) simplifies to

$$C_t = k(1 - \mu)Y_t + \mu C_{t-1} + \epsilon_t \quad \text{(where } \epsilon_t \approx C_t^T - \mu C_{t-1}^T\text{).}\qquad (1.33)$$

The role of μ is evident in (1.33): the larger it is, the weaker the influence of current income upon current consumer spending, and the stronger the tendency for the latter simply to repeat itself. Aggregate time-series evidence from the USA was soon seen to conform nicely to (1.33) (see Friedman (120)): k appeared to lie close to 0.9, and μ to exceed $\frac{1}{2}$ on annual intervals ($\frac{3}{4}$ or more on quarterly intervals).

The permanent income model has undoubted appeal, particularly in view of its empirical successes.[31] None the less, the pattern of expectations is imposed *ad hoc*. There is no explanation of why μ takes on the value it does, nor indeed why the weighting scheme in (1.30) should conform to any particular type. At bottom, (1.30) embeds a particular hypothesis about the learning process. (1.30) and (1.31) imply that

$$Y_t^P - Y_{t-1}^P = (1 - \mu)(Y_t - Y_{t-1}^P).\qquad (1.34)$$

(1.34) states that the revision in expectations (of permanent income) over a measured interval is a fixed fraction of the size of the difference between the actual current value of income and the previous date's expectations of future income. $Y_t - Y_{Pt-1}$ is the previous expectational error. (1.34) is a special case of the general condition

$$Y_{Pt} = Y_{Pt-1} \text{ if and only if } Y_t = Y_{Pt-1},$$

which states that evidence of errors is sufficient and necessary for causing expectations to change.

The question that arises is what can explain the inertia coefficient, μ. In particular, if expectations of future income are formed rationally, how will μ be related to actual observations of the income path?

Expectations for a variable are said to be *rational* when all available evidence, and the best theoretical explanation for it, are used to provide statistically optimal predictors for that variable. More detailed discussion of rational expectations, including the concept of rational expectations equilibrium, will be found in chapter 2, section VII: 4; see also chapter 7. At this stage we shall confine ourselves to trying to answer our question about μ under rational expectations step by step, taking some examples.

Suppose, first, that an individual observes that his income follows the path

$$Y_t = Y_{t-1} + u_t,\qquad (1.35)$$

where u_t is a stochastic disturbance term relating to date t with the following characteristics: a mean of zero; finite variance; each u_t distributed identically and independently (so that there is no serial correlation); stationarity in the distribution of u_t. These characteristics make u_t 'pure white noise', the simplest kind of random

---

[31] See Mayer (211) for a survey of studies; see also Hall (144).

variable. How will he form rational expectations of his future income? This process tells us that income takes a purely random walk. The best guide to the future is the most recent observation of income. More than that: he should rely *exclusively* on his most recent observation. Past observations are just water under the bridge. Income is just as likely to continue moving away from its previous observation as it is to return towards it. So he should put no weight at all on past observations. Denote expectation at date $(t + i)$ of variable x for date $(t + j)$ by $E_{t+i}x_{t+j}$. Formally, then,

$$E_t Y_{t+1} = Y_t + E_t u_{t+1}$$

and since u_{t+1} is pure white noise, its expected mean value is zero. Hence

$$E_t Y_{t+1} = Y_t. \tag{1.36}$$

Furthermore the most recent observation is the best guide to more distant future income levels, since there is no trend in our example. So

$$E_t Y_{t+1} = E_t Y_{t+2} = E_t Y_{t+3} = \ldots = Y_t.$$

From this it follows that permanent income at date t simply equals actual income at date t. The inertia coefficient μ should be zero.

Actual and permanent income only coincide, however, in this very special case. Suppose now that another individual finds that his actual income varies randomly around a constant level, a, which again exhibits no trend. Assume again, that the random component in income is pure white noise. In this case, income follows the path

$$Y_t = a + u_t. \tag{1.37}$$

How much weight should he place on the most recent observation in forming a rational expectation of income in the next, or any later period? Very little, if any. If he has m observations on Y, the constant term a (which he must presumably infer from evidence) is best estimated by

$$\frac{1}{m} \sum_{i=0}^{m} Y_{t-i}.$$

Consequently his best guess about income in any future period, and hence permanent income, at date t must be

$$E_t Y_{t+1} = E_t Y_{t+2} = E_t Y_{t+3} = \ldots = \frac{1}{m} \sum_{i=0}^{m} Y_{t-i}. \tag{1.38}$$

If past observations are very numerous, expectations of future income, and hence permanent income are effectively *independent* of the most recent observation of actual income. The inertia coefficient μ should be 1, or almost 1.

These two examples have produced limiting values of μ. In the first case, μ should be zero. Past history of income serves one purpose: it tells him that it is irrelevant. Forecasts should be based solely on the most recent observation. In the second, μ should be 1, or nearly so; past history is all-important, since deviations from trend are transitory and insigificant as far as the future is concerned. Both examples are special cases of the income path

$$Y_t = Y_{t-1} + u_t - \mu u_{t-1}, \tag{1.39}$$

which is known as a *first-order autoregressive scheme*. It is first-order, since only the one immediately previous disturbance term enters the equation (in addition to u_t); it is autoregressive, since, except in the limiting case where $\mu = 0$, Y tends to regress back, to some extent, to some (weighted) average of previous levels of Y. Now when $j > 1$, (1.39) implies

$$E_t Y_{t+j} = E_t Y_{t+j-1} \tag{1.40}$$

and

$$E_t Y_{t+1} = Y_t - \mu u_t = Y_t - \mu(Y_t - Y_{t-1} + \mu u_{t-1})$$
$$= Y_t - \mu(Y_t - Y_{t-1}) - \mu^2(Y_{t-1} - Y_{t-2}) - \mu^3(Y_{t-2} - Y_{t-3}) - \mu^4 u_{t-3}$$
$$= (1 - \mu) \sum_{i=0}^{\infty} \mu^i Y_{t-i}. \tag{1.41}$$

Combining (1.40) and (1.41) we find permanent income at date t:

$$Y_t^P = (1 - \mu) \sum_{i=0}^{\infty} \mu^i Y_{t-i}, \tag{1.42}$$

which is precisely the geometrically-declining lag distribution on past incomes proposed and employed by Friedman. Differencing (1.42) we obtain the adaptive or error-learning expectations equation

$$Y_t^P - \mu Y_{t-1}^P = (1 - \mu) Y_t, \tag{1.43}$$

which is just a rearrangement of (1.34); see Sargent (279). Strictly, equations (1.41)–(1.43) all take the individual's observation set to be infinite. They are close approximations when m is large and μ is not too high.

We have, therefore, identified conditions under which the lag structure on actual income is rationally determined. We have provided an answer to the question of what can explain the size of the inertia coefficient, μ. But as usual one question only leads on to others. What happens if income follows a second or higher order autoregressive path? What role does a trend play? How does the analysis change if 'news' about the future arrives which is not already contained in the history of the past? What is the significance of risk-aversion? Can any allowance be made for endogeneity in income? This is certainly not an exclusive list of additional questions, but it is a list of important questions. We shall try to sketch a short answer to each.

If (1.39) is replaced by a *second-order* autoregressive path

$$Y_t = Y_{t-1} + u_t - \mu_1 u_{t-1} - \mu_2 u_{t-2} \tag{1.44}$$

two things occur. Permanent income ceases to equal $E_t Y_{t+1}$, because $E_t Y_{t+1} \neq E_t Y_{t+2}$. In fact, for $j \geqslant 2$,

$$E_t Y_{t+j} = E_t Y_{t+2} = Y_t - \mu_2 u_t,$$

while

$$E_t Y_{t+1} = Y_t - \mu_1 u_t - \mu_2 u_{t-1}.$$

Secondly, the optimal weighting on previous observations alters to reflect the slower and more complex autoregressive path. All the attractive simplicity of (1.43) is unfortunately lost. The coefficients on Y_{t-k} for $E_t Y_{t+1}$ and $E_t Y_{t+2}$ are, respectively,

$$\mu_1^k(1-\mu_1) + \sum_{j=1}^{k/2} \mu_2^j \mu_1^{k-2j} \left[\binom{k-j-1}{j} - \mu_1 \binom{k-j}{j} \right]$$

and

$$(1 - \mu_1 - \mu_2) \left[\mu_1^k + \sum_{j=2}^{k/2} \mu_2^j \mu_1^{k-2j} \binom{k-j}{j} \right].$$

With an *n*th order autoregressive path, all the $E_t Y_{t+1}$, $E_t Y_{t+2}$, ... differ up to and including $E_t Y_{t+n-1}$, and the coefficients of each on Y_{t-k} are still more byzantine.

A trend may be introduced by inserting a constant term, let it be b, on the right-hand side of (1.39). This will allow for a constant absolute growth rate of b per period. A constant proportionate growth rate may be incorporated by adding b but redefining Y_t, real income at date t, in *logarithms*. In the first order auto-regressive case, when b is known, b/μ is added to the result for $E_t Y_{t+1}$ and $b/\mu + b(k-1)$ to that for $E_t Y_{t+k}$. The real novelty to which the trend gives rise is the large boost to consumption. The discounted present value of future earnings is highly sensitive to the forecast growth rate of earnings, particularly when the individual concerned is expecting to draw wages for a long time. If two assumptions made in our simple life-cycle model are imposed (namely, no bequests and a wish to consume at a constant rate), an *x* per cent increase in discounted earnings will lead to an *x* per cent rise in consumption. Friedman's empirical work (121) allowed for a constant trend in real income per head.

One issue that arises when a trend is admitted is the possibility that expectations are formed about the trend, as well as the level of income. For example, suppose

$$Y_t - Y_{t-1} = u_t + Y_{t-1} - Y_{t-2} - \mu u_{t-1}, \tag{1.45}$$

then the rational expectations predictor of Y_{t+1} at date t is

$$Y_t + (1 - \mu) \sum_{i=0}^{\infty} \mu^i (Y_{t-i} - Y_{t-i-1}). \tag{1.46}$$

Note the contrast between (1.42) and (1.46). (1.46) is an extrapolative expectations formula: the change in Y is predicted as a weighted average of present and past changes in Y. (1.42) is regressive in the level of Y. (1.46) is regressive in the change in Y, and extrapolative in the level of Y. In the context of price level forecasts (where Y_t would denote the logarithm of the price level at date t), Flemming has called (1.42) and (1.46) 'first-gear' and 'second-gear' expectations (113). The concept can be generalized: if

$$\Delta^{n-1} Y_t = u_t + \Delta^{n-1} Y_{t-i} - \mu u_{t-1},$$

the rational expectations predictor of $\Delta^{n-1} Y_{t+1}$ at date t, is

$$E_t(\Delta^{n-1} Y_{t+1}) = (1 - \mu) \sum_{i=0}^{\infty} \mu^i \Delta^{n-i} Y_{t-i}, \tag{1.47}$$

(1.47) is the 'nth gear' adaptive expectations equation. Which gear expectations are in will depend upon what past experience implies for optimal predictions. Between 1625 and 1913, for instance, Great Britain experienced no trend in the level of prices. Relative prices changed and the price level ebbed and flowed over the downswings and upswings in the business cycle; but there was no inflation. It is quite natural that for much of this period, and some time thereafter, expectations of prices should have been in 'first-gear'.

Another restriction implicit in (1.39) is that the variable Y is independent of other economic variables. There will be variables, such as levels of spending on (non-durable) consumer goods, which will be well correlated with 'permanent' income and hence with the series for current income. But the consumption data will display no *independent predictive powers* of their own.[32] Accordingly, actual and permanent income will display 'econometric exogeneity'[33] as far as previous consumption is concerned. On the other hand, suppose that there do exist variables which can be shown to improve the predictions of income, once they are added to past income data in the regression equation. In this case, the 'rational' individual will surely base his personal income predictions on these variables, as well as on past income data.

The arrival of news about future income which is not contained already in the observed time path of actual income will lead (under rational expectations) to an immediate recomputation of $E_t Y_{t+j}$ and thence of the provisional consumption programme. One important policy implication of this is that consumption spending should rise as soon as expectations of future tax rates are reduced. People

[32] Consumption takes a random walk, under certain assumptions. See Hall (144) and n. 30.
[33] That is, there will be no systematic observed association between income at one date and consumption at any previous date. Microeconomic counter-examples would be the subsequent labour supply effects of previous purchases of a dishwasher or an addictive drug.

should not wait until a promised tax cut is actually enacted before spending more; still less should they wait until it has proved to be permanent, if they believed it to be a once-and-for-all cut in the first place. If their consumption does not change in the face of an announcement of a future tax cut, the reason must be one of the following: people had expected the announcement anyway; people do not believe that the tax cut will occur; or people think that the authorities will simply have to raise tax rates in subsequent periods above what they would have been otherwise, to amortize the extra debts they will incur. Under some extremely restrictive assumptions, the arrival of news about future income prospects will have no effect on aggregate consumption. These assumptions are: a 'zero-sum game' where anyone's good news, e.g. about promotion or a lottery win, just matches everyone else's bad news; risk-neutrality; identical, homothetic preferences for all winners and losers. Just how confining these assumptions are is evident from the positive covariance in different households' incomes introduced by booms and slumps. Slumps may do wonders for those with specific skills or specific capital in the pawnbroking, sock-darning and tyre-retreading trades, but almost everyone else suffers badly. News of a political event that causes people to recalculate the probability of a slump in the future, for example, should lead to a change in consumption spending.

Aversion to risk means that individuals do not confine themselves to just the first moment of probability distributions. They care about higher moments, too: variance, skewness, kurtosis and so on. The risk-neutral individual's utility is linear in his wealth, the risk-averter's, concave. The risk-averter will typically behave as if his income expectations were lower than they really are. He will be pessimistic and conservative in his forecasting of future income. In his early years, he will save more than his risk-neutral counterpart. As he ages, his past cowardice bears fruit. His wealth grows faster than it would have done had he been neutral to risk. So his consumption rises more quickly from its lower base. If he can get actuarially fair, inflation-proofed annuities, and has decided to bequeathe nothing, uncertainty will not worry him once he retires. His last years will be spent in relative luxury. We may infer from this that risk-aversion may make negligible difference to the community's average propensity to save, when the population growth rate has been zero. If population has grown rapidly, on the other hand, risk-aversion will imply a higher community savings ratio, boosted more by the extra saving of the youthful pessimists than it is eroded by the extra dissaving of older ex-pessimists in retirement. The magnitude of these effects will vary positively with the variance of the u_t, the random elements in income, and negatively with the autoregressive coefficients, the λ_i. Note that the variance of lifetime earnings will be much higher when income takes a random walk (as in (1.34)) than when the income difference does so (as in (1.37)). Risk-averse young farmers should save less than risk-averse young bureaucrats, all else equal, since the vicissitudes of nature make for a much higher autoregressive coefficient on a farmer's income than that for the bureaucrat, for whom $Y_t = Y_{t-1} + u_t$ may be rather accurate. Finally, if we introduce uncertainty into the return available on savings, and into absolute or relative prices, as well as income, the additional positive link between the population growth rate and the savings ratio may be reinforced or controverted. Savings may be held in a safe but relatively low-yielding form, compared with the risk-neutral person, while uncertainty about future prices may well reinforce the motives to accumulate.

A final problem, already emphasized in section II: 3, is the extent to which the individual may *choose* his income. If the wage rate per hour is exogenous, as in our standard model, he chooses his hours of work. Rational expectations will then be formed about wage rates; these could take a form similar to (1.39), but with 'income' replaced by 'hourly wage rate'. One important conclusion to emerge from this is that an unexpectedly high current wage rate is quite likely to boost hours of work, and hence income, particularly when the individual expects the wage rate in future periods to be lower than this. The short-run marginal propensity to save will be high for two reasons. Not only will our individual seek to divert more of his modest increase in lifetime earnings into consumption at future dates: he will also be anxious to substitute out of (now relatively cheaper) current leisure into leisure in future periods. Against this, what may save the assumption of exogenous income is the indivisibility of jobs, or the rationing of hours of work. One interesting possibility is a negative association between the current wage rate and the hours of work anticipated in the near future. Workers may respond to a rise in the wage rate by forecasting a higher probability of unemployment.

We conclude by considering how the PIH, RIH, and LCH try to explain Kuznets's finding. The PIH attributes the greater long-run than short-run sensitivity of consumption to income to the fact that current income is treated as an inadequate proxy for future income expectations. A substantial element in current income is treated as a windfall. The same argument, that transitory and current incomes are subject to high positive correlation, explains the cross-sectional evidence as well. Those with above-average current income are likelier than not to have positive transitory income; hence their (temporarily) lower average propensity to consume.

The RIH explains inertia by habit persistence, and the cross-sectional evidence by a positive influence on consumption of some social norm for consumption. Relatively high incomes display a higher-than-average savings propensity, in both senses of 'relatively': relatively high in relation to the past and relatively high in comparison with the social average. Like the PIH, the RIH postulates long-run proportionality of C to Y, to preserve consistency with Kuznets's evidence.

The LCH offers the ratio of non-human wealth to income as an important positive influence on the average propensity to consume. Long-run constancy of C to Y is attributed to long-run constancy in two ratios: the wealth–income ratio and the expected future earnings to current income ratio. The short-run time-series evidence is explained by the hypothesis of counter-cyclical variation in these two ratios. Wealth and future earnings expectations may hold up better than current income expectations, for example. The long-run value of the average propensity to consume varies negatively with the growth rate. In one sense, this is a trivial observation, since savings are by definition additions to wealth; and the growth rates of income and wealth will not permanently differ. But there is a deeper insight. The aggregate savings ratio will be positively associated with the rate of population growth. Fast population growth implies a low average age, and a relative paucity of retired people decumulating assets.

Both PIH and LCH postulate the proportionality of consumption to a redefined version of income—either the flow concept of permanent income, or the stock concept of lifetime resources. This is in marked contrast with the cross-sectional implication of the RIH, which maintains that C/Y and Y are negatively related. Compelling evidence against the RIH in this respect has been provided by Ando and Modigliani (5). The average propensity to consume current income is, they find, entirely independent of the level of current income, when their population is classified by the value of their house. It is perhaps this evidence, as much as any other developments, which has led to the widespread acceptance of PIH and LCH as the most satisfactory macroeconomic theories of consumption currently available.

Summary of Notation in Chapter 1

A	the mean expectation of the discounted present value of income
A_0	the initial holdings of non-human wealth
B	bonds
C	consumption
DPV	discounted present value
E	total wealth: the sum of human and non-human wealth
e	work effort
h	an individual's endowment of time (except in LCH model)
L	legacy or transfer of capital
l	an individual's hours of work devoted to earning wages
M	money stock
N	the total working and retired population
P	the price level
$\dot{p}^e$	the rate of expected inflation
R	the rate of return on bonds (nominal)
R_m	the rate of return on money
S	the date of retirement from work
T	the date of death
t	the tax rate
U	utility
v	discount factor: $v_j \equiv (1 + R)^{-j}$
W	wage rate
X_i	purchase of good i
Y	income
δ	the rate of depreciation
λ	the marginal utility of money or wealth
ρ	the rate of time preference
ϕ	real wealth (in LCH model)
ψ	lump-sum tax

Chapter 2

The Producer

The second component of aggregate expenditure given by the equation $Y = C + I + G + X - M$ is *investment*. This chapter explores the theory underlying the producer's demand for capital goods. His investment decisions are in fact very closely related to his plans for output or employment, and also to the forces that govern the prices of goods and factors, and the distribution of income. Accordingly, this chapter will not concentrate exclusively upon investment. The analysis of investment occupies perhaps half of the chapter (sections II: 3, part), III: 1-4, IV (part) and V). The rest is devoted to employment, output, pricing, and distribution, all of which also constitute major aspects of the macroeconomy. In chapter 1 it was seen that optimization by households provides a common foundation for the theories of consumption, labour supply, and the demand for assets. Optimization by producers fulfils a similar function. It furnishes a common basis for the analysis of investment, employment, production, pricing, and distribution.

The chapter begins with a conspectus of models of the firm (section I). The theories of the firm may be classified according to the assumptions made about six central issues, concerning the firm's objectives and environment. Next, the competitive static model of the firm is analysed (section II). Its implications for distribution are considered in II: 2, and for output, employment and investment in II: 3. The model is dynamized in section III, where account is also taken of monopoly and monopsony. This section begins with the assumption of perfect foresight (III: 1 and III: 2), and then introduces other issues (expectations, satisficing, taxation and disequilibrium in III: 3, and adjustment costs in III: 4). Section IV generalizes the competitive static model in other directions, by focusing upon oligopoly and non-profit maximizing behaviour. A model of oligopoly is set up where firms have three goods in their objective function (wages, capital rentals and surplus); attention is directed towards the demand for labour and capital, the level of output and prices, and distribution in this framework. Section V investigates what determines the cost of capital to a firm. The Modigliani–Miller theorem and Arrow–Debreu contingent commodities are among the topics covered. Section VI considers two non-neoclassical models of distribution: those of Kaldor and Marx. Section VII returns to investment, with some further comments; the concepts of intertemporal equilibrium, and rational expectations equilibrium, are presented and discussed.

The centrepiece throughout this chapter is the *producer's demand for factors of production*. This is the common foundation of the theories of employment, investment, and distribution.

I: A Conspectus of Models

Theories of the producer can be classified conveniently according to assumptions made. There are six central areas where the assumptions differ. These are best illustrated by considering the possible sets of answers to a six-branch question:

Does the firm aim to *maximize* . . .	(q. 1)
a *unique* function . . .	(q. 2)
of only *one* variable . . .	(q. 3)
which is *profits* . . .	(q. 4)
subject to *known restraints* . . .	(q. 5)
and *parametric prices*?	(q. 6)

There are sixty-four possible sets of answers to this question, if each part admits of Yes and No answers only. But some of the sixty-four will be otiose: a negative answer to the first or second branch makes the questions that follow redundant. There are really seven substantial and distinct sets of assumptions, each of which gives rise to a recognizable group of models. These are:

Model Set I:	Yes to all
Model Set II:	Yes to qq. 1–5, No to q. 6
Model Set III:	Yes to qq. 1–4, No to q. 5
Model Set IV:	Yes to qq. 1–3, No to q. 4
Model Set V:	Yes to q. 1 and q. 2, No to q. 3
Model Set VI:	Yes to q. 1, No to q. 2
Model Set VII:	No to q. 1.

Model Set I refers to the traditional theory of the competitive profit-maximizing firm under conditions of certainty. We may call it competitive for short. This is the easiest and the oldest model. It lies in the background of most general equilibrium and macroeconomic models of the economy. It gives results quickly, and, for all its remoteness from the awkward features of reality, is a natural starting point.

Model Set II may be termed Classical Monopolistic. Prices of either inputs, or outputs, or both, are not completely outside the firm's control. The Classical Monopolistic group of models embraces most oligopoly theories, theories of monopsony in factor markets, and monopolistic competition, as well as monopoly in its strictest sense. Model Set II is usually restricted to partial equilibrium analyses of a single industry, but not always: Arrow (8) and Negishi (235) venture into general equilibrium. The term 'Classical' is added to remind us that no uncertainty is introduced; this is the preserve of Model Set III.

The Uncertainty model-group, Set III, can allow for uncertainty in the prices and/or quality of inputs and outputs, and in the production function. It consists of a number of ideas, some of which are far from new, and a disparate set of findings which have been as yet incompletely absorbed or united.

The fourth model set refers to theories of the non-competitive firm which propose some other single variable than profits as its maximand. The two best known are Baumol's model of the total-revenue maximizing firm (32) and Marris's model of growth maximization (206). Broader than Set IV, the fifth group gives the firm a utility function which depends on more than one variable: in fact, the firm has an indifference map. Two or more goods, for example, total revenue and profits, are traded off against each other, to maximize utility. An example is Williamson (334).

Model Set VI has been developed informally by Cyert and March (74), among others, to show what can happen if the firm is a coalition of agents with different objectives. Like the seventh group which is the only one to reject the optimizing approach completely, and postulate some alternative method of behaviour, Set VI has relatively sparse results to report so far. Set VII is well represented by Winter (335).

II: The Competitive Static Model and its Macroeconomic Implications

II:1 *Introduction*

Central to this and other models is the firm's production, or transformation function, $Q(..)$. For a multiproduct firm, Q links a vector of outputs to a matrix of inputs, arranged by allocation to particular products. In the simpler case of a single project producer, Q is a single-valued function of a vector of inputs. It is easiest to start by working with the latter, and then to generalize when required. The input vector is labelled $\mathbf{x}$. For simplicity, Q is taken to be (a) twice differentiable, and (b) strictly concave and increasing in each of its arguments. Assumption (a) ensures that each factor's marginal product is a smooth continuous curve; (b) that it slopes down but remains above the horizontal axis.

Analysis commences with the firm's profit function. This is

$$\pi = P \cdot Q(\mathbf{x}) - \mathbf{r}' \cdot \mathbf{x}, \tag{2.1}$$

where r_i is the price, and x_i the volume, at which input i is hired; and P the price of the (single) product. Next, (2.1) is to be maximized with respect to $\mathbf{x}$, so that

$$d^2\pi < 0 = d\pi \Rightarrow \partial\pi/\partial x_i = 0.$$

The first-order condition implies that the marginal product of each factor should equal that factor's price in terms of the product:

$$P\frac{\partial Q}{\partial x_i} = r_i. \tag{2.2}$$

Exact equality follows directly. We have assumed that P and $\mathbf{r}$ are parametric to the firm (so that they must be independent of x_i), and that $\partial Q/\partial x_i$ is always defined and positive. The second-order condition is met since, by assumption, $\partial^2 Q/\partial x_i^2 < 0$ for all i.[1] Note an important implication of (2.2): marginal products, and hence factor demands and output, are unaffected by an equiproportionate change in the prices of all inputs and outputs. Inputs and outputs are homogeneous of degree zero in all prices.

---

[1] This last is sufficient if Q is linear homogenous.

II: 2 *Implications for Distribution*

The condition (2.2) is the kernel of neoclassical theories of distribution. At the level of the firm, it is simply a profit-maximization condition to determine the volumes in which the inputs are hired. Labour, for instance, is hired up to the point where the value of its marginal product just balances its wage: below that point, an increase in employment would add more to receipts than to costs; beyond it, less. At a national level, however, in a simple economy characterized by only one product, (2.2) can be read as determining r_i for given x_i, or at least as co-determining the r_i and x_i as part of a wider system of equations and equilibrium conditions covering the demand and supply of goods and other factors, and the supply of labour.

A further insight into distribution may be gained by multiplying both sides of (2.2) by (x_i/PQ). The right-hand side now becomes the ratio of factor i's total rewards to the value of output. This is known as 'i's share'. The left-hand side becomes $(\partial \log Q/\partial \log x_i)$ which is the elasticity of Q to factor i. Now if the elasticities of Q to each of the factors are technologically-determined constants, independent in particular of the quantities of the factors, Q will be a log-linear function of the x_i:

$$Q = b \prod_{i=1}^{m} x_i^{\alpha_i}. \tag{2.3}$$

Here, b will be a constant of integration, the numerical value of which can be interpreted as an index of the quality of technology; m, which is no smaller than 2, represents the number of separate factors of production; and α_i is the elasticity of Q to x_i, or 'i's share' in competition.

(2.3) is known as the Cobb–Douglas Production Function. Its inventors constructed it (63) as the one algebraic relation for aggregate production in competitive economy that would imply that factors' shares in national incomes would be unchanging. If (2.3) were a correct description of the production function, an increase in the ratio of capital to labour employed in industry would, for instance, cut the rate of profit and raise the wage rate; but these changes in the r_i would balance exactly the change in relative quantities of the x_i so that the ratios $(r_i x_i/PQ)$ remained fixed. This characteristic of (2.3) means that the ratio (r_i/r_j) is a fraction or multiple of the ratio (x_j/x_i), as depicted by the ray in panel (*a*) of fig. 2.1. The 'elasticity of substitution' measures the proportionate change in the ratio at which two inputs are hired, in response to the proportionate change in the ratio of their marginal products. Formally, this is

$$\sigma = \frac{\partial \log \dfrac{x_j}{x_i}}{\partial \log \dfrac{\partial Q/\partial x_i}{\partial Q/\partial x_j}}, \tag{2.4}$$

which under competitive conditions equals $\{\partial \log(x_j/x_i)\}/\{\partial \log(r_i/r_j)\}$. σ takes a value of unity in the Cobb–Douglas case (see Figure 2.1). Factors of production

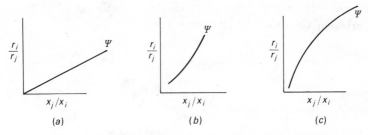

FIG. 2.1. The implication of different production functions for the factor price ratio: factor employment ratio correspondence

are neither complements nor substitutes. A final point to note about (2.3) is that, in (2.3), Q is homogenous in x of degree

$$\sum_{i=1}^{m} \alpha_i$$

and that the sum of factors' shares,

$$\sum_{i=1}^{m} \frac{r_i x_i}{PQ}, \text{ is also } \sum_{i=1}^{m} \alpha_i.$$

This is an illustration of Euler's theorem—that if Q is a function linear homogenous in x,

$$\sum_{i=1}^{m} x_i \frac{\partial Q}{\partial x_i} = Q.$$

It is necessary and sufficient for factors' shares to add up to one, that the sum of the exponents α_i also sum to one. This amounts to an assumption of *constant returns to scale* (or 'linear' homogeneity for Q). If there were increasing returns to scale,

$$\sum_{i=1}^{n} \alpha_i > 1,$$

competitive rewards to factors would exceed the value of output; if decreasing, fall short. The implication of Euler's theorem, that perfect competition requires a constant-returns to scale production function for rewards to exhaust the value of output exactly,[2] is clearly quite general, and not restricted by setting σ

---

[2] The sum of competitive factor rewards may, by happy and unlikely accident, happen to equal the value of output if the production function is not homogeneous. Let $Q = x_i \sqrt{(x_j)} + (1/x_i)$ for instance: if $x_j = 1$ and $x_i = 2$, Q equals $x_i(\partial Q/\partial x_i) + x_j(\partial Q/\partial x_j)$ at a value of 2.5. But this is a fluke. And if Q is homogeneous, it must be linear homogeneous for this to happen.

constant but not unitary. Take the competitive reduction of (2.4) and make $\partial \log(r_i/r_j)/\partial \log(x_j/x_i)$ the subject: we have

$$\frac{\partial \log \dfrac{r_i}{r_j}}{\partial \log \dfrac{x_i}{x_i}} = \frac{1}{\sigma}.$$

By integration, *with σ treated as a constant*, we find:

$$\log \frac{r_i}{r_j} = \frac{1}{\sigma} \log \frac{x_j}{x_i} + \log C,$$

where $\log C$ is a constant of integration. Taking antilogarithms:

$$\frac{r_i}{r_j} = C\left(\frac{x_j}{x_i}\right)^{1/\sigma}, \tag{2.5}$$

whence we may derive the ratio of payments to factor i to payments to factor j:

$$\frac{r_i x_i}{r_j x_j} = C\left(\frac{x_j}{x_j}\right)^{(1-\sigma)/\sigma}. \tag{2.6}$$

Now (2.5) is illustrated in Figure 2.1. Panel (*b*) shows how the factor price ratio behaves against the factor employment ratio when the two factors are complements. The production function depicted in panel (*b*) displays (relative) inflexibility between the two inputs examined. Since σ is the elasticity of ψ, it has a low value, of perhaps one-half, in panel (*b*). In panel (*c*), the two factors are substitutes; the production function displays (relative) flexibility; σ has a value of about 2.

Turning to (2.6), we can see how the factor share ratio varies with the factor employment ratio. The elasticity of the former to the latter is $(1-\sigma)/\sigma$, since (2.6) is log-linear. Consequently, if σ is less than one (as in panel (*b*)), a rise in the relative employment of a factor will reduce its share of output, and raise the share of the (relatively) declining factor. The reason for this is the relative inflexibility: the increasing factor encounters rapidly diminishing returns, which drive down its price quickly. The factor price effect dominates the factor volume effect, so that despite the increased (relative) quantity of the factor hired, its total reward has to drop as a share of output.

With σ greater than one, on the other hand, the opposite happens. The reasoning is visible in panel (*c*) of Fig. 2.1. Quite a big proportionate change in x_j/x_i has little effect to speak of on r_i/r_j. The factor price effect is weaker than the factor volume effect. The (relatively) increasing factor experiences only a slight fall in its price, and, on balance, a rise in its share of the value of total output.

Most advanced Western economies have experienced (by most definitions) a falling share of profits since the Second World War. In the UK, there is some evidence of this trend going back much earlier. The drop in profits, which has been particularly marked when they are measured net of stock appreciation and depreciation but gross of taxation,[3] has accompanied a large rise in most estimates of the ratio of capital employed to the employment of labour. This last ratio is subject to grave and complex measurement problems; but the upward trend in it is discernible enough. If all sectors of the economy could be assumed to have identical production functions these phenomena (falling profit share and rising capital-labour ratio) would be inconsistent with the implication of (2.3). This is so becasue (2.3), if applied at an aggregate level under competitive conditions, would imply a fixed profit share. But with $\sigma \neq 1$, an explanation for them may be provided easily. From (2.6), it would appear that $\sigma < 1$: capital and labour are complementary in production. Alternatively, if each industry had a Cobb–Douglas production function such as (2.3) but with different weights, the drop in profits could be explained by increasing relative output in the labour-intensive industries.

But (2.5) and (2.6), illuminating as they are, do not constitute a production function. They may, however, be derived from one: the constant-returns-to-scale version of the Constant Elasticity of Substitution (CES) production function. In a simple form, this is

$$\left(\frac{Q}{b}\right)^{(\sigma-1)/\sigma} = \sum_{i=1}^{m} a_i x_i^{(\sigma-1)/1}. \tag{2.7}$$

Here the a_i and b are positive constants, performing distributive and technology-indicating roles similar to those of the α_i and b in (2.3). The constant (c) in (2.5) and (2.6) will then be a_i/a_j. (2.7) first appeared in published form in 1961 (10), but echoes earlier work by Burk (51).

The exact form of the profit function corresponding to (2.7), from the first-order maximization conditions of which (2.5) and (2.6) follow directly, is

$$\pi = Pb \left(\sum_{i=1}^{m} a_i x_i^{(\sigma-1)/1}\right)^{\sigma/(\sigma-1)} - \sum_{i=1}^{m} r_i x_i. \tag{2.8}$$

II: 3 *Implications for Output, Employment and Investment*

In the last section, we saw that the maximization of (2.1) entailed conditions which could be treated as determining factor prices, and factor rewards, in the macroeconomy, if factor inputs (and hence output) were given. That is the essence of the neoclassical analysis of distribution. In this section we return to the micro-cosm, the individual producer, and swap endogenous for exogenous variables. This time, it is the **r**, the factor prices, that are parametric; inputs—and/or output—are endogenous. The level of technology, and one (or more) of the inputs, are fixed. The idea was first proposed by Alfred Marshall (207), who defined a 'short period' during which the producer had to take technology and his stock of capital as predetermined and outside his control. Constant returns to scale (which could only

---

[3] See Feldstein and Summers (107) for a summary of the US evidence, and Flemming *et al.* (115), Glyn and Sutcliffe, (132) and King (184) for the UK. Some interesting international comparisons are made in Clark (58).

be reaped in the long run, when all factors were freely variable) would then imply, assuming that factors were less than perfect substitutes for each other, that there were diminishing returns to the variable factors. Marginal costs of production would therefore rise with output. A parametric price $\bar{P}$ could intersect the marginal cost curve at a unique level of output Q^*; profit maximization would entail that actual output was at this level. In turn Q^* would prescribe a unique cost-minimizing set of inputs x^*, at least one element of which, the fixed factor(s), was at a pre-determined level.

The parametric price, $\bar{P}$, and profit-maximization together ensure that the firm's supply curve will be its marginal cost curve (once this is unambiguously upward sloping, and provided that $\bar{P}$ is no less than average variable costs).[4] In the important special case when the production function is as in (2.7) the elasticity of this supply curve, η, will be

$$\eta = \sigma \frac{r'x^*}{\bar{P} - r'x^*}, \tag{2.9}$$

where σ is the elasticity of substitution between the variable and the fixed factors of production. This can be seen easily in the case of a two-factor production function.[5] If subscripts N and K denote labour and capital, and only labour is

---

[4] Average variable costs are $(r' \cdot x^* - F)/Q^*$, where F represents the (exogenous) payments to the owners of the fixed factor(s).

[5] Suppose $Q = Q(x, z)$ where x is the variable factor, and z is fixed. Hence $dz = 0$, and

$$dQ = Q_1 dx \tag{2.9.i}$$

and since Q is linear homogeneous,

$$Q = Q_1 x + Q_2 z \tag{2.9.ii}$$

and

$$dQ = Q_1 dx + Q_{11} x dx + Q_{21} z dx. \tag{2.9.iii}$$

Subtracting (2.9.i) from (2.9.iii), we have

$$Q_{11} x = -Q_{21} z. \tag{2.9.iv}$$

Now differentiate totally the marginal rate of substitution between factors z and x:

$$d\left(\frac{Q_2}{Q_1}\right) \bigg/ \frac{Q_2}{Q_1} = \left[\frac{Q_{21}}{Q_2} - \frac{Q_{11}}{Q_1}\right] dx. \tag{2.9.v}$$

Using (2.9.iv), the right-hand side of (2.9.v) can be expressed as

$$-\left[\frac{Q_{11} x}{Q_2 z} + \frac{Q_{11}}{Q_1}\right] dx = -Q_{11} dx \left[\frac{x}{zQ_2} + \frac{1}{Q_1}\right] = -\frac{Q_{11}}{Q_1} dx \left(\frac{Q}{zQ_2}\right)$$

since (2.9.ii) implies

$$\frac{x}{zQ_2} = \frac{1}{Q_1}\left(\frac{Q}{zQ_2} - 1\right),$$

so

$$d \log\left(\frac{Q_2}{Q_1}\right) = -\frac{Q_{11} Q}{Q_1 zQ_2} x d \log\left(\frac{x}{z}\right),$$

or rearranging terms,

$$\sigma \equiv \frac{d \log(x/z)}{d \log(Q_2/Q_1)} = -\frac{Q_1 zQ_2}{xQQ_{11}} = -(1 - B)\frac{Q_1}{xQ_{11}}, \tag{2.9.vi}$$

variable (and infinitely elastic in supply at a given nominal wage rate, w) the price elasticity of supply (η) will be

$$\eta = \frac{\sigma[\partial \log Q/\partial \log N]}{\partial \log Q/\partial \log K} = \frac{\sigma(\text{labour's share})}{(1 - \text{labour's share})}.$$

Unlike (2.9), this formula is quite general. It relies only on constant returns to scale. But, except in the CES case, σ must now be evaluated at the current position, and only infinitesimal changes are allowed for.

(2.9) has an important macroeconomic application. If labour is the only variable factor of production; its price is given in nominal terms; producers are in equilibrium, and produce homogeneous output with identical production functions and under competitive conditions; then: *the elasticity of the 'aggregate' supply curve* is σ multiplied by the ratio of wages to profits. The elasticity depends on the substitution elasticity, and the factor shares. This will tell us, under the assumptions stated, how an increase in aggregate demand will be decomposed into rises in output and rises in the price level. A low share of the value of output accruing to labour, coupled with complementarity between capital and labour in production, will make supply highly inelastic; the greatest output effect will be felt when the opposite is true. We return to this result later, in chapter 7, section V: 4.

The formula may be generalized in various ways. If capital is freely variable at a nominal price, and labour fixed, $\eta = \sigma(\text{profits/wages})$ rather than $\sigma(\text{wages/profits})$. If a third factor, say natural resources, is introduced, which is (like labour, suppose) variable at a given nominal price, and the production function follows (2.7), $\eta = \sigma(\text{wages} + \text{natural resource costs})/\text{profits}$. If one of the factors is freely variable, but at a given *relative* price (which is fixed in terms of the product), that factor behaves as if it were absent. Its rewards are removed from the numerator. If, therefore, capital is fixed, and the other two factors, labour and natural resources are available at fixed relative prices in terms of the product, the value of η is zero. Intermediate positions are encountered if the price of (each) variable factor is given partly in nominal, and partly in real terms: suppose ω is the elasticity of the money wage rate to the price level, with $1 \geqslant \omega \geqslant 0$. If natural resources are again suppressed, and capital is fixed, η becomes $(1 - \omega)\sigma(\text{wages/profits})$. In aggregate models, $(1 - \omega)$ may perhaps be taken as an index of money illusion on the part of suppliers of labour. If labour 'stipulates for' (to choose Keynes's term (182)) a real wage, not a money wage, α may be taken to approach unity, and η will sink to zero. Output and employment will be negatively related to the real wage rate. This is

where $B = (xQ_1/Q) = 1 - (zQ_2/Q)$. Furthermore, perfect competition implies that the real wage rate for labour $w/P = Q_1$, so that (given $dw = 0$) $Q_{11}dx = w/P[(dw/w) - (dP/P)] = -(Q_1 dP/P)$. Now, using (2.9.i) to eliminate dx, we have $(Q_{11}/Q_1)dQ = -(Q_2 dP/P)$ or

$$\eta = \frac{dQ/Q}{dP/P} = -\frac{(Q_1)^2}{QQ_{11}} \tag{2.9.vii}$$

Substituting $x\sigma/(1 - B)$ for $-Q_1/Q_{11}$ (from (2.9.vi), (2.9.vii) yields

$$\eta = +\frac{x\sigma Q_1}{Q(1 - B)} = \frac{B\sigma}{1 - B}. \tag{2.9.viii}$$

Q.E.D.

the central idea underlying Classical Unemployment (see 204, 226, and 313); Keynes found it very hard to abandon.[6]

When capital as well as labour are variable factors, attention is sometimes confined to the solutions that can (often) be obtained,[7] such as the proportions between the inputs, and between each input and output. In the CES production function, (2.7), for instance, the ratio of output to factor i implied by profit maximization, when all factors are freely variable at given nominal prices, is:

$$\frac{Q}{x_i} = \left(\frac{r_i}{a_i p}\right)^{\sigma} b^{1-\sigma}. \tag{2.10}$$

Now (2.10) may be read in many ways. As it stands, it gives the average product, or 'productivity', of factor i, in terms of other variables. Alternatively, multiplication of both sides by b/r_i allows one to express the reciprocal of the share of factor i in the value of output: this will be $(r_i/bp)^{\sigma-1} a_i^{-\sigma}$ which increases (decreases) in the real price of factor i, according as the factors are substitutes (complements). Further rearrangement of (2.10) brings factor i's share in terms, not of its real price, but its average product: we find that average product and share are positively related when σ is less than one, negatively when greater. Yet another way of reading (2.10) is to move from the explanation of factor shares, to that of *employment levels*. Making x_i the subject now, we have

$$x_i = \frac{Q}{b}\left(\frac{bpa_i}{r_i}\right)^{\sigma}. \tag{2.11}$$

In words, the volume of factor i hired will vary equiproportionately with output, and log-linearly (with elasticity minus σ) in the real price of the factor i. One celebrated and hotly disputed application of a simplified version of (2.11) is Jorgenson's *'neoclassical' theory of investment* (see 172, 173, 174 and 175). Here, x_i becomes the required, or optimum, stock of capital, K^*; ϕ is relabelled Q; σ is set to unity, so that (2.7), the starting point for (2.10) and (2.11), is effectively replaced by (2.3), the Cobb–Douglas production function; r_i is the 'cost of capital', c (on which more below); P is the price of output, as before; and other parameters are constants. Jorgenson derives from a profit maximization condition with respect to capital that

$$K^* = \mu \frac{PQ}{c} \qquad \text{(where in a simple case } c = P_K[r + \delta - \hat{P}_K^e]), \tag{2.12}$$

where μ may be interpreted as the elasticity of Q to K and hence the (competitive) share of capital in output. If P, Q, and c are defined at date t, so is K^*; and Jorgenson makes his actual level of net investment $\dot{K}$ follow a freely-estimated distributed lag behind $(K^* - K)_t$. The cost of capital, c, has four components. These are: the rate of interest, r; the rate of depreciation, δ; the (expected) proportionate rate at

---

[6] In (182), Keynes still doggedly retains this critical relationship. In (183), however, he moves cautiously away from it. See also Harrod (152).

[7] The profit-maximizing output level becomes indeterminate when returns to scale are constant, and all factors are variable at fixed nominal prices. Here, $\eta \to \infty$.

which the capital good's price P_K is increasing, call it $\hat{P}_K^e$; and the current level of P_K. The common sense behind this is readily visible if one considers what a competitive, fully informed machine-rental company must charge to break even. Machines fall in nominal value at rate $\delta - \hat{P}_K$; when converted into present values, to reflect the financial opportunity cost of the machines, this becomes $r + \delta - \hat{P}_K$. For Jorgenson, r is problematic; in our example it represents the nominal rate of interest on (unindexed) corporate bond-capital, and not necessarily the (arguably more relevant) cost of equity capital, nor some weighted average. In his empirical tests, Jorgenson experiments with different definitions of r. The simple definition of c given in (2.12) abstracts from taxation; this restriction is removed later, in section III: 3.

Other queries which may be placed upon Jorgenson's work relate to the confining nature of its assumptions, to the endogeneity of Q, and to the arbitrariness of the adjustment path of K. The assumptions are narrow: to take three, a unit substitution elasticity, parametric prices for the product and the factors, and pure profit maximization can hardly be offered as universally applicable. This query need not, however, be fatal to Jorgenson's approach. In fact, we shall see below (in section IV of this chapter) that extensive generalization of (2.12) is possible not just to a non-unitary value of σ, but also to imperfect markets, and a more general objective function for the producer.

The other two queries are more telling. They are also interrelated. Q *is* an endogenous variable for the producer,[8] no less than K; indeed Marshall thought it even more flexible; hence the artificiality of skipping aside from the issue of what determines the scale of output. Yet (2.12) is at best a limited model of the *destination* (an 'optimum' stock of capital); and this is only a relative destination, K^*/Q; it is not a model of the *itinerary* that investment actually takes in relative or absolute terms. This is, in Jorgenson's model, a purely empirical matter, a set of numbers thrown up by direct observation. Could the itinerary not be explained directly? In principle, it could be; and by either of two types of approach. One is to introduce *adjustment costs*, perhaps for the scales of output, and employment, as well as for the stock of capital.[9] A recent model of investment costs is presented in section III: 4. The second method is to model investment as a dynamic optimization problem without adjustment costs. This approach will be illustrated in section III, below. Jorgenson's major contribution was to introduce two key prices— the price level of output, and the cost of capital—into the first of the two 'accelerator' equations[10]

$$\left.\begin{array}{l} K^* = \kappa Q, \\ \dot{K} = \omega(K^* - K). \end{array}\right\} \quad 1 \geqslant \omega > 0 \qquad (2.13)$$

[8] One exception to this is the exogenous constraint upon production set by the volume of sales, if the product market is in disequilibrium. Q would be taken as a 'rationing' output level, set by demand, in temporary equilibrium models, such as Malinvaud (204), and other works (38, 226).

[9] The analysis of investment recast into a model with explicit adjustment costs has been treated in depth by Brechling (46). See also Mortensen (225), Lucas (195), and Gould (137).

[10] The simplest accelerator model takes ω to be 1, so that $\dot{K} = \dot{K}^* = \kappa\dot{Q} + \dot{\kappa}Q$. If, further, κ is rigid, we derive the result $\dot{K} = \kappa\dot{Q}$. The rigidity of the required capital to output ratio κ calls for static technology and constant returns, and also for either perfect complementarity

In Jorgenson's work the parameter κ was enriched by multiplication by the ratio P/c. But he could have gone much further. He could have brought prices into the second equation in (2.13) as well, so that an undated optimum target for K could be replaced by a dated optimum trajectory $\dot{K}(t)$.

III: Dynamics

III: 1   *The Perfect Foresight Model*

When the static model of section II is replaced by one allowing for intertemporal actions and decisions on the part of the producer, the simplest assumption to make is perfect foresight. The producer has perfect knowledge, not just about the present prices of inputs and outputs, and the current transformation functions between them, but about these variables and functions for all future dates as well. As far as his objective is concerned, profit-maximization remains the easiest framework; the flow of profits needs to be replaced by the stock concept, value (V), which is maximized:

$$V = \sum_{i=0}^{n} \sum_{j=0}^{T} V_j P_{ij}(q_{ij}(Z)) \cdot q_{ij}(Z) - \sum_{k=0}^{m} \sum_{j=0}^{T} V_j r_{kj}(Z_{kj}) \cdot Z_{kj}. \qquad (2.14)$$

The first order condition for a maximum for V is that the hiring of each input at each date should be taken to the point where the discounted present value (DPV) of its marginal revenue product stream on all goods produced should balance the DPV of its marginal cost. Assuming that the input in question is perfectly flexible, so that it is hired for just one period, this condition is

$$\sum_{i=0}^{n} \sum_{j=0}^{T} V_j P_{ij} \left(1 - \frac{1}{\epsilon_{ij}}\right) \frac{\partial q_{ij}}{\partial Z_{kl}} = V_l r_{kl}(1 + e_{kl}), \qquad (2.15)$$

where $V_j = (1 + R)^{-j}$, a discount factor (R = rate of interest); r_{kl} is the reward to factor k at date l, and e_{kl} the elasticity of this to the amount hired; ϵ_{ij} (defined positive) is the elasticity of demand of product i to its own price at date j; $\partial q_{ij}/\partial z_{kl}$ the marginal product of factor k at date l on the output of good i at date j. (2.14) and (2.15) rest on the assumption that P_{ij} varies, if at all, only with q_{ij}, and r_{kl} only with Z_{kl}; under perfectly competitive conditions, e_{kl} and $1/\epsilon_{ij}$ disappear.

Provided that the second-order condition $\mathrm{d}^2 V < 0$ is met, the set of Z_{kl} that satisfies (2.15) constitutes an *optimal programme* of inputs, stretching out from the future up to and including the horizon, T (which could be infinite). The set of q_{ij} which the optimal input programme yields is an optimal programme for output and sales. Every input is hired at each date up to the point that its marginal contribution to net present value vanishes. When P_{ij} and r_{kl} are exogenous (and e_{kl} and

between capital and other factors (so that $\sigma = 0$) or rigid factor prices. The theory was proposed first by Clark (59). A further restriction in the concept is that Q and $\dot{Q}$ are assumed exogenous. The same issue arises with Jorgenson's model. One way of justifying this is to assume that firms' output levels are constrained by an exogenous 'level of demand', perhaps because the commodity market is in excess supply.

$1/\epsilon_{ij}$ disappear), it is sufficient for the second-order condition that $(\partial q_{ij}/\partial Z_{kl}) > 0 > (\partial^2 q_{ij}/\partial Z_{kl}^2)$ for each $i, j, k,$ and l where $(\partial q_{ij}/\partial Z_{kl}) \neq 0$: this guarantees that the input's net present value is *falling* when it vanishes.

The new considerations which (2.14) and (2.15) introduce are the *intertemporal* substitution opportunities between inputs and between outputs. If it is known that the price of good i will drop autonomously between years S and $S + 1$, for example, a value-maximizing production plan is most unlikely to imply higher sales of that good in year $S + 1$ than year S. If input k is known to be cheaper at date S than at $S + 1$, there will be a strong incentive to hire it when it is cheaper.

Within the confines of perfect foresight, one may manipulate the variables so as to see how the production plan would have changed, had their values been different. A lower rate of interest implies higher V_j and V_l. This will increase an input's net present value—and hence entail an increase in the input's optimal hiring rate— if and only if its costs on average *precede* its gains on the revenue side, in time. If this is so, hiring the factor is a disinvestment; gains precede costs, and the desirability of the hiring act varies positively with R. If a project as a whole has both revenue and cost streams so shaped that the net cash flow over time undulates back and forth, sometimes positive and sometimes negative, how R affects net present value will be ambiguous.

III: 2 *An Example with Perfect Foresight*

A simple example will provide an insight into how the optimal programme could look in practice, and can also serve to extend the analysis to factors of production where hiring decisions cannot be reversed; this characteristic applies to many kinds of capital good, and increasingly perhaps also to labour. Consider a firm in perfect competition in input and product markets. Its single product sells at a price P_j at date j. Labour, L, is homogeneous and flexible, hired and rehired each period for a wage of w_j. Homogeneous capital goods are bought for θ_j at date j, and they affect output from date $j + 1$ onwards by forming part of the capital stock then. For simplicity's sake, we ignore depreciation, and assume the production function to be Cobb–Douglas: $Q_j = AK_j^\alpha N_j^\beta$. A is constant, and might represent the product of a fixed technology parameter T and a fixed factor, $E^{1-\alpha-\beta}$ raised to this power to preserve linear homogeneity of Q_j. The maximand will be

$$V = \sum_{j=0}^{T} V_j [P_j A K_j^\alpha N_j^\beta - w_j N_j - \theta_j I_j] \tag{2.16}$$

where $K_{j+1} = K_j + I_j$, and $v_j = (1 + R)^{-j}$.

Maximizing (2.16) with respect to I_0 and I_1 reveals

$$\frac{\partial V}{\partial I_0} = 0 = -\theta_0 + \alpha P_1 v_1 A K_1^{\alpha-1} N_1^\beta + \alpha P_2 v_2 A K_2^{\alpha-1} N_2^\beta + \alpha P_3 A K_3^{\alpha-1} N_3^\beta + \dots \tag{2.17}$$

$$\frac{\partial V}{\partial I_1} = 0 = -\theta_1 v_1 + \alpha P_2 v_2 A K_2^{\alpha-1} N_2^\beta + \alpha P_3 v_3 A K_3^{\alpha-1} N_3^\beta + \dots \tag{2.18}$$

Subtraction of (2.18) from (2.17) yields (as $v_T \to 0$)

$$\theta_0 - \theta_1 v_1 = \alpha P_1 v_1 A K_1^{\alpha-1} N_1^{\beta}. \tag{2.19}$$

Meanwhile, maximization of V also entails $\partial V/\partial N_j = 0$, so that

$$\frac{\partial v}{\partial N_1} = 0 = -w_1 v_1 + \beta P_1 v_1 A K_1^{\alpha} N_1^{\beta-1}. \tag{2.20}$$

Substitution of (2.20) into (2.19) allows us to derive an expression for K_1:

$$K_1 = I_0 + K_0 = \left\{ \frac{\alpha P_1 A (\beta/w_1)^{\beta}}{(\theta_0(1+R) - \theta_1)^{1-\beta}} \right\}^{1/(1-\alpha-\beta)}. \tag{2.21}$$

(2.21) tells us that investment is related *negatively* to (i) the size of the capital stock inherited from the past; (ii) the current price of capital goods, θ_0; (iii) the rate of interest; and (iv) the expected future wage rate for labour. The expected future prices of the product produced and capital goods are positive influences on investment. There is no reason, of course, why all these variables should influence investment in exactly the form specified by (2.21); different assumptions about the production function, the quality of competition and the firms's objectives would have led to quite different expressions. What is helpful about (2.21) is the qualitative information it imparts about these influences, and why they work as they do. The role of P_1 emerges from the fact that postponing investment from date 0 to date 1 would sacrifice earnings at date 1 from the sale of extra goods which I_0 permits; the higher the level of P_1, the greater this sacrifice. The higher is θ_1, the more expensive investment will be at date 1, and (all else equal) the greater the incentive to invest earlier. θ_0 and R are negative influences; the higher is θ_0, all else equal, the greater the incentive to postpone the acquisition of capital goods, and the higher is R, the smaller the discounted present value of earnings sacrifices at date 1 and the greater the price of investment goods at date 0 relative to their present discounted price a year ahead. The higher is w_1, the smaller the optimal level of employment of labour in that period, hence the lower level of output and the lower the capital requirement then. (This last result is an unmistakable feature of our model, but it should be pointed out that the incentive to invest can often be sharpest when wage rates are now lower than their present discounted future expected levels: investment may be considered an attempt to *pre-empt* labour, to incur the costs of current labour at the construction stage in order to save future labour at the operation stage of a project). Lastly, K_0 is a negative influence: the higher the capital stock you inherit, the less—all else equal—you will wish to add to it. On the other hand, once depreciation is allowed for, a positive link between gross investment and the capital stock is established; and this will to some degree offset the negative effect of K_0 on I_0 so clearly visible in (2.21).

One difficulty with (2.21) is that K_0 is treated as exogenous in the 'short run'. K_0 may be treated as predetermined, when date 0 is reached. But if an investment programme is being planned at date 0 over subsequent periods, K_1, K_2 and so on will *not* be predetermined at date 0. How can we allow for this? Repeating the maximization and subtraction procedure above, we can find from $\partial V/\partial I_1 = \partial V/\partial I_2 = \partial V/\partial L_2 = 0$ that

$$K_2 = I_1 + K_1 = \left\{ \frac{\alpha A P_2 (\beta/w_2)^\beta}{(\theta_1(1+R) - \theta_2)^{1-\beta}} \right\}^{1/(1-\alpha-\beta)}$$

Subtraction of this from (2.21) reveals

$$I_1 = \alpha^{\gamma(1-\beta)} \beta^{\beta\gamma} A^\gamma \left[\frac{P_2^\gamma w_2^{-\beta\gamma}}{(\theta_0(1+R) - \theta_2)^{\gamma(1-\beta)}} - \frac{P_1^\gamma w_1^{-\beta\gamma}}{(\theta_0(1+R) - \theta_1)^{\gamma(1-\beta)}} \right] \quad (2.22)$$

where $\gamma = (1 - \alpha - \beta)^{-1}$. (2.22) may serve as a paradigm for any I_j when $j > 0$. The crucial determinants of the optimum time profile of investment are the price paths of output, labour and capital goods. The rate of interest R ceases to be a powerful unambiguous influence on I_1. A lower R for all time implies higher investment *before* the period began, as well as higher investment now, all else equal. Two influences upon I run counter to each other. If we introduce the possibility of a non-unique rate of interest, by allowing the term structure of interest rates to be other than horizontal, this changes. Let $_0R_{1,2}$ stand for the rate of interest expected (in our case known) at date 0 to apply on a one-period loan starting at date 1, the square-bracketed term in (2.22) becomes

$$\frac{P_2^\gamma w_2^{-\beta\gamma}}{(\theta_1(1 + {}_0R_{1,2}) - \theta_2)^{\gamma(1-\beta)}} - \frac{P_1^\gamma w_1^{-\beta\gamma}}{(\theta_0(1 + {}_0R_{0,1})^{\gamma(1-\beta)}}. \quad (2.23)$$

This shows that the term structure of interest rates shapes the optimum investment plan, as well as the price paths for output, labour, and capital goods.

The denominators in (2.22) and (2.23) look ambiguous in sign. Indeed, they are: θ could exceed $\theta_0 (1 + {}_0R_{0,1})$. Does this suggest that I_0 should be negative? Certainly not; in fact it should be infinite: the firm can expect to make a profit simply by buying up machinery now, holding it for a year, and selling it a year later for a profit, large enough to swamp interest costs. Introducing storage costs, depreciation and the 'lemon' problem of quality-uncertainty in used capital goods markets (see Chapter 1, section II: 4) will qualify this.

III: 3 *Expectations, Satisficing, Taxation, and Disequilibrium*

The dynamic approach treats planned investment and planned hiring of additional labour in one period as codetermined. More than that, each is found by differencing optimum stocks of capital, and optimum employment levels, between adjacent dates. There are numerous possible extensions which it can incorporate. We shall examine several shortly. Perhaps the most important is to treat time as an irreversible process, and relax the assumption of perfect foresight. If this is done, we may preserve the notion of a programme or plan for inputs and outputs. But for all save the current period, and the near future, the plan will be *provisional*. An important distinction now emerges. This is between equilibrium and disequilibrium additions to inputs.

Equilibrium additions to capital and employment merely follow the previous programme. They have been preplanned, and are undertaken accordingly.

Disequilibrium additions occur as a result of programme revision. Revisions are likely if *current* values of P, $R_{j,j+1}$, θ and w deviate from what they had been expected to be. They will also be stimulated by new information relevant for making optimal forecasts of *future* values of P, $R_{j,j+1}$, θ and w. When expectations of these latter are adaptive, there will be a regular, mechanical link between the forecast error on current values and the size of forecast revisions for future values. When expectations are rational, such a regular link between the current forecast error and the current forecast revision may still be observed. But, as we saw in chapter I, this will be so if and only if the relevant variable (call it Z) has been seen in the past to follow a stochastic path, such as

$$Z_t = Z_{t-1} + U_t - \lambda U_{t-1}, \tag{2.24}$$

where U_t and U_{t-1} are serially uncorrelated, stationary, mean zero disturbance terms. The difficulty is that wage rates, prices and interest rates are not self-determining variables in the manner suggested by (2.24). They are endogenous variables in a large system. A host of other influences could lie behind a rise in wage rates. New information about the future magnitudes of such influences should surely be employed by producers making optimal forecasts.

When such new information presents itself, we have seen, the plan will be revised. Not immediately, however; the costs of gathering information and taking decisions are rarely negligible. This points to rules of thumb as convenient devices to tradeoff between the costs and benefits of these activities. Rules of thumb are discernible behind such practices as full-cost pricing, and the setting of annual targets for sales, profits, and other variables. The concept of satisficing, proposed by Simon (297) and extended by Winter (335), need not be inconsistent with maximizing behaviour, once full recognition is given to the costs of information and decision-taking. Satisficing is traditionally defined as sacrificing the excess of the maximum possible level of a goal variable, such as profits, over its satisfactory level. In fact, the maximum possible level excludes important organizational costs, allowance for which could make the practice consistent with rational behaviour.

Delays in responding to new information will depend on the structure of the company involved. They may be considerable, when this is highly centralized. But delays in revising the input and output programme may be exacerbated by externally imposed constraints of other kinds: a lengthy order-book for new machinery, and the time-interval for job applicants to respond to job advertisements, for instance. In the next section, we examine how the costs of adjustment may influence producers' actual investment behaviour. But before proceeding to discuss this, we need to consider two further phenomena which impinge upon the producer's optimum programme: taxation, and disequilibrium. Expectations of these phenomena in future periods are no less important whether and how seriously they apply currently. The optimum programme will be sensitive to such expectations. Changes in such expectations may be just as powerful an explanation of the movement of actual investment behaviour, as (for example), the changes in interest rates. Indeed, the Keynesian tradition regards them as more powerful.

Introducing taxation is a fairly simply matter. All that needs to be done is to define the price variables P, w, θ, and R as prices *facing the producer*. Consequently P_j measures the price of output at date j excluding indirect tax and including any per-unit production subsidy; w_j is the cost of labour at date j, gross of income tax, social insurance levies upon the employer, employer pension contributions, and perks; and θ_j is net of any investment subsidy. Expectations of factor and product taxes and subsidies can now be seen as crucial determinants of the programme. A temporary investment subsidy expected from year 2 to year 4 will raise the desirability of investment within that period, at the expense of investment beforehand and later. Expectations of a temporary employment subsidy in some future year will enhance the attractiveness of employment and production in that year; they will tend to stimulate investment in the previous year so that the temporarily cheap labour may have more equipment with which to work; investment in other periods could be reduced. Just how sensitive the programme will be to such tax/subsidy expectations depends upon their incidence. If income-tax cuts or employment subsidies are passed on fully to households in the form of higher take-home pay, producers' equilibrium conditions will be independent of them. This should be regarded as a limiting possibility, not a general case; one should normally expect some impact upon the set of prices facing producers. The ratio of sellers' gain to buyers' gain from a tax cut or subsidy increase equals the ratio of the elasticity of demand to the elasticity of supply. Introducing taxation into the cost of capital equation $c = P_k(r + \delta - \hat{P}_k^e)$ given after (2.12) leads to the expression $c = P_k\{(1-s)/(1-t)\}\{r(1-t) + \delta - \hat{P}_k^e\}$, where s is the value of investment allowances and t denotes the marginal rate of corporation tax. (See Anderson (4).)

Disequilibrium resembles taxation surprisingly closely. Producers may be rationed by disequilibrium in their product market(s) by excess supply,[11] or their input current markets. As was seen at the end of section II, the traditional accelerator

[11] For example, suppose that all firms in a particular commodity market face exogenous prices of their product ($\bar{P}$), labour (w) and capital to rent (c). Suppose each has the same production function $Q = K^\alpha N^\beta$. If the level of P is sufficiently high, there will be *excess supply* in the product market. At least one firm will be unable to sell all it would like to at the going constellation of prices. The profit maximizing value of output—assuming that this level of output can be sold at P—can be found by substituting the marginal productivity-factor price equalities into the production function to yield

$$Q = \left(\frac{\alpha}{c}\right)^{\alpha/\gamma}\left(\frac{\beta}{w}\right)^{\beta/\gamma}\bar{P}^{(\alpha+\beta)/\gamma},$$

where $\gamma = 1 - \alpha - \beta$. But what happens if the firm cannot sell this amount of output? If the product market is in excess supply, it is simplest to assume that *all* sellers are constrained equally by the disequilibrium. If so, and if they have no wish to accumulate inventories of unsold output, they will all cut back output to a common level, let it be $\bar{Q}$. First-order profit maximization conditions then yield $K = (\alpha\bar{P}\bar{Q}/c)$ and $N = (\beta\bar{P}\bar{Q}/w)$. Notice that the first of these corresponds exactly to the Jorgenson equation for the optimum stock of capital. Firms will behave *as if* they had faced a lower price of output at which they could choose their production levels freely. This hypothetical, or 'virtual' price—borrowing the term from Neary and Roberts (233)—in our context is

$$P^* = \bar{P}\left(\frac{\bar{Q}}{Q}\right)^{\gamma(\alpha+\beta)}.$$

The level of $(\bar{P} - P^*)$ may be thought of as an implicit tax on production. Excess supply in the product market works like an indirect tax, or sales tax, on the product.

approach to investment, and Jorgenson's extension of it, can be made intelligible in terms of modern theory by arguing that output is demand-constrained; the firm will therefore assess its capital requirements in the light of forecasts of future levels of demand-constrained output. The firm can be endowed with a notion of 'permanent output' that parallels the permanent income approach to consumer behaviour. Evidence that the sensitivity of investment to changes in output, $I/\Delta Q$, is much smaller than the capital–output ratio K/Q can be explained by conservatism in forecasting: a high value of the inertia coefficient λ in equation (2.24), for instance, if this equation can be offered as an empirically plausible model of how output evolves over time. Typically, the ratio of $I/\Delta Q$ to K/Q is found to be about one-fifth (see Evans (101)). The de-emphasis on prices of goods and factors and also on interest rates, also accords nicely with the Hicksian notion of a 'fix-price' economy. The complex pattern of lags linking I to previous values of ΔQ may be ascribed partly to informational and satisficing lags, and partly to adjustment costs.

The antithesis of this Keynesian view is the 'monetarist' hypothesis of continuous market clearing. Results differ radically. In the fix-price world, monetary changes can exert real effects upon producers. As will be seen in chapter 7, if there is excess supply of goods and labour, a rise in the money supply will raise consumers' demand for goods, and release the demand constraint upon output; this in turn raises employers' levels of hiring new labour, and new investment. These effects are amplified by any tendency for interest rates to fall, as a result of the wider asset market repercussions of the monetary expansion. In contrast, the monetarist insistence upon equilibrium destroys the influence of money upon the 'implicit tax on production'[12] that disequilibrium brings. There is no excess of actual over virtual price: P^* and $\bar{P}$ are equal. A once-and-for-all rise in the money supply will imply higher values of w, P, and θ, for all dates; they all go up equi-proportionately. A close look at (2.21) and (2.23) will reveal that optimum levels of investment are unaffected. A once-and-for-all increase in the growth rate of the money supply will raise the rates at which w, P, and θ are expected to increase; and since R is a nominal rate of interest, the rise in R will equal that in the growth rates of nominal values of w, P, and θ, if the real rate of interest is unaffected. In this case, money will be both neutral and superneutral: neither the level of prices, nor its rate of change, exert any effect. Non-superneutrality will be observed, however, if producers have balances of cash on which no (or little) interest is payable: the higher the rate of expected inflation, the higher the real cost of such balances. Schramm (283) has produced a model in which firms have three factors: fixed capital, labour, and the services of inventories (of which money balances are an instance). This model lends itself neatly to the foregoing non-superneutrality argument.

The rate of inflation may also affect producer markets by causing excess demand. (It may also be evidence of it.) We may again apply the Neary–Roberts (233) device of virtual prices. Excess demand in the market for investment goods is equivalent to a tax—probably a temporary tax, given the queuing procedure for coping with excess demand in this market—on the investment good itself; and

[12] See footnote 11.

excess demand for labour is equivalent to a tax on wage rates. Excess supply in the goods market drags down optimal levels of capital and employment; an increase in excess supply reduces investment and leads to redundancies, or, at the least, shorter-time working or reduced hiring. Increased excess demand in one factor market leads in general to lowered demand for other factors, and invariably to lowered output. The reason for the ambiguity in the first case lies in the fact that there could be factors unrationed in supply which are relatively close substitutes for the rationed factor: if blue-eyed labour is in excess demand, and brown-eyed not, producers can substitute the latter for the former with no effect. If the production function is 'neutral' in the sense that each factor is an equally good or poor substitute for any other factor, however, excess demand for one input implies a lower hiring rate for all others, than would transpire in equilibrium.

In equilibrium, actual and virtual prices coincide. In Keynesian unemployment, which is one example of the set of disequilibrium regimes that can be reached when prices are locked away from equilibrium, they diverge: there is an implicit tax on households' wages. Producers will attempt to plan in the light of forecasts of future disequilibria, no less than evidence of imbalances in behaviour in other circumstances. Incomplete indexation of the tax system may imply a positive (or negative) link between the level of tax, and the rate of inflation. If rapid inflation brings a high probability that the authorities will attempt to combat it by such devices as credit squeezes or wage and price controls, the rational producer will come to associate inflation with a widening margin between actual and virtual prices. The same conclusion emerges if rapid inflation provokes the authorities into deflationary policies that lead, in turn, to Keynesian unemployment. For evidence on how inflation has affected investment, see Feldstein (349).

III: 4 *Adjustment Restraints*

Explicit 'speed limits' or adjustment restraints may be imposed upon the producer's policy variables. The concept of a target vector of inputs and output is replaced, in the short run at least, by an account of the *status quo ante* inherited from the past, and a set of conditions governing the movement of variables in the current period.

A recent attempt to derive the investment function rigorously from adjustment restraints has been made by Sargent (280). Sargent's model consists of a present value function,

$$PV = \int_0^\infty [e^{-rt} f(N(t), K(t), \dot{K}(t))]\, dt, \qquad (2.25)$$

subject to a given inherited stock of capital, $K(t)$. The prices of labour, machinery, and output (w, J, and P) are deemed to grow at a common rate $\hat{P}$. All three are treated as parametric. The $\dot{K}(t)$ affects f through parabolic adjustment costs

$$C(\dot{K}) = \frac{1}{2\eta}(\dot{K})^2. \qquad (2.26)$$

The shape of (2.26) means that the marginal cost of adjustment is proportional to its size, and that only when the capital stock is stationary will costs of adjustment be completely avoided. Maximizing (2.25) with respect to N, K, and $\dot{K}$ gives the optimum *rate of increase* of investment:

$$\dot{K} = \eta\left[r + \delta - \hat{P} - \frac{P}{J}Q_K'\right] - (r - \hat{P})\dot{K} \tag{2.27}$$

where δ represents the rate of depreciation, and Q_K' is the marginal product of capital. Sargent solves for (2.27): the optimum *level* of investment

$$\dot{K} = Ze^{(r-\hat{p})t} - \eta\left(1 + \frac{\delta - \dfrac{P}{J}Q_K}{r - \hat{P}}\right) \tag{2.28}$$

where Z is some constant, which must be zero if the firm's present value is to be at a maximum: given (2.26) and $r > \hat{P}$, PV must only decrease in Z.[13] (2.28) therefore yields the optimum level of investment

$$\dot{K} = \eta\left(\frac{\dfrac{P}{J}Q_K - \delta}{r - \hat{P}} - 1\right) \tag{2.29}$$

(2.29) tells us that in Sargent's model of parabolic adjustment costs and parallel price trends, the competitive firm's investment will: be unit-elastic negatively, to the size of the adjustment costs; and vary *positively* with the ratio of the demand price to the supply price of machinery;[14] and vary *negatively* with the real rate of interest $(r - \hat{P})$ and the depreciation rate, δ. In words, the marginal revenue from investment, $PQ_K - J(r + \delta - \hat{P})$, equals its marginal cost, $J\dot{K}(r - \hat{P})/\eta$.

Unfortunately, however, the results do not generalize readily. The timing of investment is indeterminate if (2.26) is replaced by a condition that gives a constant marginal cost of investment. Replacing the assumption of parallel price trends (that w, P, and J all move equiproportionately) with some other condition also destroys the result. It is intuitively clear, however, that projections of non-parallel paths for these variables will create very powerful incentives to concentrate investment at particular dates. J will be a most powerful influence on the timing of investment. If J is expected to rise faster than the rate $r + \delta$, and storage costs are set aside, it pays to pre-empt the machinery immediately, not just for one's own future requirements but for resale to other firms. Price paths for the product will also matter greatly. Suppose P is known to follow a wave pattern such as

$$P_t = e^{+rt}(\bar{P} + e^{i\omega t} + e^{-i\omega t}) \tag{2.30}$$

where ω is the frequency of the (cosine) wave, and $\bar{P}$ the mean value of the price. If the machine is known to last an integral number of waves, and can start operation after a delay α, investment decisions must be framed so that they are always installed α units of time before the price peak.

---

[13] This is known as the 'transversality condition'.

[14] This is the meaning of PQ_K/J. PQ_K is the value of marginal product of capital and J is its supply price per unit. The ratio PQ_K/J is defined as 'q' in Tobin's model of investment (321).

The exact nature of the adjustment costs, however, is no less critical. They can be classified into two types: those internal to the firm, and those external to it. External adjustment costs show up in the premium that a firm must pay its supplier to get faster delivery of machinery or other capital goods that have been ordered. They are not the premium itself, but rather the speed with which it rises, the more the firm pre-empts. These external costs can only be a reflection of monopsony power. They are known to occur for many reasons. The greater the specificity of equipment, the greater the ratio of bulk to value in the capital good,[15] and the greater the size of the enterprise considered, the more noticeable they are likely to be. The fact that there may be an upward sloping supply of building workers in an area may incline you (or your builder) to stipulate a longer construction period.

A second external adjustment cost relates to that other aspect of the cost of capital concept: the rate of interest on borrowing. Capital market imperfections may lead to an excess of rates of interest on borrowing over rates available for lending. Suppose that this is so, but that both rates are parametric.[16] The firm will now have a strong incentive to synchronize its payments and receipts. If receipts are exogenous, the stream of payments should be tailored to meet it. The revenues of a business are exogenous if (a) price is parametric and (b) the volume of sales is exogenous too. Sales may be fixed now by previous orders; or by a rationing constraint when the market is in excess supply;[17] or when inventories are impossible,[18] by previous scheduling of all factors of production; or by the fixed supply of one factor for which no other can substitute. If the costs of other factors of production are also exogenous, the time-profile of the stream of profits will be outside the firm's control; and if, by contrast, the timing of investment spending is flexible, the course that investment will take will follow quickly and depend upon that plotted by the movement in profits. Should the scheduling of investment expenditure be less flexible than that of sales and production, however, the opposite may happen. If investment payments are expected to be heavier in one period than the next, the firm facing serious capital market imperfections will try to step up sales, temporarily, in the first period, for example by running down inventories, or increasing output. The positive association between investment and cash flow, to which capital market imperfections should be expected to lead, cannot prove by itself either direction of causation. This cannot be ascertained without a precise knowledge of the relative flexibility of all the parameters that the firm can (at least to some degree) control—output; inventories; labour and other non-capital inputs; in imperfect markets, all the relevant prices; and, in particular, the ordering, delivery and installation of capital equipment. This returns us directly to adjustment costs; but costs depressingly more complex than those captured by (2.26).

Internal costs of adjustment may take a number of forms. The simplest is the cost of learning by management and employees. Arrow's concept of learning by

[15] This will govern the costs of transport, and hence increase the chance of spatial monopsony.

[16] Imperfect competition and/or imperfect information in the banking industry is almost certain to produce this. See chapter 6.

[17] See footnote 11 above.

[18] Without inventories, sales can never exceed output.

doing (6) appears in industrial economics as the 'Penrose effect'.[19] The faster the firm grows, the less experienced its personnel will be. This will mean a higher chance of mistakes, and more disruption of work while consultation takes place. These will be pronounced if growth is associated with novelty in the range of products made, or if the characteristics of work entail lengthy training for the staff. If the firm could buy in experienced labour from other firms, these difficulties might be avoided. But the problem here is that the experience provided by work in other businesses might be inappropriate; people with this experience will be few in number and hard to find; and the uncertainties involved might be greater.

IV: Employment, Capital, Output, Distribution and Pricing in Non-profit-maximizing Oligopoly

We shall now examine the firm's optimization problem in a static model without uncertainty, but with non-profit-maximizing behaviour and oligopoly. This model embraces monopoly with or without profit maximization, two traditional oligopoly models and perfect competition, as special cases; it belongs to Model Set V.

Suppose there is an industry composed of m identical firms that together produce a homogeneous product. Market demand for this is assumed to be *isoelastic*: if the price elasticity of demand is ϵ (defined positive), ϵ is a constant. Output is homogeneous of degree T in capital and labour inputs. e_1 and e_2 represent the firm's elasticities of the rental on capital, c, to the volume of capital fixed, and the wage rate, w, to the level of employment. e_1 and e_2 will both be zero if the firm is a price-taker in its inputs markets; otherwise, non-zero. The conjectural variation for other firms' output is χ. This means that each firm i thinks that total industry output Q responds to its own output q_i, thus:

$$\frac{\partial Q}{\partial q_i} = 1 + \chi(m-1). \tag{2.31}$$

In other words, every other firm is expected to raise its output by χ in response to a one-unit rise in output. Each firm's maximand is a linear combination of its capital rental payments $c_i k_i$, its wage bill $w_i n_i$, and its surplus, S_i, of income minus these factor rewards:

$$U = a_0 S_i + a_1 c_i k_i + a_2 w_i n_i. \tag{2.32}$$

The maximand may be expressed more conveniently as

$$\underset{n_i, k_i}{\text{Max}} \frac{U}{a_0} = P q_i - \left(1 - \frac{a_1}{a_0}\right) c_i k_i - \left(1 - \frac{a_2}{a_0}\right) w_i n_i \tag{2.33}$$

subject to (2.31), $q_i = q_i(k_i, n_i)$, and

$$\log Q = \gamma - \epsilon \log P. \tag{2.34}$$

---

[19] After E. Penrose (249) for whom the problem was managerial inexperience. The concept may be applied to all categories of staff. See Marris (206), and Hay and Morris (155), for a detailed analysis of the limits to a firm's growth rate. Rigorous models of the growing firm are provided by Slater (302), Solow (306), and Yarrow (337).

The first-order conditions for this are

$$\Lambda P \frac{\partial q_i}{\partial k_i} = c_i(1 + e_1)\left(1 - \frac{a_1}{a_0}\right), \text{ and} \tag{2.35}$$

$$\Lambda P \frac{\partial q_i}{\partial n_i} = w_i(1 + e_2)\left(1 - \frac{a_2}{a_0}\right), \tag{2.36}$$

where $\Lambda = 1 - \{1 + \chi(m - 1)\}/\epsilon m$. These two conditions state that the value of each input's marginal product, multiplied by a fraction Λ to convert it into the input's *marginal revenue product*, should equal the input's price adjusted by two qualifying coefficients: $1 + e_1$ or $1 + e_2$ convert the *average* cost of the input (c or w) into its *marginal* cost; and $1 - (a_1/a_0)$ or $1 - (a_2/a_0)$ to correct for the fact that capital rentals and wages may also be 'goods' for the firm. If a_2 were zero, the second equation would simply state that the marginal revenue product of labour should equal its marginal cost. It is only then that any weighted average of surplus and capital rental charges reaches a maximum.

In perfect competition Λ rises to unity, because m reaches infinity and χ vanishes. Each firm treats its fellow producers' output rates as given, and there are so many of them that its own market share, $1/m$, is negligible. Furthermore, perfect competition in the input markets makes e_1 and e_2 disappear, since all prices (w, c, and P) are parametric to the firm. Natural selection enforces vanishingly low co-efficients a_1 and a_2. Hence both factors are paid the full value of their marginal products.

In imperfect markets, Λ lies below unity. Marginal revenue lies below average revenue, since the latter 'slopes down'. Indeed, Λ equals the ratio of marginal revenue to average revenue, and (equivalently) one minus the reciprocal of the elasticity of average revenue. There are three influences on Λ: χ, ϵ and m. Apart from monopoly, when $m - 1$ vanishes and χ has no role to play, m exceeds one; so Λ varies negatively with χ. The higher the value of χ, the greater the output response from its rivals that a firm anticipates a unilateral output increase on its own part will provoke. If $\chi = 1$, perfect collusion, explicit or tacit, is reached: the firms expect to behave in union, like the managers of different plants owned by a single company. In Cournot's case, $\chi = 0$, and the firm thinks that any unilateral action of its own will go undetected. When $\chi = 1$, m makes no difference to Λ; but for $\chi < 1$, Λ and m are negatively related. The larger the number of firms, the more elastic each thinks his average revenue is. Lastly, except in the limiting competitive case when χ and $1/m$ vanish, ϵ and Λ are positively associated. The more elastic the demand for the product as a whole, the less the damage to market price done by an increase in one firm's output level.

In imperfect competition, factor owners are likely to be paid less than the value of their marginal product. Likely, yes; but not certain. Imperfect competition, as we have seen, reduces Λ. It may well lead to positive e_1 and e_2, if the firm has monopoly power in the input markets. The positive association between plant size and wage rate points to $e_2 > 0$, although evidence that little firms pay more for capital (the 'Macmillan Gap') suggests that $e_1 < 0$. But these two influences on the factor price-marginal product relation—the first necessarily negative, the second quite possibly so—could be opposed, even counterweighed in extreme circumstances by a third influence: the goals of the firm. The greater the emphasis on wages as opposed to surplus among the firm's goods, for example, the larger a_2/a_0 will be.

Can we go beyond (2.35) and (2.36) to derive solutions for k_i and n_i? The answer to this is yes, when q_i (k_i, n_i) obeys certain rules; and even if it does not, solutions for *changes* in k_i and n_i, rather than levels, can be found. Suppose, for example, $q_i = Tk_i^{\alpha}n_i^{T-\alpha}$. This is the Cobb-Douglas production function, homogeneous (as we have stipulated) of degree T. Since $\partial q_i/\partial n_i = (T-\alpha)(q_i/n_i)$, we may express (2.35) and (2.36) as

$$\left.\begin{aligned}
k_i &= \frac{\alpha \Lambda P q_i}{c_i(1+e_1)(1-(a_1/a_0))} \\[2mm]
n_i &= \frac{(T-\alpha)Xpq_i}{w_i(1+e_2)(1-(a_2/a_0))}
\end{aligned}\right\} \tag{2.37}$$

The CES production function $q_i = (ak_i^{(\sigma-1)/\sigma} + bn_i^{(\sigma-1)/\sigma})^{\sigma T/(\sigma-1)}$ is homogeneous of degree T. Here,

$$\frac{\partial q_i}{\partial k_i} = \frac{a}{T}\frac{q_i^{1-(\sigma-1)(T/\sigma)}}{k_i^{1/\sigma}}$$

and

$$\frac{\partial q_i}{\partial n_i} = \frac{b}{T}\frac{q_i^{(1-(\sigma-1)(T/\sigma)}}{n_i^{1/\sigma}} ;$$

so that substitution reveals:

$$\left.\begin{aligned}
k_i &= \left(\frac{\Lambda P}{c_i(1+e_1)(1-(a_1/a_0))}\right)^{\sigma}(w)^{\sigma}q_i^{(\sigma(T-1)+1)/T}, \\[2mm]
n_i &= \left(\frac{\Lambda P}{w_i(1+e_2)(1-(a_2/a_0))}\right)^{\sigma}(bT)^{\sigma}q_i^{(\sigma(T-1)+1)/T}.
\end{aligned}\right\} \tag{2.38}$$

(2.38) are clearly a generalization of (2.37); in the latter case, $\sigma = 1$. These two pairs of equations are seductive. They can be (and, in simpler form, have been) used to generate numerous macroeconomic 'theories'. We give three examples.

One central concept in traditional theories of investment is the accelerator. This links the *increase* in the stock of capital to the *increase* in some other variable (typically, output) or set of variables. Take the first equation in (2.37). If this is to hold continuously, differentiating with respect to time reveals

$$\hat{k}_i \equiv \frac{\text{net investment}}{\text{capital stock}} = \hat{p} + \hat{q}_i - \hat{c}_i + \hat{\Lambda} - \frac{e_1\hat{e}_1}{1+e_1} - \frac{d(a_1/a_0)}{(1-(a_1/a_0))dt} \tag{2.39}$$

or equivalently

$\dot{k} \equiv$ net investment

$$= \frac{\alpha \Lambda P q_i}{c_i(1 + e_1)(1 - (a_1/a_0))} \left[\dot{p} + \dot{q}_i - \dot{c} + \dot{\Lambda} - \frac{\dot{e}_1}{1 + e_1} - \frac{d(a_1/a_0)}{(1 - (a_1/a_0))dt} \right]. \quad (2.40)$$

The oldest hypothesis is that investment is simply a given multiple of the absolute change in output. This can be seen at once on the right-hand side of (2.40) if all variables determining k_i, except q_i, are assumed stationary. Jorgenson's model has an expanded accelerator, where not just output but also p and c are formally introduced, and allowed to vary. As was seen in section II, Jorgenson uses (2.37) to derive a target stock of capital, under the simplifying assumption of perfect competition, so that k_i shrinks to $\alpha pq/c$. The adjustment of the actual stock of capital towards its target is left, as we have seen, for the data to trace in an unconstrained fashion.

Our second example is distribution. Taking the second equation in (2.37) and multiplying both sides by w/pq_i, one derives labour's share in the value of output,

$$\frac{(T - \alpha)\Lambda}{(1 + e_2)(1 - (a_2/a_0))}$$

which reduces to $(T - \alpha)$ in the perfect competitive case. (2.34) yields that labour's share equals

$$\left(\frac{n_i}{q_i} \right)^{(\sigma - 1)/\sigma} \frac{b\Lambda T}{(1 + e_2)(1 - (a_2/a_0))}.$$

Both these expressions reveal that labour's share is related *positively* to m, the number of firms, provided that $\chi < 1$; to ϵ, when $1/m$ does not vanish; and to a_2/a_0, the relative emphasis placed on wages as opposed to surplus in the firms' utility functions. It is associated *negatively* with χ, the extent to which firms anticipate that their actions will be matched by their fellow producers; with e_2, the extent to which rising employment drives up the wage rate; and with T, the returns to scale parameter.

The third example is output and pricing. To derive an expression for changes in output and price, we may note an important weakness in the 'solutions' just obtained for investment, and the wage share: endogenous variables were included among their determinants. Total differentiation of the production function, the demand function (2.34) and the first-order condition (2.35) and (2.36) yields a system of four simultaneous equations. These are expressed in terms of changes in the four endogenous variables (output, price, employment, and capital), and changes in exogenous variables. Define q_j^* as the elasticity of q to factor j $(j = k, n)$, $\breve{y}$ as the proportionate change in variable y, and $\breve{c}$ and $\breve{w}$ as autonomous changes in the cost of capital and the wage rate *not* induced by changes in the hiring of these factors. Assuming that the three elasticities ϵ, c_1 and e_2 are fixed, we may solve for changes in capital, employment, output, and price:

$$\check{k}A = \left(\check{x} + \frac{\check{\gamma}}{\epsilon} - \frac{\check{m}}{\epsilon}\right)\left(\frac{1}{\sigma} + e_2\right) - \left(q_n^*\mu + \frac{1}{\sigma} + e_2\right)\left[\check{C} + \mathrm{d}\log\left(1 - \frac{a_1}{a_0}\right)\right] +$$

$$+ q_n^*\mu\left[\check{w} + \mathrm{d}\log\left(1 - \frac{a_2}{a_0}\right)\right],$$

$$\check{n}A = \left(\check{x} + \frac{\check{\gamma}}{\epsilon} - \frac{\check{m}}{\epsilon}\right)\left(\frac{1}{\sigma} + e_1\right) - \left(q_k^*\mu + \frac{1}{\sigma} + e_1\right)\left[\check{w} + \mathrm{d}\log\left(1 - \frac{a_2}{a_0}\right)\right] +$$

$$+ q_k^*\mu\left[\check{c} + \mathrm{d}\log\left(1 - \frac{a_1}{a_0}\right)\right],$$

$$\check{q}A = B\left(\check{x} + \frac{\check{\gamma}}{\epsilon} - \frac{\check{m}}{\epsilon}\right) - q_k^*\left(e_2 + \frac{1}{\sigma}\right)\left[\check{c} + \mathrm{d}\log\left(1 - \frac{a_1}{a_0}\right)\right] -$$

$$- q_n^*\left(e_1 + \frac{1}{\sigma}\right)\left[\check{w} + \mathrm{d}\log\left(1 - \frac{a_2}{a_0}\right)\right],$$

$$\check{p}A = \left(\frac{\check{\gamma}}{\epsilon} - \frac{\check{m}}{\epsilon}\right)\left(\epsilon A - B\right) - \check{x}B + q_k^*\left(e_2 + \frac{1}{\sigma}\right)\left[\check{c} + \mathrm{d}\log\left(1 - \frac{a_1}{a_0}\right)\right] +$$

$$+ q_n^*\left(e_1 + \frac{1}{\sigma}\right)\left[\check{w} + \mathrm{d}\log\left(1 - \frac{a_2}{a_0}\right)\right], \tag{2.41}$$

where:

$$\mu = \frac{1 - \epsilon}{\epsilon} + \frac{\sigma - 1}{\sigma T},$$

$$A = \left(e_1 + q_k^*\mu + \frac{1}{\sigma}\right)\left(e_2 + q_n^*\mu + \frac{1}{\sigma}\right) - q_n^*q_k^*\mu^2,$$

$$B = e_1 q_k^* + e_2 q_n^* + \frac{T}{\sigma}, \text{ and}$$

$$\check{x} = (1 - \Lambda[\check{m}(1 - \beta m) - \beta\check{\beta}(m - 1)]).$$

It is sufficient for second order condition for a maximum to be met that $(T/\epsilon) + 1 > T$ and that e_1 and e_2 be bounded below. Using this, coefficients in (2.41) may be signed without difficulty. Increases in employment, capital, and output, and a fall in price, will occur as a result of:

(i)   a rise in the number of firms, except when they act in unison ($\chi = 1$);

(ii) a fall in the conjectural variation parameter χ, which would occur, for example, if the oligopolists stopped colluding, or if leadership became contested;

(iii) an autonomous fall in the wage rate facing the firms (perhaps as a result of

of an employment subsidy, or income tax cut);
(iv)   an increase in the emphasis placed upon wages, as opposed to surplus, in the firm's utility function;
(v)   an autonomous fall in the cost of capital facing the firms (perhaps as a result of a fall in rates of corporation tax);
(vi)   an increase in the emphasis placed upon capital rentals, as oposed to surplus, in the firm's utility function.

There are two small caveats to this. First, for (iii) and (iv) to increase the demand for capital, and for (v) and (vi) to raise the demand for labour, μ must be negative. Given that $(T/\epsilon) + 1 > T$, this requires a sufficiently small value of the elasticity of substitution. Secondly, a rise in m, the number of firms, will increase employment, capital and output at the *industry* level, not at the level of the firm.

An autonomous increase in demand is registered by a rise in γ. This will raise output, employment, capital, and price. Price could fall, however, if (2.35) changed in such a way that the elasticity of demand increased. If an increase in γ is accompanied by equiproportionate rises in the money wage rate and the cost of capital, price increases equiproportionately—and the real variables output, employment and capital remain unchanged. The real variables are therefore homogeneous of degree zero in the set of all prices.

Another implication of (2.41) can be drawn for factor share changes. The change in labour's share

$$\hat{w} + \hat{n} - \hat{p} - \hat{q}$$

can be found directly in terms of $\hat{x}, \hat{\gamma}, \hat{m}, \hat{w}, \hat{c}$ and the changes in the firm's utility function. How labour's share reacts to autonomous changes in w or c is governed chiefly by the elasticity of substitution. When this exceeds one, a rise in w relative to c tends to lower labour's share; when less than one, labour and capital are complements, and the opposite is likely to occur. This finding echoes the competitive model-set. But there is also a role for $e_2(\epsilon - 1)/\epsilon$. Labour's share tends to be boosted by an autonomous rise in w relative to c when this is negative. The effect of changes in the firm's utility function is more clear-cut: a rise in the relative emphasis placed on wages against surplus must raise labour's share. A rise in the relative emphasis placed on capital rentals against surplus acts just like the autonomous increase in the cost of capital. One new insight that this model of non-profit-maximizing oligopoly provides is that factor shares can be affected by changes in the firm's objectives or market structure, no less than by influences visible in the perfectly competitive framework.

The model provided here is essentially static; firms are identical; there is no product differentiation and no uncertainty; the firm has a unique utility function, which is simply the weighted average of three elements in its value added—wages, capital rentals, and surplus. Some of these confining assumptions may be relaxed, but only at the cost of much additional complexity. Furthermore, attempts to go beyond Model Set V to Model Sets VI and VII tend to lead to an invertebrate string of conjectures, rather than sharp results. One must concede, however, that only an autocratically governed company can be relied upon to have a unique utility function. Managers differ in age, salary, shareholdings, time-preference rates and other preferences. Employees and shareholders are also diverse groups. There is conflict, as well as community of interest, among the individuals who together form a company. The costs of taking decisions and gathering information have sometimes been thought to be inconsistent with the notion of maximizing, although we have seen that they need not be.

V: The Financial Cost of Capital, Dividend Policy, Diversification, the Modigliani–Miller Theorem, and Arrow–Debreu Contingent Commodities

Until now the cost of capital has been treated as a rental. We saw earlier that one factor upon which this rental will depend is the rate of interest. This is the rate of return paid on financial capital. In this section, we investigate what determines the financial elements in the cost of capital confronting a firm. Attention is focused particularly upon the extent to which the firm may be able to influence the financial cost of capital by its own actions, and upon the role played by uncertainty.

If shareholders are averse to risk, it is not just the mean expected return on an asset which will interest them. They will be concerned with the range of possible outcomes as well. The simplest way to reflect this is to assume that while mean return is a desirable characteristic in an asset, the variance in that return is not. This suggests that the price of equity will be negatively related to the expected variance of dividends. The expected variance is unmeasurable. The past history of dividend variance may provide some guide, but only if this past history is itself sufficiently coherent for variance to have shown itself able to be a good predictor of later variance. Let us suppose that this is so. A negative link should now appear between the price of an equity and the past variance of the dividend stream upon it.

Three ways that may be open to a firm of reducing its cost of capital now present themselves. These are: (*a*) to avoid fluctuations in dividends; (*b*) to merge with a firm or firms with an unrelated set of products; and (*c*) to finance investment by borrowing rather than by issuing new equity. The steadier the past pattern of dividends, the greater the price of equity and hence the lower costs of servicing it. A 'conglomerate' or 'diversification' merger should lower the cost of capital to the extent that the variance of dividends declines: the variance of profits of the combined company must be less than the sum of profit variances of its constituent elements. Borrowing by issuing corporate bonds (UK: 'debentures') or from banks may often be undertaken at a lower rate of interest than the cost of servicing equity.

These three arguments have intuitive appeal. But each is open to objections. All three rely on an assumption that shareholders are less perceptive or more constrained than the firm's manager. Take the first argument. The farsighted shareholder will treat retained earnings per share as part of the yield on each share in his portfolio, no less than the dividend. Pegging the *current* level of dividends merely transfers the uncertainty of profit shocks to *future* dividends. If the shareholder and the company can both borrow and lend on the same terms in perfect capital markets and taxation is ignored, the company's manager will not be able to enhance the attractiveness of the equity by the device of postponing the volatility of dividends—any more than it could by altering the time-profile of a dividend stream with a given discounted present value.

The second argument is vulnerable to attack on parallel lines. The shareholder can diversify his portfolio. The profits of sun-hat makers and umbrella manufacturers both suffer from high variance, because the weather is fickle. Their combined variance is far less than the sum of their variances, since the weather affects them in opposite ways. So risk-averse shareholders can acquire shares in each set of firms. The Capital Asset Pricing Model proposed by Lintner (193) and Sharpe (292) predicts that the yield of equity in a company j will be the sum of two components: a risk-free rate of interest (R), and the product (ρH_j) of this security's contribution H_j to the expected variance of the overall market portfolio and the market 'price' of variance (ρ). In this model, all agents hold identical beliefs about the mean, variance, and covariance of returns on all securities, and identical preferences between mean return (a good) and variance (a bad). What matters for the cost of a company's equity is not the variance of returns expected on it, but the extent to which it is expected to contribute to the overall variance of the portfolio— a much smaller and more complicated number. In particular, it follows that mergers between companies with small profit covariance cannot secure any financial advantage not already open to shareholders themselves.

The third argument falls victim to a similar line of reasoning. Continue to suppose that shareholders can do and undo financial transactions themselves just as easily as a company's managers can: both can borrow or lend at a safe rate of interest, R per cent. Imagine the firm borrows £x at this safe rate, and issues N shares at a price of £E each. It has a total capital of £$x + N$£E, on which it will earn a random return of Z per cent. Setting aside bankruptcy and tax, the shareholders' total return will be $Z(£x + N£E) - R£x$; since $R£x$ is the interest charge to which the firm is committed. The return per share, S, will be

$$S = \left(Z - R\,\frac{£x}{N£E + £x}\right) \frac{N£E + £x}{N£E}. \qquad (2.42)$$

Now the firm's average cost of capital, c, will be a weighted average of the cost of equity, S, and the cost of borrowing, R, where the weights are provided by their respective shares in $N£E + £x$:

$$C = S\,\frac{N + E}{N£E + £x} + R\,\frac{£x}{N£E + £x}. \qquad (2.43)$$

Substitution of (2.42) into (2.43) reveals that C reduces down to Z. The cost of capital is simply what the cost of capital would be if the firm had no debt. If the firm borrows at the safe rate R, even though R is less than Z, the weighted average cost of capital is unaffected. The price of a share, £E, falls by an exactly offsetting amount. This occurs because the shareholder recognizes that he has become committed indirectly to interest charges of $R£x/N$ on each share he owns. Since he, the shareholder, could himself have borrowed at R to finance the purchase of additional equity, the firm's manager is simply taking this same step for him. Borrowing by the company does nothing to enlarge (or narrow) the opportunities available to the shareholder.

These last results constitute the Modigliani-Miller theorem. The theorem was first proved in Modigliani and Miller (221) and extended by Stiglitz (310) and (312). The theorem establishes the conditions under which the cost of capital confronting a company will be independent of its financial policy, and of the ratio of debt to equity. Financial and investment decisions are separable, since the rate of discount to be applied for the latter is independent of the former. The assumptions upon which the theorem rests are:

(i)   shareholders can borrow on the same terms as companies, namely at a safe rate of R per cent which is independent of bankruptcy considerations;
(ii) shareholders have perfect perception of companies' borrowing activities;
(iii) taxation affects all sources of capital to the firm neutrally;
(iv) shareholder have homogeneous expectations of the profits of companies.

It is important to stress that the theorem does allow for uncertainty, and can be made[20] to allow for the possibility of bankruptcy—so long as assumption (i) is not infringed. None the less, these four assumptions are very stringent. Their unrealism leads one to suspect that there is something after all to be said for the traditional view that there is an optimum debt-equity ratio for a firm. Up to this point, borrowing by the company reduces the cost of capital, essentially because the shareholders approve of being able to borrow indirectly on better terms than they could obtain themselves. Too much borrowing, however, will not just reduce the price of equity but raise the borrowing rate, too, as the probability of bankruptcy increases. This is Kalecki's Principle of Increasing Risk (180).

Capital market imperfections and/or limitations on information available to shareholders can be adduced to defend the first two arguments, as well. Shareholders will prefer dividend stability if their preferred consumption time-profile is steady, and capital market imperfections penalize borrowing and lending. Shareholders may also value the information about the manager's beliefs about *future* profits that the dividend 'signal' may be though to contain. Moreover, shareholders may well not be indifferent between dividends and retained earnings: if he surrenders his dividends, the 'principal' (the shareholders) loses an important control over the 'agent' (his manager).[21] In practice, furthermore, diversity of tax status, expectations, risk attitudes, and borrowing opportunities make for heterogeneity among shareholders (see Hart (153)). The manager may be able to influence the cost of capital confronting him by judicious financial policy. The case for conglomerate mergers as devices to lower the cost of capital might be rebuilt on the basis of fixed transaction costs facing comparisons in capital markets, or impediments stopping shareholders from obtaining the advantages of diversification in their own portfolios.

We conclude this section by considering the implications of Arrow-Debreu

[20] See Stiglitz (312).
[21] See chapter 1, section II: 2 and particularly footnote 3.

contingent commodities (7) for the prices of securities, and hence the cost of capital. Suppose an individual has wealth W_0 now which he must allocate between different assets. His attention is confined for the moment to just two: A and B. Neither asset gives a certain return over his planned portfolio holding period (say, one year). Let us imagine that there are only two states of the world that can prevail in a year's time. These can be labelled 'Democratic President of the USA' (State 1) and 'Republican President of the USA' (State 2). The two assets give returns of R_{1A}, R_{1B}, R_{2A}, and R_{2B} in the two states. There are no transactions costs.

Figure 2.2 illustrates. Point E represents initial wealth, W_0. If our individual devotes all his wealth to asset A, he can attain point A. The distance AC/EG represents R_{2A}, the return per unit is state 2; EC/EF gives the negative returns per unit in state 1, when asset A is predicted to perform badly.

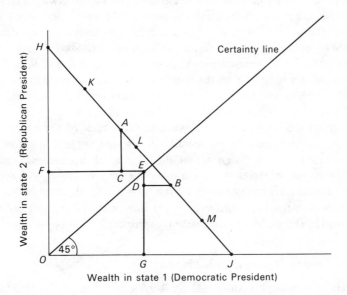

FIG. 2.2. The state-preference approach to security pricing and Arrow–Debreu contingent commodities.

Asset B, by contrast, thrives under a Democratic Presidency. The return per unit invested in B, R_{1B}, is BD/EF in state 1, while R_{2B} is negative and measured by ED/EG. If the two assets are prefectly divisible, our individual's portfolio opportunity locus is AB. If he can sell equity in A and B short—in other words, sell equity he has not got, for delivery in a year's time—this locus is extended northwest of A and southeast of B to the line HJ. Portfolio optimization involves seeking a point of tangency between the portfolio opportunity locus (AB or HJ, as the case may be) and an indifference curve between wealth in alternative states of the world. If our individual is averse to risk, these curves will be convex to the origin; if neutral, linear. Their gradient will also be governed by the probabilities he assigns to the two states of the world: the likelier is state 1, the steeper the gradient.

What distinguishes the two assets is the different ways in which the political party of the incumbent president affects the returns upon them. In fact, the prices of the two assets can be unscrambled to give the prices of the Arrow-Debreu contingent commodities of which they are implicitly composed. There are two contingent commodities in Figure 2.2: commodity 1 which pays a return only in state 1, and commodity 2, which pays only on state 2. The present prices of these commodities are OG/OJ and OF/OH respectively. Our individual can effectively bet on which party controls the White House in a year's time. The odds are $GJ\text{-}OG$ against the Democrat, and $FH\text{-}OF$ against the Republican. These are the odds available to someone who pays for his bets now, rather than when they fructify or turn sour in a year's time.

Suppose we now introduce additional assets, K, L, and M. If the securities market is efficient, the prices of all five assets will be aligned in such a way that no profit can be had from reassembling the portfolio between them. Asset arbitrage will ensure this, if transactions costs are negligible and everyone is apprised of the significance of each state for the returns on each asset. Holdings of asset A will be tantamount to a linear combination of assets K and L, or K and B, or K and M. There could of course be an asset the returns on which are affected in just the same way by the two states of the world as (for example) asset B; in this case, the two assets would not be independent and should be treated as one.

The analysis will carry over to more than two states of the world. All that matters for the determination of security prices, and implicit prices of Arrow-Debreu contingent commodities, is that the number of independent assets be no less than the number of states of the world.

Finally, this chapter has not analysed the investment behaviour of the firm (as opposed to its owners) *under uncertainty*. The interested reader is referred to Lucas and Prescott (199) for a powerful treatment of this complex subject.

VI: Other Views on Distribution: Kaldor and Marx

The models of distribution considered up to now have been, in the broadest sense, neoclassical. The centrepiece of analysis has been the production function, which we have taken to be differentiable and to display positive but diminishing returns to each input. Attention has been focused on equilibrium conditions for the producer, neglecting macroeconomic and intersectoral relationships. In this section, we explore two non-neoclassical theories of distribution, one proposed by Kaldor (179) and the other by Marx (208).

Kaldor's theory is macroeconomic. Output is defined as consumption plus investment, and consumption plus saving, and wages plus profits:

$$Y = C + I = C + S = W + \pi. \tag{2.44}$$

Savings are the weighted average of savings propensities out of wages and profits (s_w and s_π respectively), where the weights are provided by the levels of wages and profits:

$$S = s_w W + s_\pi \pi = s_w Y + (s_\pi - s_w)\pi. \qquad (2.45)$$

Employing the equality of savings with investment, and dividing through by Y, (2.45) becomes

$$\frac{I}{Y} = s_w + (s_\pi - s_w)\frac{\pi}{Y}; \qquad (2.46)$$

alternatively, making π/Y the subject:

$$\frac{\pi}{Y} = \frac{(I/Y) - s_w}{s_\pi - s_w}. \qquad (2.47)$$

Kaldor takes I/Y and the two savings propensities to be exogenous. In his view, therefore, the profit share can be found directly from (2.47). Profits increase with investment, and fall with a rise in either of the two savings propensities.

The major weakness in Kaldor's theory is that his social accounting identities can be manipulated no less plausibly to give the investment–income ratio in terms of factor shares and savings propensities. If I/Y is endogenous, and the other variables exogenous, (2.46) provides the solution for I/Y. Indeed, there are plenty of reasons for preferring this interpretation. UK cyclical evidence points clearly to the fact that profits lead private sector investment over the business cycle: the former are synchronized with GDP movements relative to trend, while the latter lags behind by three or four quarters. Furthermore, there are many reasons for expecting a dependency of investment upon profits at the microeconomic level. Imperfections in capital markets will provide an incentive for firms to make investment outlays match the time-profile of retained earnings. Unanticipated increases in profits may cause expectations of future profits to be raised, in consequence of which the net present value of investment projects not yet undertaken may rise. Unanticipated profit increases boost the price of equity, making external finance more plentiful and (at least seemingly) less expensive. The wealth of existing shareholders increases, and with it their ability to finance new expenditures. Risk attitudes, whether on the part of shareholders or managers, might alter so as to make investment more desirable. In general, it seems better to accept that I/Y and π/Y are both *jointly* determined: in a multi-sector model, the latter is likely to depend on the composition of output (see Solow (305)).

The basic elements of Marx's theory may be presented as follows. There are two sectors. One, indexed c, produces a consumption good; the other, indexed k, produces an intermediate product, 'capital'. There are fixed coefficients in the production of each good:

$$\left. \begin{array}{l} Q_k = \min[a_k K_k, b_k N_k], \\ Q_c = \min[a_c K_c, b_c N_c]. \end{array} \right\} \qquad (2.48)$$

If both labour and capital restraints bind, (2.48) may be re-expressed

$$\left. \begin{array}{l} Q_k = a_k K_k = b_k N_k, \\ Q_c = a_c K_c = b_c N_c. \end{array} \right\} \qquad (2.49)$$

The output of each sector is deemed to appear one period after the inputs of labour and capital. Hence Q_k in one period will equal the sum of the inputs of K_k and K_c which will combine with N_k and N_c to furnish outputs Q_k and Q_c in the following period. In Marx's *Simple Reproduction Scheme*, outputs repeat themselves period after period. Hence, we may write

$$K = Q_k = K_k + K_c = \frac{Q_k}{a_k} + \frac{Q_c}{a_c} \qquad (2.50)$$

$$L = \frac{Q_c}{b_c} + \frac{Q_k}{b_k}. \qquad (2.51)$$

Now (2.50) and (2.51) allow us to derive Q_c and K in terms of N: defining $\lambda \equiv a_k b_c$ and $\mu \equiv a_c b_k (a_k - 1)$,

$$Q_c = \frac{b_c \mu}{\lambda + \mu} N, \qquad (2.52)$$

$$K = \frac{b_k \lambda}{\lambda + \mu} N. \qquad (2.53)$$

(2.52) tells us that the output of the consumption good is a multiple of the labour force. The size of the multiple is governed by the four productivity variables, the a_i and b_i. Capital—the intermediate product—is also a multiple of the labour force; this multiple depends upon the productivity variables, too, but in a different fashion. Commodity and 'factor' prices are linked by the condition

$$P_i Q_i = (1 + R)[w N_i + P_k K_i] \qquad\qquad i = c, k \qquad (2.54)$$

which states that the value of each sector's output equals the sum of its wage bill and its purchases of the intermediate product, scaled up to include an interest charge of R per period, since output matures one period after inputs. If $\theta \equiv b_k \{1/(1 + R) - 1/(a_k)\}$, we may solve (2.54) for the prices:

$$\left.\begin{array}{c} P_c = w(1 + R)\left(\dfrac{1}{b_c} + \dfrac{1}{a_c \theta}\right), \\[3mm] P_k = \dfrac{w}{\theta}. \end{array}\right\} \qquad (2.55)$$

Both prices vary in proportion to the wage rate. They also vary positively with the rate of interest, R. The price ratio P_c/P_k is independent of the wage rate, but depends upon the productivity variables and (usually) the interest rate. Prices are marked up by the same proportion over direct wage costs only in the special case when the capital–labour ratios (in Marx's terminology, the 'organic compositions of capital') are equal in the two sectors. In this special case,

$$\frac{P_c}{P_k} = \frac{b_k}{b_c},$$

and the rate of surplus value in each sector,

$$\frac{P_iQ_i - wN_i - P_iK_i}{wL_i}$$

will be equal to each other at $Rb_k/\theta(1 + R)$. If capital–labour ratios differ $(a_k/a_c) \neq (b_k/b_c)$, relative prices will depend on R, rates of surplus value will diverge, and prices will not be equiproportional to direct labour costs.

The relation between w and R is negative. If R is zero, w will be at its highest. The real wage in terms of the consumption good will in this case equal

$$\frac{w}{P_c} = \left[\frac{a_k}{a_cb_k(a_k - 1)} + \frac{1}{b_c}\right]^{-1}, \tag{2.56}$$

while in general the elasticity of w/P_c to R will be

$$-\frac{R}{1 + R}\left[1 + \left\{\theta(1 + R)\left[1 + \frac{a_c\theta}{b_c}\right]\right\}\right]^{-1} < 0.$$

None the less, our analysis so far does not amount to a theory of distribution. There is merely a negative relation between the wage rate and the rate of interest; one cannot be determined without the other. In Marx's view, w would in practice be held down while manufacturing industry could expand at the expense of a low-wage handicraft or agricultural sector, but as soon as this source of cheap labour dried up, wages would be driven up. This process could be exacerbated or qualified by the increasing difficulty that Marx considered that capitalists would encounter in realizing their surplus value

$$P_iQ_i - wN_i - P_iK_i$$

in a world of scale economies, increasing concentration, and relentless competition between producers. The reader should be warned that space has precluded any but the briefest thumbnail sketch of Marx's analysis. For a much more detailed treatment, he is recommended to consult Morishima (223); for further elaboration of the ideas presented above, he may refer to Craven (71), Desai (81) or Samuelson (271). Marx's model of intersectoral relations builds upon Ricardo (263), and anticipates Sraffa (308). The Neumann model of economic growth (Neumann (237)), and the Non-Substitution Theorem (Georgescu-Roegen (130) and Mirrlees (216)) constitute powerful generalizations of Ricardian concepts. In Neumann's model, R equals the growth rate under ideal circumstances in balanced growth, while the wage rate for labour behaves like fodder to a farm animal: labour is not 'original', but instead represents a part of the process of production of goods. The Non-Substitution Theorem (see below, chapter 4, section II: 1) provides conditions under which the relative prices of goods depend only upon productivity conditions, and not demand. Its dynamic extension by Mirrlees (2.16) allows a full treatment of interest rates and the intertemporal aspects of production; see also Bliss (42), chapter 11.

VII: Investment, Intertemporal Equilibrium and Rational Expectations Equilibrium: Some Further Comments

VII: 1 *Do We Need an Investment Equation?*

In Keynesian macroeconomic models, the answer is a definite yes. Making the simplest assumptions (that all prices are fixed, the economy is closed, government plays no role and consumption is a fixed fraction MPC of national income), we derive the result

$$Y = \text{national income} = \text{investment} \frac{1}{1 - \text{MPC}}. \tag{2.57}$$

(2.57) holds provided that available productive resources can support this level of output.

The neoclassical tradition has it otherwise. If output gravitates rapidly towards a natural rate Y^* governed by technology, resource endowments, and organizational efficiency, an independent investment equation overdetermines the system. (2.57) should be re-expressed as

$$\text{savings} = (1 - \text{MPC}) Y^*, \tag{2.58}$$

which is *not* an investment equation.

The distinction between these views is brought out most clearly in the context of growth theory, as we shall see in chapter 9. It is also visible in chapter 7. We need the investment equation in Keynesian disequilibrium models, in order to determine the additional unknown for which they allow: the margin of unused capacity $Y^* - Y$.

VII: 2 *Stocks and Flows, Demand and Supply*

The traditional approach to investment has been to analyse the factors governing the demand for the stock of capital. This is the natural starting place. But there are important additional elements in the story to be brought in too.

Investment is conditional upon *excess* demand for capital. The required stock of a particular type of equipment must exceed its actual stock for it to be worthwhile adding to it. For investment to keep occurring the required stock of capital must keep growing, too.

Then there is the issue of exactly when the investment expenditure occurs. One possibility is that the actual investment outlays follows a prepared programme. Producers may have foreseen a jump in the price of their product, or an investment subsidy from the State, and planned accordingly. If their expectations are correct, the timing of the investment will match the occurrence of those events the expectations of which had caused it. But if the unexpected happens, producers will have to revise their programme, possibly in rather a hurry. Investment plans may be brought forward, postponed, increased, cut down, or scrapped. Actual investment expenditures have both equilibrium and disequilibrium components. The former merely follow the programme; the latter are responses to revisions in the programme occasioned by unexpected events. Disequilibrium investment will tend to follow such events in time. The delay may be a few days for typewriters, weeks for vehicles, months for other machinery, and even years for buildings and large scale plant. The length of these delays will be partly outside the firm's control, but sometimes inside it: the firm may have some freedom to choose between different trajectories towards its new optimum programme. Getting there quickly may lead to heavy adjustment costs, but there is the advantage of earlier additions to revenue or savings in costs. The choice between different trajectories is itself an investment selection problem; which is best will depend upon the firm's goals, interest rates, predicted price paths for inputs and outputs, and the costs of adjustment. Adjustment costs may be either internal or external to the firm.

Adjustment costs are likely to be asymmetric. It is usually harder to get rid of surplus equipment (or, indeed, labour) than to add to it. The lemon problem afflicts markets for used machinery. Plant suffers from indivisibilities. The value of the whole generally exceeds the break-up value of its parts. Legislation, strike threats, redundancy compensation and other obstacles discourage dismissals. Unexpected structural change may raise overall investment and employment because of this.

One adjustment cost external to the firm is provided by the supply conditions in the capital goods industry. It is surprising how little attention is paid to these in empirical work on investment equations. The price of capital goods plays a vital role in reconciling the theory of the demand for capital with the theory of investment. The former is related negatively to this price. Furthermore, since the rental on capital is related negatively to the expected rise in the price of capital goods, the balance between current and future expected prices of machinery acts like a valve to control the equilibrium speed of aggregate investment. Let us assume that the supply of new capital goods (per head of population) rises with their price (p_k) relative to consumption goods. The capital stock is in long-run equilibrium when the output of new capital goods just keeps pace with depreciation needs and with any growth in the labour force. At this output rate, p_k must also be in long-run equilibrium. Call this p_k^*. But when the stock of capital (per head of population) is increasing towards its long-run value, machinery output will be higher than this; and $p_k > p_k^*$. But as equilibrium is approached, $\dot{p}_k < 0$. Hence machinery output (per head of population) is also dropping back. Conversely when the capital stock is falling to its long-run equilibrium.

If we apply the principle of perfect foresight examined in section II: 1 of this chapter, these changes in the price of capital goods will be forecast accurately. Hence the actual path of $\hat{p}_k \equiv \dot{p}_k / p_k$ will have been anticipated in that of $\hat{p}_k^e$, the *expected* rates of change in the price of new capital goods. Through the formula for the cost of capital presented in (2.12)—that $c = p_k(r + \delta - \hat{p}_k^e)$—this lays down a particular time-path of the structure of capital rentals, which will ensure that at each instant the demand for the changing stock of capital keeps pace with its supply. The path towards long-run equilibrium from any starting point will probably be unique. This consideration makes one wonder what would happen if a chance disturbance pushed the economy off this path. Would there not be at least a grave chance of instability? This is the fear expressed by Harrod in his famous knife-edge problem of the warranted growth rate, which we examine in chapter 9, section III. The answer is that these fears of instability are ungrounded, *within the confines of the perfect foresight assumption.* The chance disturbance must have been anticipated.

VII: 3 *Intertemporal Equilibrium*

The concept of intertemporal equilibrium can apply at various levels: the individual household; the producer; the aggregate economy. Imagine a Robinson Crusoe economy. All decisions are taken by just one person. One such decision is how much of current output to allocate to current consumption, and what to leave over for the future. This is the essence of the investment decision. The concept of inter-temporal equilibrium is quickly grasped in the one-person case. But it extends to a many-person economy, too. Intertemporal *personal* equilibrium becomes inter-temporal *general* equilibrium. In this case, it is convenient to assume that all agents are price-takers, and that every price in the system takes the value it does so that every market can clear. In a dynamic model, some—with continuous time, virtually all—of these markets and prices relate to the future, not the present. Figure 2.3 presents the simplest possible framework to illustrate intertemporal

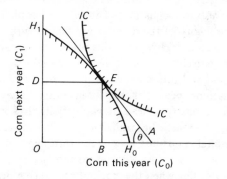

FIG. 2.3. Intertemporal general equilibrium: the simplest model.

equilibrium, personal or general: a two-period, one-good model. The good is corn, which is capable of being consumed or invested to growth corn next year. H_0 represents this year's harvest. The concave curve $H_1 H_0$ depicts the frontier of trans-formation between current corn consumption and next year's corn harvest. Its concave shape reflects the fact that this year's investment of seedcorn suffers diminishing returns, given (for instance) an exogenous stock of land. Curve *IC* displays a community indifference curve between current consumption and future consumption of corn. (An indifference map for depicting a *society's* aggregate consumption behaviour is unique if each individual has a unique indifference map and faces the same set of prices, and two or three of the following conditions hold: (a) all have the same preference map; (b) all have homothetic preferences; (c) the distribution of incomes between them is locked.) Point *E* illustrates competitive equilibrium and Pareto efficiency. The gradient of the double tangent (tan θ)

equals $-(1 + R)$, where R is the real rate of profit from investing corn and the real rate of interest on lending corn from period 0 to period 1. Had preferences been more directed to consuming in the second period, equilibrium would have occurred to the north-west of E, where R was lower.

Figure 2.3 simplifies intertemporal equilibrium in numerous ways. The current harvest is taken to be exogenous at H_0; this abstracts from the inputs of other factors, such as labour—not merely this period, but next period too. There is only one good at each date; the entire future is collapsed into a single future date; there are no spot or future money markets. There are only two markets—for present and for future corn. The price ratio of spot corn for immediate delivery to future corn for delivery a year ahead is $1/(1 + R)$. In more complex models, it is improbable that R remains unique. Trees grow with time, and wine improves; but milk grows sour, so that the own-rate of profit on milk *as a capital good* will be heavily negative, unless it can be converted into very highly priced Stilton cheese. In a particular activity R will be unique if costs unambiguously precede (or follow) returns in time; if not, there may be multiple values. An activity with net cash flow of -1, $+3.3$, -3.62 and $+1.32$ in successive years, for example, has internal annual rates of return[22] of 0, 10 per cent, and 20 per cent. There are two other respects, of course, in which R is or may be non-unique. There is no reason why the term structure of interest rates need be horizontal; and there is no reason why all prices should be expected to remain stationary. This implies that nominal and real rates of interest can diverge and, further, that real rates of interest can differ according to the commodity (or index of commodities) used as numeraire. The own rates of interest on oil and computers differ very widely.

VII: 4 *Rational Expectations Equilibrium*

A *rational expectations equilibrium* fulfils the following conditions:

(i)   at least one relationship governing variables in the economic model is subject to random disturbances;
(ii) agents form expectations on the basis of all available information and in conformity with the model itself;
(iii) all current and planned activities are consistent in aggregate.

The third of these conditions defines an equilibrium path for the variables in the system. The second stipulates that agents optimize in their predictions of future events no less than in any other aspect of their behaviour. It is the first assumption that distinguishes a rational expectations equilibrium from a perfect foresight equilibrium. The latter requires that all relationships in the model be deterministic. A rational expectations equilibrium must include stochastic elements.

An attractive example of this in a non-competitive framework comes from the game of 'Stone, Scissors and Paper'. This is a two-person game, with a zero-sum

[22] The *internal rate of return* on an investment project is that rate of interest, or discount, at which its net present value vanished. The equation

$$-1 + 3.3(1 + R)^{-1} - 3.62(1 + R)^{-2} + 1.32(1 + R)^{-3} = 0$$

has solutions for $R = 0$, $R = 0.1$ and $R = 0.2$.

Table 2.1. *Payoff matrix in the Stone–Scissors–Paper game:
an illustration of rational expectations equilibrium*

Player II strategies

		Stone	Scissors	Paper
	Stone	0	+1	−1
Player I strategies	Scissors	−1	0	+1
	Paper	+1	−1	0

of payoffs if played for money. Each person declares a symbol simultaneously; the payoff matrix from Player I's standpoint is shown in Table 2.1. The optimal strategy for each player is to randomize, around equal steady-state playing probabilities $(\frac{1}{3}, \frac{1}{3}, \frac{1}{3})$. Any other plan of action will lead to an expectation of loss. The game has a solution where both players employ their optimal strategies. The probabilities of one's rival's strategy selections which are leant from experience are mutually consistent. The aggressive player will search for evidence of a pattern in his rival's play: if there is any evidence of serial correlation (for example, if I observes that II is likelier than not to repeat a strategy which proved successful), he will exploit it to his own advantage. Serial correlation in play, like bias in strategy selection, will be punished. The Darwinian mechanism of natural selection may drive out such players from the economic game, or reduce their 'weight' in determining its outcomes by depriving them of wealth. So long as serial correlation of biased strategy selection persist, the game is out of equilibrium. In this example, there is a unique solution, where mixed strategies are employed, and, in probabilistic terms, expectations are fulfilled. In general, however, rational expectations equilibria need not be unique, or indeed optimal.[23] It is interesting to note that the stochastic disturbances in the Stone–Scissors–Paper game are *endogenous*. The random element in behaviour is itself the product of optimization by the agents themselves. In most economic contexts, rational expectations equilibria are analysed in models that take the random elements to be exogenous, like the weather.

We turn next to an illustration of a market out of rational expectations

---

[23] In an uncertain economy, prices transfer information between agents. Grossman (138) has shown that traders have incomplete and diverse information but rational expectations, and additively separable utility functions (such as (1.5) in chapter 1), and there is a complete set of markets for both current and *contingent* commodities (see chapter 2), a rational expectations equilibrium will exist; and the equilibrium will resemble one where everyone had complete information, by virtue of the information contained in the set of prices. But there may be multiple equilibria, one of which will be Pareto-efficient. However, if information is costly for agents to gather, the set of markets will cease to be complete, and rational expectations equilibria will *not* be efficient (Grossman and Stiglitz (139)).

equilibrium: the cobweb, as traditionally propounded. This is a partial equilibrium model of a good with a gestation lag. Its supply in one period has to be planned in advance. Demand, however, is responsive to price at once. The current price preserves equilibrium between current demand and predetermined supply. Supply is assumed to depend upon the previous period's price. For simplicity, linearity is assumed

$$Q_{dt} = a_0 - a_1 P_t + u_t, \qquad (2.59)$$

$$Q_{st} = b_0 + b_1 P_{t-1} + v_t. \qquad (2.60)$$

$$Q_{dt} - Q_{st} = 0. \qquad (2.61)$$

Variables u_t and v_t are stochastic disturbance terms, with zero mean value, no serial correlation and no mutual correlation. The equilibrium price (where $P_t = P_{t-1}$) equals $(a_0 - b_0)/(a_1 + b_1)$. It is reached by convergence if and only if $a_1 > -b_1$, so that demand is more elastic than supply. What is unattractive about the model is (2.60), which is in fact a collapsed version of

$$Q_{st} = b_0 + b_1 E_{t-1} P_t + v_t, \qquad (2.62)$$

and

$$E_{t-1} P_t = P_{t-1}. \qquad (2.63)$$

It is (2.63) that conflicts with rationality unless

$$P_t = P_{t-1} + \epsilon_t \qquad (2.64)$$

is shown to be the stochastic process for the price (ϵ_t again is a stationary zero-mean disturbance term with no serial correlation). So far from last period's price being an optimal predictor of the current price, however, it is an extraordinarily bad predictor: a high P_t stimulates a large Q_{st+1} and therefore, by (2.59), leads to a low P_{t+1}. By contrast, with rational expectations and neutrality to risk, the price will converge swiftly to its equilibrium value with rather different restrictions on parameters.[24]

One final point is worth noting. It is highly convenient to assume that the relations governing variables in a model with rational expectations are *linear*, or linear in the logarithms of the variables. The reason for this is that, in general, the expected value of a function relating variables is *not* equal to the function of those variables' expected values. Suppose $f(x, y) = x/(1 + y)$, and that x is equally likely to be 1 or 3, and y equally likely to be 2 or 4. The expected value of $x/(1 + y)$ is 19/30, while the ratio of the expected value of x to the expected value of $1 + y$ is 1/2. With linearity, however, the expected value of $f(x, y)$ *does* equal the fraction of the expected values of x and y. The cobweb model above displays linearity, as do the macroeconomic models considered in the context of rational expectations in chapter 7. Linearity of course implies that the random disturbance terms, such as u_t and v_t in (2.59) and (2.60), are additively separable from the deterministic part of the equations.

[24] See Muth (228) for the classic demonstration of this, and Schiller (294) for a valuable survey on rational expectations. See also Beenstock (36).

Under linearity, the role played by the random elements is therefore separated from the rest of the model. This separation means that a rational expectations equilibrium is simply a probabilistic extension fo the corresponding perfect foresight equilibrium that the model would yield had the random elements been banished. This close resemblance between the two equilibria is the reason why many builders of rational expectations models accept that convergence to equilibrium will proceed along a unique 'saddle' path from which deviations would be cumulative if they occurred. We saw in section VII: 2 that instability would not arise along the perfect foresight path to equilibrium. Whether such optimism is justified in the context of rational expectations is still controversial, particularly (but not exclusively) in the context of non-linear models, or of a transition to a new rational expectations equilibrium after a structural change in the model about which agents are still imperfectly informed.

Summary of Notation in Chapter 2

C	consumption
c	the cost of capital
I	net investment
J	the price of machinery
K	capital stock
N	labour
P	price
Q	output
r_i	the price of input i
S	savings
s_i	savings propensities out of i
$\mathbf{x}$	the vector of inputs
α	the elasticity of Q to x
β	the elasticity of Q to N
γ	parameter reflecting the level of demand
ϵ	price elasticity of demand
η	the elasticity of the supply curve
κ	the accelerator
μ	the elasticity of Q to K
π	profit
ρ	the price of variance
σ	the elasticity of substitution in production
χ	the conceptual variation for other firm's output
ψ	the correspondence between the factor input ratio and the factor price ratio
ω	the elasticity of the money wage rate to the price level

Chapter 3

Government

We have now arrived at the third term in the equation $Y = C + I + G + X - M =$ direct government spending on goods and services. When added to transfer payments by the public authorities, this amounts to over two-fifths of national income in the contemporary UK. Indeed, governments have many economic roles. Two dominate all. These are to provide public goods, and to influence the distribution of income. In Chapter 1 we saw how government might affect the behaviour of the household, but its public goods provision and redistributive taxation. The impact of taxes on the producer was noted at various stages in Chapter 2. It is the function of this third chapter to investigate the concepts and arguments that underlie these two roles of government. Section I analyses the theory of public goods; section II surveys the different meanings that can attach to the notion of the optimum distribution of income. Both sections present simplified models of the aggregate economy. These are needed to illuminate the purposes of (or claimed for) government economic activity. They provide an essential foundation for the chapter on the aggregate economy, chapter 7. Particularly in sections II: 3, V, and VI, chapter 7 shows the interplay between the key fiscal policy variables and the rest of the macroeconomy, under varying assumptions about expectations and whether or not markets clear.

I: Public Goods

A strict public good has two characteristics. It may be consumed by everyone; and no one may be excluded from it. Contagious disease is a strict public bad since it meets both criteria. Consequently, expenditure on hospitals that will check it is, at least in part, a public good. Defence is another celebrated example. It is a good for many people, and probably for most; for the pacifist, unfortunately, it represents a bad. Yet, good or bad, it is collectively consumable, and non-excludable. By contrast, public health is in large measure a private good. Public provision or subvention of medical costs is often motivated by an elemosynary case for relieving the ill of some of their triple burden (medical costs, loss of earnings and disutility of illness). This case falls under the heading of redistributive taxation.

It is helpful to start with a formal model. We assume:

(A1) a society composed of n egocentric agents, with exogenous incomes;
(A2) tastes are identified, well-behaved (convex indifference curves) and homothetic;
(A3) agents take decisions independently, and behave, in the Cournot fashion, by treating the actions of others as parametrically given;

(A4) there are two goods, y_1 and y_2, of which y_1 is a strict private good, and y_2 a strict public good;

(A5) the Non-Substitution Theorem assumptions[1] hold for y_1 and y_2, implying a unique marginal rate of transformation (MRT)[2] between them. There is perfect competition. The price ratio P_1/P_2 is therefore a parameter μ.

Figure 3.1 illustrates the model, with n chosen as a very small number, seven. This permits graphical illustration.

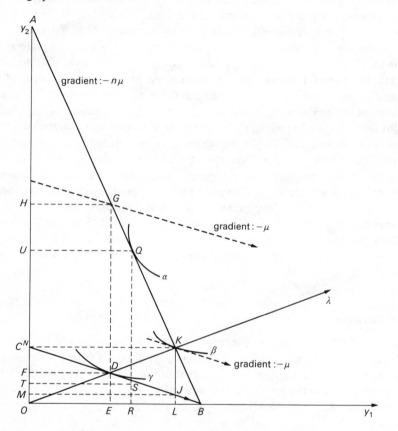

FIG.'3.1. Cournot equilibrium and the optimum solution to the public goods problem.

AB represents each person's consumption possibility frontier given that all seven in the society are behaving alike. BC is the individual's 'provision' possibility frontier. B and C are found by dividing his exogenous income by P_1 and P_2 respectively.

We start by assuming that no one knows that y_2 is a public good. This leads to everyone providing for himself at D, where BC is tangent to indifference curve γ.

---

[1] See chapter 4.

[2] The marginal rate of transformation between a pair of goods equals the ratio of their marginal costs of production (when the relevant factor markets are perfectly competitive). Dunne and Smith (347) analyse the allocative efficiency of government spending.

But D will not be the consumption equilibrium: each consumes what the other six provide of y_2 (not y_1), just as much as his own. So the individual's consumption occurs at point G. Here, he is out of equilibrium: the price ratio he sees is μ, and, by homotheticity (A2), if his marginal rate of substitution (MRS)[3] equals μ at D, it must differ from it at G. Only on ray λ will the MRS be constant at a value of μ. So everyone will try to provide more y_1, the private good, and less y_2. And since they behave identically, provision and consumption equilibria must move down CB and AB towards B. At B, of course, no one provides any y_2 at all. But the private-enterprise economy will, in general, stop well short of B. The individual is in equilibrium if his consumption occurs along ray λ. This is so because his own private MRS will equal μ on this ray.

If the individual must consume on ray λ and frontier AB, equilibrium is defined by their intersection at point K. Consumption at K corresponds with provision at J. Each person provides OL of y_1 and OM of y_2; and he consumes n times as much y_2 (ON) as he consumes. This must occur, at least, under the Cournot behavioural assumption of individual decision-taking, with others' behaviour regarded as given. In the Cournot equilibrium, the individuals' MRS are each of them equal to the MRT.

But Cournot's equilibrium is inefficient. It is, in fact, a Prisoner's Dilemma. Individuals optimize—or think they do—and society as a whole sub-optimizes. K is not a point of tangency between the individual's consumption possibility frontier and his highest attainable indifference curve. It cannot be, since the gradient of BC and AC differ.

This point of tangency must lie north-west of K, from A2. In Figure 3.1 it is drawn at Q. Q corresponds with provision at S: everyone provides OR of y_1, and OT of y_2. Then they may consume OR of y_1 and OU ($= n \cdot OT$) of y_2. Q and S are the social optima for consumption and provision. In this case, the MRT between y_2 and y_1 equals the sum of all n individuals' marginal rates of substitution.

Where Q lies in relation to G (the first-stage consumption point in the Cournot convergence upon K) depends upon the elasticity of substitution in consumption. If this is unitary (Cobb–Douglas tastes) G and Q are the same point. If the public and private goods are substitutes in consumption Q lies north-west of G; if complements, south-east. In the limiting case of perfect complementarity between the public and private goods, Q becomes the same point as K. It is only in this extreme case that society avoids its Prisoner's Dilemma of public goods.

Figure 3.1 illustrates our model without much loss of generality. We have seen how important the substitution elasticity is between y_1 and y_2, and what happens with different ranges of values. The other parameter that had to be frozen in the illustration was the number of members of the society. Had this been 700, not 7, AB would have been one hundred times steeper than in Figure 3.1; and the gain to everyone in moving from the Cournot equilibria at J and K to the social optima at S and Q would have become much greater.

Some of the assumptions of the model may be relaxed without difficulty.

[3] A consumer's marginal rate of substitution between a pair of goods equals the ratio of his marginal utilities for them.

Relaxing A5 to introduce an endogenous price ratio does not upset the qualitative nature of the results, except in the limiting case of a rectangular social production possibility frontier—complete joint production of y_1 and y_2—which dissolves the difference between the Cournot equilibrium and the social optima at once. Relaxing A4 to bring in more goods does no damage to the reasoning upon which Figure 3.1 is based although the figure itself needs amendment. Introducing excludability for good y_2 would imply that much more y_2 would be produced in the Cournot equilibrium. Actual markets in y_2 would start to operate successfully. An example could be opera seats. Charges could be made for these. Group decision-taking (relaxing A3) could bring us directly to the social optima. Heterotheticity of tastes (A2), unlike concavity of indifference curves, would not be a serious nuisance; it would imply that λ was no longer a ray from the origin. Differences in tastes (again A2) would pose a serious difficulty: how are the interests of the defence-lover and the pacifist to be reconciled? Relaxing egocentricity (A1) gives rise to the possibility of equilibria under altruism which comes closer to the social optima: members of society now start to place some emphasis on the good to others that their own provision of y_2 brings. So in Figure 3.1, the λ ray pivots counterclockwise.

An intriguing problem arises when the assumption of exogenous incomes is relaxed. For simplicity, we now take a Cobb–Douglas case (so that G and Q coincide in Figure 3.1), but introduce an hours-of-work variable, x; y_1 and y_2 both display constant returns to labour, which is homogeneous and constitutes the only factor of production. If h denotes an endowment of leisure, $h - x$ is the leisure the household retains. The household utility is assumed to be log-linear in $h - x$ as well as in y_1 and y_2. The wage rate, in units of y_1, is w. Figure 3.2 displays the social optima (which must coincide under Cobb–Douglas tastes with what an individual would choose to do if he did not know that y_2 was a public good). Plane ABC is the individual's provision frontier', or the consumption frontier he thinks he faces when he still thinks y_2 is private. DBC is the consumption frontier he actually faces, if there are three members of society ($OA = \frac{1}{3}OD$).

The vector OK shows the individual's provision of y_2 (OL) and consumption of leisure (ON) and y_1 (OQ) in a social optimum. With three members of society, his consumption of y_2 is OE. OE is his consumption vector in a social optimum. The provision and consumption vectors are highlighted as the two boxes in Figure 3.2.

The major problem posed by Figures 3.1 and 3.2, to which we now turn, is how the government should proceed to ensure appropriate provision of the public good y_2.

Can it rely upon voluntary contributions? Unfortunately, not. If we return to the formal model underlying Figure 3.2, the government will receive only OM units of the public good from everyone. This is so since voluntary contributions imply a return to the Cournot equilibrium. Back come the problem of egocentricity (why should I provide for others?) and the associated 'free-rider' problem (why should I not rely upon what others provide?)

So the government must coerce, if it is to provide the social optimum level of y_2 (OU in Figure 3.2). Everyone must be made to contribute. There is, it seems,

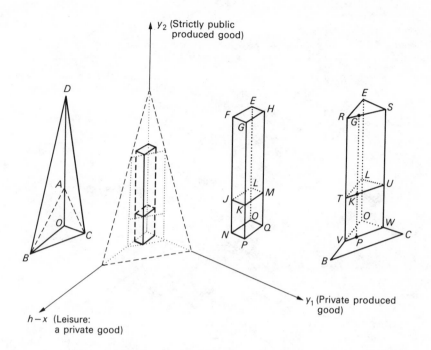

FIG. 3.2. Social optima with a labour input and pure private and public produced goods.

an inescapable cost in liberty forgone that the public goods problem imposes. This cost is still more unappealing when the assumption of identical tastes is removed: suppose society is composed of a large majority of defence-lovers and just one pacifist. Everyone must unfortuantely be coerced into contributions towards defence, defence-lover and pacifist alike. If pacifists were exempted from contributions, or, more generously, compensated for the loss in their welfare that defence spending brings, defence contributions would be undermined by the incentive defence-lovers would see to lie, and pretend to be pacificists too.

Another facet of the government's task is to determine the appropriate means of payment for public goods. In Figure 3.2, payment is made by lump-sum tax. The truth of this can be seen by considering the gradients of *RS, TU, VW* and *BC*. The first three equal the fourth. The individual perceives the same trade-off between leisure and the private good, y_1, as the true MRT between them.

Yet lump-sum taxation is almost certain to be highly inegalitarian. The rich man pays a lower share of his income in tax than the poor man, once the assumption of equal incomes (part of A1) is removed. It might seem that public goods may extract costs in the form of increased income inequalities as well as liberties forgone. Yet they need not. Figure 3.3 shows how a proportional income tax rate may be set to gather the revenue necessary to provide society with *CE* units of y_2.[4] An income

[4] In Figure 3.2 *OU* units represent an optimum provision for society, under first best conditions; in Figure 3.3 this is *OE* units.

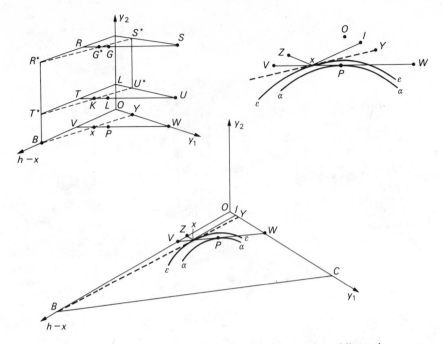

FIG. 3.3. The inefficiency of using income tax to pay for public goods.

tax with a positive marginal rate creates the distortion illustrated in Figure 3.3. It twists the relative prices of leisure and goods (in this context, leisure and *private* goods) as perceived by individuals and households away from the true social marginal rates of transformation between them.

Now suppose that the government decides to provide OE units of y_2. OE constituted the optimum provision, to each and all, in Figure 3.2. Paying this by means of a proportional income tax will alter the individual's choice set from the plane ERS, as in Figure 3.2, to ER^*S^* in Figure 3.3. R^*S^* illustrates a much lower relative price of leisure, measured in units of y_1. Examining R^*S^* in the $(h - x, y_1)$ plane only, the tax has changed the individual's budget line from VW to BY. BY is constructed so that the point of tangency x between it and indifference curve ϵ lies on VW. VW is, and remains, the $(h - x, y_1)$ plane representation of everyone's actual consumption frontier (the full frontier is, of course, the plane ERS).

The individual chooses point G^* on RS (i.e. X on VW) despite the fact that G (P on VW) yields a higher level of utility.[5] He does so because of the distorting effect of income tax. The problem with income tax is its lop-sidedness: it taxes (private) goods, but not leisure. In fact, income tax turns leisure into a public bad. Indeed, if income tax is to be relied upon as a revenue source, despite this disadvantage and because of its relatively attractive implications for income-distribution, it

---

[5] In the $(h - x, y)$ plane in Figure 3.3, this higher level of utility is shown by indifference curve α rather than ϵ.

is likely that the 'second-best' level of public goods expenditure will be below its 'first-best' level (*OU* in Figure 3.1 and *OE* in Figure 3.2).[6]

Figures 3.1, 3.2, and 3.3, and the analysis that has accompanied them, serve to illuminate the fact that society has a three-dimensional trade-off: economic efficiency, equality and liberty are each to some degree in mutual conflict. Economic efficiency for the provision of public goods called for restrictions on liberty, and quite possibly some adverse effects on equality if secondary inefficiency (in the labour–private good trade-off) was to be avoided.[7] A vivid example of this is military conscription. If y_2 is defence, and defence provision calls for labour inputs, one way of achieving a social optimum is to require everyone to give *BV* units of labour-time to the State. Although strongly coercive, this measure at least has the merit of avoiding the inefficiency introduced by income tax.

Further light on the nature of the economic efficiency–liberty–equality trade-off will be thrown by the next section, on the optimum distribution of income.

II: The Optimum Distribution of Income

It is best to start with a simple set of assumptions where there is no 'optimum' distribution of income. These assumptions are then relaxed in turn. Different sorts of arguments for a particular distribution can be derived. An analysis is then made of the issues posed by optimum taxation of income.

Model 1 consists of the following assumptions:

(A1) every person has a constant and equal marginal utility of income;
(A2) social welfare is the sum of all individuals' utilities;
(A3) the sum of each person's income is exogenous: aggregate income is a fixed number;
(A4) no person's utility is affected by any other person's income.

These four assumptions may be termed CEMU (constant and equal marginal utility) for A1; Utilitarian for A2; Constant Sum Game, for A3 and Egocentricity for A4; they are illustrated for a two-person society in Figure 3.4.

The bottom left quadrant illustrates A3: where Y_i is person i's income, A3 states that $\Sigma_i Y_i$ equals a constant. This is the equation of the line *AB*, labelled ϕ. ϕ has a gradient of -1. The top left and bottom right quadrants depict A1. Both 1 and 2 have linear utility functions in income, with the same derivative dU_i/dY_i.

---

[6] Likely, but not certain. y_2 could, for example, be a better substitute for leisure than for y_1.

[7] But it should not be thought that the gain to welfare which arises from moving from the Cournot equilibrium to the social optimum is trivial. An example can dispel such impressions immediately. Suppose we return to the formal model with exogenous incomes and impose Cobb–Douglas tastes and a cardinal utility function with linear homogeneity. The ratio of the individual's utility in the social optimum to that in the Cournot equilibrium will now equal $n^{1-\alpha_1}[\alpha_1 + (1 - \alpha_1)/n]$, if α_1 is the elasticity of utility to the private good. For example, if there are one hundred million people in society, and the elasticity of each person's utility to the private good is 15/16, utility is nearly trebled by moving to the social optimum. The general formula, and others for variant assumptions, are found by maximizing utility subject to the consumption possibility frontier for the social optimum, but subject to the provision frontier (and then substituted into the first frontier) for Cournot.

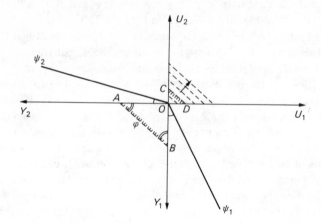

FIG. 3.4. The independence of social welfare from the distribution of income in Model 1.

A4 is obeyed, given that the function Ψ_i are seen to be invariant with respect to the income of another. The top right quadrant is depicted in the space of utilities. *CD* is the utility possibility frontier. In Figure 3.4, it is linear and has a gradient of -1 as a result of Model 1's assumptions. The dotted lines in this quadrant represent social welfare indifference curves, in the space of individuals' utilities. These embody the linearity—and gradient of -1—implicit in assumption A2. *CD* is coincident with one of these social welfare indifference curves.

This coincidence means that all feasible income distributions between 1 and 2 are equally valued by society. Social welfare is quite unaffected by any redistribution of income, from rich to poor or poor to rich. This result accords with a right-wing liberal outlook on economic policy.

Quite the opposite view, that an equal distribution of income is clearly better than all others, may be derived in different ways. One possibility, let us call it Model 2, is to repeal assumption A1, and replace it by

(A1■) everyone has an identical utility function in income, which shows diminishing marginal utility of income,

while retaining A2, A3 and A4 from Model 1. A1■ changes the ψ_i functions in Figure 3.4, and—as a result—turns the utility possibility frontier *CD* into a concave curve whose most north-easterly point lies on a ray from the origin λ with unit gradient. Figure 3.5 illustrates.

Instead of lines with constant derivatives dU_i/dY_i, the ψ_i functions in Fig. 3.5 are concave. This means that the marginal utility of income diminishes as income rises—and, in Model 2, in exactly the same way for both (all) people. The political imperative to which Model 2 points is to equalize the marginal utilities of income. As it happens, under A1, marginal utilities of income are equalized at identical income levels: each person receives equal income ($OJ = OK$). The concavity of the

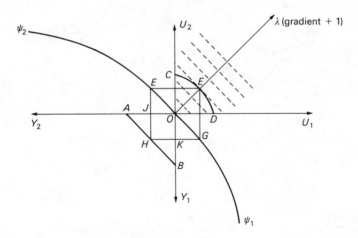

FIG. 3.5. The social superiority of income equality, with concave identical utility-income functions in Model 2.

ψ_i causes *CD* to be concave; but since A2 has not been altered from Model 1, the social welfare indifference curves remain linear.

There are two other ways of reaching the result that an equal income distribution is best, while retaining all but one assumption of Model 1. One is to replace A2, and put in its place:

(A2■) Social Welfare is a symmetrical function of weighted individuals' utilities, with less than infinite elasticity of substitution between these utilities.

A2■ may be captured most easily by either of the following equations:

$$\text{S.W.} = (\sigma - 1) \sum_i a_i (U_i)^{(\sigma-1)/\sigma}, \tag{3.1}$$

$$\text{S.W.} = \left[\sum_i a_i (U_i)^{(\sigma-1)/\sigma} \right]^{\sigma(\sigma-1)}. \tag{3.2}$$

These two equations generate identical social welfare indifference curves, the $(\sigma - 1)$ coefficient in (3.1) and the $(\sigma - 1)/\sigma$ exponent on S.W. in (3.2) are different ways of ensuring that social welfare is always increasing in individuals' utilities. Both equations are members of the CES family. (3.2) is linear homogeneous. A2■ in fact stipulates that $\sigma < \infty$ and that the a_i are all equal (this last being the implication of symmetry). In the single case of $\sigma = 1$, (3.1) and (3.2) shrivel up: in (3.1), S.W. vanishes, while (3.2) dissolves into the statement that the a_i sum to unity. So the unit value of the substitution elasticity calls for (3.1) and (3.2) to be replaced. In their stead comes the Cobb–Douglas equation

$$\text{S.W.} = \Pi U_i^{\alpha_i} \tag{3.3}$$

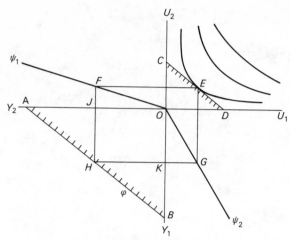

FIG. 3.6. The social superiority of income equality, with concave identical utility-income functions, in Model 2.

with the restriction that the α_i are equal (the symmetry property).

Model 3 consists of A2■, plus A1, A3, and A4 all unamended from Model 1. Figure 3.6 illustrates the case where the substitution elasticity for social welfare between individuals' utilities is cut from infinity (as in A2 in Model 1) to unity: the Cobb–Douglas case.

Once again, the optimum distribution of income is unique and equal: 1 should receive OK, 2 OJ; E is the point of tangency between the utility possibility frontier (now linear again) and the social welfare indifference curves (which are not rectangular-hyperbolic, in accord with (3.3) subject to the α_i being equal).

The third possible justification for an equal income distribution may be found by replacing A3 by

(A3■) The sum of incomes is variable and maximized at equality.

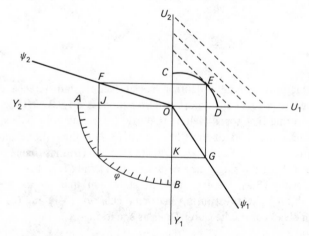

FIG. 3.7. The social superiority of income equality, when this maximizes the sum of incomes.

A3■, together with A1, A2, and A4 from Model 1, constitute Model 4. Figure 3.7 illustrates.

In Figure 3.7, *CD* is concave not (as in Model 2) because the ψ_i are concave, but because the income function ϕ is concave. The size of the cake varies with its distribution: in Model 4, its size is assumed to be greater when that division is equal.

So Models 2, 3, and 4 prescribe a unique distribution of income, and, in each case, this is income equality. Yet it is curious how sensitive the precise income-division recommendation is to the exact character of the assumptions. Let us explore this in each of these three models.

Suppose we retain the concavity of the ψ_i in Model 2, but remove the identity. Now, ψ_1 and ψ_2 are allowed to look quite different, apart (that is) from the concavity they share. We might call the modified model Model 2*. Suppose the utility value for any income level is five times higher for person 1 than 2. Panel (*a*) of Figure 3.8 illustrates this. Here, person 1 is a much better 'happiness machine' than 2: he is simply more successful at converting pounds or dollars into units of felicity. Model 2* is very inegalitarian: it prescribes a high income for those who can enjoy it, and much less for those who cannot. Equalizing *marginal utilities of*

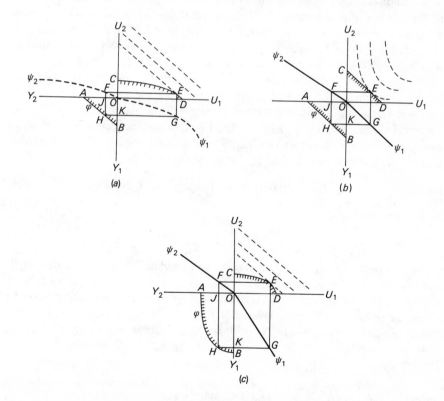

FIG. 3.8. Various assumptions which yield an unequal optimum distribution of income. (*a*) Unequal utility-income functions; (*b*) Unequal weights in social welfare; (*c*) Unequal earning abilities with total income variable.

income (as models 2 and 2* both stipulate) cannot entail equalizing utilities, or incomes, unless the ψ_i are identical.

Now Model 3. Retain limited substitutability for the social welfare indifference curves, which makes them convex to the origin. But remove their symmetry property. Call this Model 3*. Panel (*b*) of Figure 3.8 shows what can happen. If the social welfare function places more weight on person 1's utility than on 2's, the optimum income distribution moves across in 1's favour.

Model 4 can be amended easily to recommend an unequal income distribution, too. The symmetry property in the income function ϕ needs to be removed: that is enough. Panel (*c*) of Figure 3.8 shows the effects of doing this. This illustrates Model 4*. Again, the optimum income distribution is tilted strongly towards person 1.

Models 2*, 3* and 4* illustrate various possible arguments for unequal income distribution. Some people have a higher capacity to enjoy income than others, Model 2* assumes; put another way, some people may have greater need for income than others.[8] Model 3* allows society to place higher emphasis on some people's economic welfare than others: national heroes perhaps; or minorities disadvantaged in some non-economic respect; or in a non-democratic system, the rulers themselves in their own eyes; or residents in marginal constituencies whom a political party needs to woo sedulously to be assured of power. Model 4* introduces differences in earning capacities between people; and it presents the notion that income re-distribution, at some stage at least, imposes a cost in total income forgone. So unequal incomes may be defended on the ground that the reduction of inequality would reduce the size of national income.

These arguments against equality of income call for a deeper probe. We shall concentrate upon Models 3* and 4*. The four-quadrant diagram presented up to now may be reduced to two quadrants, by expressing social welfare directly in terms of each individual's income. In algebra, we may state[9]

$$\text{S.W.} = f(\psi_1(y_1), \psi_2(Y_2), \ldots, \psi_n(Y_n)) \tag{3.4}$$

as the maximand, and

$$g(Y_1, Y_2, \ldots, Y_n) = 0, \tag{3.5}$$

as its restraint. (3.5) is the function ϕ in the preceding figures. First-order conditions for the maximization are $f_i \psi_i' = \xi g_j$, and $g = g(..)$, where ξ is a Lagrange multiplier. If a solution to these equations is to be optimal, g must be concave to the social welfare indifference hypersurface implied by (3.4). This is quickly said, and so general as to be sterile. Everything depends upon the shapes of f and g. It is these two which we shall now investigate in detail. Of the two, f is largely familiar already.

---

[8] At an abstract level, 'utility' is a versatile concept. There is no reason why it need not be defined to include or even represent what is meant by 'need'.

[9] (3.4) still preserves A4 of Model 1 (egocentricity). Allowing for altruism or envy, (3.4) may be redefined as S.W. $= f(\psi_1(Y), \ldots, \psi_n(Y))$, and the term $f_i \psi_i'$ for the first-order condition becomes $\Sigma_j f_j \psi_{ji} = \xi g_i$.

The exact shape of f depends, above all, on three factors: the elasticity of substitution between different individuals' utilities in social welfare (symbolically, σ); the weights placed upon these people's utilities (the a_i in (3.1) or (3.2), or the α_i in (3.3)); and the shapes of the ψ_i.

Figure 3.9 presents some instances of f, in the two-person case. Panel (a) keeps the a_i all equal, assumes that the ψ_i are similar, and imposes a zero value on σ. Different individuals' income levels are perfect complements in social welfare.

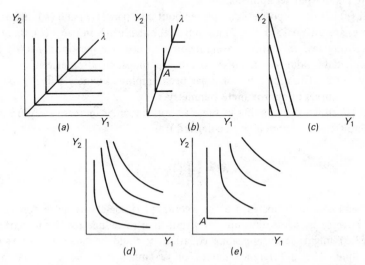

FIG. 3.9. Various social welfare functions depicted in income-space. (a) Absolute inequality-aversion; (b) The conservative social welfare function; (c) The biased Utilitarian function; (d) Intermediate inequality-aversion; (e) Variable inequality-aversion.

Absolute aversion to inequality in incomes emerges from a combination of the rectangularity of the indifference curves ($\sigma = 0$) and the fact that the λ ray has a unit-gradient (a_i all-equal). Panel (a) is frequently associated with Marxist political attitudes. It has also been proposed by Rawls (261), on the ground that if everyone were unaware of his economic circumstances, he would assent to that contract or set of social decisions that gave as much as possible to the least advantaged: if everyone were sufficiently averse to risk, he would be too afraid of landing in the poorest set to agree to anything else. While Rawls's argument is put forward as an explicitly non-utilitarian defence of (qualified) equality, it can be translated easily into utilitarian terms by recalling the Neumann–Morgenstern approach to choice under uncertainty. This equates risk-aversion with a declining marginal utility of income, and hence with concave ψ_i.[10]

Panel (b) shares with (a) a zero value of σ, but imposes either unequal a_i, or unequal ψ_i, so that the preferred income distribution is unequal. Corden has termed it the 'conservative social-welfare function' (see (65)). For what it implies is that

[10] The more pronounced the concavity of ψ_i, the lower the elasticity of substitution along a social welfare indifference curve drawn in the space of individuals' incomes.

departure from, for example, position A can bring forth an increase in social welfare only if there is no one in the society that suffers from the change; and if anyone does lose, social welfare has clearly fallen. (Contrast this with Pareto's value judgement: if the departure from A brings loss to one and gain to another, social welfare cannot be said to have risen or fallen.) But (b) could result from different ψ_i, not different a_i: the old nostrum 'to each according to his *needs*' shows that there need be no inconsistency between (b) and socialism, if individual needs are taken to differ appreciably.

Panel (c) has the opposite assumption about σ to panels (a) and (b): it is infinite. But the a_i are unequal (or the ψ_i are unequal but linear). In panel (c), there seems to be a strong case for concentrating income on just one person. Panel (d) depicts an intermediate value of σ, close to unity perhaps, or alternatively concave ψ_i (perhaps both). The unit value of σ has been employed widely.[11] Panel (d) shows indifference curves of approximate symmetry.

Panel (e) shows σ increasing in value as both incomes increase away from point A. The indifference curves might be derived from

$$\text{S.W.} = \prod_{i=1}^{n} (Y_i - \gamma_i)^{\alpha_i} \tag{3.6}$$

where point A's coordinates are the vector $\boldsymbol{\gamma}$. If society is more concerned to remove poverty by some absolute definition than to reduce relative income differences, (3.6) might be an appealing equation. γ could be taken to represent the poverty line. The indifference curves in (e) might also be explained by any tendency for the fall in the marginal utility of income to decelerate very rapidly as income rose, such as with $U = a - Y^{-10}$.

The shape of f is governed therefore by political value-judgement. But g is another matter. Its properties are governed by positive factors. Consider the following model (call it the Standard Income Tax Model):

(A1) all income is earned;
(A2) the value of output is the sum of all labour inputs, expressed in efficiency units: person i chooses to work h_i hours at efficiency rating e_i; total output $= \Sigma_i h_i e_i$; the pre-tax hourly wage rate for person i is e_i;
(A3) an income tax rate t is applied to all earnings and its total proceeds

$$t \sum_i^n h_i e_i$$

are distributed back equally to everyone as a lump sum;

---

[11] It forms the basis for Champernowne's measure of income inequality (56). Phelps (253) is another author who makes use of it in the context of the optimum distribution of income. Equation (3.6) on which it is based may be treated as a convenient social democratic compromise between the right-wing liberal utilitarian view shown in Model 1, and the priority accorded to equality in panel (a) of Figure 3.9.

(A4) hours of work are chosen by i to maximize

$$U_i(h_i, y_i) + \lambda\left[y_i - e_i(1-t)h_i - \frac{t}{n}\sum_j^n h_j e_j\right], \tag{3.7}$$

where $U_{i1} < 0 < U_{i2}$, and i treats j hours of work as given parametrically for $i \neq j$;

(A5) e_i varies across the population n;

(A6)
$$\sum_i^n y_i = \sum_i^n h_i e_i$$

(a market clearance condition for the aggregated commodity).

Figure 3.10 displays an individual's choice of hours of work and consumption of y, as t varies from 0 to 1. When t is at zero (panel (a)), he optimizes at A, on a

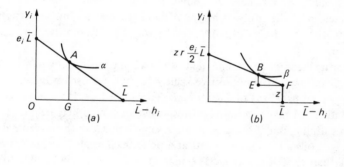

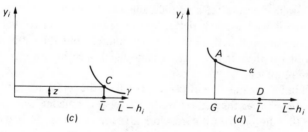

FIG. 3.10. Endowment effect of income taxation: leisure is a public bad. (a) $t = 0$; (b) $t = 0.5$ with $n \to \infty$; (c) $t = 1$ with $n \to \infty$; (d) $t = 1$ with $n \to \infty$.

budget restraint which starts on the horizontal axis at his leisure endowment level, $\bar{L}$. The vertical intercept for his restraint is e_i, the maximum volume of y he could earn by sacrificing at his leisure. In panel (b), the income-tax rate is pitched at one-half. This does two things: it halves the gradient of the budget restraint, doubling the relative price of y in terms of leisure; and it also shifts the endowment point, from $\bar{L}$ on the horizontal axis, to point F above it. $F\bar{L}$, shown as distance z, is the social dividend $(1/n)\Sigma_i e_i h_i$, which is parcelled out equally to everyone. In the figure, it has been assumed that our representative individual is less productive than the average, because the vertical distance BE (which with tax at 50 per cent represents what the government receives from him through income tax) is a little smaller than z. A final point about panel (b), which is valid also for (c) and (d): n has been set at ∞. Strictly, the gradient of the budget restraints is not $-e_i(1 - t)$, but $-e_i[1 - t(n - 1)/n]$ which tends to $-e_i(1 - t)$ as $n \to \infty$. In (b), the individual optimizes at B.

In panel (c), t has risen to 100 per cent. Again assuming that $n \to \infty$, this makes the budget restraint horizontal. The individual chooses point C, given (A4) that the marginal utilities of the Hicksian 'commodity',[12] and leisure, are both positive. But in fact panel (c) contains a contradiction. Since our individuals do not work, by A1 and A2 there will be no aggregate output; tax receipts by the State are zero; so the social dividend $(1/n)\Sigma_i e_i h_i$, which depends upon work effort, is zero too. Distance e shrivels away to nothing. Panel (d) illustrates the true predicament of our individual. He chooses D. All leisure, and no output at all. With $n < \infty$, the situation is minimally better; here the individual realizes that he receives a tiny but positive fraction of the fruits of his own labour, so that the budget restraint has a slightly negative tilt, hours of work may be very slightly positive, and z could be positive too.

The linear income-tax regime that we have modelled provokes a Prisoner's Dilemma. It occurs with any positive value of t, but is most easily seen with $t \to 1$ and $n \to \infty$, as in panel (d) of Figure 3.10. To work harder is a dominated strategy for each individual taken separately; irrespective of how others behave, it will not increase his utility. But if all agree to work some hours (say the horizontal distance DG), average consumption may occur at a point such as A. Here, everyone can be better off than if all were at D. The high ability person will be able to sacrifice relatively low-valued leisure for a considerable earned income. The low ability person, who is faced with a much flatter budget restraint closer to that in panel (c) of Figure 3.10, may not perhaps work much himself; but the social dividend will stll be much higher than at D (where it is negligible), so he too can reach a much higher consumption level of y.

There will in fact be one rate of tax, t^*, at which the social dividend is at a maximum. This rate achieves the highest welfare level for someone with earning ability low enough that he chooses not to work. If, for example, differences in e_i are trivial, and everyone has identical Cobb–Douglas tastes between leisure and y (with α representing the elasticity of utility to leisure, and $1 - \alpha$ to y), t^* equals $n/[(n - 1)(1 + \sqrt{\alpha})]$. This tends to about $58\frac{1}{2}$ per cent if a is one-half and n tends to infinity. These, and other results for different assumptions and parameter values, may be found by the following procedure: (a) specify a probability density function for the e_i; (b) allow each person to maximize (3.7) where the restraint may be (helpfully) re-expressed as

---

[12] y is a Hicksian composite commodity.

$$h_i \geqslant 0 \text{ and } y_i - e_i \left[1 - t\,\frac{n-1}{n} \right] h_i - \bar{z} = 0;^{13}$$

(c) solve for h_i; (d) find $\bar{z}$; (e) find t^* to maximize $\bar{z}$. Analytic solutions are often unavailable: here solution by computer is necessary, frequently with grids of particular values for variables. This is especially true when the number of people for whom the $h_i \geqslant 0$ restraint binds is endogenous as it is most likely to be when the ability distribution function is continuous.[14]

In this model, and variants upon it, the income-tax rate t has three effects upon the hours of work of individuals who do work. First, there are two conventional effects—the substitution and income effects—that arise from the counter-clockwise rotation of the budget restraint, through point $\bar{L}$ in panel (a) of Figure 3.10. Of these, the substitution effect is uni-directional. Unless the indifference curve is kinked at the relevant point (in which case h_i are unaffected), there must be a substitution into leisure. So h_i can never rise. Then there is an income effect, which will raise h_i if leisure is a normal good, cut it if (improbably) inferior. These two effects will be self-cancelling if tastes are Cobb–Douglas; with homothetic tastes, the substitution effect will overhaul the income effect, if and only if the substitution elasticity exceeds one. But even if, as seems likely, this substitution elasticity is often less than one, this does *not* imply that an increase in t will raise h in our model. For there is also a third effect. An increase in t—if it raises receipts from taxation—will lead to a rise in the social dividend (z in Figure 3.10, panels (b) and (c)). Assuming that leisure is a normal good the north-eastward displacement of the budget restraint that must accompany a rise in t cannot fail to exert a negative effect upon the hours of work. It is this third effect on incentives—the 'social dividend effect'—that is ultimately so corrosive. It must combine with the substitution effect to defeat the income effect if leisure is a normal good. Eventually it leads to the chaos shown in panel (d), if t is pitched at its upper limit of unity. The essential point is that the social dividend effect neutralizes the income effect, leaving the pure substitution effect as the only consequence of a change in t.

We must now see exactly what all this implies for the income function g (equation (3.5)). Suppose we take a two-person society, where 1 is much more able to earn than 2. Persons 1 and 2 may, without loss of generality, serve as representatives for large groups (Figure 3.11 illustrates). Panel (a) of Figure 3.10 showed equilibrium where income tax was zero: this may be taken to correspond with T, or even U, in Figure 3.11. At S, g is horizontal: S is achieved by the tax rate t^* that maximizes the social dividend—assuming that 2 does not work when $t = t^*$. So S^* must maximize 2's income. The origin, O, corresponds with point D in panel (d) of Figure 3.10. As in panel (a) of Figure 3.9 the ray λ represents the line of complete income-equality. Under the standard model assumptions, g cannot cross λ.

[13] Where z is i's share of that (vurtually 100 per cent) part of the social dividend that depends upon taxes paid by everyone else.

[14] The computation becomes much more intricate in this case. See Mirrlees (217) for a detailed discussion on this point, for the more sophisticated problem of deriving an optimum non-linear income tax system. Mirrlees's article is the pioneering paper in this area. See also Atkinson (13), Phelps (253), Seade (286) and Stern (309).

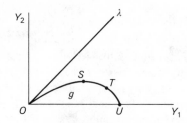

FIG. 3.11. The function g in the standard model.

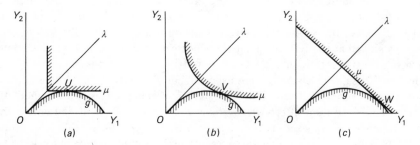

FIG. 3.12. Various distributive optima, achieved by income taxation in the standard model.

Combining g in Figure 3.12 with f from the various panels of 3.9, we may see that there are many possible optima. The Rawlsian, Cobb-Douglas and Liberal Utilitarian are contrasted in panel (a), (b), and (c) of Figure 3.12. The Rawlsian maximizes the absolute income of the worst off: λ is the line of equality, and μ a rectangular indifference curve derived from (3.4).[15] In panel (b) μ has become a rectangular hyperbola, asymptotic to the axes derived from (3.6); point V maximizes the geometric mean of Y_i. W, in panel (c), maximizes their sum, and corresponds with point E in panel (c) of Figure 3.8. W will occur where $t = 0$.

Before finishing this section, we must ask whether there is any way of escaping from the ugly conflict between equality and economic efficiency to which the standard model points. In fact there are four: altruism, coercion, the Protestant Ethic, and tagging. Altruism amends A4 in the standard model, so that the

---

[15] The following three-group example illustrates. For convenience take a society where the population n is so enormous that everyone who works treats t/n as vanishingly small. Everyone has identical Cobb-Douglas tastes; δ is the elasticity of utility to leisure and $(1-\delta)$ that to y. There are three groups: proportion α of n work with efficiency rating e_α; proportion β of n, with e_β; and $1 - \alpha - \beta$ with e_γ. $e_\alpha > e_\beta > e_\gamma$. Otherwise, the assumptions of the standard model apply. If $e_\beta > e_\alpha / [1 + (1/\alpha)\sqrt{\{(\alpha + \beta)/\delta\}}]$, the second group will continue to work, and if $e_\gamma < (\alpha e_\alpha + \beta e_\beta)/[\alpha + \beta + \sqrt{\{(\alpha + \beta)/\delta\}}]$ at all, in the Rawlsian optimum. So the third group, if these conditions are met, will consume only the social dividend. The Rawlsian optimum linear tax rate in this case, t^*, equals $1/[1 + \sqrt{\{\delta(\alpha + \beta)\}}]$, which clearly varies negatively with utility-elasticity of leisure and positively with the proportion of the population in the third group. Note, however, that Rawls's analysis is open to various objections. For example, why should individuals' liberty be given the priority that Rawls accords it? May the worst off not be concerned with relative as well as absolute income? And why should everyone be very risk averse behind the veil of ignorance? For further comments, see Barry (29).

individual's utility function in (3.7) depends not just on his 'income' or consumption y_t, but on that of others, too. With altruism the fact that some of the benefits of one's own work are dissipated in a general increase in other people's social dividend is a source of pleasure. The introduction of altruism is similar to a reduction in the size of the population n. It strengthens the incentive to work.

Coercion may avoid the conflict between egalitarian income tax and economic efficiency completely. Consider panels (*c*) and (*d*) of Figure 3.10. Constraints upon the individual's liberty may disrupt the continuity of the restraint so that his choice set consists of *D* and the striped rectangle *OHGJ* in Figure 3.13. Here the social dividend $\bar{z}$ is made conditional upon working a minimum of *JD* hours. This guarantees that all coerced groups do, in fact, work: there is, in consequence, positive

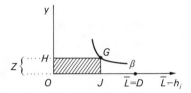

FIG. 3.13. Coercion improves the equality–efficiency trade-off.

work, positive tax receipts (even with a 100 per cent income-tax rate, illustrated by the horizontal line *HG* in Figure 3.13) and therefore a positive social dividend $\bar{z}$ for all. Complete equality can be guaranteed, given coercion, and without necessarily any cost in aggregate output. On the other hand, society may deem that the cost in liberties forgone is excessive. Most likely, society may choose to apply some qualified coercive condition for $\bar{z}$, such as a rule that adult males below the age of retirement shall receive unemployment benefit or negative income tax, only if they are genuinely seeking a full-time job.

The Protestant Ethic questions the sign of the marginal utility of leisure. Suppose that this is negative after some position values for leisure, K. In that case, positive output, tax receipts, and social dividend are compatible with a 100 per cent marginal tax rate in a society where population is large enough for all to treat t/n as negligible. Figure 3.14 shows this. The individual depicted here chooses to work

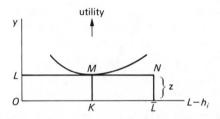

FIG. 3.14. Equality and efficiency reconciled by the Protestant Ethic.

K hours; if he is sufficiently representative, a unit value of t will still lead to an appreciable value of $\bar{z}$. $\bar{z}$ will vary positively with the coefficient of correlation between efficiency and incidence of the Protestant Ethic (see Scitovsky (285)).

The fourth and final[16] escape route from the efficiency–equality dilemma that we consider here is the concept of tagging introduced by Akerlof (2). Suppose e_i is measurable accurately by the Government. Then the warping effects of income taxation are entirely unavoidable: income tax can be replaced by ability tax. Everyone can be 'tagged': a vector of lump-sum transfers, summing to zero, can be calculated by the government; complete equality of income could be achieved. Figure 3.15 illustrates this. Panel (a) shows an individual with low earning capacity for

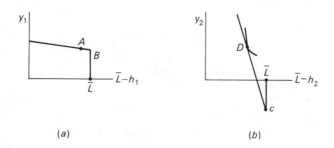

FIG. 3.15. The lump-sum transfer with tagging.

whom the ability tax is a negative lump sum $B\bar{L}$. For the individual in panel (b) the lump sum is positive, $C\bar{L}$. Both consume equal quantities of y. And both face a marginal tax rate of zero: the gradients of AB and CD represent their different marginal wage rates per hour.[17]

Intriguing although these four escapes from the efficiency–equality dilemma are, they are not very compelling. Altruism and the Protestant Ethic do not seem far from ubiquitous. Most societies have fought shy of directing labour, as the coercive solution requires. And (differential) ability tax at least in the form illustrated in Figure 3.15, relies upon the authorities' ability to measure earning capacity. This notion skates over serious practical problems, such as the incentives it would give to understate earning ability and underinvest in human capital. So the efficiency–equality conflict is hard to escape. We conclude with some observations on what factors govern the shape of optimum tax systems. The *marginal* tax rate (if not linear) is found to vary negatively with the income level (although the *average* rate must rise with income if the system is to be at all progressive). This is so because the marginal benefit that society receives from an extra hour's work by the

[16] Another way out of the problem would be to repeal A1 and A2 in the standard model. Assume that labour is a dispensable factor of production, its place taken by robots not subject to depreciation.

[17] Tagging may also be very useful in other ways: it may be easy to identify necessitous groups easily, with only slight danger of fraud. Some social benefits can be, and are, made conditional on factors such as age, certified medical characteristics, and number of dependents.

most efficient income-earner is particularly high, and with it the cost of any work-disincentive operating upon him. The marginal tax rate (or rates) are negatively related, too, to two elasticities of substitution: between leisure and goods,[18] and between different individuals' utilities, or incomes, in social welfare.[19]

Summary of Notation in Chapter 3

e_i efficiency rating of hours worked

h_i hours worked by individual i

n agents in the society

P prices

t tax rate

U utility

y_1 strict private good

y_2 strict public good

z social dividend

σ the elasticity of substitution between different individuals' utilities in social welfare

---

[18] Because a high value makes hours of work, and tax receipts, fall away quickly as t is raised. Mirrlees (217) assumed this elasticity to be unity; recomputation of Mirrlees' optimum tax schedule for an elasticity of 0.5 raises the marginal rate considerably. See Stern (309).

[19] The influence here runs from the shape of f (equation (3.4)). See Figure 3.9. For Mirrlees (217) this elasticity was infinite. Atkinson (13) using a variant of (32) derives higher tax rates with lower values of this elasticity.

Chapter 4

The Overseas Sector

I: Introduction

In the previous three chapters, we have analysed the economic behaviour of households (the personal sector), producers (the corporate sector) and governments. It is now time to open the economy to international influences. The equation $Y = C + I + G + X - M$ reminds us of the importance of the current account surplus on the balance of payments, $X - M$, in the determination of Y. Although the ratio of $X - M$ to Y is usually rather modest (mostly within the range of plus three per cent to minus three per cent, among member countries of the E.E.C.), the ratio of exports to national income is often over one-third.

In section II, we consider the trade flows between countries. In II: 1, trade is assumed to be balanced; at this stage, the central question to be answered is what explains the composition of exports and imports. In II: 2, unbalanced trade is introduced. The various potential explanations for this are scrutinized. In section III, attention transfers to the capital account of the balance of payments: in III: 1, a simple comparative static model of international capital movements is established. Section III: 2 relaxes the assumptions of the simple model. Section III: 3 examines portfolio movements and the interaction of spot and forward exchange rates with international interest differentials.

II: Trade in Goods

II: 1 *Equilibrium: Balanced Trade*

Arbitrage is the riskless exploitation of opportunities for profit provided by *price discrepancies*. International trade in goods is most easily explained by arbitrage in commodities. Ignore all barriers to trade (tariffs, international transport costs, monetary complications), and assume that a trader can buy and sell at identical prices. In this case, there will be opportunities for profitable trade when these equalities do *not* hold:

$$P_{iA} = E_{AB}P_{iB} \tag{4.1}$$

and

$$\frac{P_{iA}}{P_{jA}} = \frac{P_{iB}}{P_{jB}}, \tag{4.2}$$

where i and j index goods; A and B are countries; E_{AB} is the price of one unit of A's currency in terms of B's currency; and P_{ik} means the price of good i in country k measured in units of country k's currency.

To see this, suppose $P_{iA} > E_{AB} \cdot P_{iB}$. Profit can be made from sending good i from country B to country A, selling it there for the high local price of P_{iA}, and selling the resulting sum in A's currency for what it will fetch in B's to pay for the initial purchase of good i there. If $P_{iA}/P_{jA} > P_{iB}/P_{jB}$, it will be worthwhile to export good j from A to B and import good i in return. In the first case, commodity-money arbitrage is profitable; in the second, commodity-commodity arbitrage.

Our initial assumption that trade barriers were negligible is disagreeably strong for some commodities such as bricks or haircuts (because of high transport costs), or consumer durables subject to high tariff duties; but for others, such as grain, oil, and (especially) diamonds, it comes much closer to the truth. Many models impose a logical distinction between goods for which trade barriers are prohibitive ('non-traded' goods) and those for which they are negligible ('traded' goods).[1] We shall concentrate attention in this section upon the traded goods.

Arbitrage will ensure that (4.1) and (4.2) are valid for these goods if traders are sufficiently numerous and informed and trading costs really are negligible. The direction of commodity trade in a competitive world where these conditions are met will be governed by one thing: the direction of profit if the trade did not take place. So country A will export (import) those goods which, in the absence of trade, would have been *relatively* cheap (dear): relatively cheap—relative to its trading partner. Trade is explained by 'pre-trade'[2] price–ratio differences.

The simplest explanation of international differences in pre-trade price ratios is technology differences. This is illustrated by the assumptions of the Non-Substitution Theorem:[3]

if (i) each good i is produced under conditions of constant returns to scale (CRS);
   (ii) there is no joint production (NJP);
and (iii) each scarce primary factor is *employed equiproportionately* in every sector and is perfectly mobile between sectors (EE);

then the frontier of production possibilities is a hyperplane, and (in competitive equilibrium) relative prices depend exclusively upon technology.

Figure 4.1 illustrates this case, in two dimensions representing outputs of goods y_1 and y_2. The production set for country A has a linear outer boundary CD and in panel (a), while B's is GH (also linear) in panel (b). Let E describe A's autarkic competitive equilibrium one Tuesday evening,[4] and consider a shift in tastes from

---

[1] The classic models were devised by Salter (266) and Pearce (248). See also Oppenheimer (244) and for evidence on failures of (4.1), see Frenkel (351).

[2] 'Pre-trade' means autarkic', or 'in the absence of trade'.

[3] See Georgescu-Roegen (130) and Samuelson (269), (272). Its dynamic extension was first analysed by Mirrlees (216). See also Bliss (42), chapter 11. The theorem's results are not invalidated by the introduction of intermediate goods: indeed it was constructed explicitly to analyse these.

[4] If E is the point of tangency between CD and a social indifference curve, the question arises of what conditions permit a unique set of social indifference curves to be drawn. Two of the following three conditions are sufficient, if each individual's preferences are uniquely given, and Pareto-efficiency in exchange is met: (a) identical tastes (across the population); (b) homothetic tastes; (c) fixed income distribution.

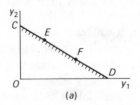
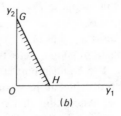

FIG. 4.1. Autarkic relative prices in two countries, under Non-Substitution Theorem assumptions. (a) Country *A*'s production set; (b) Country *B*'s production set.

y_2 to y_1, on Tuesday night. Next morning, autarkic equilibrium will have moved south-eastward along *CD* to *F*, where more of y_1 is consumed and produced than before, and less of y_2. But the marginal rate of transformation, and relative price, between the two commodities is unchanged. The partial equilibrium analog of Figure 4.1 is the horizontal supply curve, showing the independence of price from demand.

The algebra underlying Figure 4.1 is as follows;

$$y_j = b_j N_j \qquad (4.3)$$

where b_j, a parameter, is the productivity of labour (direct and indirect) and N_j is employment in sector *j*. Since the sum of all industries' labour allocations may not exceed the labour force,[5] $\bar{N}$, we have

$$\bar{N} \geqslant \sum \frac{y_j}{b_j}, \qquad (4.4)$$

which is the equation of the set of feasible 'final' or 'net' output combination in as many commodity dimensions as one wishes. With $j = 1, 2$ (4.4) will appear like *CD* or *GH* in Figure 4.1. Equation (4.3) displays CRS since labour productivity is a parameter independent of scale; since y_j is independent of N_i, the NJP condition is fulfilled; and finally, there is only one factor of production, so that the EE condition is met. If (44) holds as equality, labour is fully employed, and the price ratio P_2/P_1 equals $-dy_1/dy_2$.[6] This is b_1/b_2. Price ratios are simply the reciprocals of labour-productivity ratios. Technological differences between countries are necessary and sufficient for trade. In Figure 4.1, country *A* has a lower autarkic relative price (and hence a relative technological lead) for commodity 1. Free trade without trade barriers will (as (4.2) asserts) equalize commodity price ratios, so that the social consumption set is expanded beyond its old autarkic levels (ΔOCD for *A*, ΔOGH for *B*). Figure 4.2 illustrates this. Forced with an equilibrium world relative price (the gradient of *JD* or *GK* equals $-P_1/P_2$), producers will maximize the value of aggregate income by specializing, at *D* in *A* and *G* in *B*. If trade is balanced, and c represents the vector for consumption, $\mathbf{P}(\mathbf{y} - \mathbf{c}) = 0$ for all countries.

---

[5] This is assumed to be supplied inelastically, and therefore to be given parametrically. This assumption is retained throughout this chapter for all productive factors.

[6] Assuming competitive equilibrium.

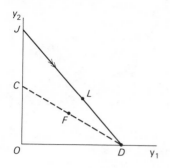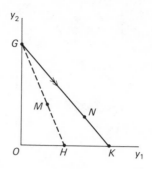

FIG. 4.2. Free trade enlarging the social consumption set. (*a*) Country *A*'s consumption set *ODJ*; (*b*) Country *B*'s consumption set *OGK*.

In Figure 4.2, consumption moves from *F* to *L* in *A*, and *M* to *N* in *B*. In *A*, more of both goods is consumed; in *B*, less of 2 and much more of 1. Assuming that the distribution of income is unchanged—which it must be, given assumption (iii) of the Non-Substitution Theorem and perfect competition—panel (*a*) points to inelastic demand for 2, and (*b*) to elastic demand. Both are possible. Everyone in *A* and *B* gains from the move from autarky to free trade, unless he consumes non-positive amounts of the good that has (locally) fallen in relative price.

Two other possible explanations for the existence and direction of trade appear when the third assumption (EE) of the Non-Substitution Theorem is relaxed. Suppose, now, that there are two priced primary factors, labour (*N*) and land (*F*), and that these are used in different proportions in the two industries; but the other Non-Substitution Theorem assumptions are retained, and with them the assumption of perfect competition.

The production possibility frontier (in this two-dimensional case) must now be concave. Panels (*a*) and (*b*) of Figure 4.3 illustrate this for the case where there are variable coefficients in production—the isoquants are not L-shaped in at least one of the sectors.[7] Contrast Figure 4.3(*a*) with Figure 4.1(*a*): imagine *E* is, again, an autarkic equilibrium in *A* before demand for good 1 increases. The economy-wide demand for the factor employed intensively in the expanding industry (good 1) rises; and that for the other factor will fall. So the price of the first factor rises relative to that of the second. This must increase the *average costs of production* of the expanding commodity, relative to those of the other. Since, under perfect competition, price equals average cost, the ratio P_1/P_2 must rise. This implies a steeper relative price target to the production possibility frontier than at *E*. Output of good 1 must rise, and that of good 2, fall; so, since the new autarkic equilibrium position must lie south-east of *E* (e.g. at *F*), the frontier of production possibilities is concave between *E* and *F*, and, by generalization and symmetry throughout the frontier *CD*.

The two possible explanations for the direction of trade are international *demand*

[7] Panel (*c*) illustrates the fixed coefficient case. The factor employed intensively in sector 1 is free if production occurs to the left of *K*, the other factor is free if to the right.

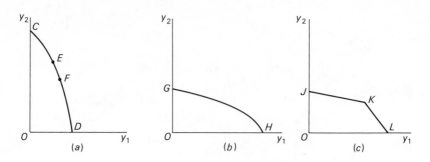

FIG. 4.3. Repealing the equiproportionate employment assumption: the Heckscher–Ohlin model. (*a*) Country *A*, well endowed with *N*; variable coefficients in production; (*b*) Country *B*, well endowed with *F*; variable coefficients in production; (*c*) Fixed coefficients in production factors employed equiproportionately.

differences, and international *factor endowment* differences. It is clear from Panel (*a*) of Figure 4.3 that two economies alike in all respects save tastes will have different autarkic relative prices. The price of good 1 will be higher, relatively, where the demand for it is relatively stronger. Secondly, factor endowment differences will influence the shape of the production possibility frontier. This must be elongated somewhat in the dimension of a commodity produced intensively by a locally plentiful factor of production. The panels of Figure 4.3 depict as intensive good 1 in *F*, and good 2 in *N*: *B* is said to be well-endowed with *F*, and the relative *F*-intensity of 1 can account for *B*'s much flatter production possibility frontier. (There is, of course, an alternative explanation: that *B*'s producers have a relative technological lead in the production of 1 (as they had in good 2 in Figure 4.2).) Industries may be ranked by factor-intensity, when there are just two factors, and industries have the same degree of flexibility[8] in production between these factors.

The Non-Substitution Theorem model of trade is usually attributed to Ricardo, in recognition of his famous illustration of the Principle of Comparative Advantage with England, Portugal, cloth, and wine.[9] The variant reached by introducing *non-equiproportionate* employment of two-priced primary factors is labelled Heckscher–Ohlin (H–O).[10] In its strict form, the H–0 model imposes identical technology for each good world-wide, an invariant ranking of industries by factor intensity,[11] a unique autarkic equilibrium,[12] and identical demand between

---

[8] i.e., the same elasticity of factor-substitution in production.

[9] Ricardo's model of distribution (263), however, places heavy stress on the differences in factor proportions between agriculture and industry.

[10] After Heckscher (156) and Ohlin (243). For generalizations, see Dixit and Woodland (346).

[11] This precludes a reversal of factor-intensities, which must occur if two industries have different but constant elasticities of substitution. See Minhas (215).

[12] If, for instance, points *E* and *F* were both possible autarkic equilibria for *A* in Figure 4.3(*a*), there could be no guarantee which good would be exported if, 'on the stroke of midnight', *A* were allowed to trade. The world price ratio might be steeper than the target to *CD* at *E*, but flatter than that at *F*. *E* and *F* could both be possible autarkic equilibria if, for example, those who owned factor *N* (used intensively in the production of 2) had a stronger demand for good 2 than *F*-owners. This sort of assumption can introduce income-transfer effects from

countries[13]—these assumptions are jointly sufficient to prove (in a two-factor world) that each country exports those commodities that are produced relatively intensively by its relatively plentiful factor.

The H-O theory points to an inter-dependence between trade and the distribution of income. In Figure 4.3, trade between A and B will tend to raise the price of factor N in A, and that of F in B: we saw that the price of N rose as production moved from E to F in panel (*a*). But the price of the other factor will fall, denominated in terms of either good. A movement from autarky to free trade will raise the incomes of those who own only the factor used intensively in the export industry; it will lower all incomes derived exclusively from ownership of the other factor; and although those who own some of both factors are likelier than not to gain, their chance of loss is higher if their tastes are biased towards the exportable good (the relative price of which must rise). Compared with autarky, free trade will also lower all incomes derived exclusively from ownership of a factor of production employed *specifically*[14] in a contracting (importable) sector. So if our assumption of perfect competition is amended to allow (for instance) fixed labour allocations to sectors 1 and 2, a decline in sector 2's output in 1's favour must cut the competitive wage rate in 2 (and increase it in 1).[15] If all factors of production employed in an industry are specific to that industry, their owners will have a perfect community of interest in pressing for an export subsidy (if the industry produces an exportable) or a tariff against imports (if an importable). Both can improve the dividends to shareholders *and* the wages (or employment prospects) of the work-force. The burden of these gains, coupled with the economic inefficiencies in production and consumption to which they give rise, will be borne less conspicuously by other citizens in the economy.

So far, we have seen why certain goods will be exported, and why others are imported—and what, in competitive equilibrium, will help to determine the volumes of this trade. A small country can trade as it will at parametrically given prices but a large country cannot. The world equilibrium price vector for traded goods is found where two vectors sum to zero: that for home excess demands, and the rest of the world's excess demands.[16]

---

price changes that undermine the uniqueness, and stability, of general equilibrium. See Arrow and Hahn (11) for the general point, and Kemp (18) for its application to this context.

[13] In order to remove the possible influence of international demand differences on autarkic price ratios. See above.

[14] The H-O theory relies upon perfect mobility of factors within a country, and none between. So factor-specificity calls for an explicit relaxation of this assumption.

[15] This result was well known to Marshall (207), who assumed short-term specificity of capital and enterprise. Its application in the context of international trade has recently been developed by Neary (230). See also Basevi (30).

[16] If the home country is large enough to influence world prices, there is a monopoly-power-in-trade argument for its government to tax exports and imports (if its traders are insufficiently few or united to do this optimally themselves).

II: 2 *The Causes of Unbalanced Trade*

The values of a country's export receipts and import payments frequently differ. It is not uncommon for one of these to be as much as 10 per cent more than the other, when measured annually. On a monthly basis, discrepancies tend to be proportionately greater still. How are these imbalances to be explained? Why should they be of concern to policy makers? The second question is easier to answer than the first. A deficit on the current account of the balance of payments implies that the home country's citizens are accumulating net liabilities to the rest of the world: assets are being sold, or debts incurred. If repeated, or in large amounts, these mounting obligations may be felt to impose an intolerable cost in future consumption opportunities forgone. Large or persistent surpluses on the current account may imply that society is deferring too much of its consumption of jam until tomorrow. This leaves the first question: what can explain imbalances between export receipts and import payments?

Walras's Law provides a useful key to unlock the various possibilities. Walras's Law is defined thus:

$$\sum_{j=1}^{h} P_j \sum_{i=1}^{m} z_{ij} = 0, \tag{4.5}$$

where i indexes agents (m in all), j indexes goods (including goods and factors for all dates, and money), and z_{ij} is agent i's excess demand for j. Equation (4.5) is usually defined[17] to hold for all price vectors, in and out of equilibrium. It is sufficient for Walras's Law to hold that all agents obey linear and parallel budget restraints. One implication of (4.5) is that if there is one good (or set of goods) k for which

$$\sum_{i} z_{ik} > 0,$$

there must be at least one other good (or set of goods) l such that

$$\sum_{i} z_{il} < 0.$$

Disequilibrium cannot occur in just one market: it must infect two markets at least, if any.

An excess of import payments over export receipts at the present date must, if Walras's Law is to hold, co-exist with excess supply in some other market or group of markets. Of many possible locations for this excess supply, we shall consider four: non-traded goods, labour, money, and claims upon goods for future delivery. Figure 4.4 illustrates the problems of excess supply in the market for non-traded goods (here, treated as a Hicksian composite commodity, NT (see Hicks (162)). Traded goods are also aggregated into T.

---

[17] See Patinkin (247). In this interpretation, what distinguishes Walras's Law from Say's Law is that Walras's Law *includes money* in n and Say's Law excludes it.

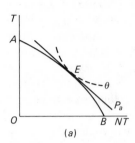
(a)

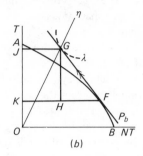
(b)

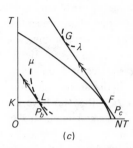
(c)

FIG. 4.4. Equilibrium and disequilibrium in traded and non-traded goods. (a) Equilibrium;
(b) Disequilibrium: excess supply of NT goods and current account deficit; (c) Removing the
current account deficit by deflation.

Panel (a) of Figure 4.4 shows competitive equilibrium, where a social indifference curve θ is tangent to the production possibility frontier AB at E. Since AB
is drawn concave here, we should suppose that one at least of the Non-substitution
Theorem assumptions fails. The double tangent has gradient (minus) P_a. Here,
(minus) P_a is the ratio of the price of non-traded goods, P_{NT}, to that of $T(P_T)$.
P_T is determined by the commodity-money arbitrage equation, (4.1); P_{NT}, by a
market clearing condition

$$\sum_i z_{iNT} = 0.$$

The middle panel depicts what can happen if P_{NT} is stuck at an excessive level,
above equilibrium. The price tangent is steeper. Producers will (initially at least)[18]
set out to produce at F, which maximizes the value of aggregate output at these
prices. If we may assume that output actually occurs at F, however briefly, national
income should be parcelled out to households in such a way that consumption
occurs at G on social indifference curve λ.[19] The vector FG represents disequilibrium. Its vertical component GH or (JK) is the current account balance of
payments deficit. The horizontal component is the excess supply of non-traded
goods.

Disequilibrium calls out for a cure. Under ideal, competitive assumptions, it
would remove itself automatically. Walras's adjustment hypothesis for disequilibrium has it that price turns in the direction of excess demand. In the case of NT,

[18] Since, as we see later, F implies excess supply of NT, producers of NT are likely to react
to growing inventories by cutting back output.
[19] This is assuming that the market value of the sum of all other excess demands (e.g.
labour, money, and future good claims) is zero. If, for instance, there was an excess demand for
money—and the other markets cleared—households' expenditure could be somewhere south
and/or west of G. With homothetic tastes, it would lie between O and G on ray η. Any expenditure by the government needs to be included, and allowance made for any cut in household
expenditure that taxation implies. For the conditions under which social indifference maps are
uniquely defined, see chapter 2, section VII: 3, immediately after Figure 2.3.

this implies that P_{NT} must fall. The price tangent will flatten towards P_a, and keep doing so until the disequilibrium had vanished. In the presence of Keynesian rigidities that prevent the nominal price of NT from coming down—perhaps, because the nominal wage rate is inflexible downwards, too—the disequilibrium will not be automatically self rectifying. If P_{NT} won't fall, E is given and the overseas prices of T are given in foreign currency, the ratio P_{NT}/P_T is locked at P_b.

If the authorities are unwilling to accept the large current account deficit (equal to JK), they do have the means to remove it. One way of doing so is to generate an excess demand for money. This can be done by cutting the domestic nominal money supply, for example, by large sales of bonds on the open market, or a large rise in the banks' compulsory reserve-deposit ratio. The excess demand for money that results will tend to cut the demand for goods, including (assuming that they are not inferior) T.[20] Another method of reducing demand for T is fiscal deflation. The government may reduce its own spending (especially useful, if the cuts can be concentrated upon the T it buys); and it may increase tax rates. The effects of monetary or fiscal deflation are portrayed in panel (*c*) of Figure 4.4. If demand is cut so that expenditure contracts to L, the balance of payments deficit on current account can be removed. The disagreeable aspect of this 'solution' to the problem is the *increase* (as there must be if NT are not inferior) in the excess supply of non-traded goods. In panel (*c*), government action has merely removed the external symptom of the disequilibrium. This cosmetic change conceals a worsening of the implication that the disequilibrium has for the home economy's non-traded industries. At L, the price ratio of NT to T is still as it was in panel (*b*) (P_b).

By contrast, a superior policy decision in the circumstances shown in panel (*b*) of Figure 4.4 is go to the heart of the distortion and alter relative prices. If the producers of NT (or their employees) prevent P_{NT} from falling, its price to consumers can be cut by the imposition of a consumption subsidy. The consumers' price of T, on the other hand, can be raised by a consumption tax. As far as producers are concerned, the output of T can be stimulated, and that of NT restrained, by an appropriate assignment of production subsidy and tax. The right consideration of all four changes can (generally) restore equilibrium at E, as in panel (*a*). Devaluation is equivalent to uniform taxes on production (positive on NT, negative for T) and on consumption (the opposite). Import tariffs confine the production subsidy and consumption tax to importable elements in T, and export subsidies to the exportables. Devaluation amounts to generalized import tariff and export subsidy, at the same rate.[21]

The second possible explanation for a current account deficit given Walras's Law, is an excess supply of labour. This is an example of excess demand for goods with excess supply of labour—classical unemployment.[22] The simplest way of

[20] The current account deficit will in any case tend to reduce the money supply, unless large enough imports of capital or official sterilization stop this.

[21] A devaluation of k per cent is equivalent to an increase in the price of foreign currency measured in unit of home currency of $k(1-k)^{-1}$ per cent and this latter fraction is the equivalent generalized import tariff/export subsidy. Depreciation, with a floating exchange rate, would also tend to remove the disequilibrium.

[22] See pp. 219–20; and also Malinvaud (204), Dixit (88) and Dixit and Norman (89), and Muellbauer and Portes (226), Heffernan (157) and Neary (231).

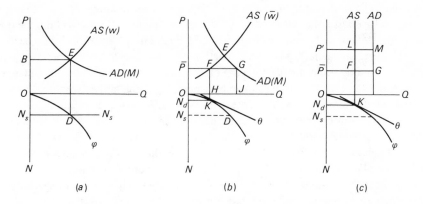

FIG. 4.5. Equilibrium and Disequilibrium in goods and labour markets. (*a*) Equilibrium in goods and labour markets; (*b*) Disequilibrium that an exchange rate change can correct; (*c*) Disequilibrium: an exchange rate change triggers hyper-inflation.

illustrating this is to employ the commodity–money arbitrage equation (4.1), to fix the price level in a one-good economy, otherwise characterized by a parametric money-wage rate and nominal money supply. Figure 4.5 illustrates.

The upper quadrant in each panel depicts the aggregated goods market, where aggregate supply is shown sloping upward (this presumes a fixed money wage rate,[23] and competitive equilibrium among producers,[24] with diminishing returns to labour), and the aggregate demand curve downward. The commodity markets as a whole are in equilibrium at E in panel (*a*), when the price index is at B. This conjuncture also brings equilibrium to the labour market, in the lower quadrant, where the production function ϕ intersects the (assumed exogenous) labour supply line at D. Given perfect competition, the ratio of w to P at B equals $\partial\phi(N)/\partial N$.

Panel (*b*) illustrates what happens when the price level dictated by (1) is lower than B, e.g. at $\bar{P}$. Production occurs at F, demand at G. The horizontal gap FG (or HJ on the Q axis) measure the excess demand for commodities which will be plugged, typically, by net imports.[25] The level of employment will be given by point K, on the production function ϕ; if producers are to be in equilibrium; it is here that the marginal product of labour, θ, equals the ratio of the exogenous money wage rate, w, to the price level $\bar{P}$. With the real wage rate so high, firms can only hire a small level of labour at maximum profit. The demand for labour, N_d, is measured vertically downwards from the origin; this falls some considerable way short of the supply of labour, N_s. With the price level set exogenously by (1) above E, however, there would be excess supply of goods (hence a trade surplus on the balance of payments) and an excess demand for labour.

[23] Or, at least, some money illusion, so that the money wage is less than unit elastic to the price level.

[24] So that producers are not constrained in the labour or commodity markets.

[25] The reduction in employment, indicated by point K, will sooner or later exert downward pressure on demand which may or may not counterweigh the expansionary influences (from the lower price level upon spending via real balances and interest rates). But, even allowing for this, there must still be an excess demand for goods when $P = \bar{P}$.

The problems depicted in panel (*b*) of Figure 4.5 call for an increase in the price level as a first-best policy. Reduction of the money supply can help to eliminate the payments deficit, as it could in Figure 4.4. In Figure 4.5, it does this by squeezing the *AD* curve to the left. The same direction of effect would occur if government spending were lowered, or tax rates raised. But none of these measures would contribute at all to the alleviation of unemployment. If anything, they would aggravate it (this would certainly be so if there were a non-traded goods sector lurking behind the bold aggregation over commodities depicted in Figure 4.5). Benefit would be felt for employment and the balance of payments as a result of a rightward movement of aggregate supply, whether due to a fall in the money wage rate, or to rises in the supplies of the fixed factors, capital, or to improvement in the quality of employment.[26] But none of these changes is plausible in the short run, especially if Keynesian asymmetries make the nominal wage rate inflexible downwards.

How, then, may a rise in the price level be achieved? Devaluation is an attractive means of doing so. By (4.1), it must raise the price of exportables *and* importables in domestic currency. Ignoring time-lags for the present, and assuming that the home country is small enough to be a price-taker for its tradable goods in overseas markets, the price rises in exportables and importables must be equiproportionate in home currency. (If the country is large, its terms of trade will improve—with the price of exportables rising relative to that of importables—if the product of the home and overseas import demand elasticities exceeds that of the export supply elasticities, and worsen if less.[27] If, as is assumed, the money wage rate is given, these price rises will lower the real wage rate, and raise the demand for labour, employment (since there is unemployment), and output. On the demand side, the price rise will lower real balances if the nominal money stock is given, and hence squeeze expenditure; furthermore, there is the Keynesian effect of a higher demand for money to finance transactions at a higher price level upon the rate of interest—this should serve to lower private sector expenditures as well.

Semi-devaluation may also help to lower unemployment and remove the payments deficit. An import tariff will work, by raising the price of importables. It acts as a production-subsidy cum consumption-tax. Since the good is an importable, this combination raises revenue for the State. It will also tilt income distribution in favour of owners of factors specific to the protected industries, or hired intensively in them. Under ideal conditions, a tariff on imports will be inefficient, since it will raise the social marginal cost of producing importables at home (and the

---

[26] Labour-augmenting technical progress could lower the demand for labour: it will do so (when the real wage rate is fixed) when the substitution elasticity is less than the profit share. See Heffernan (157) and Sinclair (301).

[27] Let 1 denote home country exportables, and 2 importables; let subscript *f* denote the rest of the world, and *E* be the price of foreign currency in units of home currency. *S* represents supply, *D* demand, and * denotes elasticity. Home exports are foreign imports, so that $S_1(P_1) = D_{1f}(P_1/E)$; similarly, $S_{2f}(P_2/E) = D_2(P_2)$. Totally differentiating these and rearranging, we find

$$\frac{\hat{P}_1 - \hat{P}_2}{\hat{E}} = \frac{\text{proportionate gain to terms of trade}}{\text{proportionate devaluation of home currency}} = \frac{D_1^* D_2^* - S_1^* S_2^*}{(S_1^* - D_1^*)(S_2^* - D_2^*)}.$$

With $D_i^* < 0 < S_i^*$ the stated condition for devaluation to improve the terms of trade is proved.

price to domestic consumers) above the marginal cost of imports.[28] But this ceases to be true in the situation in Figure 4.5(*b*). This is because the unemployment of labour implies that the 'shadow' wage rate may be very low, and in any case a good deal below the 'private' marginal cost of labour forced by the employer. What is, however, likely to be unsatisfactory with a tariff levied upon importables in these circumstances is that it does *not go far enough*. Why only subsidize employment and production in import-competing industries? Why not go further, to stimulate them in export industries as well, either by outright devaluation, or an economy-wide subsidy for the employment of underutilized variable factors of production? The import tariff taken by itself may raise the output of importables, but cut that of exportables: resources may be transferred there from exportables as well as from unemployment. Demand, too, may be switched away from importables (the relative price of which must rise with a tariff) to exportables, particularly if they are substitutes in consumption. So a tariff on imports could cut exports as well as imports; this would weaken its impact on employment and the balance of payments. The same arguments apply *mutatis mutandis* to an export subsidy in isolation, which (by raising the domestic price of exportable *only*) is quite likely to raise imports.

The real worry with devaluation is shown in panel (*c*) of Figure 4.5.[29] If the aggregate supply curve is vertical, devaluation cannot affect output or employment. It will be vertical if the real rewards to all variable factors are exogenous (in our case, if the real wage rate is fixed). There could be two reasons for an exogenous real wage: either the labour market is kept in continuous equilibrium, as at *D* in panel (*a*), by whatever adjustment in the money wage rate (*w*) would be needed to achieve this; or the real wage rate may be pegged, e.g. by legislation in real minimum wage rates, or a trade-union labour monopoly. So if devaluation is accompanied by a compensating rise in nominal wage rates so as to keep real wage rates unchanged, output and employment cannot respond. They remain as at *K*. If, at the same time, the money supply is also raised in nominal terms to avoid any cut in real expenditure—this is quite possible, if the nominal money supply is sufficiently endogenous, or sufficiently impotent in affecting real spending; or, simply, if the authorities aim to peg the *real* (not nominal) quantity of money—devaluation has no demand-reducing effect, either. The fall in the exchange rate becomes neutral in real terms—it is just a milestone in the process of rapid inflation. $LM = FG$; all that has happened is a rise (from $\bar{P}$ to P') in the price levels.

The third potential source of disequilibrium unveiled by Walras's Law is an imbalance in the market for money. Consider general equilibrium at home, suddenly disturbed by an unexpected rise in the supply of money. The chain of events to which this gives rise is complex. Its first effects will probably be the appearance of excess demand in markets for other assets and for commodities. The first of these is a Keynesian portfolio effect, the latter a pure real balance effect. At the same time,

[28] Assuming the country is small enough to be a price-taker in world market for its importables.

[29] But not the only worry. Devaluation reduces the value of the country's money stock in terms of traded goods. A payments surplus may result, if there is now an excess demand for money. But the surplus will be gradually whittled away by the growth of foreign exchange reserves, and holdings of domestic money, unless sterilization is completely effective.

as soon as the rise in the money stock is noticed, it will give agents cause to think. Should they recalculate their expectations for future money stocks? Wage rates? Prices? Exchange rates? To the extent that they do, there will be a sharp incentive to pre-empt.

In some cases, the excess demand will be met with price rises. The market, if there be one, for assets not marketed internationally will perhaps react most.[30] Wage rates and non-traded goods prices should rise as quickly as contracts and lags in perceptions permit. But for goods and assets traded internationally, overseas supply can meet the domestic excess demand: if the home country is small, in virtually limitless amounts at unchanged prices, as long as the exchange rate does not change. Capital will be exported, and tradables imported; and any new expectatiosn of exchange rate depreciation will be vehement stimuli. Official gold and convertible currency reserves should start to drop, or, at the very least, start rising at a greatly reduced rate.

If a fall in reserves does occur, the money supply may start to contract. Only two things could stop it falling: the willingness of overseas payees who have sold the extra goods and assets to accept a home currency bank deposit in the home country; and deliberate action by the central bank (such as open market bill or bond purchases, or manipulating reserve ratios for banks) to keep the supply of money up. The second is usually attempted, and often (at least partly) successful. The first is highly improbable. So there may well be some downward pressure on the money supply, but probably smaller in magnitude and even later in timing than the fall in reserves. In the absence of attempts by the central bank to sterilize it, the rise in the money supply will tend to be self-eliminating. The excess money simply will be exported. If, as we have assumed up to now, the home country is only small, the international repercussions are trivial. But if the excess supply of money occurs in a large country, the mechanism we have sketched will tend to raise money stocks and prices in all countries—or at least in those with exchange rates fixed in terms of this large country's currency.

This is the essence of the 'monetary approach to the balance of payments'. Pioneered by David Hume (168), it is basically an open-economy version of the Quantity Theory of Money. Its major claims are that payments imbalances have monetary origins and are (given time) self-rectifying.[31] The theory also maintains that the only reason for a continuing payments imbalance (on current and capital accounts combined) between two parts of the world would be that one was growing faster than the other. The faster growing area would, all else equal, exhibit the faster rise in the demand for money. Given a positive association between the domestic demand for money and the demand for international reserves, the faster-growing area would keep bidding for a rising share of the world's reserves. To make this bidding effective, an overall payments surplus would be needed.

Proponents of the monetary approach would argue that the situation depicted

---

[30] See Branson (44) for an analysis of this idea.

[31] See Frenkel and Johnson (116) for a clear exposition of different facets of the approach, and Hahn (142) for a critical review. Dornbusch (91) and (92), Kuska (186) and Mussa (227) also have important papers on certain aspects of the subject.

in panel (*b*) of Figures 4.4 and 4.5, where a current account deficit was shown coinciding with excess supply of non-traded goods or labour, was impossible given sufficient price flexibility. As we saw, if P_N (or w in the case of Figure 4.5) was flexible downwards the disequilibrium would disappear. So rival theories to the monetary approach must stand or fall on the rigidity of prices. This is a familiar result: the claims of the Quantity Theory of Money depend upon price flexibility in both its domestic open-economy applications. In the context of Figures 4.4 and 4.5, supporters of the monetary approach could also claim that an earlier excess supply of money could have underlain the rises in P_N or w; and, moreover, that the payments deficits (*JK* in Figure 4.4, *HJ* in 4.5) would tend to disappear—unless, that is, the authorities deliberately recreated the money supply that falling reserves would tend to lower, or a large enough inflow of capital on the capital account kept reserves from falling. Both of these claims are valid, provided that the conditions on which they depend do in fact hold.

But there is a fourth possible explanation for the current deficit: an excess supply of claims on future goods. This would occur if domestic citizens as a whole were borrowing, on the capital account of the balance of payments, to finance an excess of current expenditures over current income. This is quite possible, and is indeed perfectly consistent with equilibrium in the markets for money, labour, and non-traded goods. We analyse this case in detail in the section on the capital account below. Before attention is switched to this, however, two points remain to be considered.

We have employed Walras's Law to pry open several potential explanations for current account imbalances in a country's external payments. Is this a legitimate application of the Law? There is a major difficulty with the use of Walras's Law in disequilibrium. At least one agent must be rationed in any market where it occurs. If there is excess demand, one buyer (or more) must be unable to buy all he can; if in excess supply, at least one seller must be constrained. The concept of price is not unique in disequilibrium. So not everyone's budget restraint can be linear.[32]

Yet this argument *does not* impugn the use of the Law to identify possible disequilibrium. All it does is to warn us that positions of disequilibria (such as panel (*b*) in Figures 4.4 and 4.5) are more complex than they seem at first glance. This was, in fact, hinted at in our discussion: we saw why point *F* in Figure 4.4 could not for long represent an actual production vector, nor (correspondingly) *G* a vector for consumption. Production will drift leftwards along *HF*, consumption downwards down the Engel curve *OG*. If the prices for non-traded goods and labour and foreign currency remain really locked, consumption may fall as far as *L* in panel (*c*). In panel (*b*) of Figure 4.5, we noted that aggregate demand would tend to drop below *G* (or *J*) at a price of $\bar{P}$, as a result of the reduction in employment to *K*. Some workers—perhaps even all, if the 'unemployment' is shared out evenly

---

[32] The linearity of budget restraints is a member of the set of conditions jointly sufficient for Walras's Law to hold. For a powerful attack on the use of Walras's Law in disequilibrium, see Clower (60); and for another on its use in monetary models of the balance of payments, Tsiang (325).

as a cut in hours of work—will recalculate their commodity demands in the light of the rationing constraint they face in the labour market. This, and related issues posed by the new 'temporary equilibrium' approach to macroeconomic disequilibrium, are discussed by Dixit (88) and Dixit and Norman (89).

Our second point is related to this. We have just seen that whatever causes external disequilibrium has complex internal ramifications. As far as policy is concerned, therefore, analysis of the effects of different ways of removing an external imbalance must take these internal ramifications, and the underlying cause of the imbalance fully into account. External balance policy may never be discussed *in vacuo*. Monetary (and perhaps fiscal) measures are appropriate instruments for removing a payments deficit attributable to excessive domestic aggregate demand, itself the product of an excess supply of money. When there is evidence of unemployment of labour, or slack in the non-traded goods industry, that accompanies the external deficit, an exchange rate change is more likely to be required. Or, if not an outright devaluation, at least an instrument that reproduces some of its effects, such as export or employment subsidy. Yet it must be emphasized that the need for policy intervention by the authorities is itself debatable: if the source(s) of excess supply can be relied upon to remove themselves quickly, as a result of price flexibility and/or reserve losses, action by the government can be otiose and even damaging. We shall return to the debate about the merits and demerits of active government intervention in chapter 7.

III: Capital Movements

III: 1 *A Simple Comparative Static Model*

Capital can be exported from one country to another in two senses. A's citizens may sell existing assets to B's. Or A's citizens may add to the stock of capital in B, by for example building new factories there. In both cases, A exports capital to B. The first is a *portfolio* capital export, and has no implications for the international location of capital stocks. The latter is a *direct* capital export. Portfolio capital movements are merely a change in ownership of title-deeds to existing wealth.

We examine the effects of a direct capital export from A to B first. Assume (for a 'Basic Capital Movement' Model):[33]

(A1) output is aggregable in each country, into functions ϕ_A and ϕ_B, with given technologies;

(A2) labour is a fixed factor in each country, given in supply and internationally immobile;

(A3) $\phi_i = \phi_i(K_i)$ with $\phi_i' > 0 > \phi_i''$ (positive but diminishing marginal product of capital in each country);

(A4) perfect competition, with perfect foresight and no externalities;

(A5) costless transfer of capital between countries, on and after date t, prohibited before t;

(A6) Country i's social welfare function is increasing in its own national income only;

[33] See MacDougall (201) and McCloskey (202) for applications of this kind of model.

(A7) no taxation;

(A8) capital is homogeneous and infinitely durable;

(A9) a common currency.

Figure 4.6 illustrates these assumptions, and the implications they support. Panel (*a*) depicts the capital stock in *A* (horizontal) against its marginal product (vertical); panel (*b*) shows the same for country *B*. Before date *t* (from A5), capital movements between *A* and *B* were prohibited. Equilibria for the two countries are depicted at *C* and *F*: *A* has a large stock of capital and (given competition, A4) a low rate of interest, *OE*. In *B*, the interest rate is *OG*. Output in *A* is the area under ϕ'_{iA} between the origin and *D*. *B*'s output is

$$\int_0^H \phi'_{iB}(K_B)dK_B.$$

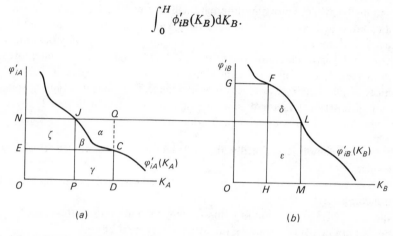

FIG. 4.6. A direct capital export from one country to another. (*a*) Country *A*; (*b*) Country *B*.

At date *t*, capital is allowed to transfer. The process continues costlessly (A5), and in the absence of tax (A7), until the rates of interest are equalized. This happens at *ON* (since *PD* = *HM*). The capital stock in *A* shrinks from *D* to *P*, while *B*'s rises from *H* to *M*. Output increases in *B* by area $\delta + \epsilon$. In *A*, it falls, by $\beta + \gamma$. The world's output must have risen: indeed, the new distribution of the capital stocks maximizes it. The problem

$$\text{Max} \sum_i \phi_i(K_i) \text{ s.t. } \sum_i K_i - \bar{K} = 0 \tag{4.6}$$

has the first order condition $\partial\phi_i/\partial K_i = \partial\phi_j/\partial K_j$ for all *i* and *j*, and the second-order condition that $\phi''_i < 0$. The new world interest rate (at *ON*) meets the first-order condition, while A3 fulfils the second-order one.

It might seem that although world output has risen, *A*'s welfare might have fallen. This is not so: national income (the sole determinant of social welfare, given A6) actually rises in *A*. This is because the capital shipped over to *B* (volume: *HM*) earns a profit yield of ϵ over there, which must be defined as part of *A*'s national income. Given that $HM = PD$ (from A5) ϵ exceeds the loss in output $(\beta + \gamma)$ by area α. A's national income rises by α, and B's by δ, which is of course much smaller than the output rise there $(\delta + \epsilon)$.

The positive side of the theory predicts that capital—once free to move— migrates to earn the highest return it can. This process continues until interest rates have been equalized (when expressed in a common currency, by A8). Yet neither this result nor the predictions of gain for all remain unaffected if the assumptions are relaxed.

III. 2 *Relaxing the Assumptions*

Suppose A1 is relaxed to allow two or more commodities which can be traded internationally, while factors are internationally immobile. Then it might turn out that a country such as B which is ill-endowed with capital may compensate for this deficiency entirely by concentrating on the output and export, of goods which call for little capital in production. A, on the other hand, might export capital-intensive goods. In fact, if the following conditions hold, free trade in goods will equalize the prices of all factors of production everywhere. Such a result would obviate the need for international factor migration: interest rates would be equal, anyway.[34] These conditions for factor price equalization are:

(i) at least as many internationally immobile factors of production as freely traded goods;

(ii) each commodity continues to be manufactured everywhere (i.e., specialization is incomplete);

(iii) the same, CRS production function for any good in every country;

(iv) perfect competition, including full internal factor mobility;

(v) all industries have an identical elasticity of substitution between factors of production, but different mixes of factor employment.

If these five assumptions hold, factor prices will be equalized across national boundaries by trade in goods, and the effects shown in Figure 4.6 would not occur.

If A2 is relaxed, and the other assumptions of the basic model retained, the possibility of international labour migration is introduced. If labour migration equalizes the wage rate between countries—and technologies are identical in the two countries, with the same composition of output—it will succeed in equalizing rates of profit (and interest) too. Under weaker assumptions, this would certainly not follow as a matter of course, but it could by fluke.

While A3 is not a restrictive assumption, A4 certainly is. Imperfect competition would unhinge the rates of interest from their equality with the marginal product of capital, ϕ'. If market imperfections led to the 'overpayment' of capital in one country, that country would tend to get more than its correct allocation of capital,

---

[34] The rate of interest equals the rental on capital and the marginal product of capital under the following conditions: perfect competition; negligible expected change in the price of any good; no depreciation of the capital over time or by use. See chapter 1, p. 30 and chapter 2, p. 66.

and others less. Imperfect foresight is an important possibility: capital will tend to move—with neutrality to risk—until its *prospective* yields have been equalized in each use.[35] But prospective and actual yields can and do differ. One argument for a country's government placing a limit on direct capital exports could be that it has good reason to believe that their estimate of profits on overseas investment is too optimistic. The political risk of expropriation, for instance, may have been under-calculated. There is also the possibility that a domestic investor overseas may have been duped, for instance by local partners in a joint venture or local vendors (when the capital export has a portfolio element). The introduction of externalities introduces another possible argument against unrestricted international capital movements. World optimization entails the worldwide equalization of *social* marginal products of capital;[36] the arbitrage process equalizes prospective *private* marginal products (under perfect competition). A last element in perfect competition is the characteristic of full price flexibility. If this is impaired, weighty Keynesian arguments appear against capital emigration. Since this will tend to lower equilibrium wage rates, sticky actual wage rates may well imply falling employment. Furthermore, the international movement of capital in practice usually takes the form of successive periods of low capital formation in the capital-exporter, and heavy capital formation in the capital-importing nation. So the emigration of capital may spell the threat of deficiency in Keynesian aggregate demand in the capital-exporting country.[37]

If there are costs to exporting capital (although it is not easy to see why there shuld be) the process of interest-rate equalization depicted in Figure 4.6 will stop short of exact equality. A6 is a more interesting assumption than A5. It embeds social indifference to the source of domestic citizens' incomes, and indifference to the division of national income between them. In contrast, a socialist government may place a higher weight on its citizens' wage income than profits. If it does, it will be likely to *discourage* capital exports and *encourage* capital imports. The former will tend to depress, and the latter raise, the marginal product of labour. A socialist government in country A will not regard area ϵ in Figure 4.6(b) as adequate compensation for the output loss $\beta + \gamma$—still less for the loss in wage income $\beta + \zeta$.[38]

Another phenomenon that A6 banishes (and its repeal might introduce) is a utility-interdependence between countries or their citizens. If A's government is for some reason ill-disposed to the government of B, it may wish to restrict or prevent the exportation of capital which must (given the model's other assumptions) bring benefit to B. This 'international externality' is probably reflected in the

---

[35] What Keynes calls the 'marginal efficiency' of capital.

[36] Propositions that the *inflow* of foreign capital has unpleasant consequences for the recipient country can be considered under this head.

[37] Unless the capital-exporter's current exports of goods and services are pulled up sufficiently as a result. See Reddaway (2.62) for an analysis of the effects of capital exports on current exports for the United Kingdom.

[38] If there are just two factors of production, labour will receive the 'surplus' enclosed between ϕ_i' and the ruling rate of interest. So $\beta + \zeta$ represents A's fall in wage bill, as a result of the capital export.

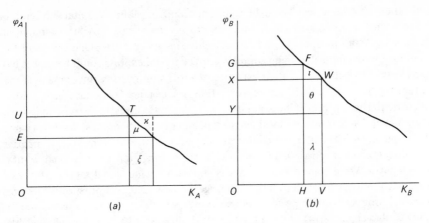

FIG. 4.7. International capital movements with taxation imposed by the recipient country. (a) Country A, levying no tax; (b) Country B, levying a tax at rate XY/OX on profits.

existence of sanctions and boycotts, and perhaps also customs union preferential trading arrangements.[39]

The introduction of taxation (with the repeal of A7) has interesting effects. Portfolio equilibrium (with risk-neutrality) will ensure the equality of *after-tax* prospective marginal yields on all assets. So if B places a tax of t on profits, the pre-tax and post-tax rates of interest must diverge. Figure 4.7 illustrates. The post-tax rate rules in A, the pre-tax rate sets the marginal product of capital in B. B's output rises (with the same starting point, a capital endowment of OH, as before) by areas $\iota + \theta + \lambda$; λ must be paid over, now, in capital earnings to A, bearing a national income increase of $\iota + \theta$. In A, output falls by less than before (only $\mu + \xi$) and income rises by less than before (only κ).

But Figure 4.8 portrays the imposition of taxation by one of just two large

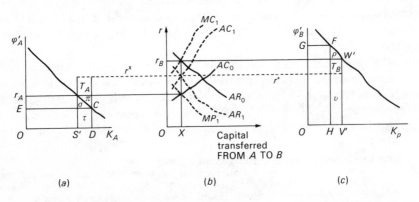

FIG. 4.8. Lender and borrower countries both tax optimally. (a) Country A; (b) World capital movement; (c) Country B.

---

[39] Those phenomena may also be explained by the threats or bribes that sometimes become advisable in a games-theoretic context. See Bacharach (18).

countries, with the other levying none. A number of questions are provoked. What constitutes an optimum rate of tax on capital exports or imports? How does it vary between small and large countries? How does the danger of foreign retaliation alter this optimum level of tax? What Figure 4.8 shows is that the borrower may reduce the rate of interest at which he borrows by restricting his borrowing— provided that he has monopsony power in the market for loans, as B clearly has. Suppose by contrast, B were a perfect competitor in the international capital market, facing a parametrically given international interest rate, F. In this case, his optimum rate of tax on capital would be zero, assuming that all the other assumptions of the Basic Capital Movement Model were retained. A positive rate of tax could only lower output and income; a negative one would raise output but cut income.

So for B the optimum rate of tax depends on monopsony power. Assuming that A does not retaliate at all, it equals the rest of the world's (i.e. A's) elasticity of supply of capital to the (after tax) rate of interest it receives. *Mutatis mutandis,* A has an incentive to restrict its overseas lending—once it has monopoly power— in order to raise the rate of interest its citizens receive on the income derived. In this case, again assuming no retaliation, the optimum lender's tax rate is the reciprocal of the excess of the elasticity (defined positive) of the rest of the world's *demand* for capital over 1.[40] At the world level, of course, such restrictions can only reduce aggregate output: they must infringe the rules derived from (4.6).

If both of two countries apply what they see as optimum taxes, the situation may well resolve into that depicted in Figure 4.8. Here, there are three interest rates: the 'world' interest rate, r^*, represented by the dotted line, that would prevail in any third (and very small)[41] country introduced into the model if it levied no taxes; r_A, the after-tax interest rate inside A earned by A's residents on their capital; and r_B, the rate earned on domestic and foreign capital in B before deductions of tax. T_A and T_B are taxes received by A's and B's governments upon the income derived from the capital that does transfer, which is measured by OX in panel (b) (equal to $S'D$ in (a) and HV' in (c)). In the middle panel, OX is determined thus. A sees its income maximized by a tax at rate $r^* - r_A$. (This equates *its perception of* the marginal revenue for capital movement, MR, with the opportunity cost or marginal product inside A (AC_0). B sets tax at $r_B - r^*$, to equate its marginal product inside B (r_B) to its *perception* of the marginal cost (MC_1). This curve MC_1 is A's supply curve with A's tax added, AC_1, scaled up by the reciprocal of its elasticity. Figure 4.8 depicts a Prisoner's Dilemma: it pays each to levy a tax irrespective of the other's actions; yet aggregate output is not maximized, and both countries could gain by allowing more capital to transfer from A to B.[42] As it is, the capital transfer that does occur brings national income

[40] A second-order condition requires that this elasticity exceed one. Analogously for the borrower's optimum tax rate. The analysis resembles that for optimum import tariffs and export taxes. See, for example, Corden (65).

[41] It would have to be small enough not to affect world interest rates.

[42] Given a Paretian social welfare function, every member of the two societies would have to be compensated by lump-sum transfers from any income-reducing effects (such as, for instance, that on wage rates in A).

increases of $\rho + T_B$ to B and $\sigma + T_A$ to A.[43] The area in panel (c) enclosed below AR_0, above AC_0 and to the right of x is a measure of world income foregone.

The eighth assumption made capital homogeneous and infinitely durable. Repealing this gives rise to numerous possibilities. Disaggregating capital and output into sundry objects distinguished by date and other characteristics, 'the' rate of interest disintegrates into a myriad of own rates in return, which all too often differ from each other.[44] By contrast, introducing depreciation is a simple matter of defining ϕ' as the sum of the rate of depreciation *and* the rate of interest. When there is no expected change in any price, and depreciation is simply a function of time, at least, competition will ensure that this equality is met.[45] But there is one important possibility that arises when assumptions 1 and 8 are relaxed together: *technology* may be transferred, along with the capital. This will generally be of benefit to B, but there can be exceptions. In a two-factor competitive model, technical progress will reduce the real wage rate for labour at a given employment level (or reduce the level of employment at a given real wage rate) if it is labour-augmenting and the elasticity of substitution between the factors is less than the profit share.[46] It can also damage the terms of trade, if concentrated in an exportables industry where the country has international monopoly power. By changing the allocation of resources between and within sectors, and leading to new work-habits, it may also cause temporary social strains in a country where traditions die hard.

II: 3 *Portfolio Capital Movements*

If the ninth assumption of the simple model is relaxed, different currencies are introduced. Provided that the exchange rate between them is locked, and everyone concerned knows this, this makes no difference to the analysis. What if the exchange rate is flexible? The commodity–money arbitrage equation (4.1) will tell us that the nominal prices of a particular good will not move together if the exchange rate changes, when these prices are quoted in the local currencies. Expectations of exchange rate changes will be consistent with expectations of price changes, provided expectations are rational. Logarithmic differentiation of (4.1) with respect to time yields

$$\hat{P}_{iA} = \hat{E}_{AB} + \hat{P}_{iB} \tag{4.7}$$

and rational expectations will require that

$$\hat{P}^e_{iA} = \hat{E}^e_{AB} + \hat{P}^e_{iB} \tag{4.8}$$

where e denotes a single-valued expectation. If we can assume that money is both neutral and super-neutral, we may still employ the analysis of the Basic Capital

---

[43] The tax receipts are included here, since they may be redistributed to the citizens as income (or as public goods).

[44] See chapter II, section VII: 3; and, for more detail, and Dixit (87) and the work he is reviewing there, Bliss (42).

[45] See chapter 9, Figure 9.4 and surrounding discussion, for further analysis of this.

[46] See Heffernan (157) and Sinclair (301).

Movement Model to govern *real* interest rates.[47] Nominal interest rates in the two countries can be explained by Fisher's equation for equilibrium:[48]

$$\text{nominal rate in } j - \text{real rate in } j = \hat{P}_j^e \qquad (4.9)$$

where j denotes country, and $\hat{P}_j^e$ is the expected level of inflation in j, measured in its own currency; so *nominal* interest rate differences between countries are simply equal to expected exchange rate changes when real rates are equalized. Note that (4.7) related to the price of a single traded good, while (4.9) is a statement about price indices. This step may well be illicit unless all goods are traded, and the two countries' price indices are identically weighted.

Portfolio (as opposed to direct) capital movements are likely to be highly sensitive to these factors. The simplest kind of portfolio capital movement is covered-interest-arbitrage. This is the riskless exploitation of any nominal interest rate differentials between countries, when correction has been made for exchange rate risk. They are best analysed in terms of a simple Basic Portfolio Model. Assume:

(A1) interest rates are known and parametrically given to all market participants;
(A2) no taxation;
(A3) no transactions costs in asset, spot, or forward exchange markets;
(A4) no default risk;
(A5) speculators have uniform expectations and are numerous and risk-neutral.

Under these assumptions, portfolio returns will be maximized (in terms of country A's currency, the numeraire) by lending for t periods in currency j if

$$\frac{{}^0E_{Aj}^t}{E_{Aj}^0}(1 + {}_0r_t^j)^t \qquad (4.10)$$

is the highest for all j. In (4.10), ${}_0r_t^j$ is the annualized rate of interest, at date 0, on a t period loan in country j in j's currency; E_{Aj}^0 is the spot price of j's currency in A's at date 0; and ${}^0E_{Aj}^t$ is the forward price (at date 0) of a unit of j's currency expressed in units of A's, for delivery at date t. The t-period forward premium (discount if negative) on j's currency in terms of A's is

$$\frac{{}^0E_{Aj}^t}{E_{Aj}^0} - 1. \qquad (4.11)$$

An investor will have an incentive to switch funds from country j to country k if and only if

$$(1 + {}_0r_t^j)^t \, {}^0E_{kj}^t < E_{kj}^0(1 + {}_0r_t^k)^t. \qquad (4.12)$$

An example illustrates. Suppose there are 14 Austrian schilling per Australian dollar on the spot exchange rate, and 14.50 on the three-month forward market. Australian Government Treasury bills maturing in three months' time for $A100

---

[47] Money is neutral if the values of all real variables, such as quantities and relative prices, are independent of the level of the money supply. It is super-neutral if they are also independent of its rate of growth. See chapter 8 for greater discussion of this, and in particular of the way $\hat{P}^e$ may affect real variables.

[48] See chapter 8, for further discussion of this equation.

stand at $A98. So 'the' three-month rate of interest, annualized, is $\{(2/98)+1\}^4-1$, or nearly 8.417 per cent. If 'the' three-month rate of interest is also about 8.5 per cent per annum in Vienna, it will pay to sell Viennese three-month bills (or borrow on the three-month market there), sell Austrian schillings spot for Australian dollars, buy three-month Australian bills, and *pre-sell* Australian dollars on the three-month forward market for forward Austrian schillings. The annualized Austrian interest rate at which this is no longer worth while is a massive 24.754 per cent. With the Austrian rate above this, the opposite becomes profitable. Funds should be transferred to Vienna, not away from it.

Inequality (4.12) gives the direction for profitable covered-interest arbitrage. The profit is guaranteed, given our model's assumptions. The forward currency transaction ensures that whatever happens to the spot exchange rate by the time the contracts expire (date t in (4.12)) the investor has complete cover. By contrast, uncovered-interest arbitrage is a transfer of funds from country j to country k in pursuit of a higher nominal rate of interest ($_0 r_t^j < {_0 r_t^k}$). This is risky (since the spot exchange rate between j and k at date t can never be known for certain beforehand. It may even have a negative (mean) expected yield: if k's currency is expected on average to fall against j's by a larger proportion than the interest-rate differential, a risk-neutral investor could switch funds in the opposite direction.

Covered-interest arbitrage on a large enough scale must cause (4.12) to hold with strict equality.[49] The slightest divergence between *covered* interest-rate differentials would provoke a flood of capital from the lower to the higher rate centre: this would tend to raise rates in the former and cut them in the latter, and raise the latter's spot (and cut its forward) exchange rate in terms of the former's currency. All four changes would serve to cut back the discrepancy that occasioned the capital flow in the first place.

Under the assumptions of our model, the forward exchange rates, $^0E_{rj}^t$, will be set by speculative expectations of future spot exchange rates. A5 guarantees this. How will these be formed? If (4.1) holds, (4.8) allows us to resolve expectations of change of E into forecasts of inflation differentials between the countries concerned. Further analysis calls for some explanation of these price movements.

If money is neutral, output is independent of the nominal money stock. The former is governed by changes in factor supplies and technology; the latter by the central bank and a host of exogenous variables, which will be considered in Chapter 5. Assume the money market can be described by a clearance condition between the exogenous nominal money stock, $\bar{M}$, and the demand for nominal money $L = P\psi(Y, \mathbf{Z})$. L here is homogeneous of degree one in prices, respecting the neutrality of money; Y is, as usual, income, and $\mathbf{Z}$ a vector of exogenous variables. Logarithmic differentiation with respect to time establishes that

$$\hat{P} = \hat{M} - \psi_1^* \hat{Y} - \frac{P}{M} \sum_i \frac{\partial \psi}{\partial Z_i} \dot{Z}_i \tag{4.13}$$

---

[49] Empirical evidence suggests that covered interest differentials are small, but rarely negligible. They are particularly low in Euro-currency markets. See Beenstock (35) for recent evidence, and Hewson and Sakakibara (161). The first major tests were conducted by Grubel (140).

and rational point expectations will then require that

$$\hat{P}^e = \hat{M}^e - \psi_1^* \hat{Y}^e - \left[\sum_i \frac{\partial \psi}{\partial Z_i} \dot{Z}_i \right]^e \left(\frac{P}{M} \right)^e. \tag{4.14}$$

(4.14) allows us to express the $\hat{E}^e$ terms in terms of $\hat{M}^e$ and $\hat{Y}^e$, if changes in **Z** can be ignored. It therefore appears that a sudden rise in the expected growth of the money supply in a country, or a sudden drop in the output growth forecast for it, will—all else equal—provoke an outflow of short-term capital. Forecasts of the future value of its exchange rate will be lowered, and (4.12) will dictate at least an increased probability of an outward movement of covered-interest arbitrage funds. If, however, the change in $\hat{M}^e$ or $\hat{Y}^e$ is accompanied by the required rise in the domestic nominal interest rate, capital need not flow abroad at all. Indeed, this will happen under the assumptions of the Basic Capital Movement model:[50] if real interest rates are equalized everywhere, the nominal interest rate differential should —given equation (4.9)—react directly to the change in inflation forecast. In this case, the nominal r and $^0E_k^t$ terms would respond at once in (4.12) to preserve strict equality. This line of argument is internally consistent, and clear in its implication: international differences in nominal interest rates and inflation speeds, as well as exchange rate changes, can almost wholly[51] be ascribed to international differences in money supply growth and output growth.[52]

Under extreme Keynesian assumptions on the other hand, money wage rates are exogenous. It is changes in the expected value of these that govern 'rational' inflation rate forecasts, when allowance is made for expected changes in labour productivity and profit rates. If the identity $(PY - wN)/wN = $ profit mark up $\equiv m$ is time-differentiated, we derive

$$\hat{P} = \hat{w} - \hat{z} - \frac{m}{m+1} \hat{m} \tag{4.15}$$

[50] It is interesting to see that real interest rate equalization may result from a combination of zero covered-interest differentials (353) holds as a strict equality) and Fisher's equilibrium condition (that the nominal rate of interest equal the real rate of interest, plus expected inflation: see chapter 8).

[51] Not entirely: the $\dot{Z}_i$ in (4.14) may not be negligible.

[52] The hypothesis receives at best highly qualified empirical support. See Eltis and Sinclair (98), in particular the contributions by Beenstock *et al.*, and Haache and Townend; and also by Begg (340). The reason for this may be that the actual exchange rate path is driven by expectations of *future* changes in the money supplies, income, and other variables, and that these expectations are not directly observed. If the demand for money in each country is negatively related to the nominal rate of interest there, it must also be negatively related to the expected speed of exchange rate depreciation, due to the covered arbitrage condition. Consequently, a sudden fall in the expected growth of one country's money supply should cause a jump in its forward exchange rate, a fall in the nominal rate of interest, and a *rise* in the demand for money. With the supply of money fixed, and a clearly floating exchange rate, a sharp appreciation in the spot rate should ensue. This will succeed in reducing the domestic price level and thereby preserve money market equilibrium by restraining the domestic demand for nominal money. This kind of 'exchange rate overshooting' is discussed at greater length in the author's concluding comments in (98). Another kind of overshooting has been proposed by Dornbusch (92): if prices are sticky in some markets, prices, and therefore the exchange rate, must temporarily overrespond to shocks in those (traded goods) markets where prices are flexible.

and its rational expectations conjugate

$$\hat{p}^e = \hat{w}^e - \hat{h}^e - \frac{m}{m+1}\hat{m}^e \tag{4.16}$$

with $h \equiv$ labour productivity. Rational predictions made under these assumptions will cause a sudden deterioration in expectations for a country's exchange rate if there is a jump in the expected rate of rise of money wage rates uncompensated by cancelling changes in $\hat{h}^e$ or $\hat{m}^e$. The issues raised by the contrast between (4.14) and (4.16) are considered at greater length in chapter 7, section IV: 2.

We can see other characteristics of capital movements by relaxing the Basic Portfolio Model's assumptions. If the interest rates are not known, the covered-interest arbitrage results just considered break down, unless those participating are risk-neutral and have uniform expectations (conforming to the speculators assumed in A5). In this exceptional case, the $_0 r_t^i$ are as good as known. Risk-neutrality is incompatible with diverse expectations of returns, if the other assumptions of this model are retained: for then there will be no means of ensuring market equilibrium. The introduction of uncertainty of returns with aversion to risk brings into play the forces that determine closed economy portfolio optimization. Aversion to risk implies that agents will pay some respect to a 'matching' principle: all else equal, it is unwise to have positive net assets denominated in one currency and negative net assets in another. There must be considerable confidence that the yields on the former will exceed the cost of the latter, when both are expressed in a common currency; otherwise the exchange risk (that the latter's currency will appreciate more or depreciate less than expected in relation to the former's) will be unacceptable. The forward foreign exchange markets provide the formal mechanism for removing this exchange risk.

Another implication of aversion to risk is the incentive to diversify the portfolio. International diversification is likely to achieve this. The covariance of returns on equity or bond investments in different countries is considerably lower than on two such investments in the same country. Equity yields and prices in the one country are likely to be affected similarly by changes in taxation, exchange rates, local interest rates, and wage rates; this will be much less true of equity investments in different countries. The desire to reduce risk by international investment may be a potent force behind cross-national company take-overs and mergers, no less than direct portfolio diversification by individual wealth-holders.

The purchase by a resident of one country of a particular title-deed to wealth from a resident in another is certain to involve at least one of the parties in handling an asset located or issued in a foreign country. In a world of uncertainty, such a transaction will probably be explained by changes in their expectations of future yields. It is most unlikely that the expectations of both of them will have altered in the same way, because why then should one sell, and the other buy? If everyone (for instance) suddenly revised upwards his expectations of profits earned by a specified German electronics company, the equity value of that company would rise at once. The nationality of particular buyers and sellers could hardly be affected directly by this.

Summary of Notation in Chapter 4

A, B	countries
b	the productivity of labour
c	consumption vector
E	the exchange rate
F	land
K	capital stock
$\bar{M}$	exogenous money stock
N	labour
NT	non-traded good
P_{ik}	the price of good i in country k ($k = A, B$) measured in units of country k's currency
$\hat{p}^e$	the expected rate of inflation
r	the rate of interest
T	traded good
U	unemployment
w	wage rate
z_{ij}	agent i's excess demand for j
ϕ	production function

Chapter 5

The Demand for Money

We have now completed our analysis of the key sectors that together shape the real side of the macroeconomy: households, producers, the government, and the overseas sector. We turn now to monetary aspects. In this chapter, we examine the demand for money. After an introduction (section I) we proceed to investigate the theory of the transactions demand for money (section II), and then the asset demand (section III).

I: Introduction

The traditional definitions of money make it an asset held through time, and used as numeraire and in exchange and payment. Some other assets perform one or even two of these functions. Exchange may be effected by a promise, payment by barter or 'in kind'. Gallons of petrol might be thought of as a numeraire, and even used as such in transactions. There is a vast spectrum of assets held over time as a form of wealth. Unlike everything else, however, money can perform all these functions. It is the only component of wealth that serves also as numeraire and as means of exchange and payment. By its narrowest definition, money is also an asset which gives an explicit return of zero in terms of itself. Notes and coins carry no interest. Nor, typically, do current (or demand) bank deposits. Why should an asset with no interest ever be held?

Therer are three answers to this question. Money is held because this avoids transactions costs; because other assets are expected to give a negative yield; and because money may be safer than other assets. These answers are the basis of the three types of demand for money identified by Keynes:[1] the transaction demand, the speculative demand, and the precautionary demand. The dividing line between the categories is hard to draw in theory, and even more difficult in empirical work.[2] But they are a very useful way of classifying the kinds of influence operating upon the demand for money, and the reasons for them. In the household optimization model of chapter 1, the first of these three arguments for holding money was invoked to justify the inclusion of real money balances in the household's utility function. It is to this argument that we now turn.

II: The transactions demand

The standard model of the transactions demand for money was developed by Baumol (31). The following assumptions are set forth:

[1] See J. M. Keynes (182), ch. 15.
[2] The earliest empirical tests retained a Keynesian division between transactions and asset balances: see, for example, Tobin (318). It has been discarded by subsequent investigators.

(A1) an agent receives his annual income (Y) in discrete amounts of known size and at regularly spaced known dates; his expenditure is even and continuous;

(A2) money (M) bears no interest, and must be held in non-negative amounts;

(A3) all receipts and payments are made in money;

(A4) an alternative asset, B (bonds), with positive and known yield R, may be bought and sold at will, but there is a fixed and known cost of C per transaction in B;

(A5) the agent optimizes by choosing the character and number of transactions involving B that maximizes interest received less transactions costs paid.

Suppose Y is received in w instalments, and that x is the number of transactions involving B—purchases or sales—per payment period. There will be w payment periods each year.

Three questions are now prompted. If holdings of M are ever to be switched into B, should this be done the moment income is received, or after a delay? Should any M be held the moment before sales of B are realized or income receipts are due? Should any sales of B be made in equal or unequal amounts? The answers to these three questions help to determine the optimum pattern of transactions in B. The first is straightforward. There is no case for delaying purchase of B after income has been received. Every day's delay means a sacrifice of interest: M yields nothing (A2) while B gives a positive yield (A4); all income is received in money (A3); and the transactions cost can never be lower tomorrow than today (A5). The second is also clear. Receipts of income are completely predictable, in timing and amount, and expenditure is predictably even (A1). Since M bears no interest while B does (A2 and A4), even a modest balance of cash the instant before bond sales are realized represents waste. So the cash balance must be at zero at the moment income and proceeds from selling B are received. Panels (c) and (d) of Figure 5.1 illustrate these points. A delayed purchase of B leads to a wasteful transfer of area from B to M in panel (c); the effects of selling too early, and having positive holdings of M at this time, lead to the wasteful transfer shown in panel (d). Given the assumptions of the model, it would also be silly to sell B in different amounts at different times. This could also only raise the average holding of M and (because the average holdings of M and B sum to a constant) thereby lower the interest receipts. For any given number of transactions in B interest receipts must be maximized and this is done by selling B—if at all—in equal amounts and at regular intervals. Panel (b) of Figure 5.1 also illustrates this. Premature sales of B, and unequally sized sales of B, are most likely to lead to the same type of waste.

Interest receipts will be directly proportional to the average bond-balance held and hence to the horizontally striped areas in Figure 5.1. The volume of each striped box represents the total holding of bonds multiplied by the duration of the holding; interest receipts (per unit time) will be proportional to this volume. (If sales of B are to be of equal size and at regular intervals, and the timing of transactions in B avoids the wasteful delay or prematurity shown in panels (c) and (d), the exact number of these transactions remains to be determined.) In panel (a), $x = 0$; B is never held. In (b), $x = 2$ and in (e), $x = 4$. In panel (b), an individual

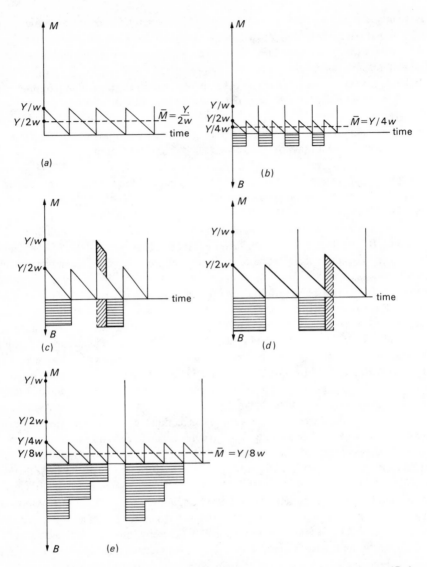

FIG. 5.1. The profiles of cash balances (*M*, upper quadrant) and bond balances (*B*, lower quadrant) under different assumptions. (*a*) Time profile of cash balances with no transactions in *B*; (*b*) The cash-balance profile with $x = 2$, no delay in purchasing *B*, no wasted holdings of *M*, and equal sales of *B*; (*c*) The effects of a delay in purchasing *B*, when $x = 2$; (*d*) The effects of selling *B* too early: wasted holdings of *M* (again, $x = 2$); (*e*) The cash-balance pfofile when $x = 4$.

puts half his income receipt of Y/w into *B* as soon as he gets it, then sells this exactly half-way through his payment interval. In (*e*), if $w = 4$ and $Y = 16,000$, he buys 3,000 worth of *B* as soon as he receives his 4,000 income, and then sells off *B* in three lots of 1,000, each lot every 365/16 days.[3] In (*e*), his average holding

---

[3] Ignoring such complications as week-ends and leap-years.

of money would be 500, and his average holding of B, 1,500. The sum of 500 and 1,500 is the 2,000 his average cash balance would be, if x were zero (as in panel (a)).

Generalizing, we can see that when x is an integer of two or more, the average holding of M (labelled $\bar{M}$ in Figure 5.1) is $Y/2xw$. The average bond holding, $\bar{B}$, equals the excess of $Y/2w$ over $Y/2xw$, since $Y/2w$ equals $\bar{M}$ if $x = 0$. Annual interest receipts are therefore $(RY/2w)[1 - (1/x)]$, since B gives a known yield of R (A4). Transactions costs are simply Cx per payment interval, or Cxw per year. The function to be maximized is therefore

$$\phi(x) = \frac{RY}{2w}\left[1 - \frac{1}{x}\right] - Cxw. \tag{5.1}$$

Differentiating (5.1) with respect to x and setting ϕ' to zero, we have

$$(wx)^2 = \frac{RY}{2C}, \text{ or } wx = \sqrt{\frac{RY}{2C}}. \tag{5.2}$$

Since $\phi = -RY/2wx^3$, the second-order condition requires that the negative root for wx be disregarded. Since $\bar{M} = Y/2xw$, we can substitute using (5.2) to derive the *optimum* mean holding of money:

$$\bar{M}^* = \frac{Y}{2xw^3} = \sqrt{\frac{CY}{2R}} \tag{5.3}$$

Taking logarithms and differentiating, (5.3) implies

$$\tilde{M}^* = \tfrac{1}{2}\tilde{C} + \tfrac{1}{2}\tilde{Y} - \tfrac{1}{2}\tilde{R}, \tag{5.4}$$

where $\tilde{z}$ is the proportionate change in z. Equation (5.4) gives the following results: the elasticities of the optimum mean holding of money to income and to the level of transactions costs are both plus one-half, and the interest-elasticity of the demand for money is minus one-half. These results are arrestingly precise. They merit close examination.

The transactions cost term, C, may be thought of as the cost of a telephone call to a stockbroker, plus the commission, taxes, and dealer's fees,[4] and the value of (to himself) the time and energy expended by the individual concerned. This is how it might be for a rich individual who employs a stockbroker directly. For the more representative household, B are perhaps better thought of as time-deposits (UK: deposit accounts), or savings and loan deposits (UK equivalent: building society deposits, or trustee savings banks deposits). The transactions costs in this case are shoe-leather, time, nuisance, perhaps other transport costs, and the various restrictions and penalties that may be imposed on withdrawal.[5] These are for the most part psychic rather than explicitly pecuniary;[6] they are likely to differ too, person from person. One interesting feature is that they are for the most part fixed rather

---

[4] In the United Kingdom, 'dealer's fees' are 'jobber's fees'. Both are generally captured by the spread between 'bid' and 'ask' prices; but these are (largely) proportional costs. These costs are introduced in equation (5.8).

[5] Such as sacrifice of interest, or requirement to give advance notice.

[6] This makes testing very difficult.

than proportional: it probably 'costs' as much to place a week's income in an interest-bearing deposit, as a year's income. This is fortunate, given A4. But the psychic elements in C have a very important implication. They are highly likely to vary with income, Y. When income is all earned, and taxation can be ignored, the cost of time taken on 'banking chores' may be proportional to income. If tastes are heterothetic, it is not inconceivable that the convenience afforded by cash balances might turn out to be a luxury. If C do depend on Y, the true income-elasticity of demand for money will differ from the figure of $\frac{1}{2}$ presented in (5.4): (5.3) will yield

$$\frac{\partial \log \bar{M}^*}{\partial \log Y} = \tfrac{1}{2}(1 + \text{elasticity of } C \text{ to } Y),$$

which could certainly equal, even exceed, unity.[7]

No definition of Y has been attempted so far. Is it current or permanent? Real or nominal? Pre-tax or post-tax? In the case of a self-employed person, or especially a shopkeeper, is it a measure of turnover or profit? And what would it mean in the context of a business?

Several of the issues opened up here are discussed at length below: they are large subjects. The brief answer in the context of the standard model is: Y is nominal current income after tax[8] for the household-employee, and nominal pre-tax turnover for all other agents, domestic and corporate. Both are nominal; consequently a doubling of the price level and all nominal earnings that leaves C u-changed will multiply the demand for money by $\sqrt{2}$. A purely neutral rise in the price level that raises C (which is also nominal) equiproportionately must, however, raise the demand for money in the same proportion. So A4 does not do violence to the postulate of homogeneity.[9]

The interest rate term, R, must be interpreted as covering a *safe and short-term* rate of interest. But which rate? That on interest-bearing bank deposits—if so which? Treasury bills? Short-term bonds? Although this multitude of rates moves in reasonably close harmony, aggregation of such assets may be highly problematical. In principle the ideas inherent in the standard model may be capable of giving us a hierarchy of different assets within the 'aggregate' B, ranked by R and C. The inventory-theoretic approach to the demand for money could then explain how narrow money was split between currency and non-interest bearing bank accounts;[10] how broad money was split between interest-bearing and non-interest bearing bank accounts;[11] how 'liquid' assets were split between broad money on the

[7] Indeed, it is perfectly possible that the frequent switching of assets to maximize returns is like walking to work to save train fares or motoring costs: a consumption technology for the household that is often rejected as an inefficient activity, dominated on the frontier of choice between leisure and other goods by some set of alternatives. The probability of this in the case of money must rise with the level of income.

[8] Assuming that tax is fully deducted from income at source.

[9] Which, in the context of money, implies independence of $\bar{M}^*/P$ from the price level.

[10] C would be bank charges plus psychic costs of visiting the bank; R would arise from the lowered probability of theft from bank deposits.

[11] Here, C would be the measure of the 'illiquidity' cost of non-interest bearing deposit (such as delay or penalty for withdrawal) and R the interest rate on time-deposits.

one side, and other kinds of deposit (e.g. savings and loan, or building society) on the other. A properly developed model of all this would be very complex, but its intuitive character is clear. On each frontier of choice, the marginal yield, net of marginal cost (explicit and psychic) would be equalized when *all* assets were held (an 'interior' solution). In a corner solution, at least one asset would not be held. The remainder's marginal net yields would be equalized. Figure 5.2 illustrates for the simple *M*, *B* choice posed in the standard model.

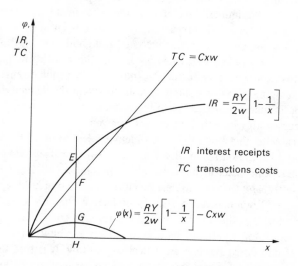

FIG. 5.2. The optimum number of bond transactions.

The interest receipts function (IR) is a branch of a rectangular hyperbola, asymptotic to $RY/2w$ as $x \to \infty$. The transactions cost function (TC) is a ray from the origin, given A4. The optimum number of transactions in the asset per payment periods (variable: x) is given by H, where ϕ reaches it maximum. This corresponds to the equalization of marginal cost (gradient of TC) with marginal interest receipt (gradient of IR at E). $EF = GH$.

We have discussed the solution to the standard model, and the significance of variables Y, C and R. Before considering the effects of relaxing the assumptions, one or two messy difficulties need to be considered. Easily the most important of these concerns the variable x. This must be restricted to integer solutions of 2 or more, or to zero. Unit, fractional, or irrational values are absurd. This means that, in practice, often

$$\frac{1}{w}\sqrt{\frac{RY}{2C}} \neq x. \tag{5.5}$$

Now if $(1/w)\sqrt{(RY/2C)}$ exceeds 2 and is not an integer, our agent will select whichever of the nearer two integers gives the higher value for ϕ. From (5.1) it can be seen that x will be 2 if $(1/w)\sqrt{(RY/2C)}$ lies between 2 and 1.

If (5.2) gave a 'nonsense' value for x of less than one, x collapses to zero and $\bar{M}^*$ is simply $Y/2w$, as in Figure 5.1(a).[12] One implication of (5.5) is income is received frequently—if w is high—is that there is an appreciable chance that the agent will never hold B. The probability of this varies positively with the ratio of C to Y, as well as w. Inequality (5.5) therefore shows why low-paid income-earners who receive their pay weekly (rather than monthly or quarterly) are much less likely to have bank accounts and the like than the rest of the population. Another inference that may be drawn is that an increase in income will tend to lessen the adverse effect of the indivisibility that x must be an integer. Doubling Y will, for example, raise the interval between the limits for $\bar{M}^*$ given by (5.5) *by a smaller proportion*. A person with a very large income has a good chance of overriding most of the indivisibility problem that (5.5) poses. For those with low income that are paid frequently, on the other hand, the indivisibility problem ensures that they always hold temporary cash surpluses as cash: for them the demand for money will be unit-elastic in income, insensitive to the interest rate, and inversely proportional to the frequency with which their income is received.

By contrast with the indivisibility problem presented by x, there is the minor difficulty posed by the omission of ϕ from the cash flow itself. We need to assume that the transactions costs in bond sales and purchases—if incurred at all—are paid continuously, and that the interest receipts on any bond-holdings to each lump sum of income (Y/w) makes no real difference. With these observations made, we may at last feel that the standard model is internally consistent.

It is now consistent, yes; but hardly complete. We now survey the effects of relaxing its assumptions. A1 is a great deal to swallow. It is true that households receive their earned income in reasonably regular, evenly spaced lumps. Seasonal employment and overtime working, holiday and Christmas and 'Thirteenth Month' payments, Maigeld, profit-related bonus payments, and yearly or twice-yearly dividend and interest income all upset the picture to varying degrees. So do irregularities due to tax rebates and payments, illness, and the unequal length of months. Household income is also imperfectly predictable. But for the self-employed, and for businesses, the pattern of receipts will be much more continuous, probably less regular, and certainly subject to considerable uncertainty, in timing and size.

Suppose, instead, that receipts and outlays are continuous and evenly spread over time. If the model's other assumptions are retained, there will now be no incentive to hold money, no matter how small the level of transactions costs. Imperfect synchronization of receipts and disbursements is necessary, therefore, if money is to be held. The transactions demand for money returns, however, if spending is discrete and receipts are even and continuous. In this case, which could well apply to a business with a steady flow of receipts from trading and a commitment to pay wages at discrete intervals, the saw-tooth pattern of cash holdings seen in Figure 5.1 will simply be reversed. Figure 5.3 illustrates

[12] If (5.2) gives a value of x less than 2, the individual must choose whether to make 2 bond transactions per period, or none. He will choose the former if and only if ϕ is positive at $x = 2$, since ϕ must vanish at $x = 0$.

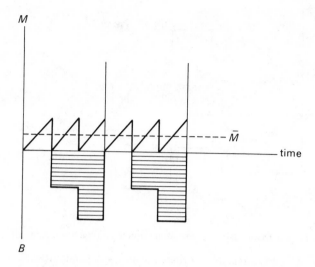

FIG. 5.3. The cash-balance profile under continuous receipts and discrete outlays, with $x = 3$.

this, with x (now defined as the number of bond transactions per *outlay* interval) equal to 3.

The introduction of uncertainty into cash-flow was pioneered by Whalen (331), Miller and Orr (213) and (214), and Orr (245); Eppen and Fama (99) and (100), Girgis (131) and Neave (234) all generalized the mathematical basis for the results obtained in the earlier papers, and Vial (328) made the crucial breakthrough from discrete to continuous time. Further work has been done individually and together by Barro and Santomero.[13] The uncertainty models set out to analyse the appropriateness, characteristics, or conditionality for existence or uniqueness of what is known as the '*simple two-bin optimal inventory policy*'. This policy consists of a pair of rules: if a variable M drifts up to a ceiling M_{max}, cut it to $M^{\square}$; if it drifts down to a floor M_{min} raise it to $M^{\blacksquare}$. In this context, M is an inventory—in our case, cash balances.

The essence of this approach is that M carries an opportunity cost—typically, the (higher) rate(s) of interest available on an asset or set of assets, B. Switching M between its ceiling or floor and its starting values $M^{\square}$ or $M^{\blacksquare}$ is costly. The picture is completed by a description of the random walk that M takes over time, and of how trouble arises if M drops too low. Figure 5.4 gives a visual example, when M is constrained to being positive.

In Figure 5.4, the vertical distance θ in the lower panel represents bond sales and equals $M^{\blacksquare} - M_{min}$. Similarly, when M rises to M_{max} and is cut back suddenly to $M^{\square}$, bond holdings rise by λ.

It can certainly not be taken for granted that the simple two-bin policy is optimal in every case, nor that finding the ceiling, floor, and starting values (if they

---

[13] See various articles by Barro and Santomero, singly (23), (276), or together (28). The central idea goes back at least as far as Edgeworth (97).

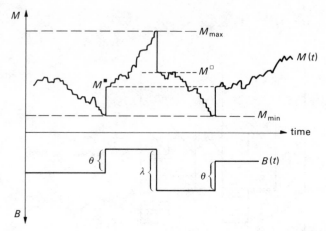

FIG. 5.4. The stochastic cash-balance and the simple two-bin optimal inventory policy.

exist) is easy. As always, results—if there are any—depend critically upon assumptions. For example, the Miller–Orr model (214) takes a discrete-time view of $M(t)$, making $(M_t - M_{t-\delta})$ equiprobably a positive or negative number that depends on Y. The time-interval, δ, also varies with Y. The optimum cash-management policy is defined to be of the two-bin type, and, armed with assumptions otherwise identical to the standard model, solutions are found for M_{min}, M_{max} and the starting values $M^\square$ and $M^\blacksquare$. The last two are in fact equal, at 1/3 of M_{max}. M_{min} is zero. The optimum mean holding of money turns out to be 4/9 of M_{max} The interest-elasticity of the optimum mean cash balance is found to be $-1/3$, while the income elasticity depends on how δ and $(M_t - M_{t-\delta})$ vary with Y. One-third and $1\frac{1}{2}$ are limiting plausible values.[14]

Further discussion of uncertainty is postponed until section II of this chapter, where the asset-demand for money will be examined specifically. But before we return to the task of relaxing the standard model's other assumptions, we should note that the transactions demand has been 'crossed' with uncertainty in two other ways. Niehans (241) has considered models that differ from the standard model by making R (the return on B) a random variable, and (in one of two cases) by replacing the fixed cost of making transactions in B by proportional costs. The Tobin–Hicks mean-variance approach to uncertainty is adopted—and the optimum mean cash balance varies negatively with the variance of R, in addition to the other variables. The second 'mongrel' model is due to Shell (in 315)).

Shell's model[15] maximizes an agent's expected utility (where this depends on 'end-of-period' real wealth) with respect to proportions of the portfolio devoted to M, B, and a risky asset, A. Ratios of current wealth (W_0) to these three are $1 - a - b$, b and a. End of period real wealth, W, is

$$W_0[(1 + R_R)a + (1 + R_B - \hat{P})b + (1 - a - b)(R_M - \hat{P})] - C \qquad (5.6)$$

---

[14] The elasticity of $\bar{M}^*$ to income is $(2\beta + \delta)/3$ where β is the income-elasticity of $(M_t - M_{t-\delta})$ and $1/\gamma$ the income elasticity of δ.

[15] The version presented here is a slightly expanded variant on the model given in (315).

where R_R and $\hat{P}$ are random variables signifying the real rate of return on A, and the rate of inflation. B and M give known nominal returns R_B and R_M; C represents transactions costs, and is deemed to depend upon both M and B. $\partial C/\partial M$ is clearly negative, and $\partial C/\partial B$ is non-positive.[16] Optimization entails setting the derivatives of Φ with respect to a and b to zero,[17] where $\Phi = E(u\,[w])$.[18]

This gives first-order conditions[19]

$$E\{u'\cdot w[r_B - r_M + C'_M - C'_B]\} = 0,$$

$$E\{u'\cdot w[x + \hat{P} - r_M + C'_M]\} = 0,$$

which may be rewritten as

$$r_B - r_M + C'_M - C'_B = 0, \tag{5.7(a)}$$

$$E\{u'\cdot w[x + \hat{P} - r_B + C'_B]\} = 0, \tag{5.7(b)}$$

since in the first equation every component of the square brackets is known. (5.7(a)) expresses the tangency condition of Figure 5.2, that the marginal revenue from holdings of B should balance their marginal cost in transactions. Equation (5.7(b)) is a portfolio equilibrium condition on the frontier of choice between assets whose nominal return is secure (B) and those for which neither nominal nor real return is secure. If transactions costs are unaffected by this choice (so that C'_B is zero), (5.7(a)) and (5.7(b)) become separate conditions: the demand for money depends exclusively upon the relative nominal return on it and the safe, short-term alternative to it (and the marginal cost of transactions), while expectations of neither the inflation rate nor the nominal return on other assets has any direct relevance for it. On the other hand, (5.7(b)) may help to determine equilibrium asset prices for A and B, given their relative supplies; and there would therefore be some roundabout link through from the expected real return on A, and from inflation expectations on to the demand for money.

Relaxing the second, third, and fifth assumptions of the standard model is not the source of difficulty it was with the first. Introducing a rate of return on M means that the *relative* return is the relevant concept of opportunity cost. The Shell model shows this; (5.7(a)) needs to replace the simpler case of $R_B + C'_M = 0$ illustrated in Figure 5.2. Introducing overdrafts complicates the analysis little; if the overdraft rate is pitched above R_B, negative holdings of money will usually be a dominated strategy (except when a brief bridge between payments and receipts is needed, to avoid the double transactions costs involved in selling and then repurchasing B). If, on the other hand, the overdraft rate lies below R_B, arbitrage will be profitable: borrowing at one rate and re-lending (entirely safely) at a higher rate will be so appealing that market equilibrium will require the overdraft rate to rise up to or beyond R_B.

---

[16] This allows for the possibility that temporary surplus of cash can be held in A as well as B, with transactions costs in A no lower and perhaps higher than in B.

[17] Assuming that $1 - a - b$, a, $b > 0$ (i.e., that some of all assets are held).

[18] $E[..]$ is the expectations operator.

[19] Defining C'_M and C'_B as $\partial C/\partial M$ and $\partial C/\partial B$.

Bringing receipts and payments in assets other than M into the analysis is unrealistic. The effect of doing so would clearly be to cut the average optimum holding of money, in favour of these other assets, if there were any transactions costs in buying or selling them. But for these transactions costs, the results would carry through unamended.

The fifth assumption is also unexceptionable. But relaxing the fourth (that transactions costs in buying and selling B are fixed) produces some major changes. We start by assuming that transactions costs are partly fixed and partly proportional in the value of the quantities of B to be bought or sold.

We start by defining α as the proportion of the agent's income receipt, Y/w, which is retained initially as cash. α must lie between 1 and 0. For the fraction α of the payment period, his holdings of B will be stationary at $(1 - \alpha)Y/w$. After this, he will sell bonds in equal amounts at regular intervals. His average holding of money will be

$$\bar{M} = \frac{Y}{2w}\left[\alpha^2 + \frac{(1 - \alpha)^2}{x - 1}\right]$$

and his receipts of interest on B each year, net of both fixed and proportionate transactions costs, will equal

$$\phi(x) = (1 - \alpha)\frac{YR}{2w}\left(1 + \alpha - \frac{1 - \alpha}{x - 1}\right) - Cxw - 2DY(1 - \alpha). \tag{5.8}$$

Here, D is the rate of proportionate transactions costs. Then maximize (5.8) with respect to α and x; solve for α and x; and substitute into the new expression for $\bar{M}$, giving

$$\bar{M}^* = \frac{Y}{2}\left\{4w\left(\frac{D}{R}\right)^2 + \left(1 - \frac{2Dw}{R}\right)\sqrt{\frac{2C}{YR}}\right\}. \tag{5.9}$$

(5.9) holds provided that $R > 2Dw$, otherwise $\bar{M}$ will be $Y/2w$ and B will never be held. Note that the interest and income elasticities are now higher than before.

If assumption A4 of the standard model is relaxed still further to remove fixed transactions costs entirely, the interest-elasticity rises (in modulus) to -2, and the income elasticity increases also, to unity. This is so because once fixed transactions costs have gone the incentive to keep sales of bonds reasonably few and regularly spaced also vanishes. In contrast, time-profiles for money and bond holding are as illustrated in Figure 5.5 (when the cash-flow profile is assumed to be the same as in the standard model).

In Figure 5.5, the individual receives Y/w, of which he keeps z in cash and turns $(Y/w) - z$ into bonds. So he incurs a transactions cost here of $D\{(Y/w) - z\}$. After certain time has elapsed, his money balance becomes exhausted; but subsequent expenditures are paid for (until his next income receipt) by continuous bond sales, and immediate transfer into cash. Total transactions costs per payment

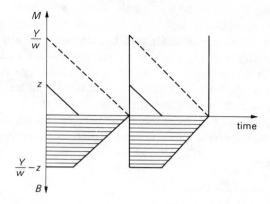

FIG. 5.5. Bond holding and money holding with exclusively proportional transactions costs.

interval are $2D\{(Y/w) - z\}$, since bonds are both bought and sold; and interest receipts are

$$\frac{R}{w}\left[\frac{z}{Y}\left(\frac{Y}{w} - z\right) + \frac{1}{2}\left(\frac{1}{w} - \frac{z}{Y}\right)\left(\frac{Y}{w} - z\right)\right].$$

per payment period. (The horizontally striped pentagon consists of a rectangle of height $(Y/w) - z$ and base z/Y, and a triangle of base $(1/w) - (z/Y)$ and height $(Y/w) - z$.) The annual value of interest receipts net of transactions costs is therefore

$$\phi(x) = \frac{R}{2}\left(\frac{Y}{w} - z\right)\left[\frac{1}{w} + \frac{z}{Y}\right] - 2D\left[\frac{Y}{w} - z\right]. \tag{5.10}$$

Differentiating (5.10) with respect to the unknown z reveals that $z = 2DY/R$ and

$$\bar{M} = \frac{z^2 w}{2Y} = \left(\frac{D}{R}\right)^2 2wY \tag{5.11}$$

Logarithmic differentiation of (5.11) shows greatly increased elasticities of the demand for money to Y and R. Given that Y is linear homogeneous in the price level, and that D (which is of course a proportion) and R are independent of it, (5.11) is still consistent with the neutrality of money.

If D is sufficiently high, ϕ in (5.10) would become negative. This state of affairs would emerge if z became so high that it exceeded Y/w. In fact, z may not exceed Y/w, if negative holdings of B are precluded, as Figure 5.5 will confirm. So, since in the optimum $z = 2DY/R$, the boundary condition for *any* bonds to be held is that $D < R/2w$, the probability of which increases with R and decreases with w and D. Frequent income payment, high transactions costs and a modest rate of interest will serve to keep the holdings of money at $Y/2w$ just as in the standard model with fixed transactions costs.

In sum, the nominal transactions demand for money will vary positively with transactions costs; it should be unit-elastic in the price level. For those with frequent income payment, it will be proportional to income, independent of interest rates and inversely proportional to the frequency of income receipts. If income is paid rarely enough, and the transactions costs are low enough, the demand for money will be negatively related to the interest rate on an alternative safe asset, typically shorter term bonds; the elasticity to this interest rate will be lower if transactions costs are predominantly fixed than if chiefly proportional. The income elasticity of demand will be a half under certain strict conditions, the relaxation of which generally raises it substantially, even above unity in certain cases.

III: The Asset Demand for Money

III: 1 *Keynes's Speculative Demand for Money*

The starting point for the asset demand is Keynes's speculative demand for money, in (182). Money is desired for speculative purposes when the alternative asset(s) give(s) a *negative* net yield. This will happen if the expectations of capital loss is large enough to counterweigh the (necessarily non-negative) interest yield upon the asset. If a bond is expected to fall in price from 100 today to 90 this time next year, the annual interest yield must be less than 10 for the expected net return on it for that year to be negative.

The basic Keynesian model of the Speculative Demand for Money is constructed on the basis of the following assumptions:

(A1) agents choose between two assets, money (M) with zero yield and irredeemable bonds (B) with a known coupon of c per period;

(A2) no one may borrow;

(A3) transactions costs in buying and selling B are negligible;

(A4) each agent holds firm expectations about the rate of interest in one period's time on B, with no variance;

(A5) each agent attempts to maximize the nominal return on his wealth, over a one-period planning horizon.

Let $R_0 \equiv$ the current rate of interest on B, and A_0 be its present price. If the next interest payment is not made until the end of the current period, and the present date is the start of a period,

$$A_0 = \frac{c}{(1+R_0)} + \frac{c}{(1+R_0)^2} + \frac{c}{(1+R_0)^3} + \ldots = \frac{c}{1+R_0} \frac{1}{1-1/(1+R_0)} = \frac{c}{R_0}.$$

$$(5.12)$$

The bond described here is completely 'clean'. If the bond were completely 'dirty' with its first interest payment of c on the point of being paid, A_0 would be $(c/R_0) + R_0$. In practice, therefore, A_0 climbs steadily up from its floor of $\bar{R}_0$ to its ceiling of $(c/R_0) + R_0$, only to fall back as soon as the interest payment—or eligibility for the interest payment—has passed. Define z_0 as the net return on B which is expected now (at date 0) over a one-period holding interval. Then, assuming henceforward that B is always completely clean, $z_0 = R_0 + (E_0A_1/A_0) - 1$ where E_0A_1 is the price of B expected at 0 to rule at date 1. Consequently $E_0A_1 = c/E_0R_1$, since the bond is irredeemable (A1). So

$$z_0 = R_0 + \frac{R}{E_0R_1} - 1 = r_0 \frac{[E_0R_1 + 1]}{E_0R_1} - 1 \gtreqless 0 \text{ as } R_0 \gtreqless \frac{E_0R_1}{1 + E_0R_1}.$$

Given the assumptions of the model, one agent's portfolio action will be

Hold all wealth in money if $z_0 < 0$,

Hold all wealth in bonds if $z_0 > 0$,   } Rule I

Hold indeterminate quantity of each asset if $z_0 = 0$.

In Keynes's view, E_0R_1 (the present point expectation of the interest rate at date 1) is a fickle, subjective variable, which varies person from person and is often strongly influenced by the history of actual $R(t)$. But further results can only be made on the basis of assumptions about E_0R_1. We now examine three kinds of simple discrete-time adaptive expectations assumptions for E_0R_1: *generalized linear*, *regressive*, and *extrapolative*.

The *generalized linear* equation will be

$$E_0R_1 = u_0 + \sum_{i=0}^{T} a_iR_i. \tag{5.13a}$$

Now E_0R_1 will clearly depend on R_0. To see how, recall that

$$z_0 = 1 + \frac{R_0}{E_0R_1} - 1 = R_0\left[1 + \left(u_0 + \sum_{i=0}^{T} a_iR_i\right)^{-1}\right] - 1.$$

The effect of a change in present R_0 upon present z is

$$\frac{\partial z}{\partial R_0} = 1 + (E_0R_1)^{-1} - a_0r_0(E_0R_1)^{-2} = (E_0R_1)^{-2}\left[(E_0R_1)^2 + u_0 + \sum_{i=0}^{T} a_iR_{-i}\right].$$

This shows that for a rise in R_0 to riase z_0, it is sufficient that neither u_0 nor any a⟨ be negative, and that at least one be positive.

Under *regressive* expectations, with geometrically declining weights

$$E_0R_1 = (1 - \lambda)[R_0 + \lambda R_{-1} + \lambda^2R_{-2} + \lambda^3R_{-3} + \ldots]. \tag{5.13b}$$

where λ, the coefficient of inertia in expectations, is positive and less than unity. If (5.13b) is valid generally, it must have been valid one period ago; hence

$$\lambda(ER_0) = (1 - \lambda)[\lambda R_{-1} + \lambda^2R_{-2} + \lambda^3R_{-3} + \ldots]. \tag{5.14}$$

Subtraction of (5.14) from (5.13b) establishes the Koyck transformation:

$$E_0R_1 - \lambda(E_{-1}R_0) = (1 - \lambda)R_0.$$

If δ is defined as last period's mean expectation for today's interest rate $(E_{-1}R_0)$, the error-learning adaptive expectations equation is derivable:

$$E_0R_1 - \delta = (1 - \lambda)(R_0 - \delta). \tag{5.15}$$

(5.15) allows us to solve for z_0, recalling that $z_0 = R_0 + (R_0/E_0R_1) - 1$

$$z_0 = r_0 + \left[1 - \lambda + \frac{\lambda\delta}{R_0}\right]^{-1} - 1. \tag{5.16}$$

(5.16) is negative for sufficiently high δ and low R_0. Indeed,

$$\text{sn } z_0 = \text{sn}\left[1 + \frac{1}{\lambda}\frac{R_0}{1 - R_0} - \frac{\delta}{R_0}\right].$$

Differentiation of (5.16) with respect to r_0 gives

$$\frac{\partial z_0}{\partial R_0} = 1 + \frac{\lambda\delta}{[(1 - \lambda)R_0 + \lambda\delta]^2}. \tag{5.17}$$

Now (5.17) is unambiguously positive. There is therefore no chance of a perverse response of the speculative demand for money to current interest rates. An increase in the current rate of interest increases the prospective interest yield directly; this is always true—but the consequence of assuming regressive expectations is that it also has an important secondary function—it raises the mean expectation that the rate of interest will fall back. This can only increase the prospective net return on the asset still further, by raising the expectation of capital gain.[20]

Under *extrapolative* expectations for E_0R_1, however, results change. Again geometrically declining weights are assumed, but now we move from levels to rates of change. It is the forecast of the proportionate *change* in the rate of interest that is a weighted average of present and past observed *changes* in interest rates (and not, as in the regressive model, the expected *level* a weighted average of present and past *levels*). Formally:

$$E_0\frac{R_1}{R_0} = (1 - \lambda)\left[\frac{R_0}{R_{-1}} + \lambda\frac{R_{-1}}{R_{-2}} + \lambda^2\frac{R_{-2}}{R_{-3}} + \ldots\right], \tag{5.13c}$$

where $1 > \lambda > 0$ and λ is, again, a coefficient of inertia.

(5.13c) implies

$$\lambda\left(\frac{E_{-1}R_i}{R_{-1}}\right) = (1 - \lambda)\left[\lambda\frac{R_{-1}}{R_{-2}} + \lambda^2\frac{R_{-2}}{R_{-3}} + \ldots\right]. \tag{5.18}$$

Subtraction of (5.18) from (5.13c) yields

$$E_0R_1 = \frac{R_0}{R_{-1}}[(1 - \lambda)R_0 + \lambda\delta] \tag{5.19}$$

and substitution of (5.19) into $z_1 = R_0 + R_{-1}[(1 - \lambda)R_0 + \lambda\delta]^{-1} - 1$ yields

$$z_0 = R_0 + R_{-1}[(1 - \lambda)R_0 + \lambda\delta]^{-1} - 1. \tag{5.20}$$

---

[20] Or lowering the expected capital loss.

The sign of (5.20) is indeterminate. For it to be positive,

$$R_{-1} > (1 - R_0)[R_0 + \lambda(\delta - R_0)],$$

which is rather likely if $R_{-1} > R_0$ (i.e. interest rates have been dropping).

Differentiation of (5.20) with respect to R_0 reveals that

$$\frac{\partial z_0}{\partial R_0} = 1 - (1 - \lambda)R_{-1}[(1 - \lambda)R_0 + \lambda\delta]^{-2} \gtrless 0;$$

but introducing $\epsilon = \text{Max}[\delta^2, R_0^2]$ and considering all but very high values of λ,

$$\frac{\partial z_0}{\partial R_0} \leqslant 1 - \frac{(1 - \lambda)R_{-1}}{\epsilon} = \frac{1}{\epsilon}[\epsilon - (1 - \lambda)R_{-1}] < 0. \qquad (5.21)$$

(5.21) suggests that with extrapolative expectations, there is a substantial likelihood of a perverse response of the demand for money to the rate of interest. A sudden rise in the rate of interest is taken as an indication of an upward trend, not hitherto (fully) suspected; this implies increased expectation of capital loss.

Keynes's discussion of the issue takes *regressive* expectations, with high inertia, as typical. If expectations of future interest rates are shared by all wealth-holders, the 'liquidity trap' is reached in the limit as λ tends to unity. These shared expectations of future interest rates are held so firmly and so insensitively to any new evidence about actual interest rates, that alterations in the available stocks of money or bonds will have no effect on 'the' interest rate, at all. Keynes was ambiguous on how likely this was. On p. 207 of the *General Theory* he writes 'There is the possibility . . . that, after the rate of interest has fallen to a certain level, liquidity preference may become virtually absolute. . . . But . . . I know of no example of it hitherto', while on p. 309 we find, 'But the most stable, and least easily shifted, element in our contemporary economy had been hitherto, and may prove to be in future, the minimum rate of interest acceptable to the generality of wealth-holders'.

We have been considering Keynes's model of the asset demand for money— what he termed the speculative demand—through the medium of adaptive expectations of various kinds. One question this begs is whether interest rate expectations are formed rationally. Recalling the analysis of rational expectations in the context of the permanent income hypothesis for consumption in chapter 1, we can see that the regressive expectations model (5.13b) will be rational when the interest rate is observed to follow the path

$$R_0 = R_{-1} + v_0 - \lambda v_{-1}, \qquad (5.22)$$

where the v_i are stationary stochastic disturbances with zero mean and no serial correlation. Similarly, (5.13c) is rational when the interest rate path has been

$$\frac{R_0 - R_{-1}}{R_{-1}} = \frac{R_{-1} - R_{-2}}{R_{-2}} + v_0 - \lambda v_{-1}.$$

Unfortunately, the conditions that must hold for either path to be observed are extraordinarily restrictive, and, worse still, distinctly unrealistic. There are two major reasons for this. First, interest rates are endogenous variables determined jointly with other variables (such as output, employment, prices and so on). They do not follow an independent path that can be written down in a single auto-regressive equation, unless—by the merest accident—the precise way in which the endogenous variables depend upon the exogenous variables, and the latter's observed time paths, just happen to imply this. Besides, information about the likely future values of exogenous variables, such as the authorities' predictions of money supply growth or budget deficits, may be available in its own right. If it is, rational expectations cannot be collapsed into a simple 'backward-looking' formula such as (5.13b) or (5.13c). Second, the evidence drawn from securities markets[21] suggests that the prices of stocks and bonds follow a 'martingale',[22] with no autoregressive features at all. The presence of serial correlation would imply an unexploited opportunity for speculative profit. Hence the value of λ in (5.22) should be negligible. This is clearly at variance with the notion of a liquidity trap.

Another difficulty with Keynes's model of the asset demand for money is this. Its claim to explain the demand for *money* is weakened once A1 is generalized. Suppose we introduce a set of bonds, distinguished by date of redemption, in addition to the irredeemable bond. If, as A5 requires, the agent does wish to maximize the nominal return on the portfolio between now and a specified future date, why on earth should he ever hold non-interest bearing money? The irredeemable bond may give a negative net return, if it falls steeply enough in capital value for this to exceed the running interest yield. So may bonds with maturity dates after the portfolio holding horizon. But a bond maturing at, or very close to, this horizon will never give a negative net return between the present date and then. Money is surely a dominated asset.

Once a large enough spread of redeemable bonds has been allowed into the model, the demand for money evaporates. Money can never be as good a refuge for wealth that is fleeing long-term or irredeemable bonds as a bond maturing at the holding period horizon. Even if this period is very short, or uncertain in length, money (narrowly defined) must be dominated by such assets as interest-bearing deposits with near-banks. Only implausibly large transactions costs could prevent this.[23] Keynes's speculative demand for money, then, belongs more to the theory of the term-structure of interest rates than to the theory of money, at least in any narrow definition of money. This holds just as true for other asset-demand theories, to which we shall soon turn, as for Keynes's.

It is not just a wide selection of bonds that an agent's asset choice needs to include along with money and irredeemable bonds. Equities, real estate, and commodities (particularly durables) also belong. Friedman, in his classic reformulation of the Quantity Theory of Money (125), repaired this deficiency. Keynes's omission of these other assets is explained partly by his understandable wish to simplify, but

[21] See, for example, Fama's classic survey (102).

[22] If prices follow a martingale sequence, the present discounted expected value of next period's price, based on all information currently available, should equal the current price. See Samuelson (273).

[23] And the greater these transactions costs, the greater the portfolio holding period the individual will wish to select, if he has any freedom in the matter.

partly too by the circumstances of his day: transactions costs in buying and selling real estate were (and remain) prohibitively heavy in relation to a holding period of less than a year; and with nominal interest rates on short-term alternatives to money of typically 2 per cent per year or less, even the idea that money could be a refuge from bonds expected to depreciate in value was a less unreasonable simplification than it appears later in the twentieth century.

III: 2 *Mean-variance Analysis and the Demand for Money*

One phenomenon that Keynes's analysis cannot explain is the fact that wealth-owners typically hold *both* bonds *and* money. Keynes's agents plump for one or the other; only when z is exactly zero could the possibility of holding both arise. The first serious attempt to explain simultaneous asset-demands for money and other assets was made by Hicks (164). It was extended by Tobin (320), whose analysis we summarize here. Money gives a predictable nominal return, of nothing or (usually) next to nothing. Bonds (and equities) promise a positive interest or dividend yield and usually a capital gain which may be positive or negative. The mean expectation of net return here is usually (though not always) positive; but there is inevitably some variance in that expectation—unless the holding period coincides exactly with the bond's term to maturity, and default is out of the question. Tobin argued that equilibrium in the portfolio could be achieved where the wealth-owner's marginal rate of substitution between mean return (μ) and the standard deviation of return (σ) equalled the gradient of the restraint on portfolio choice. Figure 5.6 illustrates. Variance (σ^2) is the square of standard deviation.

Most wealth-holders were, in Hicks's and Tobin's view, averse to risk, so that σ (depicted horizontally in Figure 5.6) was a bad characteristic of an asset. Mean expected return should be a good one, however; so utility (u) should usually increase north-westwards, as in panel (a). Risk-neutrality is shown in panel (b).

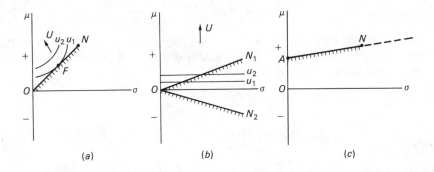

(a)   (b)   (c)

FIG. 5.6. Mean-variance analysis. (a) Risk-aversion, and a linear portfolio restraint. The risky asset's mean return and variance are given by the gradient of ON: N represents a portfolio devoted exclusively to the risky asset; (b) Risk-neutral, horizontal indifference curves. ON_1 shows a positive mean expected return for the risky asset; ON_2, a negative mean expected return; (c) Positive mean expected return on both safe and risky assets. Points on dashed locus right of N may be achieved by issuing claims on the safe asset.

The portfolio choice restraint can be constructed from a knowledge of the mean and variance of expected returns from the assets between which the agent chooses. If money has zero μ and σ, an all-money portfolio is shown by the origin O. In a two-asset model, the alternative of a portfolio with no money is given uniquely by point N, whose position shows the combination of μ and σ obtained when the agent specializes in this single risky asset (call it B). A positive mean return on B is shown in panel (a), and by point N_1 in panel (b). N_2 in panel (b) shows a negative μ for B. Keynes's model can be shown as a special case, in panel (b). The agent chooses the origin when μ or B is negative, and an all-B portfolio when positive. In (a), risk-aversion can explain why both M and B are held. With equilibrium at F, the proportion of the portfolio in money is given by FN/ON. Panel (c) depicts the effects of introducing positive μ for money (so that the vertical intercept for the restraint moves up from O to A). The portfolio locus is AN is both assets must be held in non-negative accounts. If negative holdings of M are allowed, the line AN may be produced. A proportional cost to issuing these liabilities would create a concave kink at N; an increasing cost would make the restraint itself concave to the right of N.

Formally, Tobin's model is as follows:

Retain assumption A1, A2, and A3 from Keynes's model (see p. 158).

Assume A4■: each agent has a quadratic utility function in wealth, $U = a + b_1 W_T - b_2 W_T^2$ with $b_1, b_2 > 0$, and maximizes expected utility for date T, the end of the holding period.[24]

Assume A5■: each agent forms a mean expectation for the net return on asset B (call it $\bar{e}_B$), which equals $\Sigma \pi_j e_{jB}$ (here π_j is the probability of the jth outcome for the end of the holding period, and e_{jB} is the proportionate return on B in that outcome).

From A4■,

$$E(U) = \sum_j (a + b_1 W_{jT} - b_2 W_{jT}^2). \tag{5.23}$$

Now (5.23) may be simplified. Recalling that the probabilities must sum to unity, and defining $\bar{W}_T$ as the mean expected wealth at the end of the holding period, we may express the maximand as

$$E(U) = a + b_1 \bar{W}_T - b_2 \sum_j \pi_j [W_{T_j} - \bar{W}_T + \bar{W}_T]^2$$

$$= a + b_1 \bar{W}_T - b_2 \sum_j \pi_j [(W_{T_j} - \bar{W}_T)^2 + 2\bar{W}_T(\bar{W}_T - \bar{W}_T) + \bar{W}_T^2]. \tag{5.24}$$

Now $\Sigma_j \pi_j (W_{T_j} - \bar{W}_T)$ is zero; and $\Sigma_j \pi_j (W_{T_j} - \bar{W}_T)^2$ may be defined as the variance of wealth at the end of the holding period, symbolically σ^2. So (5.24) reduces to

$$E(U) = a + b_1 \bar{W}_T - b_2 \sigma^2 - b_2 \bar{W}_T^2. \tag{5.25}$$

[24] Assuming that expected utility under uncertainty is the sum of utility in each outcome multiplied by its *a priori* estimated probability of occurrence.

Equation (5.25) is the equation of a circle in the space of $(\bar{W}_T, \sigma)$. It is centred where (U) reaches its unconstrained maximum: from $U' = b_1 - 2b_2 W_T$; this happens where $W_T = b_1/2b_2$. Now (5.25) is to be maximized subject to the portfolio restraint. From A5, this is provided by

$$\left.\begin{aligned}
\bar{W}_T &= W_0[1 + (1 - m)\bar{e}_B], \\
\sigma^2 &= (1 - m)^2 W_0 \sigma_B^2,
\end{aligned}\right\} \tag{5.26}$$

where m is the proportion of the portfolio invested in M, and σ_B is the standard deviation on unit of currency invested in B. Maximizing (5.25) subject to (5.26) yields the following expression

$$1 - m = \frac{\bar{e}_B}{b_2} \frac{b_1 - 2b_2 W_0}{\sigma_B^2 + \bar{e}_B^2 W_0}. \tag{5.27}$$

Equation (5.27) implies that the proportion of the portfolio devoted to money (m) increases with wealth and the variance in the risky asset, and responds ambiguously to the mean return on the risky asset. The elasticity of $1 - m + {}_0\bar{e}_B$ is $\sigma_B^2 - \bar{e}_B^2 W_0$. So a rise in the rate of interest on the risky asset B—provided that it does not engender expectations of a large fall in B's capital value,[25] or increase the perceived riskiness[26] of B—will reduce the demand for money if $\sigma_B/\bar{e}_B > \sqrt{W_0}$. If, on the other hand, the mean expected return on B already exceeds its standard deviation multiplied by the square root of wealth, any further rise in it will induce the portfolio-owner to opt for a safer portfolio in which money has a *larger* share. These two cases are shown in Figure 5.7, panels (a) and (b).

Four possible portfolio restraints are shown: ON_1, ON_2, ON_3, and ON_4, in ascending order for the mean expected return on B. When $\bar{e}_B$ is reasonably small in

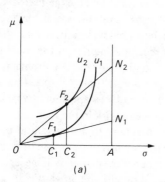
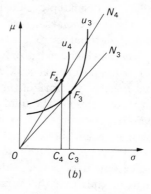

(a) $\qquad\qquad\qquad\qquad$ (b)

FIG. 5.7. The ambiguous effect of a rise in the mean expected return on the risky asset upon the demand for money. (a) A rise in $\bar{e}_B$ lowers the demand for money: substitution effect outweighs utility effect; (b) A rise in $\bar{e}_B$ raises the demand for money: utility effect outweighs substitution effect.

[25] i.e., provided that expectations are not extrapolative.
[26] Defining 'perceived riskiness' by σ_B.

relation to σ_B, as in panel (a), the substitution effect dominates the utility effect: the demand for money falls from $W_0(AC_1/OA)$ to $W_0(AC_2/OA)$. In panel (b), $\bar{e}_B > \sigma_B\sqrt{W_0}$, so that any further rise in $\bar{e}_B$, *ceteris paribus*, increases the demand for money.

Part of the reason for this surprising possibility of a perverse response of the demand for money to the expected yield on the risky asset alternative to it is the way the demands for M and B respond to wealth in Tobin's model. Bonds are always an inferior good. As manipulation of (5.27) shows, it is not just the share of bonds in total wealth $(1 - m)$ that falls as wealth increases: it is the absolute holding of bonds, too. This feature of the quadratic utility function—and the fact that it behaves sensibly only if wealth is less than $b_1/2b_2$, which represents a point of bliss—where satiation occurs—make it unappealing. So is there any alternative to it?

Which alternatives exist depend entirely upon the purposes for which we wish to have them. If it is to legitimate the mean-variance approach to the analysis of the portfolio, we have three options:

(a) to assume that U is quadratic. Then only the mean and the variance of the portfolio's returns will be relevant; in a world with more than one risky asset, the information required from each will be its means and variance, and all the co-variances;

(b) to assume that the probability distribution for the portfolio's returns is fully described by only two parameters—its mean, and variance;[27]

(c) to require small variance and similar mean returns for all risky assets, and a thrice-differentiable utility function in wealth.[28]

In different ways, (b) and (c) are as unappealing as (a). There are very few assets for which the returns distribution is not truncated by the condition that the price will never be negative. Limited liability legislation ensures this for the individual shareholder, and bankruptcy rules imply the same for companies and self-employed persons. Fiscal phenomena, such as capital gains taxation, are liable to turn a symmetrical distribution of pre-tax returns into an asymmetrical one after tax. Bond prices may be bounded above by their redemption price, if the issuer has the right to redeem earlier at will. All this—and the aggregation problem that a weighted average of normal distribution is itself normal only by fluke—make (b) an unattractive option. The third option is a coward's escape route, which works as an approximation only by trivializing the sources of risk in the first place.

A second reason for wanting the utility function to be quadratic is that it permits *aggregation over many risky assets.* Suppose it is our purpose to find where this aggregation is permitted. Stiglitz (311) has proved that it is necessary and sufficient for this that the marginal utility of wealth be isoelastic in a linear function of wealth.

---

[27] The distribution has to be normal for this to be true. Note an awkward problem: in a model with more than one risky asset, normal probability distributions for the returns on each will *not* generally yield a normal distribution for returns on the portfolio as a whole. See Feldstein (104) and Borch (43).

[28] And also a ban on any significant negative holdings. See Stiglitz (311).

$$\frac{\partial U}{\partial W} = [\alpha + \beta W]^\gamma \tag{5.28}$$

is the characteristic of utility functions for which we are seeking. The following utility functions are special cases of (5.28):

(i) The constant elasticity of substitution function,

$$U = b_1 W^{b_2} \tag{5.29}$$

(where the substitution elasticity equals $1/(b_2 + 1)$ and b_1 has the same sign as b_2);

(ii) The Bernoulli,[29] or Cobb–Douglas function,

$$U = a + b \log W; \tag{5.30}$$

(iii) The negative exponential[30]

$$U = a - b_1 e^{-b_2 W}; \tag{5.31}$$

and (iv) The quadratic, assumed in A4■.

These four are not exhaustive, but they do include the most widely-employed functions for utility in wealth.

III: 3 *State-preference Theory and the Demand for Money*

The last model of the demand for money is due to Arrow (9). This is an important generalization of Tobin's work. Basic assumptions (some of them relaxable) are:

(A1) agents choose between n assets, one of which, M, is 'safe', with a known return,

(A2) no one may borrow: no asset may be held in negative amounts;

(A3) transactions costs are negligible;

(A4) each agent knows the returns $R_{i\theta}$ on each asset i that will materialize in each 'state of the world' θ;

(A5) each agent attempts to maximize expected utility, which is given by the utility from wealth in each state of the world multiplied by the probability (confidently known) of its occurrence.

Note that A2 and A3 are the same as in Keynes's model; A1 is a straightforward extension of Tobin's basic model; A5 is the now familiar expected utility hypothesis; and only A4 calls for comment. As will be recalled from chapter 2, the number of states of the world is in principle limitless. In fact, θ may be a continuous or a discrete variable. Figure 5.8 shows the simplest case, where there are just two states of the world, θ_1 and θ_2. W_{Ti} is the wealth that materializes at date T (the end of the holding period) in state i. Five assets are shown in Figure 5.8. M, the safe asset, brings a guaranteed gross return of A if all wealth is invested in it. Point A lies upon the 'certainty line' (the ray from origin λ, of unit gradient).

---

[29] After Bernoulli's suggested solution to the St. Petersburg Paradox. Here, $b > 0$.
[30] Here, $b_1, b_2 > 0$.

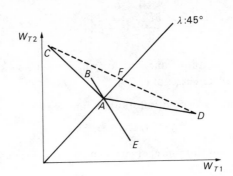

FIG. 5.8. Asset yields in the state-preference theoretic model of portfolio choice.

B, C, D, and *E* also represent portfolio specialization—in assets 2, 3, 4, and 5. Asset 5 does respectably in θ_1 but atrociously in θ_2. Asset 4, specialization in which produces higher returns in *both* states, must dominate asset 5. A linear combination of assets 3 and 4, illustrated by the dotted line from *C* to *D*, represents an efficiency locus: in Figure 5.9, both *M* and asset 2 will be dominated, like 5, but this time by some combination of 3 and 4. Point *F* can be achieved by placing *CF/CD* of initial wealth W_0 into 3 and the remainder into 4.

The general solution to the Arrow model, with θ discrete, is derived from maximizing

$$\sum_{\theta} \pi_{\theta} U(W_{\theta})$$

subject to

$$W_{\theta} = W_0 \left[R_M \left(1 - \sum_{i=2}^{n} s_i \right) + \sum_{i=2}^{n} s_i (1 + R_{i\theta}) \right],$$

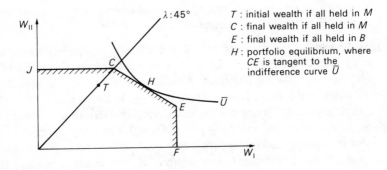

FIG. 5.9. Portfolio optimization in state-preference theory. *T*: initial wealth if all held in *M*; *C*: final wealth if all held in *M*; *E*: final wealth if all held in *B*; *H*: portfolio equilibrium, where *CE* is tangent to the indifference curve $\bar{U}$.

where s_i is asset i's share in the portfolio (money labelled as asset 1).[31] This gives n first-order conditions

$$E[U'(R_{i\theta} - R_M)] = 0, \qquad (5.32)$$

which state that the expected marginal utility of each asset is equalized. Let us consider a simple example, using the various utility functions satisfying the aggregability condition (5.28). Suppose there is only one risky asset, B; where M_0 and B_0 are initial holdings of the two asset, suppose the portfolio returns (all known) will be in each of two states θ_I and θ_{II}:

	State I	State II
M:	$M_0(1 + R_M)$	$M_0(1 + R_M)$
B:	$B_0(1 + R_M + G)$	$B_0(1 + R_M - L)$

Let π be the probability of State I, and m (as before) measure the fraction of present wealth, W, invested in M. Under A2, $1 \geqslant m \geqslant 0$. Figure 5.9 illustrates the portfolio choice frontier $F E C J$. The horizontal and vertical facets of the frontier will be straightened out to have the same gradient as CE if A2 is relaxed to allow an unconstrained m.[32] Table 5.1 presents the solutions for $1 - m$ under each utility function, in terms of: the relative probabilities of occurrence for the two states, π and $1 - \pi$; the 'safe' return on money, R_M; the return on B in the (good) state, θ_I, which is $R_M + G$; and B's yield in θ_{II}, $R_M - L$. 'G' may be thought of as gain, and 'L' loss. It also shows how m varies with initial wealth, R_M, G, L, π, and two important parameters that capture the degree of risk-aversion ($1/(b_2 + 1)$ for the constant elasticity of substitution (CES) function (5.29), and b_2 for the negative exponential (5.31). The symbol $h \equiv \pi G/(1 - \pi)L$ is introduced to simplify the results. It is worth seeing that if $h > 1$ a risk-neutral person will hold all B (and all M if $h < 1$). Therefore, h corresponds to Keynes's z_0, under risk-neutrality.

The results are illuminating, and can in several cases be generalized. Portfolio allocation between M and B displays homotheticity—m is independent of W_0 in the CES and Bernoulli cases. In Arrow's terms, these two functions (and these alone) display constant relative risk-aversion (RRA): RRA is defined as $U''W/U'$; this turns out to be $1 - b_2$ and 1, in these two cases. Where they differ is in the *degree* of risk aversion: for the Bernoulli is in fact the special case of the CES where $b_2 = 0$. Figure 5.10 illustrates these two functions in panels (a), (b), (c), and (d). The NE has *increasing* RRA, which explains why a rise in wealth raises the proportion of the portfolio held in money. But another of Arrow's measures, absolute risk aversion (ARA) is constant for the NE. ARA is defined as $-U''/U$, which is simply b_2 in the case of the NE. In the quadratic case, both ARA and RRA increase with wealth: they are respectively $[(b_1/2b_2) - W]^{-1}$ and $[b_1/(2b_2W) - 1]^{-1}$.[33] Arrow's

---

[31] Other symbols have their usual meanings.

[32] Equilibrium southeast of E would (for example) call for $m < 0$.

[33] The second-order condition $U' > 0 > U''$ confines attention to $W < b_1/2b_2$, so that both these expressions are positive.

Table 5.1 *Effects of various parameter changes upon the demand for money, with different utility functions*

	Utility function			
	CES	Bernoulli/ Cobb–Douglas	Quadratic	Negative exponential (NE)
Equation for U	$b_1 W^{b_2}$	$a + b \log W$	$a + b_1 W - b_2 W^2$	$a - b_1 e^{-b_2 W}$
Solution for $1 - m$: proportion of wealth placed as money	$\dfrac{(h^{1/(b_2+1)} - 1)(1 - R_M)}{Lh^{1/(b_2+1)} + G}$	$(h-1)\dfrac{1-\pi}{G}(1+x)$	$\dfrac{(h-1)\dfrac{1-\pi}{G}\left[\dfrac{b_1}{2b_2 W_0} - 1 - R_M\right]}{\pi G^2 + (1-\pi)L^2}$	$\dfrac{\log h}{(L+G)b_2 W_0}$
Effect on m of increase in:				
W_0	0	0	>0	>0
R_M	<0	<0	>0	0
G	?	<0	?	?
L	>0	>0	>0	>0
π	<0	<0	<0	<0
(CES only) $1/(b_2 + 1)$	<0			
(NE only) b_2				>0

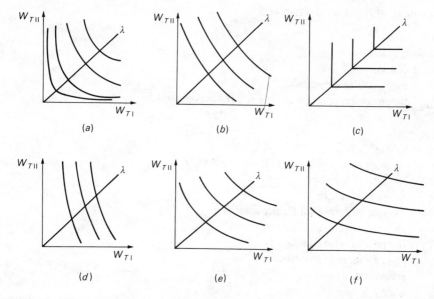

FIG. 5.10. The implications of different utility functions and probabilities for preferences under uncertainty. (a) The Bernoulli with $\pi \approx \frac{1}{2}$; (b) The CES with $b_2 \approx \frac{1}{2}$ and $\pi \approx \frac{1}{2}$; (c) The CES with $b_2 = -\infty$; (d) The CES with $b \approx \frac{1}{2}$ and $\pi \approx 0.8$; (e) The NE with $\pi \approx \frac{1}{2}$; (f) The NE with $\pi \approx 0.2$.

central result is a generalization of these findings:[34] he proves that the elasticity of demand for money to wealth is not less than unity if and only if RRA increases with wealth, and that the demand for the risky asset cannot decline with a rise in wealth unless there is increasing ARA.

The other parameter shifts considered in Table 5.1 are simpler to see. An increase in R_M leads to a parallel displacement north-eastwards in CE in Figure 5.9. With the constant RRA utility functions (CES and Bernoulli), the new point of tangency lies closer to the B-specialization cone (and further from λ) than before, because of the homotheticity property. The quadratic, with its violently increasing risk-aversion as (terminal) wealth rises, displays a shift in the equilibrium towards λ, which implies an increase in holdings of M. A rise in L means that point E is lowered vertically. This leads to a rise in the holding of money in every case. Strangely, however, a rise in GG (in the diagram, a rightward movement of point E) has ambiguous effects with the quadratic and the NE, and also with the CES if b_2 is low enough. A rise in the probability of State I steepens the indifference curves' gradients, as shown in the difference between panels (b) and (d) of Figure 5.1.

---

[34] See Arrow (9).

Summary of Notation in Chapter 5

B	bonds
C	transactions costs
c	coupon
E	expectations operator
$\bar{e}_B$	the mean expectation for the net return on asset B
G	gain
L	loss
M	money
m	the proportion of a portfolio invested in M
$\hat{P}$	the rate of inflation
R	the rate of return
R_R	the rate of return on a risky asset A
R_M	the rate of return on money
R_B	the rate of return on bonds
s_i	asset i's share in the portfolio
T	transactions costs
U	utility
W	wealth
w	the instalments of Y received
x	the number of transactions involving B
Y	income
θ	state of the world
λ	the coefficient of inertia in expectations
μ	mean return
π_j	the probability of the jth outcome for the end of the holding period
σ	the standard deviation of return

Chapter 6

Banks and the Supply of Money

The last chapter investigated the demand for money. We turn now to its supply. After a brief introduction to the subject (section I), the chapter examines the theory of banks (section II). A 'Standard Banking' Model is set up (II: 1) and its assumptions are then relaxed (II: 2). Having considered the behaviour of banks, we then proceed to the determination of the money supply (section III).

I: Introduction

Money consists of two kinds of asset owned and held by economic agents. These are notes and coins on one hand, and bank deposits on the other. The ratio of the latter to the former has risen sharply in most countries in the nineteenth and twentieth centuries, with the spread of banking habits. The definition of the money supply is difficult, because there are now so many sorts of bank deposits.

There are deposits against which cheques may be drawn at will (UK: 'current accounts': US: 'demand deposits' or 'checking deposits'), and also those against which cheques may not necessarily be drawn without notice (UK: 'deposit accounts'; US: 'time-deposits'). The former only are included in narrow definitions of the money supply (M1); both appear in broader ones (e.g., M2 and M3). Other ambiguities relate to foreign currency deposits, deposits by foreigners, deposits by public authorities and other public agents, such as nationalized industries, cheques 'in transit' awaiting clearance, and above all, the width of the definition of 'bank'.

Banks were at one stage offices where valuables might be consigned for safe-keeping. The banker charged a handling fee, related (presumably) to storage space and time, not unlike the lessor of an airport luggage locker. The demand for this kind of primitive banking service varied, one imagines, with the probability of theft, the costs of carriage, and the transactions technology and social norms of everyday life, which dictated the duration and extent of stock-holdings with which banks were concerned.

There must have been one day when a bank's owner saw that the chance of all his depositors calling for their deposits together was low enough, and the return from lending out some of these deposits high enough, to justify a reserve of less than 100 per cent. That day a bank in the modern sense was born. Banks create money, to the extent that deposits exceed reserves. This had certainly happened in classical Roman times.[1]

---

[1] Excavations at Herculeum and Pompeii have revealed banks where in the first century AD, loans seemed to bear an appreciable ratio to deposits.

II: The Standard Banking Model

II: 1 *The Model Itself*

Two ways of modelling the economic behaviour of a bank present themselves. One is to focus attention on the unknown variables: for instance, the probability of a borrower's default; the distribution of probabilities of withdrawal and deposit at different dates in different amounts by different depositors; the probability of being able to alter total lending by various amounts quickly, in case of need; the probability of distribution for returns in investing in equity. The other is to de-emphasize the stochastic character of the bank's environment, and treat it instead as a business that tries to optimize some objective function in which the unknown plays a subordinate role. There are arguments for and against each approach; of course, they may be combined in some respects. We shall now examine the second approach in detail. It gives us a surprisingly clear picture of what may determine the bank's ratio of reserves to deposits, its lending and deposit interest rates, and the scale of its branches. What we may term the Standard Banking Model can be set up with the following assumptions:

(A1) profit-maximization;
(A2) either impotence of unwillingness to practise price discrimination in loans or deposits;
(A3) reserves (R), deposits (D) and loans (L) are each homogeneous;
(A4) banking costs (C) are increasing in the number of branches (X) and in L, and decreasing in R. Branch costs are simply γX;
(A5) D are increasing in the rate of interest paid to depositors (δ), and in X, and are non-decreasing in R;
(A6) L are non-decreasing in X and R, and decreasing in the rate of interest charged to borrowers (λ);
(A7) R bears interest at rate $\beta \geqslant 0$;
(A8) government does not constrain the banks in any respect.

We may now form the bank's objective function, profits (given A1). The fact that bank's utility is linear in profits makes it neutral to risk. The profit function is:

$$\pi = L\lambda(L, R, X) - D\delta(D, R, X) + \beta R - C(L, R) - \gamma X, \qquad (6.1)$$

which may be maximized with respect to parameters L, R, X, and D subject to the balance sheet condition $L + R - D = 0$. From A6, $\lambda_1 \leqslant 0, \lambda_2 \geqslant 0, \lambda_3 \geqslant 0$; A5 gives us $\delta_1 \geqslant 0, \delta_2 \leqslant 0, \delta_3 \leqslant 0$ while A4 implies $C_1 > 0 > C_2$.[2]

Before proceeding to derive results, we may note certain features of the analysis. The assumptions on λ_1 and δ_1 permit us to consider monopoly, determinate-oligopoly and competition in parallel. In competitive conditions λ and δ will be parametric to the bank itself; otherwise, not. The λ_2 and δ_2 terms are introduced to allow for the fact that knowledge of a high reserve ratio may attract both lenders

---

[2] x_i refers to the partial derivative of x with respect to its ith argument.

and borrowers to the bank: the chances of delay in securing withdrawals for depositors, and in renegotiating loans for borrowers, will both vary negatively with R. A high value for X, whatever its cost to the bank, should at least entice large custom, because of the time and trouble saved for the bank's users. C_1 is positive to capture the sheer effect of scale on the wage bill and rent payments that the bank incurs; it also reflects the peculiar cost of processing loan-applications, of which sight may be lost given the bland, simplifying and unreasonable assumption A3. High reserves have a negative effect on the bank's costs: this is seen most clearly when there are transactions costs that the bank must face in recalling loans.[3] γ is clearly positive, given the unmistakable indivisibilities in cash-flow management as well as bank service provision. For simplicity, branch costs are modelled linearly.

The first-order conditions for a maximum for π lead to the following results:[4]

$$\frac{\text{loan rate}}{\text{deposit rate}} \equiv \frac{\lambda}{\delta} = \frac{1 + \delta_1^*}{1 + \lambda_1^* - (C_1/\lambda)}. \tag{6.2}$$

Here, x_i^* is defined as the elasticity of x with respect to its argument. Furthermore,

$$\frac{\text{reserves}}{\text{deposits}} \equiv \frac{R}{D} = \frac{\lambda_2^* - \delta_2^* \dfrac{\delta}{\lambda}}{\lambda_2^* - \dfrac{\beta - C_2}{\lambda} + \dfrac{\delta}{\lambda}(1 + \delta_1^*)} \tag{6.3}$$

and the number of branches (if, by happy accident, the RHS of (6.4) is an integer) is

$$X = \frac{L\lambda}{\gamma} \left\{ \lambda_3^* - \frac{\dfrac{\delta}{x}}{1 - \dfrac{R}{D}} \delta_3^* \right\}. \tag{6.4}$$

Only under very strict conditions will (6.2), (6.3), and (6.4) amount to exact solutions for the LHS variables; if λ and δ are log-linear, and the ratios of β, C_1, and C_2 to λ can be treated as parametric, we shall have found precise solutions. Otherwise, there will generally be a problem of endogeneity on the rhs of one (or more) equation.[5]

Even with this qualification, which can be made about most formulae in economics, (6.2)–(6.4) give plentiful insights. Take an example: if $\delta_1^* = + 1/9$, $\delta_2^* = -\lambda_2^* = -1/30$, $\lambda_1^* = -1/6$, and the ratios of β, C_1 and C_2 to λ were $1/10$, $1/6$,

[3] These transactions costs may proxy the damage done to the firm's present value by discouraging future borrowers, as well as the more direct costs of frequent placings and recalls of loans.

[4] Assuming that the second-order conditions are met, and that absurdities (such as negative reserves or branches) are ruled out.

[5] (6.3) and (6.4) build, of course, on the 'solution' for λ/δ, and (6.4) on that for R/D.

and $-1/18$, we should find that the deposit rate was 26 per cent below the rate that the bank charged on loans, and that, of its deposits, some 9 per cent were allocated to reserves and the rest to loans. Further numerical assumptions would enable us to solve for the number of branches the bank had in terms of its gross earnings from loans. Generalizing, it appears that the gap between the lending and borrowing rates depends chiefly upon the extent to which the bank may act as a rate-setter: δ_1^* is the reciprocal of the elasticity of supply for deposits to the deposit interest rate (δ_1^* is zero in perfect competition, otherwise positive), and λ_1^* that of the demand elasticity for loans to λ (negative apart from perfect competition, where λ_1^* will again be zero). Figure 6.1 illustrates this, in a simplified case where reserves and banking costs are ignored. If $R = 0$, $L = D$; if banking costs are negligible, the π function (6.1) shrivels up to

$$\pi = L\lambda(L) - L\delta(L), \tag{6.5}$$

and a maximum entails the equalization of marginal revenue (here $= \lambda[1 + \lambda_1^*]$) with marginal cost ($= \delta(1 + \delta_1^*)$), with the latter cutting from beneath. The dotted curves in Figure 6.1 illustrate these marginal curves, which may be derived from the

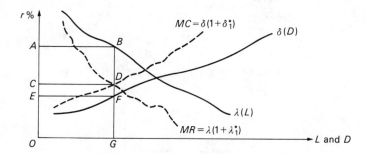

FIG. 6.1. The determination of lending and borrowing rates with monopoly and monopsony power for the bank

'average' curves for λ and δ. λ lies above MR, since the granting of additional loans calls for a cut in the loan rate, not just for the additional borrowers but for everyone else, too. Similarly, attracting additional deposits entails a rise in δ, which is paid (given A2) to all depositors alike. In Figure 6.1, the equilibrium volume of banking activity is given by OG. The lending rate will be OA, the deposit rate OE; and the bank will earn profits attributable to its monopoly position ($ABDC$) and its monopsony power ($CDFE$). The area beneath λ but above line AB might be taken to indicate the surplus of the bank's borrowers, while rent or surplus for depositors is

$$OE - \int_0^G \delta(D)\mathrm{d}D.$$

Extensions can be made to other market forms. Oligopoly (under Cournot's assumptions) is an interesting case. We assume now that there are n banks. Let δ and λ be linear in the total volume of loans, L^*; let each of the banks treat its rivals' outputs as parametric; and reintroduce bank costs, which must be a uniform multiple $\gamma L_i (\gamma \geq 0)$ of L_i, where L_i = bank i's volume of loans. Bank i's profit function therefore is:

$$\pi_i = L_i \frac{\left[a_0 - L_i - \sum_{j \neq i}^{n} L_j \right]}{b_0} - L_i \frac{\left[a_i - L_i - \sum_{j \neq i}^{n} L_j \right]}{b_1} - \gamma L_i. \qquad (6.6)$$

(6.6) is now maximized with respect to L_i, with zero 'conjectural variation'[6] by i for L_j (so that $\partial L_j / \partial L_i = 0$). In (6.6), $\lambda = (a_0 - L^*)/b_0$ and $\delta = (a_1 - L^*)/b_1$. The solution for $\lambda - \delta$ is straightforward: from the first-order condition for (6.6), and a symmetry condition on banks,

$$\lambda - \delta = \frac{a_0/b_0 - a_1/b_1 + \delta n}{n + 1}, \qquad (6.7)$$

which implies that the interest-rate gap is a linear function of the number of banks. In the limit as $n \to \infty$ the competitive break-even result is reached: $\lambda - \delta \to \gamma$. This result also emerges from (6.2), since competition eliminates δ_1^* and λ_1^*, so that

$$\frac{\lambda}{\delta} \to \frac{1}{1 - \dfrac{C_1}{\lambda}}, \text{ i.e. } \lambda \to \delta + C_1,$$

where C_1, the marginal cost of loans, corresponds with γ in (6.6) and (6.7). One familiar difficulty appears, however: the individual bank's output is indeterminate, if at a negligible volume, in Cournot's convergence to competition; while in the standard theory of the competitive firm, marginal cost is not parametric: the bank has to be assumed to adjust L so that $C_1 = \lambda - \delta$, with the second-order condition further requiring that $\partial^2 C / \partial L^2 \equiv C_{11} > 0$. In contrast, the monopoly-or-monopsony bank has a unique volume of deposits and loans, if the MR and MC curves in Figure 6.1 intersect only once, and (in the case of the more complex equation (6.1)) π are concave in R and X as well as L in the neighbourhood of equilibrium.

Results (6.2), (6.3) and (6.4) may also be generalized beyond the rather uncomfortable assumptions of parametric ratios of β and the C_i to λ. At least when $\beta = \gamma = 0$, (6.2) becomes

$$\frac{\lambda}{\delta} = \frac{(1 + \delta_1^*)(A + B)}{(1 + \lambda_1^* - C_1^*)(B + C_2^*) + C_1^*(C_2^* + \lambda_2^*)} \qquad (6.8)$$

where $A = C_2 - C_1^*$ and $B = 1 + \delta_1^* + \delta_2^*$; while

$$\frac{R}{D} = \frac{B + C_2^*}{(1 + \delta_1^*) + (\lambda/\delta)(C_2^* + \lambda_2^*)}. \qquad (6.9)$$

[6] See chapter 2, section IV.

Taking our previous values as an example, and assuming $C_1^* = 1/2$ and $C_2^* = 0$, we derive $\lambda/\delta \simeq 1.63$ and $R/D \simeq 7.45$. The values of λ/δ obtained from (6.2) or (6.8) are perhaps rather likelier in an oligopolistic framework than (6.7): there are a number of factors at work in the banking industry which make collusion rather easier to operate. Entry costs are very high: indivisibilities in cash-flow management with some fixed transactions costs are one reason,[7] the huge incentive to inertia facing the banks' customers (especially when they have acquired a good credit standing with their bank), another. A new bank will be a magnet to high-risk borrowers; this will force it into abnormally high credit-appraisal costs. A second factor making for easier collusion is the important point that an *existing* bank which tries to expand at its rivals' expense is also likely to attract high-cost high-risk business on the loan side. A third is the reliance governments are inclined to place upon quantitative restrictions on banks' lending or deposit-taking.[8] This can help to fossilize market shares, and lead banks to *expect* fossilized market shares. In these circumstances, perceptions of δ_1^*, and λ_1^*, will come close to their total-industry values, and not the much higher elasticity values which a bank would expect under zero conjectural variation.[9] Finally, interest rates (at least for depositors) are so well publicized that there is vanishingly little opportunity for a bank to expand deposits by raising δ secretly. On the other hand, a banking system at one date may be more competitive than others or the same system at another date; in some aspects, such as use made of the wholesale money markets, banks are highly competitive; and the uniformity of δ and (minimum levels of) λ across banks could be evidence of perfect competition no less than collusive oligopoly!

Before looking at the uncertainties of the environment in which banks operate, we should look briefly at some implications of relaxing the assumptions of the Standard Banking Model.

II: 2 *Relaxing the Assumptions of the Standard Banking Model*

A1 may be repealed in many directions. A sales-maximizing bank would, if sales meant λL and no profit or other constraint prevented this, aim at zero marginal revenue: L would be pitched where $\lambda_1^* = -1$. This would certainly imply higher L and lower λ than under A1. Presumably, R and X would have to be removed as arguments of λ, or else constrained, e.g. to extreme levels, because otherwise with λ_2 and $\lambda_3 > 0$ the bank will only see an incentive to expand R and X without limit. If, for instance, D is constrained, and X suppressed, the sales-maximizing bank will set L and R where $1 + \lambda_1^* + \lambda_2^* = 0$.

A richer set of results emerges if the bank maximizes a multi-argument utility function. Consider

---

[7] See Edgeworth's analysis of banking (97) and the role played there by scale economies.

[8] This relaxes A8. British governments applied almost continuous limits on banks' lending from 1960 to 1971, and a progressive tax on the growth of interest-bearing deposits at various times since November 1973 (the 'corset').

[9] If a bank's managers think it can expand loans and deposits without stimulating its competitors to alter the scale of their banking activity, it must expect δ_1^* and λ_1^* to be closer to zero (and the reciprocals larger in absolute value) than if they believe market shares to be fixed.

$$U = U(\pi, L\lambda) \qquad (6.10)$$

maximized under risk-neutrality (or equivalently, with U linear),[10] with π and $L\lambda$ expressed as in (6.1).[11] In this case, (6.2) becomes

$$\frac{\lambda}{\delta} = \frac{1 + \delta_1^*}{(1 + \lambda_1^*)E - \dfrac{C_1}{\lambda}}, \qquad (6.11)$$

where η is the elasticity of the bank's utility to total sales, or loan interest receipts, λL and $E = 1 + (\pi/L\lambda)\{\eta/(1 + \eta)\}$. (6.3) changes to

$$\frac{R}{D} = \frac{\lambda_2^* - \dfrac{\delta}{\lambda}\delta_2^*}{\lambda_2^* E + \dfrac{\delta}{\lambda}(1 + \delta_1^*) - \dfrac{\beta - C_2}{\lambda}}. \qquad (6.12)$$

The greater the value of η, the higher the emphasis on sales as an objective, the higher the value of E; and a higher value of E must imply a lower rate of λ to δ, and very probably also a lower R/D.

Other ways of relaxing A1 allow for risk-aversion (which is captured most easily by having utility increasing but concave in π and independent of the other variables) and for a positive dependence of utility on reserves. We shall return to the first below: the major implication of introducing the latter is an unsurprising rise in the optimal reserve ratio.

The introduction of discrimination in loans and/or deposits[12] follows from the repeal of assumption A2. In terms of Figure 6.1, the excess of MC over δ and the shortfall of MR below λ must now (one of these, at least) decline. Figure 6.2 depicts perfect discrimination in both markets, under profit maximization. The bank usurps all the 'surplus' of borrowers and lenders. Its total profits (ignoring bank costs reserves and the like, as in Figure 6.1) are reserved by the sum of the two striped areas: diagonally striped, to represent the excess of actual loan interest receipts

$$\int_0^c \lambda(L)\mathrm{d}L$$

over the volume of loans OL multiplied by the marginal loan rate, OA; and the horizontally striped, to indicate the transfer from depositors' surplus that emerges from perfect discrimination in the rates paid to depositors. As usual, discrimination raises the discriminator's output and profits. The important point here is that banks (unlike most other 'producers') *do* practise discrimination regularly between different classes of borrowers, and on different sizes of loan; and there is also some discrimination in rates paid to depositors of large sums. There are excellent reasons why they should be expected to, as we shall see later.

[10] Under the expected utility hypothesis. See (238) and Bacharach (18).
[11] Monti (222) uses a utility function $U = U(\pi, D)$ with not dissimilar results.
[12] See Shull (195) for an interesting analysis of discrimination by banks.

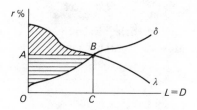

FIG. 6.2 Perfect loan and deposit discrimination by a monopoly bank.

A3 is a helpful but unreasonable assumption. Banks may hold R in several forms: balances at a central bank, cash reserves of their own (US: 'vault cash'; UK: 'till money'); and holdings of short-term government debt are examples of assets often included within governments' statutory minima for reserves.[13] Loans vary not merely in rate but duration, quality of collateral, purpose, and estimate of riskiness. Usually between 3/4 and 9/10 of L are lent to corporations, with the household sector a substantial net creditor at banks. In addition to formal loans and advances, banks have other non-reserve assets: holdings of medium-term and long-term government debt, and holdings of equity stock, together forming the largest part. Equity holdings account for a very substantial part of German banks' non-reserve assets. Deposits are characterized everywhere by an important distinction between demand- and time-deposits. The current (or demand) deposits usually bear no interest,[14] which is reserved for time-deposits. To compensate for their lack of interest, current (demand) deposits, unlike time-deposits, have unconditional and immediate encashability. The long inflationary boom after 1945 slowly raised time-deposit interest rates, which are, of course, nominal; the rate of interest gap between demand and time-deposits grew from 2 per cent per year or less to over 10 per cent in the three decades after 1950. Banks reacted by starting to pay implicit interest on demand deposits in the form of bank-charges remission, if the average or minimum balance were greater than a certain modest figure, and then, eventually, by the first moves towards explicit interest. If A3 is repealed to formalize recognition of all these points, it will still remain true[15] that each type of asset or liability will be taken to the point where the bank's perceptions of marginal receipts and marginal cost are equal.

Assumptions A4, A5, A6, and A7 contain little controversial, except perhaps the linearity of bank-branch costs, γ. This can be modified without damage: if $C = C(L, R, X)$ then (6.4) merely becomes

---

[13] In the UK before September 1971, the first two of these had to sum to not less than 8 per cent of D (the 'cash ratio'); and these two plus treasury bills and loans at call or short notice to discount houses, not less than 28 per cent of D (the 'liquidity ratio'). After 1971, banks had to hold not less than 1/8 of D in short-term government debt, balances at the Bank of England, loans at call or short notice to discount houses, and (not more than 3/200 of D first-class commercial bills. These regulations were abolished in 1981.

[14] Since 1979, interest has been payable for the first time in the US on demand deposits.

[15] Assuming that the other assumptions of the Standard Banking model holds.

$$X = \frac{L\lambda}{C_3} \left\{ \lambda_3^* - \frac{\dfrac{\delta}{\lambda}\delta_3^*}{1 - R/D} \right\} \tag{6.13}$$

This needs the ratio of C_3 to λ to be parametric before X is soluble in terms of exogenous variables. But there is one major omission: the subdivision of transactions costs (in A4) into a generalized function where their significance is only implicit. In a path-breaking study of the portfolio behaviour of US banks subject to different sorts of transactions costs over their spectra of assets and liabilities, Hester and Pierce (160) find that a once-and-for-all arrival of new deposits leads to a sudden jump in R, which takes two months to return to equilibrium. In the meantime, banks add to their holdings of rather liquid non-reserve assets, continuing to do so for a further three or four months. Eventually loans pick up, returning to their equilibrium proportion of total assets some six months or more after arrival of the new deposits. These authors also found a pattern of lags similar but less easily discerned, in another model where the banks were treated as forecasting deposits adaptively with experience. The Hester and Pierce work shows the size and broad regularity of the deviation from equilibrium that (6.13) and more disaggregated portfolio ratios take.[16]

The most disagreeable of our Standard Model's assumptions is A8. Governments do constrain banks' behaviour in numerous ways. It usually begins with an attempt to formalize control over total D by placing limits on the ratio R/D. Banks before this had previously chosen their own value of this ratio, much on the lines of the Standard Model. But government regulation through its central bank would always take the form of prescribing minima; banks could optimize by holding a higher ratio if they wished.

Actual ratios of R to D usually exceed the statutory minima by between 1/2 per cent and 2 per cent of D: this is certainly true of the UK's 'eligible reserve assets' ratio after September 1971, and the two cash and liquidity ratios in force before that. The banks' desire for a cushion of supererogatory reserves is partly explained by a combination of differential transactions costs and expectations of policy change: there is always some chance (and sometimes a definitely quantifiable probability) that the central bank will call for Special Deposits;[17] this is equivalent to raising the statutory ratio; and since loans take time to expire, and may only be reduced quickly at the risk of provoking customer defection and bankruptcy, it is wise for the banks to hold this cushion of 'second reserves'. Two other factors help to explain the level of and changes in the cushion: the demand for banks' credit (a sudden fall in which will expand the cushion), and

---

[16] The theory of the dynamic portfolio behaviour of banks owes much to Cohen and Hammer (64). See also Fama (348).

[17] These are compulsory balances deposited with the central bank, which are ineligible as reserve assets.

the vector of relative yields the bank sees on assets: an increase in β, the yield on R (or some of its components)[18] will also tend to raise it.[19]

We now proceed to examine the significance of uncertainty for banks. As with individuals and companies, the analysis of choice under uncertainty calls for three types of information: on the expected probabilities of the uncertain variable or event; on how different outcomes may affect quantifiable characteristics of aggregates of direct concern, such as wealth; and on attitudes to such characteristics. The simplest approach is to start with risk-neutrality. This confines attention to the mean expectation of uncertain variables. Even here, there is much to be said.

The most direct type of uncertainty confronting a banker concerns the good faith, ability, and luck of prospective borrowers. Prospective borrowers are not a random sample of the population: their set contains higher than average proportions of the mendacious, the feckless, and the unlucky. The first question to strike the banker when confronted with a loan application is, 'Why can't he finance his expenditures from some other source?' Law Number One of credit markets is 'You can always get an overdraft if you prove you don't need it'. Proof of collateral is proof that the individual could have provided his own finance, if necessary; all the bank does is to save him some transactions costs, and impose fees of its own for doing so.

It might be thought that the prospective borrower without acceptable collateral could, none the less, obtain funds freely, but at a higher rate than the borrower with it. This is questionable, for two major reasons. First, the higher the interest rate levied by the lender, the greater the probability that the borrower will go bankrupt. There is a legal obligation upon corporations to cease trading as soon as interest charges exceed operating surplus. In probabilistic terms, there is an efficiency interest rate for each borrower, above which the increased expectation of bankruptcy and consequent loss for the bank of much of its initial investment, overtakes the increase in expected interest received. The second reason is the difficulty of disentangling the banker's estimate of credit worthiness from the applicant's offer of interest rate. By revealing his preparedness to borrow at a high rate, the applicant signals his diffidence in his own credit-rating. He may also, unwittingly, start the banker thinking that the loan application may already have been refused by others. In many other markets where the quality of the commodity or service is not in dispute, an increase in price may be relied upon to call forth an increase in provision. In credit markets this is not necessarily so.[20] The supply of credit to a prospective borrower may become completely inelastic beyond some point, and even start to bend backward. These two arguments for expecting credit markets to behave pathologically are clear enough not to need formal demonstration; but they are important. They do not depend upon risk-aversion: that would only make them apply with greater force.

[18] R is, of course, heterogeneous in most banking systems; but most definitions contain at least one element on which interest is paid.

[19] Teigen (316) has estimated the elasticity of *supply* of bank deposits as a whole, and components of banks' liabilities, to different interest rates in the US. Teigen confirms that R/D will rise following a rise in β relative to λ.

[20] Asymmetric information is the central issue here. See Akerlof (1).

Another direct implication of risk and uncertainty for banking is visible when the preceding two arguments are applied in reverse. Banks are not *net* lenders; they are financial intermediaries, whose loans are governed by what they can borrow. In the Standard Banking Model it was assumed (A5) that D was increasing in δ. Our previous arguments suggest that this may become questionable, at least for small unknown banks at high values of δ. The putative depositor may start to doubt the bank's reliability if, as he sees it, it has to offer a higher deposit interest rate than its competitors. The esteem in which the bank is held by its actual and prospective depositors is an absolute precondition of continued operation by the bank. If once this fails, a run on the bank will start; the failure of the bank will then prove a self-justifying prophesy, unless the bank can liquidate its loans fast enough or borrow enough from other sources and thereby meet the falls in D fully in cash. This is the case for including R as an argument of δ in (6.1).[21]

This is one of several reasons for expecting banks to experience scale economies.[22] The bigger the bank, the more unthinkable its collapse, the more likely it would be for the central bank to intervene to prevent it. Furthermore, diversification in loans is likely to go with size; and banks that diversify their loans widely to different firms in different industries will have an overall variance of λL vastly less than the sum of variances on each $\lambda_j L_j$ where j indexes borrowers, because of the low covariance. Yet another argument relates to the variance of depositors' withdrawals, which should increase less than in proportion to the volume of deposits—assuming that the volume of deposits is approximately a multiple of the number of accounts. This should mean that R/D can vary negatively with the size of D, on the analogy of Baumol's celebrated square-root[23] law for optimal inventories. Since β will typically be much less than λ, the ratio of π to D will vary positively with D, at least over a range. This, coupled with other transactions-cost arguments,[24] forms the basis for thinking that the banking system tends to evolve towards increasing concentration, unless checked by deliberate government policy. These scale-economy arguments do not depend upon risk-aversion among depositors, but their significance may be heightened by it.

Risk-aversion on the part of the bank or its employees also has a role to play. A large bank is a bureaucracy. Employees will concern themselves with promotion prospects. In the UK it is almost unknown for employees to switch from one bank to another; and it is unusual in the US and other developed countries. So banks have internal labour markets. Bureaucratic promotion criteria are frequently negative. Keep someone down if he has failure to his discredit. If a loan officer sanctions what later becomes a bad debt, he may suffer a considerable diminution in lifetime earnings prospects. So promotion criteria may induce caution in the granting of

---

[21] In the US, federal deposit insurance removes much of the force from this point, at least for all those financial intermediaries covered by its provisions.

[22] See Edgeworth (97) for the first demonstration of the likelihood that banks experienced economies of scale.

[23] See Baumol (31).

[24] Concerning the fixed transactions cost element in buying and selling non-R assets such as equity or government debt, and the overhead savings that high volume may bring in scrutinizing loan requests and carrying out the banking services.

loans. If the employee is risk-averse himself, he will sanction still fewer applications. In the absence of the costs of monitoring individual employees, the banks' owners could perceive a financial advantage in fostering a risk-neutral attitude to loan sanctions. But costly and necessarily imperfect information about their own employees leads to the imposition of incentives skewed against risk-taking; and if the bank's owners or employees are themselves risk-averse, this bias will be still stronger. Employee risk-aversion will be the more powerful influence of the two, since the bank's owners will be concerned with the variances of aggregate variables. The variance of aggregated profits for the bank will be much less than the sum of variances of profits from each branch. Much less, indeed; but still not negligible, however. Bankruptcies have a pronounced cyclical pattern. In the middle to late phase of a macroeconomic recession, business failures are typically three to four times as high as in the comparable phase of the upswing. The real estate and construction sectors are peculiarly vulnerable so the covariance of returns on bank loans to two corporations is certainly not zero. Furthermore, if a bank has a substantial concentration of loans in a particular region or group of interrelated businesses, the knock-on effect of one business failure upon others may be considerable. Again, covariance could be appreciable. There is a third reason for not dismissing covariance between returns on different components of banks' assets: the fact that interest rate fluctuations (which can be substantial, incompletely predictable, and often synchronized across the maturity spectrum) have important ramifications. A general rise in interest rates brings all but the shortest bond prices down; it also tends to accompany a fall in equity prices, as a company's stream of net earnings must now be capitalized at a lower value; and as debt servicing charges mount and threaten to engulf a company's trading surplus, it will accentuate the volume of bankruptcies. So an interest rate rise brings widespread capital losses and an increased chance of bad debt provisions. Yet, uniquely for banks, it brings the gain of higher λL through a rise in λ, which tends to offset the rise in δD upon π comfortably: λ is typically 2 per cent to 6 per cent higher than δ,[25] and, of course, there are some D upon which δ is zero.[26] Interest rate fluctuations are therefore more of a mixed blessing for banks than a source of unrelieved gloom.

Rigorous treatment of banking decisions under uncertainty requires the translation of the theory of risky choice into a banking framework. This can be done straightforwardly, given simplifying conditions. For example, assume:

(i) a unique utility function in wealth, ϕ;
(ii) a unique horizon, date T, for wealth;
(iii) the net return on investment i at date t, in state of the world δ_j; r_{ij} is known confidently for all i and j;
(iv) the probability of each state of the world (p_j) is known confidently;
(v) no transactions costs, and all asset prices parametric.

[25] Taking δ here as the (mean) interest rate on time-deposits.
[26] This is known as the 'endowment effect' of an increase in interest rates.

The bank will set out to maximize

$$\sum_j p_j \phi \left(W_0 \sum_i \mu_i (1 + r_{ij}) \right), \tag{6.14}$$

given the expected utility hypothesis that $E(u) = \Sigma p_j \phi[E(W)]$ and where μ_i is the proportion of present wealth W_0 invested in asset i, so that $\Sigma\mu_i = 1$. Maximizing (6.14) with respect to the μ_i should yield a determinate optimum portfolio, $\boldsymbol{\mu}^*$, given $\phi' > 0 > \phi''$ (risk-aversion). Some assets may well be held in negative amounts. To stop this happening, assumption (v) may be relaxed to prohibit any μ_i outside the closed interval (0, 1). W_0 must be treated with care: if it is identified with deposits, D, the r_{ij} must be reduced by the estimated full cost of servicing them, that is $\delta + C/D$ per unit of deposit when these are known for certain and $\delta_i + C_j/D$ when not. If W_0 is on the other hand the bank's net worth on a perfect equity market, then the ban on negative asset holdings must be relaxed to allow the bank to accept deposit liabilities.

(6.14) is in some ways a very general approach; its first-order conditions

$$\sum_j p_j \phi' W_0 (1 + r_{ij}) = 0 \tag{6.15}$$

(m in all if there are m kinds of asset) allow a very wide diversity of possibilities. No direct solution can proceed unless ϕ has been specified exactly; as was seen in the context of the demand for money,[27] there are many possible functions worth considering. But there are some respects in which this approach is very confining. First, W_0 (or D_0) must be taken as exogenous; this is unreasonable if it is D_0 that governs the scale of banking activity. Second—a related point, since it may help to determine this (presumably) endogenous scale variable—not all the r_{ij} are likely to be parametric. Transactions costs and information costs are responsible for this. So (6.15) might be rewritten

$$\sum_j p_i \phi' W_0 [1 + r_{ij}(1 + r^*_{ij}/\mu_i)]$$

(where r^*_{ij} is the elasticity of the net return on asset i in state j to the proportion of wealth held in asset i) if such elasticities could be treated as exogenous variables.

The Hicks-Tobin (see Hicks (164) and Tobin (320)) approach to risky choice would make banks focus upon the mean, and the variance, of their total net returns (and possibly also skewness and kurtosis as well). This has one distinct advantage over the Arrowian treatment: mean and variance are measurable characteristics of different assets, given enough observations in the past; and if banks are to be rational, expectations must at least to some degree reflect these moments of *a posteriori* probability distributions. So the Hicksian view lends itself to testing in a way that Arrow's cannot. To this it may be countered that any such test would confirm or reject a joint hypothesis—that banks were concerned just about the

[27] See chapter 5, section III: 3.

mean and the variance of return, and also that probability distributions for returns were based upon experience in some precise manner. This second element in the hypothesis becomes quite overbearing when change over time in the structure of the variance–covariance matrix is fully taken into account. There is also the familiar problem that the exercise calls for an aggregated two-parameter distribution for returns or a quadratic utility function, and, unless due allowances are made, the unrealism of assuming parametric asset prices and negligible transactions costs.

There is one final respect in which risk attitudes affect banks' behaviour. This is in the 'matching' of liabilities with assets. A bank's liabilities are on average more liquid than its assets; current deposits may be withdrawn at call, time-deposits at very short notice, such as one week; but loans and advances are given for specified periods, often of several years. But some assets are more liquid than others; some loans fall due for repayment earlier than others; some assets (such as government debt and equity holdings) can be sold quickly if needs be, albeit at a price that cannot be predicted ahead. And while any individual deposit is highly volatile, the total volume of bank deposits is proportionately much less so, particularly on a month-by-month basis. Yet there is always some uncertainty about the movement of total bank deposits, and this will increase with the period considered.

Risk-aversion will therefore imply that the bank will usually seek to phase the repayment of its loans and advances as evenly as possible.[28] All else equal, it will prefer short-term to long-term loans, because of the increased flexibility this gives; so λ may vary positively with term to maturity. Furthermore, banks' demand for government or corporate-sector debt will vary negatively with its term to maturity, all else equal, because the sensitivity of capital value to the interest rate rises with term to maturity.[29] The attempt to match the maturities of assets and liabilities is also applicable to such institutions as mortgage banks (UK: 'building societies'), and life-insurance and pension companies. While the former try to encourage medium-term deposits with especially high interest rates so as to match their medium-term assets, the latter display a marked preference for long-term assets to match their long-term liabilities.

III: The Determination of the Money Supply

III: 1 *The Basic Money Supply Model*

Having surveyed the behaviour of banks, we must now turn attention to the determination of the monetary aggregates. As usual, it is best initially to simplify. Accordingly, let us assume, in a 'Basic Money Supply Model':

(B1) R consists exclusively of non-interest bearing liabilities of the State;

(B2) government debt is either interest-bearing bonds (B) or non-interest bearing (H); both are homogeneous;

(B3) H equals R plus currency in the banks of households and corporations (CU);

---

[28] For it must meet the statutory minimum ratio of R to D, let alone prudential limits, at frequent and regular intervals. So it needs to plan asset-composition continuously.

[29] The elasticity of a pure (no-coupon) bond to the gross rate of interest $(1 + r)$ is simply minus the term to maturity.

(B4) the monetary aggregate is defined as $CU + D$;
(B5) the economy is closed.

R and D retain their previous bearings (bank's reserves, and total bank deposits). From $H = CU + R$ (B3) and $M = CU + D$ we derive

$$D = M\left(1 - \frac{CU}{M}\right) = \frac{D}{R} - R = \frac{D}{R}(1 - CU) = \frac{D}{R}H - \frac{D}{R}\frac{CU}{M} \cdot M$$

whence

$$M = \frac{\dfrac{D}{R}H}{1 + \left(\dfrac{D}{R} - 1\right)\dfrac{CU}{M}}. \tag{6.16}$$

(6.16) is just a tautology. But it is a useful way of taxonomizing various influences on the money stock. In this model, there are three: the banks' reserve ratio (R/D); the public's ratio of currency to money holdings (CU/M); and the supply of non-interest bearing liabilities of the State, H. H is often known as 'high-powered money'. M is proportional in H, and decreasing in the two ratios R/D and CU/M. We shall focus attention on each of these three determinants of M in turn.

H may change for either of two reasons. The *scale* of government debt may increase, as a result of a budget deficit. Or its *composition* may alter, following (for example) a purchase of bonds by the central bank. In this case, H will rise and B fall. If h is defined as the ratio of H to B, differentiation with respect to time reveals that

$$\hat{H} = \hat{z} + \frac{\dot{h}}{h + 1}. \tag{6.17}$$

The first term on the RHS of (6.17) is the scale effect of the budget deficit (since this equals $\dot{z}$), and $\dot{h}$ is the compositional term. Time-differentiating (6.16), and substituting for H from (6.17) establishes that the proportionate growth of the money supply,

$$\hat{M} = \hat{z} + \frac{\dot{h}}{h + 1} - \frac{H}{M}\left[\left(1 - \frac{CU}{M}\right)\frac{d\frac{R}{D}}{dt} + \left(1 - \frac{R}{D}\right)\frac{d\frac{CU}{M}}{dt}\right]. \tag{6.18}$$

Although (6.17) and (6.18) point to a budget deficit as a possible source of money supply growth, they show, too, that it is neither necessary nor sufficient. If $\dot{z}$ is positive, there are two points on which the authorities may intervene to prevent monetization of the new debt: open market operations to sell bonds (so that $\dot{h} < 0$), or action to raise banks' reserve ratios (since $1 > CU/M$, a positive value of $d(R/D)/dt$ will exert negative pressure on $\hat{M}$). The fact that $\dot{z} > 0$ is not necessary for $\hat{M} > 0$ is also clear: monetary expansion can occur because of open market bond purchases ($\dot{h} > 0$), or falls in either of the ratios in (6.16).

There are several reasons why $\dot{h}$ might not be zero. First, a budget deficit (surplus) calls for sales (purchases) of bonds for monetization of the new debt to be stopped: if H is to be held at zero, $\dot{h}$ must equal $\hat{z}(h + 1)$. In this case, the first two terms in the RHS of (6.18) cancel. Then the authorities may consciously desire to alter the mix between H and B: if they want to aim for a particular value of $\hat{M}$, acting on the $\dot{h}$ term will be much simpler and quicker and more reliable than trying to change R/D, and the other terms (the changes in z and CU/M) may be regarded as almost wholly outside the authorities' control in the short run.

Another reason for changes in h is that the authorities may set interest rates, rather than some monetary aggregate, as the prime target for financial control. There are a number of arguments for suggesting that they should do so. The demand-for-money function might be volatile. If it is, keeping (some definition of) the money supply exogenous will lead to large swings in interest rates, and therefore in aggregate demand, and hence in prices and/or output;[30] but keeping interest rates exogenous would enable the authorities to prevent random movements in the demand for money from having any real effects. The Keynesian view of the transmission mechanism (the route by which a change in the money supply affects aggregate demand) gives pride of place to interest rates: it is they that changes in the money supply primarily affect, and they that help to determine investment expenditure. If this be accepted, two further arguments for controlling aggregate demand through interest rates appear.

Controlling interest rates directly may save time, if there is any delay in interest rate changes following a change in the money supply.[31] Also, since the interest-elasticity of the demand for money cannot be known accurately in advance (leaving aside the complex problem of defining the rate and money supply), the interest rate is a more reliable variable to control.[32]

All in all governments may be attracted by these three arguments; if they are, h will depend upon changes in market interest rates which the central bank wishes to counter.

There are several points at which the case for controlling interest rates is vulnerable to attack. The demand-for-money function was asserted by Keynes (182) to be volatile—highly susceptible, in his view, to changes in market sentiment about the future path of long-term interest rates. But empirical evidence (at least until the early 1970s) has found little volatility in the aggregate demand-for-money function.[33] If the demand for money is less volatile than planned expenditures of government and private sectors combined, a policy of controlling interest rates will lead to *more* volatility in aggregate demand than one of controlling the stock of money. In simple terms, if the *IS* curve is more volatile than the *LM* curve, the variability of real aggregate demand will be a decreasing function of the gradient

---

[30] The final decomposition of the effects of changes in aggregate demand on prices and output depends on the elasticity of aggregate supply to the price level.

[31] Keynes argues that long-term rates of interest may be difficult to change quickly, because of inelastic expectations. See Keynes (182). See also chapter 5.

[32] A final argument for fixing r is that it might enhance the marketability of government debt if its capital value is seen to oscillate little.

[33] See Laidler (189) for a summary of empirical findings on the demand for money.

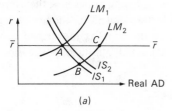

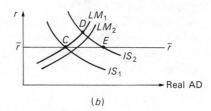

FIG. 6.3. Relative volatility in the expenditure and demand-for-money functions, and its implications for whether interest rates or the supply of money should be controlled. (*a*) The Keynesian case; (*b*) The Monetarist case.

of *LM* curve. Fixing rates of interest makes *LM* horizontal: and this will leave aggregate demand most exposed to the dangers of random movement.

Figure 6.3 illustrates. Panel (*a*) depicts the Keynesian curve, where the *LM* curve is more volatile than the *IS* because of large random movements in liquidity preference. The *IS* curve fluctuates only between IS_1 and IS_2 but the *LM* curve is the much wider band LM_1 to LM_2. In panel (*b*), the Monetarist case, the LM_1 to LM_2 band is much narrower than the gap between IS_1 and IS_2. Consider a fall in the demand for money: the money markets, if hitherto in equilibrium, must now witness excess supply in response to which interest rates will fall. So imagine that the *LM* curve shifts downward from LM_1 to LM_2. Intersection with an assumedly unchanged *IS* curve will occur now at *B* instead of *A* if the money supply remains fixed. But if the interest rate is pegged at its old level *F*, there is no reason for aggregate demand to change. Panel (*b*) shows the disadvantage of a fixed *r* if the curve shifts appreciably, e.g. from IS_1 to IS_2, there will be a large jump in aggregate demand, illustrated by the horizontal distance *CE*. But if the money stock had been held unchanged, the new conjuncture would be at *D*. The expansion in aggregate demand is checked by the fact that the demand for money must rise, and that this, in the fixed money supply case, must raise interest rates—with consequently dampening effects on expenditure plans.[34]

Two more arguments against attempts to control aggregate demand by interest rates can be offered. It may be argued that the Keynesian predilection for control by interest rates is no more firmly grounded than the Keynesian transmission mechanism (money supply to interest rates to investment and other spending). If a real balance mechanism is added (so that the position of the *IS* curve also depends on the level of the money supply), the analysis changes radically. This is shown in Figure 6.4. Consider a fall in the demand for money, with an accompanying rise in the demand for bonds, that causes the *LM* curve to move from LM_1 to LM_2 when the money supply is fixed. If instead, *r* is fixed at *F*, the authorities must lower *h* (by open market bond sales). But this will cause a leftward movement in the *IS*

[34] See Poole (257) for the original demonstration of the argument, and for an extension that introduces covariation in the *IS* and *LM* curves. The two policies (controlling *r* and controlling *M*) were christened 'Keynes-neutral' and 'classical-neutral' monetary policy by Tsiang (324), where the dependence of the size of the multiplier upon the interest-elasticity of the money supply is shown clearly. Courakis (69) has a very thorough treatment of the issue.

curve, (from IS_1 to IS_2) given the real balance effects. Fixing r does not, therefore, insulate aggregate demand from stochastic stocks in the demand for money: it just ensures that aggregate demand moves in the same direction as the demand for money (from A to C) and not, as with a fixed money supply, in the opposite direction, from (A to B).[35]

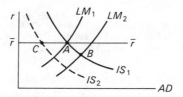

FIG. 6.4. Fixing M or r when real balance effects are present: a disturbance in the demand for money.

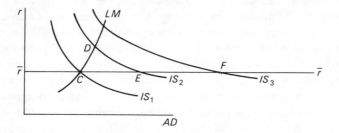

FIG. 6.5. Fixing M or r when real balance effects are present: a disturbance in the expenditure function.

If, on the other hand, a wobble now occurs in the IS curve, the case for controlling M rather than r becomes even more powerful. Freezing the interest rate variable at $\bar{r}$ entails *increasing* the supply of money in response to the rise in the demand for it, which must accompany a spontaneous rightward shift in the IS curve, from IS_1 to IS_2 (see Figure 6.5). But if the money supply rises, the IS curve must move out again, for example to IS_3. A 'fix-r' policy will exaggerate the disturbance to aggregate demand that follows a random change in planned expenditure, not for just one reason but two: the dampening effect on AD of the rise in r that would normally follow under a 'fix-M' policy is nullified; and, in addition, aggregate demand is

---

[35] There is no general way of being certain whether AC is a longer distance than the horizontal component of the vector from A to B. If E is aggregate demand and $g(.\,.)$ the demand for money, so that $E = f(r, M)$ and $M = g(r, Y)$, the question resolves itself into the sign of:

$$f_2^* - \frac{1}{2g_2^* - (g_1^*/f_1^*)}$$

which is ambiguous. (Here the $f_i^*(g_i^*)$ represent the elasticity of $f(g)$ to its ith argument). It is quite likely to be positive if expenditure is as highly sensitive to real balances as, for example, Morishima finds for consumption $(.\,.)$ and the IS curve is a good deal less elastic than the LM. Otherwise, it is not likely.

given a secondary upward twist by the 'accommodating' monetary expansion itself.[36]

The most devastating argument against controlling interest rates, however, is the instability to which this can give rise. Open market operations to alter h change *nominal* rates of interest unless government debt is indexed. The distinction between nominal and real rates of interest becomes appreciable with inflation (or strictly, with expectations of inflation). Suppose that expectations of inflation ($\hat{P}^e$) are linear in expected monetary expansion ($\hat{M}^e$) with a unit coefficient; that expected monetary expansion is increasing in actual monetary expansion; and that the nominal rate of interest (r_N), is the sum of three components, an exogenous real rate of interest (F_R),[37] expected inflation and a function ϕ of h (where $\phi' < 0$, and ϕ is rather small). In this case, suppose that the equilibrium value at date 0 of r_N ($= F_R + \hat{P}^e + \phi_0$) is higher than the authorities like: so, whether to cut national-debt servicing charges, or to stimulate investment, or to avoid bankruptcies, or to solicit votes from debtors, the government tries to bring r_N down. The central bank must raise h to cut ϕ. But, by (6.18), this will increase the instantaneous growth of the money supply. In response to this, $\hat{M}^e$ rises, and, with it, $\hat{P}^e$; and this must raise the equilibrium nominal rate of interest! Indeed, it might be said of the two-and-a-half or three decades after 1950 that the sharp rise in nominal interest rates experienced by most countries occurred partly *because the authorities tried to hold them down*. An unwillingness to accept nominal rates bloated by fears of inflation led indirectly to increased monetary expansion, and a further upward twist to inflation itself. Which of the two rival groups of argument (those for fixing r, and those for fixing M) prevails will be of crucial significance for the behaviour of h. We must now pass on to the remaining terms in (6.18): the changes in R/D and CU/M.

R/D was found, in (6.3), (6.9), or (6.12), to depend upon a number of variables, elasticities, and derivatives. Once A8 of the Standard Banking Model was repealed, the crucial signficance of the statutory minima set by the central banks became apparent; and transactions costs, risk attitudes and expectations of government policy continued to influence the safety 'cushion' of excess reserves for which a bank would aim. There are four respects in which further implications of our previous analysis need to be brought out.

The central bank can help to determine the value of β, the rate of return on R. In the Standard Banking Model, it was an arbitrary, non-negative parameter (A7); in the Basic Money Supply Model, β was zero (from B2 and B3). By raising β

---

[36] The 'fix-r' policy is markedly inferior to 'fix-M' when stochastic shifts occur in planned expenditure, and possibly inferior, possibly superior when they occur in the demand for money. The introduction of real balances therefore weakens the overall case for a 'fix-r' policy, given both kinds of random disturbance.

[37] Two possible rationalizations of this may be offered. First, r will equal the marginal product of capital, if depreciation and relative price changes are ignored, and perfect competition assumed in a single one-sector economy; and the marginal product of capital in such a model will be determined by input supplies and technology which may both be invariant with respect to inflation, at least in the short run. Second, the *IS* curve may be infinitely more elastic than the *LM* curve: the former is related to r, the latter to i; this would make r independent of $\hat{P}$.

relative to λ, the bank's *optimum* ratio of R to D will rise; so must its actual ratio, unless this is constrained by the statutory minimum. Suppose now R is not homogeneous, and contains some elements for which β is necessarily zero (e.g. 'vault cash. (UK: 'till money')), and some for which it is positive.[38] Given imperfect substitution between the two, a large rise in expectations of inflation (which tends to be reflected in parallel movements in all rates) may tend to reduce β relative to other interest rates, such as λ. An increase in loan rates relative to the yield, if any, on reserves will act as a strong incentive upon banks to economize on reserves.

A second way in which R/D may be affected indirectly by other variables is through C_2 and C_2^*, which measure the cost-saving that reserves bring. This is, as we saw, primarily a saving of transactions costs. Government can clearly affect the values banks will tend to place upon them. Frequent and unpredictable policy changes, with heavy reliance on open market operations or special deposit changes or changes in the statutory minimum R/D ratio, will create a strong demand for the safety cushion. Infrequent and minor use of these intervention techniques—or *easily predicted* use of these instruments—will lower it. Given the numbers involved (R/D is a fraction usually closer to a tenth than a half) even a small change in the target cushion will have a large potential effect on the equilibrium money supply. A fitful, Pavlovian central bank may keep aggregate nominal demand at a lower level than if policy is pursued in a more sanguine vein. And the transition from one kind of policy stance to another may bring a surprisingly large effect on R/D and hence, given R on M.

A third possibility is the effect of the quality of competition for deposits. From (6.3), (6.9), and (6.12) we may see that R/D is decreasing in δ_1^*. Strong competition for deposits will make δ_1^* low. This is not counter-intuitive: the more competitive an industry, the more it tends to produce. But this gives us one insight into the subtle relationship between changes in microeconomic efficiency and macroeconomic controllability of the banking system. Another is provided by the fact that the authorities may gain a more immediate and complete grip on monetary aggregates by quantitative restrictions on the volume of loans and advances by banks. They may also use these to push government debt interest rates down by placing pressure on the banks to buy it, where the loan ceiling binds.[39] Yet these measures all have probable microeconomic costs: they introduce, or widen, infringements of the Pareto efficiency conditions applied to capital markets.[40] Furthermore, it is not merely δ_1^*, that R/D is influenced by in this context; since λ/δ depends upon λ_1^* (inter alia), and R/D upon λ/δ, the quality of competition in the loan market affects R/D as well.

Lastly, R/D may differ bank from bank, perhaps because their safety-cushions differ, or even because the regulations prescribe different minima. In this case, changes in the shares of total deposits enjoyed by the banks will alter the total

[38] For example, bankers' balances at the central bank, assuming that these bear interest (actual systems differ in this respect).

[39] The objective of lowering national debt servicing charges is one argument advanced by Courakis (68), in his proposal for a government debt ratio for banks.

[40] By creating differences in the marginal cost of capital facing different producers (in the absence of a competitive auction of overdrafts), and by reducing inter-bank competition.

quantity of D for given R. Since (on Edgeworth's argument, at least) a large bank may opt for a smaller R/D than a small one, an increase in concentration in the banking industry could expand the money supply as a whole. This effect is previously contrary to its influence through δ_1^* and λ_1^*, noted above.

We turn now to the fourth term in (6.18): the change in CU/M. A rise in this would, it was seen, exert downward pressure on the overall money supply. The reason is this: a rise in CU/M must entail an equal fall in deposits and in banks' reserves; in order to restore the former (presumably optimal) ratio of R to D, banks must now contract L; the process continues (*ceteris paribus*) until M has fallen by a large multiple of the initial transfer from D to CU. What does CU/M depend upon? An application of Baumol's inventory model is appropriate and eloquent here: CU/M should vary negatively with δ, the return on bank deposits, since δ represents an opportunity cost of currency holdings; positively with the transactions costs—post, time, shoe leather, travel costs, bank charges—associated with cashing a cheque; and negatively, perhaps, with the level of income, if the optimum mean inventory of currency varies with something such as the square root of income as the Baumol model implies. Other possible influences include transitory expenditures, and tax evasion, which tend to raise CU/M, and three factors that can dampen it: the extent of banking hours,[41] the incidence of payment by credit card, and, perhaps most sinister of all, the rate of expected inflation. This last will affect the cost of currency holding directly, and tend to be reflected, in part at least, in the level of δ and in other interest rates. Inflationary expectations are a powerful incentive to economize on currency holdings; so an increase in them will tend to raise the money supply.[42]

III: 2 *Relaxing the Assumptions of the Basic Money Supply Model*

It remains now to consider the consequences of relaxing the assumptions of the Basic Money Supply Model. If B1 is relaxed, a new possibility emerges: a spontaneous growth in those elements of R which are not directly part of the government's non-interest bearing debt. In the UK monetary system operating after 1971, for instance, first-class commercial bills (up to a maximum of $1\frac{1}{2}$ per cent) were included within R. This built into the system a possible source of endogeneity: if a bank were to persuade a first-class company to which it had made L to replace this debt by commercial bills, the bank could manufacture its own reserves.[43] A still bigger source of endogeneity is the historic role as lender of last resort accorded by the 1844 Bank of England Act, whereby the Bank guarantees that it will supply cash to discount houses whenever requested, normally at a ('penal') rate.[44] In the US, the Federal Reserve Board has a similar obligation to supply R to

[41] A particularly high CU/M is observed at the Christmas period for most of which banks are closed.

[42] And since there is a strong likelihood that they will reduce the demand for it, there is a curious positive feedback mechanism on aggregate demand, and the level of prices, which should rise as a result.

[43] Provided that the $1\frac{1}{2}$ per cent ceiling was not already met.

[44] Until the 1981 reforms, this was the Bank Rate ('Minimum Lending Rate' since 1972), which was in general somewhat higher than the current Treasury bill rate. In the UK, this

the banking system. Whether or not the lender of last resort function means that the central bank has to forgo control of R depends on the interest rate at which it lends 'as a last resort'. If this is high enough, at least this source of endogeneity will be blocked. If not, the central bank will have committed itself, however unwittingly, to a policy of 'fix-r'.

B2 is not a particularly restrictive condition, but the notion that B and H are each homogeneous is, of course, a radical simplification. B can be arranged in a spectrum, varying by date of maturity. Also, most B are explicitly interest-bearing, in the form of coupons: this makes them a linear combination of pure (i.e. couponless) bonds. An exception to this is Treasury bills, which are redeemed at par but issued without coupon below par. In some monetary systems, Treasury bills (and also government bonds nearing maturity) are eligible as R.[45] This means that R may jump when a government source crosses the threshold of proximity to maturity, or as a result of an exchange of very short-term for longer-term government debt with another market participant.[46]

B3 is innocuous, if the admission of elements inside R but outside H is treated as a relaxation of B1. B4 is less so. No definition of the money supply excludes CU, but each differs, as we saw, in the width of D admitted. If D is defined as total deposits with classified banks by domestic residents (including public bodies) in domestic currency—this is the conventional 'M3' definition, in terms of which the ratio is generally expressed—then narrower definitions (such as M1) will depend upon the public's choice between time-deposits and current (demand) deposits. Fluctuations in the ratio of M1 to M3 seem to depend chiefly on rates of interest, and particularly, upon the rates available on time-deposits.[47]

We come now to the last assumption, B5: the closed economy. If the economy is open, a new potential source of monetary endogeneity appears: the balance of payments surplus. If domestic residents have an overall payments surplus, they must (definitionally) receive net payments in foreign or domestic currency from foreign residents. Suppose, first, that it is foreign currency that is received. Domestic residents (assumedly in portfolio equilibrium before these receipts) will now bank it. D will rise correspondingly, and, with it, banks' holdings of foreign currency. If banks were also in portfolio equilibrium before these changes, they must now have excess holdings of foreign currency. These they will presumably sell to the central bank, in return for which bankers' balances at the central bank (an element of R) will rise.

A more direct increase in R will follow if the payments surplus is paid in the form of domestic money, drawn upon a foreign bank deposit. Only if the foreign residents effect payment by drawing upon a bank deposit denominated in domestic

possible source of endogeneity was important to the banks because discount houses borrow at call and short notice from banks, and these loans have counted as part of R since 1971. Before that, they were included as liquid assets but not as reserve assets.

[45] In the UK, R has included Treasury bills and government debt within one year of maturity.
[46] Such as a discount house, in the UK framework.
[47] A rise in time-deposit rates coincides with a fall in M1 relative to M3. This has been especially pronounced in periods which saw sharp rises in interest rates (such as 1972–4 and 1978–80 in the UK and the US).

money and located in the home country will R not tend to change (except that of course in this case the definition of D probably will).

It is, therefore, highly likely that a balance of payments surplus leads to an increase in banks' reserves, of similar magnitude. But matters are not necessarily allowed to rest there. In both the US and the UK, the central bank attempts to sterilize the payments surplus by selling bonds or Treasury bills on the open market. In the UK this is done formally under the Exchange Equalization Account, which was established in April 1932 with the express purpose of trying to insulate the domestic money supply from overseas payments. In West Germany, sterilization techniques include high incremental ratios of foreign currency holdings to deposits imposed upon banks, so that the problem of multiple-deposit creation, the basis of the extra reserves, is severely curtailed. There is little doubt that the authorities can prevent much of the full increases in M that would otherwise accompany a surplus in overseas payments. But sterilization may be far from 100 per cent effective. This is particularly true if the exchange rate is fixed, or allowed to float 'dirtily'. The large rise in M3, well above the targeted growth rates then newly in force, that occurred between August and October 1977 in the UK is a recent instance of this: it accompanied a substantial inflow of short-term capital of some $US14,000 million, at a period when the Bank of England was attempting to hold the exchange rate down. The traditional device of open market bond and bill sales merely served to increase sterling short-term interest rates, which strengthened the capital inflow. Eventually the authorities were forced to choose between the exchange rate target and the monetary target; they chose to adhere to the latter and let the exchange rate appreciate. It may, therefore, be concluded that the influences of overseas payments upon the domestic money supply may require nothing short of a floating exchange rate to block them completely.

Summary of Notation in Chapter 6

B	interest bearing bonds
C	banking costs
D	deposits
CU	currency
H	non-interest bearing debt
L	loans
$\dot{p}^e$	the expected rate of inflation
p	probability
r	interest rate
r_N	nominal rate of interest
r_R	real rate of interest
S	state of the world
T	date
W	bank's wealth
x	number of bank branches
x_i	the partial derivative of x with respect to its ith argument

x_i^* the elasticity of x with respect to its ith argument
β the rate of interest on reserves (R)
γ branch banking costs
π profits
ϕ a utility function in wealth

Chapter 7

The Aggregate Economy

I: Introduction

The time has now come to assemble the separate elements of the economy considered in previous chapters. The personal sector was examined in chapter 1, the corporate sector in chapter 2, and the government in chapter 3. Households, producers and the State were considered largely in isolation from each other, although sometimes simple models of the aggregate economy (such as the Standard Income Tax Model of chapter 3) were presented to illuminate essential points. This provided us with a clear impression of the essential influences on at least the first two groups' spending behaviour, and of the factors underlying the supply and demand for labour, and commodities. In chapter 4 (the external sector) several links between these and other markets were established in the context of a single economy; this permitted us to contrast different economies, and consider the causes and effects of trade, capital movements, and both equilibrium and disequilibrium in external payments. In chapters 5 and 6 attention moved from the real to the monetary sector of the economy. The demand for money and the supply of money constituted the two major elements of this.

In chapter 7, our task is to integrate all, or nearly all, the results achieved so far. We examine the interaction of households, producers, and the government; the interaction of real and monetary aspects of equilibrium and disequilibrium; the consequences of decisions taken at one date for variables both then and later. We begin, in section II, with an analysis of a miniature general equilibrium model. This miniature model is expanded in section III to allow variety among households and among commodities; to introduce the effects of government spending and taxation which builds upon the Standard Income Tax Model of chapter 3; and to incorporate intertemporal economic activity. Section IV expands the analysis to include the effects of random shocks, and the formation of expectations. The concept of rational expectations has been encountered already, in chapters 1, 2, and 5. Section IV develops this further. In section V, we return to the miniature one-period model to demonstrate the consequences of disequilibrium (in the sense of non-market-clearance) in labour and product markets; these are considered in a dynamic setting in section VI. Sections V and VI provide a set of answers to effects of various parameter disturbances which differ considerably, both from each other (depending on the type of disequilibrium assumed) and from the equilibrium case. In section VII, we examine the different explanations for unemployment, and present and assess some of the arguments for and against different kinds of stabilization macro-economic policies that governments can pursue. The positive and normative aspects of inflation are considered in chapter 8 (optimum monetary policy in the long run);

meanwhile long-run mechanisms operating on the real side of the macroeconomy are considered in chapter 9, the chapter on growth.

This chapter provides a panoply of different models. All start from only slightly differing sets of assumptions, yet they yield intriguingly divergent conclusions. What distinguishes the models is fundamentally whether or not markets are taken to clear, and, if not, what type of disequilibrium occurs.

Finally, the reader is warned that the term 'disequilibrium' in macroeconomic contexts has two related, but distinct meanings. First, there is the sense in which we have used the word in the last two paragraphs; the failure of a market, or a set of markets, to clear. The second meaning is a state of affairs that cannot persist: equilibrium is a state which will persist if not perturbed. The two meanings are related, or at least arguably related, if it is accepted that there is some tendency for a market to move eventually towards clearance. If a market is in excess demand, for example, individual buyers and sellers have an incentive to trade, to their mutual advantage, at prices higher than those currently prevailing; these trades can be prevented only if the agents are kept apart or remain in ignorance of each others' potential offers. We shall use the term disequilibrium throughout this chapter in the first sense, of non-market-clearance.

II: A Miniature General Equilibrium Model

II: 1 *Outline*

In conventional general equilibrium models, all markets clear.[1] Demand equals supply for each commodity, for each factor of production, for each asset and for money. Every agent succeeds in trading as he wishes at the prevailing price vector. There is no involuntary unemployment, no involuntary holding of inventories, no shortages. The concept of general equilibrium can be extended to include an arbitrarily large number of commodities, factors and assets, and any number of time periods. In chapter 4 a model of international trade was presented. This was a highly simplified world with just two commodities and two factors of production, and only one period. It was a two-sector general equilibrium model in miniature.

In what follows, we shall examine an even simpler model, with only one produced commodity, two factors (one of which is exogenous), and a second commodity, money. The variable factor is labour, N, supplied by households to the firms, who convert this input, under a given technology and with a given stock of capital, into units of the produced commodity, 'bread'. There are constant returns to scale. The households maximize utility which depends on real money holdings, (M/P), leisure retained $(h - N)$ and bread (b).[2] The households have identical tastes and endowments (of money, time, and capital). Firms, too, are alike in all respects.

[1] There can also be *non-market-clearing* models, such as those produced by Barro and Grossman (26), which share at least some of the characteristics of general equilibrium. All relations governing the endogenous variables are solved simultaneously for these variables, given the value of the exogenous variables. Where these non-market-clearing models depart from conventional general equilibrium models is in treating prices as exogenous, not endogenous.

[2] As in chapter 1, the assumption that utility depends on real balances is most easily justified by the argument that money holdings save on transactions costs. See section I: 4.

All households and firms are price-takers. Governments neither spend nor tax. There is no foreign trade. This highly simplified general equilibrium model unites our previous models of the household (chapter 1) and the producer (chapter 2); strictly speaking, it unites abbreviated, one-period versions of them in their simplest form.

Figure 7.1 presents the model in a diagrammatic form. The top right-hand panel depicts the bread market. Demand is related negatively to the price of bread, positively to the wage rate, the level of nominal money holdings and the level of profits. Households maximize $U(b, h - N, M/P)$ subject to the budget restraint $Pb + M - wN - \bar{M} - \bar{\pi} = 0$. Here, $\bar{M}$ denotes the household's endowment of nominal money holdings and $\bar{\pi}$ its receipt of nominal profits. We assume that $b, h - N$ and M/P are all normal goods: this guarantees that the household demand for bread behaves as expected.

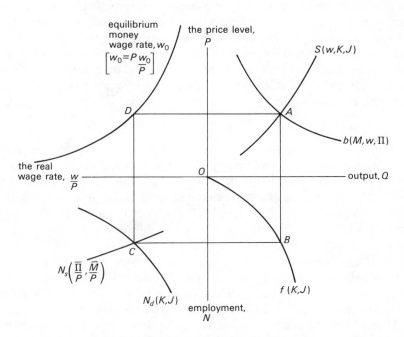

FIG. 7.1. The effects of a higher money supply.

Commentary: f is a production function, showing positive but diminishing marginal product of labour. Increases in K (capital) or J (a parameter reflecting technology) tend to swivel f counterclockwise from the origin. Perfect competition equates the marginal product of labour with the real wage rate (w/P). The negative relation between the demand for labour (N_d) and w/P follows from this and the assumed shape of f. Rises in K or (usually) J move the N_d curve southwestward. N_s (labour supply) is shown here varying positively with w/P; it need not. Increases in households' endowment of real money balances $(\bar{M}/P)$ or real non-wage income $(\bar{\pi}/P)$ tend to shift N_s northward. The labour market clears at C. Curve S is the representative competitive firm's marginal cost curve, sloping upward for given money wage rate (w), K and J. Rises in K and J move S eastward, while a higher w would imply the reverse. b is the representative household's demand curve. Rises in nominal money endowment $(\bar{M})$, w or nominal non-wage income $(\bar{\pi})$ would all move b rightwards. The product market clears at A. A and C are linked by equilibrium values of $N, Q, \bar{\pi}, P$ and w/P and hence by the equilibrium money wage rate, w_0, shown as a rectangular hyperbola.

The supply of bread is positively related to the price of bread, P, negatively to the nominal wage rate, w, and positively to both the stock of capital K and the level of technology J. The elasticity of supply will equal the ratio of the wage bill to total profits, multiplied by the elasticity of substitution between labour and capital in the production function.[3] The bottom right panel depicts the production function, f, which displays a positive but diminishing marginal product of labour. The position of the function is governed by K and J. The bottom left panel illustrates the labour market. There is a negative relation between the real wage rate w/P and the aggregate demand for labour N_d; the relation is derived directly from the production function. The aggregate supply of labour, N_s, is related negatively to the level of profits and the holdings of real money balances, and varies ambiguously[4] with w/P. The association between N_s and w/P is drawn positive in Figure 7.1; it could have been negative. N_s also varies positively with the economy's total population. The top left panel displays the equilibrium money wage rate, w_0 as a rectangular hyperbola—it is definable as the product of the price level and the real wage rate. Equilibrium in the goods market at A and the labour market at C are mutually consistent, given the money wage rate w_0 and the production function f. The prices w and P are at equilibrium levels given exogenous values of K, J, $\bar{M}$, population and preferences.

II: 2 *Comparative Statics in the Miniature Model*

Consider now the implications of different values of the exogenous parameters K, J, $\bar{M}$, population and preferences. We begin with *preferences*. Suppose the demand for money balances had been higher. Three possible cases present themselves: higher demand for M at the expense of bread; higher demand for M at the expense of leisure; and higher demand for M with lower demand for both bread and leisure, in such a way that the marginal rate of substitution between bread and leisure was the same as before. Call these cases A, B, and C.

Case C is the easiest to deal with. Both w and P would be equiproportionately lower. All real variables (w/P, the real rate of profit $\partial Q/\partial K$, the output level Q, and the total employment level N) would be the same as before. In case A, P would be lower in equilibrium, as a result of the lower demand for bread. Bread output would also be lower. In case B, labour supply would be greater, the nominal wage rate lower, and output higher. The differences in the nominal wage rate in case A, and the price level in case B, would be indeterminate. In whichever direction output differed (lower in A, higher in B), employment and the real rate of profit differ in the same direction, and the real wage rate in the opposite direction. Output would vary positively with the ratio of wages to profits if the elasticity of substitution exceeded unity, negatively if less.

Consider now a reduction in the preference for bread, accompanied first by a rise in the demand for leisure, which leaves the demand for money unchanged

---

[3] See chapter 2, section II: 3.
[4] In what follows, we shall assume—unless specified to the contrary—that all goods are gross mutual substitutes. This entails a positive association between the real wage rate and the labour supply.

(case D) and then, instead, by rises in the demands for leisure and money, which leaves the marginal rate of substitution between these two unaffected (case E). In case A and C, we have already covered other circumstances in which the demand for bread could have been lower.

In both cases, the output of bread would be lower, implying lower levels of employment, the price level, and real and nominal rates of profit. The reductions in the real variables Q, N, and $\partial Q/\partial K$ would be greater in case D than E. The fall in P, however, would be larger in the second case. This is because of the additional price-deflationary effect of a rise in the demand for money. This is reinforced by the smaller reduction of labour supply in case E—this would imply a higher output level at a given level of P. The real wage rate rises in both cases, and by more in D. The money wage rate rises in case D, with the greater scarcity of labour relative to the stock of money, while in case E, assuming gross substitution, the opposite occurs.

The final case of changed preferences we consider is a rise in the demand for both money and bread, which preserves the marginal rate of substitution between them, at the expense of a fall in the demand for leisure. Here, output and employment will both rise, raising the real rate of profit and reducing the real wage rate. The money wage rate will also be lower, but the implications for the price of bread are unclear. The increased demand for bread would tend to imply a rise in P, but this direct effect is subject to a contrary influence from both the higher employment level (which enlarges output) and a higher demand for money.

A higher level of population would imply higher N, and higher Q, but a lower average product of labour Q/N. Both w and P would be lower, since the increased population would otherwise imply an excess demand for money and an excess supply of bread and labour. The real wage rate would also be lowered, by virtue of diminishing returns and perfectly competitive pricing of labour. The rate of profit would be larger in real terms. If and only if capital and labour are complementary in production, the share of profits would be increased as well. A higher *stock of capital* would have implied a lower price level, a higher output level, a higher real wage rate and (assuming that the labour supply is not reduced as a result of the higher real wage rate and the disincentive effect of higher profit income) at least as large an employment level as well. The real and nominal rates of profit ($\partial Q/\partial K$ and $P(\partial Q/\partial K)$) would both be lower; the implications for the money wage rate ($P(\partial Q/\partial N)$) are ambiguous, since P would be lower, but $\partial Q/\partial N$, the real wage rate, higher.

Most of the effects of higher levels of technology are similar to those of higher levels of population or capital. Writing the production function f as

$$Q = f(AK, BN) \qquad (7.1)$$

allows us to distinguish between two technology parameters: A, which is 'capital-augmenting', and B, which is 'labour-augmenting'. A rise in A has the same effects as a rise in K on everything except the rate of profit per unit of capital, which is now highly likely to *rise* in real terms.[5] By contrast, we saw that a higher level of K

---

[5] If the level of employment is unchanged, the real rate of profit will rise following an increase in A if and only if the elasticity of substitution between capital and labour exceeds

brought a lower real rate of profit. Similarly, a rise in B is similar to a rise in population in all respects save upon the wage rate, at least when the employment level is given. The real wage rate must fall with a rise in population, but rises with labour augmenting technical progress with a given employment level if, and only if, the elasticity of substitution exceeds the profit share (see Sinclair (301) and Heffernan (157)).

Lastly, the implication of a larger *supply of money*. At the equilibrium constellation of w and P that would have ruled had the money supply been lower, there would be excess demand for labour and excess demand for bread. Figure 7.2 illustrates. The equilibrium values of w and P are in fact equiproportionate to the money supply since labour supply and commodity demand depend on the level of *real* balances possessed by individuals, equiproportionate rises in w, P, and M leave the supply of labour curve in the bottom left panel unaffected. The demand and supply of bread in the top right panel are unchanged in real terms, so that the curves representing them against the nominal price level are raised vertically by proportions equal to the rise in the money supply.

The distance CC^* illustrates the notional[6] excess demand for labour that would

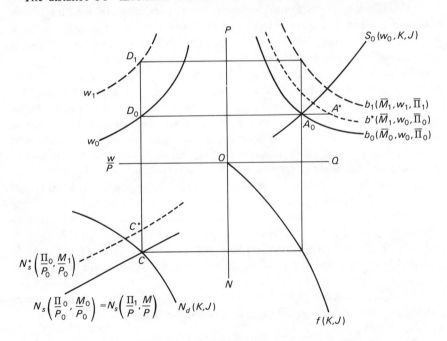

FIG. 7.2. The effects of a higher money supply.

labour's share in output. This condition for $\partial^2 Q/\partial A \partial K$ to be positive can be illustrated easily with the CES production function: $Q = [a(AK)^{(\sigma-1)/\sigma} + b(BN)^{(\sigma-1)/\sigma}]^{\sigma/(\sigma-1)}$ (see p. 63). It is always fulfilled by the Cobb–Douglas production function, where the qualitative distinction between the two parameters vanishes: $Q = c(AK)^{\alpha}(BN)^{\beta} = cA^{\alpha}B^{\beta}K^{\alpha}N^{\beta}$.

[6] Notional excess demand or supply represents the extent of the disequilibrium in the market in question, if one assumes the absence of any feedback effects upon the market as an indirect result of the disequilibrium. See section V below.

have arisen if the nominal values of P and w had been those consistent with equilibrium and a nominal money supply of M_0. The higher real balances of households (M_1/P_0) encourage them to increase their demand for leisure, from N_s to N_s^*. The distance A_0A^* represents the notional excess demand for bread in the same hypothetical circumstances.[7] The equilibrium values of w and P are w_1 and P_1 if the money supply is $\bar{M}_1$. This equilibrium position is shown at A_1 in the bread market, and D_1 in the nominal wage panel. Note that the nominal money supply has not affected the real variables Q, N, and w/P. Labour market equilibrium at C and output at B are independent of the nominal money stock. This is the classical *neutrality* result: the equilibrium values of all real variables (quantities and relative prices) are independent of the money stock. The nominal price of any good or factor, however, is determined in equilibrium *solely* by the condition of equilibrium in the market for money. For a given structure of preferences, and set of factor and technology endowments, the nominal value of w or P (or of any element which the indices w and P must be thought of as embracing, in a disaggregated model) depends exclusively upon the nominal supply of money. Money is neutral; equilibrium can be dichotomized into its real and nominal aspects. All that is necessary for this is the homogeneity property of equilibrium conditions for households[8] and producers.[9] These entail independence of the demand for real money supply from the nominal price level in equilibrium.[10] There must be no money illusion for these conditions to hold.

As we shall shortly see, there are other circumstances in which money is not neutral. We do not need to invoke money illusion to derive it. Instead, we can assume the presence of disequilibrium. When wage rates and prices are fixed, a rise in the money supply will tend to raise output and employment when goods and labour markets are in excess supply ('Keynesian unemployment') or excess demand ('repressed inflation'). Alternatively, an *unexpected* increase in the money supply in a society where agents have incomplete information about the set of current prices may mislead them into thinking that relative prices have changed. This important case is known as the Lucas Surprise Supply Function, after Lucas (196). Disequilibrium or, more strictly, non-market clearing models are introduced in section V, and the Lucas Surprise Supply Function is discussed at the end of section VI.

III: Extensions to the Miniature Model

III: 1 *Introducing a Second Produced Commodity*

Suppose there are two commodities produced: cheese, as well as bread. Figure 7.1, and the results of the miniature model, carry over with no modification in one special case. This is when the cheese and bread industries can be relied upon to have the same (cost-minimizing) ratio of capital to labour, and the two industries enjoy

---

[7] Recall the effect of higher wealth upon labour supply and commodity demand in chapter 1, section I: 7.

[8] See chapter 1, section I: 3. [9] See chapter 2, section II: 1.

[10] See chapter 5, footnote 9, and the accompanying discussion in the text.

constant returns to scale with no jointness in production. In these circumstances, the assumptions of the Non-Substitution Theorem hold (chapter 4, section II: 1). The price ratio between cheese and bread is entirely supply-determined. Aggregation over commodities is possible because their relative prices are independently fixed.[11] Introducting third to nth commodities makes no difference either, so long as the three Non-Substitution Theorem assumptions (identical input mix, constant returns, and no jointness in production) continue to hold.

If the bread and cheese industries differ in capital-intensity, however, there is a link between factor prices and the structure of demand between commodities. The higher the demand for bread, the higher the demand for (and price of) the factor used intensively in bread. As was seen in chapter 4, the transformation curve between bread and cheese is concave, and the unit cost function for each good is positively associated with its own output rate. Q and P are now indices, related by the condition

$$PQ = \sum_{i=1} P_i q_i \qquad (7.2)$$

if P_i and q_i denote the price and output level of good i.

III: 2 *Introducing a Second Type of Household*

If two or more of the aggregability conditions (homotheticity of preferences, identity of preferences, and fixed distribution of income) hold, and everyone faces the same set of prices, community tastes are unique when individuals' tastes are unique. From a positive standpoint, the addition of new individuals can alter the community's tastes if more than one of the aggregability conditions fail, or if the prices confronting individuals differ.

There is one respect in which prices facing individuals certainly do differ. They face different opportunity costs of leisure, unless each is offered the same hourly wage rate. Strictly speaking, different individuals' time endowments are distinct potential factors of production. It is not enough to assert that those with high hourly wage rates merely have a more valuable endowment of earnings opportunities, since differences in wage rates create differences in relative prices confronting individuals as well. The price of leisure in terms of bread must differ. The equilibrium set of hourly wage rates will, however, be an endogenous variable; if a unique equilibrium exists, it will be possible to construct arithmetically weighted average wage rate

$$\frac{\sum\limits_{i=1}^{n} w_i h_i}{\sum\limits_{i=1}^{n} h_i}. \qquad (i = 1, \ldots, n \text{ individual})$$

[11] It would have been possible, too, had the relative *quantities* been fixed. But unless either relative prices or relative quantities are fixed—we may call this the 'fix-price' or 'fix-quantity' condition—the relative prices and relative quantities are endogenous variables. Aggregation

The problem is that the weights (the h_i) are endogenous variables, too. They will be locked only in very special circumstances.[12] The aggregation problem posed here is evident on the production side, too. Only when different individuals' labour inputs are perfect substitutes or perfect complements in production can we be sure that an invariant aggregate labour input index is available.[13] When they are perfect substitutes, the w_i are exogenous; when perfect complements, it is the h_i which are fixed in relation to each other. Unless the 'fix price' or 'fix-quantity' solutions to the aggregation problem can be made, a unique labour aggregate cannot be constructed. It is an interesting paradox that the difficulties of aggregating labour have received less attention than those of aggregating capital. In fact, there is formally no difference between the two.[14] If labour is heterogeneous, the labour theory of value disintegrates. It falls apart no less completely than the notion of a unique rate of interest and profit related negatively to a unique aggregate for capital when capital is itself heterogeneous.[15]

Household incomes can differ because individuals face different hourly wage rates. They can also differ for another reason. Households may differ in the source of their incomes. The classical approach of Smith and Ricardo, followed and amended by Marx, is to partition society into subsets. Each subset owns a distinct factor: labour, capital, or land. The pattern of demand between goods now depends on the way national income is distributed between wages, profits, and rents, if (typical members of) the subsets differ in their preferences. An interesting threat of non-uniqueness and instability presents itself, once we allow more than one produced commodity. If the labour-intensive commodity is liked much more by those who own labour than by the rest of the citizenry, a rise in the price of the good may *raise* the excess demand for it: the income redistributive effect of a rise in its price will act in labour's favour, and unless there is some sufficiently high degree of substitution between the commodities on the part of wage earners and the rest of the community, the demand for the good will increase.

III: 3 *Introducing the Government*

So far, the government has been set aside in the miniature model. Its existence can be inferred from the fact that there is a paper currency, $\bar{M}$. $\bar{M}$ is the government's debt. In an expanded model, it is the non-interest-bearing component of the government's debt;[16] or at least part[17] of $\bar{M}$ satisfies this description.

Allowing the government to spend and to tax introduces several new features. The curve b in the top left panel of Figure 7.1 needs to be redefined to include the spending of government; household labour supply, demand for money, and cannot proceed independently of the solution of the full model where all endogenous variables are jointly determined.

[12] Such as Cobb–Douglas tastes when all income is earned (for then the h_i are independent of the w_i), or when all individuals are deprived—by law for example—of the right to choose their hours of work.

[13] See Bliss (42).　　　　　　　　　　　　　　　　　　　　[14] See Bliss (42).

[15] See Morishima (223), for a discussion of the effects of assuming heterogeneous labour, and Dixit (87) for the probable non-uniqueness of interest rates in a general equilibrium model.

[16] Once government interest-bearing bonds are admitted.

[17] The monetary base of 'high-powered' or 'outside' money. See chapter 6, section III: 1.

commodity demand need to be modified in the light of the government's expenditure and taxation; producers' actions in factor and goods markets are also very likely to be affected.

These consequences of government spending and taxation are illustrated in Figure 7.3. To simplify matters, let us assume that there is only one type of household;[18] that all commodities are produced under identical capital–labour ratios at all wage–rent ratios, with no joint production, and subject to constant returns;[19] that the government 'spends' G in nominal units, of which G_1 consists of outlay on public goods, and G_2 is a social dividend, or transfer, paid as a lump sum to every household $(G = G_1 + G_2)$; $G = tPQ$, so that the budget is balanced by a uniform rate of tax t on all income (wages and profits). Finally, we assume that government spending has no effect on the production functions of producers, and that labour supply is an increasing function of the real wage rate received by households. Later, we shall note some consequences of relaxing these assumptions. The variable w denotes the money wage rate paid by firms, inclusive of tax.

In Figure 7.3, there are three panels in which government's spending and taxing lead to changes. In the labour market, the labour supply curve N_s is repositioned, and a wedge (equal to tw/P, and measured by the distance JL or CF) is driven

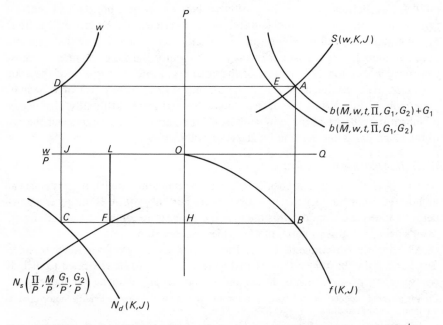

FIG. 7.3. The effects of introducing government expenditures on public goods (G_1/P) and negative lump-sum taxes (G_2/P), financed by a proportional income tax at rate t.

[18] This allows us to employ unique functions for labour supply and commodity demand, which are scaled up from any individual's functions for these.

[19] The Non-Substitution Theorem assumptions, therefore, hold, allowing us to employ a unique production function and a unique price index, P. See chapter 4, section II: 1.

between employers' and employees' perceptions of the real wage rate. In the product market(s), private and social demand are both altered. Thirdly, the money wage rate in the top left panel is liable to change.

The wedge in the real wage rate is governed by t: t equals CF/CH. Taken by itself, this effect lowers output and employment, because of the positive association between labour supply and the after-tax real wage rate that we have assumed. Had this association been negative (absent), output and employment would have been stimulated (unchanged) by the tax wedge. The repositioning of the labour supply curve occurs for two reasons. N_s will fall (increase) as a result of the provision of public goods G_1/P, if these are complementary with (substitutes for) leisure. Secondly, the real lump-sum transfer G_2/P will unambiguously lower N_s, assuming that leisure is not inferior. This effect was observed first in chapter 1, section I: 7, and then examined in detail in the Standard Income Tax Model of chapter 3, section II. It establishes that *the size of national income* is likely to vary negatively with *the degree of progressivity of income tax*. Note, however, that profit income —which the household treats as exogenous—is also liable to tax. To this extent, income tax acts as a *positive* lump-sum tax, with the opposite effect on labour supply.

In the product market, social, national demand is augmented by the government's direct expenditure, G_1. The private sector's demand for commodities (curve b) is boosted by the social dividend, G_2 (barring inferiority). It is increased or lowered by G_1, depending on whether private commodities are seen as complementary with, or substitutes for G_1. It is certainly lowered by t, unless private commodities are Giffen goods: an increase in t can be thought of as equivalent to a rise in the price of a Hicksian composite commodity, inducing both substitution and income effects. The first of these cannot raise, and the second may reduce, the demand for it.[20] Lastly, there is an effect operating on and from the demand for *money*. As was seen in chapter 5, Walras's Law allowed us to suppress the clearance condition for any one of a set of interrelated markets in general equilibrium: so far, we have availed ourself of this freedom to set aside the money market in the diagram. But when considering the consequences of government spending and taxation, we should be wrong not to incorporate all the monetary effects. It is not the supply of money which changes; it is the demand for money. The demand for real balances will be related positively to G_2/P (barring inferiority), and negatively or positively with G_1/P depending on whether G_1 and money are substitutes or complements. The income-tax rate t may raise or reduce the demand for money: as we saw earlier (chapter 1, section II: 7), this depends on a balance of considerations and cannot be determined *a priori*. In the context of the present one period model, however, the opportunity-cost argument for a positive association looks rather forced. Since there are no bonds, it has to rely upon portfolio equilibrium governing the relative demands for M/P and K, the former yielding nothing and the latter $P(1 - t)\partial Q/\partial K$ in nominal terms. This positive association is reinforced by any need for balances to effect tax 'transactions', but opposed—and probably counterweighed—by the negative effect of t upon the household's income $(wN + \bar{\pi})(1 - t)$.

[20] The second must reduce it, barring inferiority.

It is the net effect on the demand for money that governs what happens to the nominal magnitudes of w and P.

Some of the implications of altering the assumptions underlying Figure 7.3 are as follows. Introducing heterogeneous households provides a motive for redistributive taxation ($G_2 > 0$), which otherwise only serves to subvert allocative efficiency. If individuals differ in earnings ability, redistributive taxation of this kind may imply that the least able are unlikely to supply any labour.[21] If arguments such as Baumol's square-root law for inventories of money apply, so that the demand for money is concave in income for a population that differs in income level, the tendency to equalization of incomes to which redistributive taxation leads will bring a rise in the demand for money.[22]

If commodities differ in capital-intensity, P is no longer a unique index. Relative commodity prices and relative factor prices will depend upon the pattern of production. If the government provides public goods which are relatively capital-intensive, and if, as a result, the overall production pattern moves in favour of such goods,[23] the economy-wide factor prices of labour and capital will fall and rise respectively. There will be a positive association between the level of government spending and the rate of interest.[24] Government will also drive up the relative price of the goods it provides, unless private demand for them falls to an equal extent.[25] The practical likelihood of an offsetting decline in private demand depends chiefly on how 'public' the public goods in question are. In education and health, for example, at least some fall in private provision should occur if government provides more. In defence, this is much less likely, since most individuals will opt to spend next to nothing on such goods, as was seen in chapter 3.

If government expenditure on public goods does alter the household's marginal rates of substitution between leisure, private commodities, and money, we face a richer set of effects than those depicted in Figure 7.3. If the government provides national parks, private demand switches from lawn-mowers to climbing boots. If roads, we spend longer at work; opera or golf courses, probably less. If the State spends more on streetlighting and police, demand may switch from bank deposits to currency. These everyday examples may not be intrinsically very important; but they remind us that the repercussions of the State on less obvious aspects of the private sector's behaviour than 'total demand' should never be ignored.

One or two observations on taxation are in order here. We have assumed the capital stock to be exogenous. At the other extreme, had its elasticity of supply been infinite, not zero, and its real rental been defined net of *corporation tax* at rate t_c, the production function in the lower right panel of Figure 7.3 would have been linear, and the N_d curve in the lower left panel, vertical.[26] The real wage

---

[21] See chapter 3, section II, and Mirrlees (217).   [22] See chapter 5.

[23] This might not happen, e.g. if private demand fell by an offsetting amount, or were diverted away from other capital-intensive goods.

[24] Contrast the traditional '*IS–LM*' link between these variables: see section VI: 3, below.

[25] This is an example of the public sector 'relative price effect'. See Bacon and Eltis (19).

[26] Provided that the equal capital-intensity, no joint products and constant assumptions are retained.

rate (before tax) and the average product of labour would both have been negatively related to t_c; assuming a positive association between N_s and the real wage rate after tax, output and employment would have varied negatively with both t_c and t. Moving from corporation tax to rates of *indirect taxation*, we may note that the only differences between a uniform sales tax on all goods and a uniform tax on all incomes are twofold. The former is much likelier to raise the demand for money than the latter, since transactions occur at prices that include sales taxation. Secondly, in a dynamic model (which ours so far is not) the latter implies taxation on the interest earned on savings. The former does not. Taxing interest conflicts *prima facie* with intertemporal efficiency.[27]

Lastly, we might assume that government spending affects producers' equilibrium conditions directly. It could act like a change in a parameter reflecting technology, such as A or B in our earlier discussion in section II: 2, or the Hicks-neutral parameter J in Figures 7.1 to 7.3. If so, output and employment would both tend to increase,[28] all else equal, provided that government spending affected curves f and N_d favourably. Barro and Grossman (26) allow for this effect.

III: 4 *Allowing for Intertemporal Economic Activity*

The simplest equilibrium concept in a dynamic model is balanced growth. Balanced growth occurs if all growing variables grow equiproportionately. In the context of our model, this requires that technology be unchanging, and that the levels of output, capital, and labour aggregates grow uniformly. Balanced growth equilibrium may be illustrated simply by dividing Q, N, and K in Figures 7.1 to 7.3 by population; equilibrium positions simply repeat themselves in *per caput* terms. But this is a cheat, and conceals many important issues. We shall now examine some of these here; but a fuller scrutiny of the mechanisms and theories of economic growth is postponed until chapter 9.

How can our miniature model be amended to incorporate the intertemporal choices of households and producers?[29] Chapters 1 and 2 considered these choices separately, in a detailed and very general manner; we now combine them in a highly simplified two period framework.[30] Figure 7.4 illustrates. This shows the labour supply and demand, and product demand and supply decisions in the period *previous* to the one displayed in Figure 7.1 (denoted 1). In this earlier period, denoted 0 and by subscript 0, producers and consumers chose plans for the two periods 0 and 1. Labour supply in period 0 varies negatively with the expected real values of the wage rate, profit income and money balances in the subsequent period, assuming only that leisure at date 0 is a normal good. The demand for labour at 0 varies positively with the price level expected for date 1, and negatively (unless the two periods' labour inputs are complementary) with the money

---

[27] For example, the dynamic version of the Pareto conditions, and efficiency rules (such as the Keynes–Ramsey Rule) derived from them. See chapter 9.

[28] The demand for labour could fall if the government spending were equivalent to labour saving technical progress, however.

[29] The reader may wish to return to section VII: 3 in chapter 2 to refresh his memory of these.

[30] This resembles the model of Muellbauer and Portes (226).

wage rate then. In the product market, household demand (now b^h) is combined with an investment demand (b^f) to obtain the total demand for goods. (We are now returning provisionally to an anarchic state.) b_0^f is zero at point F. If P_0 is sufficiently high, firms run down their stock of capital, rather than adding to it. b_0^f varies positively with P_1: the higher the expected selling price of bread next period, the higher the profitability of inventories. It is also linked positively to w_1, since capital can be seen as stored-up labour: the higher the expected future cost of labour, the greater the incentive to buy the fruit of current, relatively cheaper labour, whether in the form of fixed investment goods or merely inventories. b_0^h varies positively with the future period's expected wage rate, profit income and money holdings, and ambiguously with the expected price level in the next period. The higher is P_1, the lower the real expected values of w_1, π_1 and M_1; on the other hand, the greater the incentive to buy present goods, if present and future goods are substitutes.

In Figure 7.4, equilibrium conditions establish w_0 and P_0, and implicitly w_1 and P_1 as well. The distance AE, or GH, represents real investment by producers at date 0; OG measures real consumption then. Since real income equals OH (at date 0), GH depicts both savings and investment, the equality of which is achieved by the price system (w_0, P_0, w_1, P_1). Real rates of profit also emerge. These are $\partial f_0/\partial K_0$ at date 0, and $\partial f_1/\partial K_1$ at date 1. Profit incomes in the two periods are found by multiplying these by $P_i K_i$ for each date ($i = 0, 1$). Lastly, the nominal interest rate, R_N. This appears as soon as we introduce bonds. There is a difference between the values of w and P that prevail in period 0's forward markets for date 1 (call these $_0w_1$ and $_0P_1$) and the actual spot values of w and P which will actually occur, if foresight is perfect, at date 1. If w_1 and P_1 are defined as the latter, we have the conditions $_0w_1 = w_1/(1 + R_N)$, $_0P_1 = P_1/(1 + R_N)$. This is by no means a complete framework; but it suffices to demonstrate several interesting results, particularly in the context of disequilibria which we shall examine in section VI.

Our dynamic extension to the miniature model has so far avoided considering the role of government. It has also adhered stoutly to the device of treating a parameter disturbance as a counterfactual change in the initial conditions; and it has effectively imposed perfect foresight. In section IV we shall attempt to repair these latter two deficiencies. But before this, we should consider the effects of injecting government activity into a two-period or multi-period equilibrium analysis.

There is no reason why a government must cover all its disbursements by taxation in each period. If its outgoings exceed its tax receipts in one year, it can, and will, borrow the difference. This borrowing can take either of two forms: an increase in $\bar{M}$, the stock of non-interest bearing government debt; or an increase in $\bar{B}$, the stock of interest-bearing debt. $\bar{B}$ denotes bonds. In most societies, government bonds are largely not indexed; they ar promises to pay at some future date a sum expressed in money terms. If B_{-i0} denotes the number of bonds outstanding at date 0 which were issued at date $-i$, and c_{-i} the coupon attached to them, interest obligations at date 0 net of tax at rate t_0 are

$$\sum_{i=0} c_{-i} B_{-i0} (1 - t_0).$$

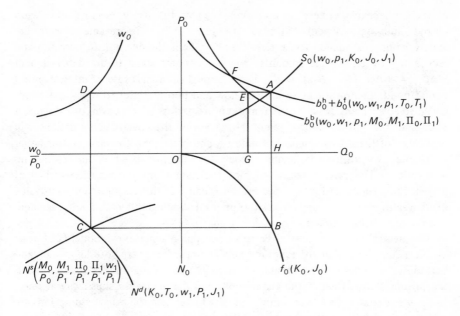

FIG. 7.4. The miniature general equilibrium model extended back one period.

Call this Z_0. In the notation of section III: 2, we have

$$Z_0 \quad + \quad G_{01} \quad + \quad G_{02} \quad = \quad t_0 P_0 Q_0 \quad + \quad \Delta \bar{M} \quad + \quad \Delta \bar{B}, \quad (7.3)$$

interest charges	+	public goods provision	+	net lump-sum transfers	=	income tax receipts	+	increase in currency debt	+	increase in interest-bearing debt

which holds for date 0, and any other date. Income tax receipts will be supplemented by any indirect and corporation tax receipts, and amended to allow for any non-linearities and discrimination in t, the income-tax rate. $\Delta \bar{M} + \Delta \bar{B}$ represent the public authorities' net disposal of financial assets. This figure may be positive, negative or zero. It will equal the private sector's net acquisition of financial assets, plus that of the rest of the world, if the economy is 'open':

$$\Delta \bar{M} + \Delta \bar{B} \quad = \quad S_0^h \quad + \quad S_0^f \quad - \quad I_0^h \quad - \quad I_0^f \quad + \quad CAS_0.$$

public authorities' net disposal of financial assets	=	household savings	+	corporate savings	−	household investment	−	corporate investment	+	current account surplus on external payments

$$(7.4)$$

In (7.4), I_0^h represents housebuilding expenditures incurred by the personal sector (the only kind of investment which national income statisticians usually allow it to undertake) and S_0^f the retained profits of the corporate sector.

What are the implications of a bond financed deficit? It seems at first sight that all the (contingent) advantages of government spending are preserved, and some of the disagreeable effects of taxation—such as the likely negative effects on output and employment—avoided. In fact, these disagreeable effects are merely being postponed. The easiest case to take is the decision to raise G_{02} and reduce G_{j2} by equivalent amounts (where j denotes some future date); in fact $-\Delta G_{j2} = +\Delta G_{02}(1 + R_{0j})^j$ if R_{0j} is the annual (nominal) rate of interest on a j period bond. Lump-sum taxes are cut now and boosted later to repay the bonds issued to cover them. Now if capital markets are perfect, so that everyone discounts at R_{0j}, if the private secttor is entirely aware of the government's actions—in particular, of their consequences at date j—and behaves in the far-sighted manner of chapter 1's utility-maximizing model, the bond-financed deficit carries no implications. The private sector anticipates future lump-sum taxation in lieu of present lump-sum taxation, and perceives no change in the discounted present value of its wealth, nor any change in relative prices. Labour supply commodity demand, and producer behaviour are all completely unaffected.

This neutrality result, seen in Barro's overlapping generations model (22), rests on the assumptions that the taxes cut now and raised later are both lump-sum, and that capital markets are perfect; and a flattering degree of cognitive skill is ascribed to the private sector. Change the assumptions and the neutrality slips away at once. If *income-tax* rates are lowered now and raised later, and the other assumptions are retained, there will be planned substitution out of this period's leisure into leisure at the date with the higher income-tax rates. Perceived relative prices have changed. Current output will tend to be raised, and output at some future date repressed. If households or companies face capital market imperfections, the replacement of one tax 'programme' by another will alter the preferred programme of consumption or investment. This is because capital market imperfections penalize non-synchronization of payments with receipts.[31] If public goods output is raised now and reduced later, there are likely to be complex reactions in supply and demand programmes in both factor and goods markets. Lastly, if the private sector is not credited with intelligence, government bonds will *not* be seen as tax threats, or public goods threats, for future years. They could be treated as an element in net wealth, by the aggregated private sector as a whole. In this case, an increase in their provision will tend to raise the demand for money and leisure and commodities. The first of these three effects is deflationary, but the latter two will tend to raise the equilibrium price level of commodities; the net effect of these repercussions will probably reduce the real capital value of outstanding bonds, from which—it might be claimed—the private sector will learn and cease treating bond issues in such a sanguine manner.

Finally, we may ask how a budget deficit affects interest rates. There will be no effect if the neutrality assumptions hold, and lump-sum taxes are merely being postponed by the issuance of bonds. Otherwise, there could be substantial and highly intricate effects. If the budget deficit has arisen because of a rise in government investment expenditure, and the private sector does not react in reducing its savings to compensate, the capital stocks in at least some activities will grow faster. This will tend to point the competitive rate of profit downwards, at least in a

---

[31] See chapter 1, section II: 8 and chapter 2, section III: 4.

simple model where capital and output are aggregable. This will imply a less steeply rising or more steeply falling trajectory for interest rates. Similar effects could follow if the income-tax rate has been cut now and is to be raised later. Any boost to current labour supply will tend to raise the current rate of profit on existing capital, but create an incentive to replace scarce future labour inputs (inhabited by higher income-tax rates) by more plentiful labour in this period. Private sector investment spending will therefore tend to rise; the extra savings from the household sector will be forthcoming because the increase in their current incomes is, and will be seen as, transitory.

There is no reason why a budget deficit need exert downward medium-term pressure on interest rates, however. In the short run, additional public goods expenditure could (temporarily) raise capital rentals if the industries providing them were relatively capital-intensive. A deficit visibly 'financed' by $\bar{M}$ will inevitably increase rational expectations of future price levels; this will tend to raise nominal interest rates, especially if further injections of $\bar{M}$ are now thought likelier. The markets may find it hard to digest large additional volumes of $\bar{B}$ without rises in rates of interest. Even if expectations are homogeneous and held with confidence, and transactions cots and taxes can be set aside so that Fisher's condition (110) on nominal interest rates

$$R_N = (\hat{P})^e + \frac{\partial Q}{\partial K} \tag{7.5}$$

holds, there is the chance the current high values of $\Delta\bar{B}$ may portend high future values of $\Delta\bar{M}$ as the government tries to save itself debt servicing charges. When risk-aversion is general, moreover, real and nominal assets will not be regarded as perfect substitutes; (7.5) will cease to hold, and increasing quantities of $\bar{B}$ will only be accepted at the price of rising R_N. Expectations of *future* bond sales by the authorities will then translate themselves into expectations of high interest rates in the future; these will be reflected, in their turn, in higher implicit forward rates and consequently higher spot rates, now. It has been usual[32] for economists to examine the proposition that government spending (or deficits) crowds out private spending within the framework of an implicitly disequilibrium model for goods and factor markets, such as the *IS-LM* system[33] or some expanded version of it. This leads to a detailed treatment of equilibrium conditions in the bond and other asset markets, but at the unfortunate price of excluding some of the other effects.

IV: Random Events and Expectations

IV: 1 *Disturbances*

There are four major differences between modern and traditional macroeconomic theory. For Keynes, capital was exogenous, at least in the short run; economic agents had 'propensities'; expectations were exogenous; and the influence of

[32] For example, Christ (57), Buiter (50), and Friedman (118). See Currie (73) for a valuable analysis of the growing literature on this important topic and also Feldstein (350).
[33] See section VI: 3 below.

random events on economic variables was fully recognized, but set aside. Harrod (147), Solow (304) and J. von Neumann (237) pioneered colourful, and startlingly different, ways of endogenizing a society's stock of capital: we consider these in chapter 9. Friedman (121), Hicks (162), Jorgenson (174), Lucas (196), Modigliani (220, 221), and Tobin (320) are among many who have attempted to provide macroeconomic theory with firm choice-theoretic foundations.

We have examined these in chapters 1, 2, and 5. The tasks of endogenizing expectations, and incorporating stochastic elements into macroeconomic theory, have only recently been undertaken on a large scale; it is to them that we now turn.

Disturbances may arise in any of the fundamental parameters of an economic model: preferences; technology; resources. Tastes change. New processes and new products are born. Population grows or declines; natural resources are discovered, or rendered sterile by sabotage, drought, or flood. Taxes, money stocks, and laws are altered by public authorities. The central distinction that presents itself is between *expected* and *unexpected* changes in the economic environment. The determinist will argue that most events that strike one as unexpected could have been foreseen, with enough information: most, indeed perhaps all. The sceptic will reply that the domain of the *currently* unknowable includes *all* future events. There is a view that 'uncertainty' about future events cannot be reduced to quantifiable 'risk', as in a game of tossing coins. This position has been put forcefully by Davidson (77), and persuasively by Shackle (291); it descends from Knight (185). Between them and the determinist, statistical theory can offer an appealing and practical compromise. This is the concept of the random disturbance, u_t at date t. Changes in variables are either systematic or random. If they are systematic, they can *in principle* be understood and anticipated. The random elements represent the irreducible minimum uncertainty: 'white noise'. The real difficulty is how to represent reality in a suitable model. Information is patchy, expensive, and unreliable. Computational complexity soon explodes if the number of relationships included is increased. If the number of observations is small, the statistical significance of parameter estimates will also drop steeply. In practice, therefore, many of the systematic changes in variables will not be perceived as such. Impressions will be confined to a small number of discernible aggregates, where the trade off between the benefits and costs of predictions seems appropriate.

IV: 2 *Expectations, Adaptive and Rational*

The first attempt to model expectations was built on the idea that they adapted over time in the face of errors. Predictive accuracy is evidence of success; however expectations are being formed, rarely they will not alter if success is achieved. When errors are experienced however, there is an incentive to revise expectations. The simplest hypothesis is that the size of the revision is proportional to the size of the error (and, of course, in the same direction):

$$E_t x_{t+1} - E_{t-1} x_t = (1 - \mu)(x_t - E_{t-1} x_t) \tag{7.6}$$

We saw earlier (chapter 1, section III) that (7.6) is an optimal predictor of x_t if and only if x_t is seen to follow the stochastic process

$$x_t = x_{t-1} + u_t - \mu u_{t-1}. \qquad (7.7)$$

Unfortunately, few economic variables can really be treated as self-determining in a manner such as (7.7). In the macroeconomy, all variables are interdependent, or at least potentially so. Only the weather follows its own course, independent of other variables; and even this may not remain true. When x_t is determined within a *system* of equations, optimal predictors of x must be constructed to incorporate this knowledge and to direct attention to the primary task of predicting the future values of parameters that will influence x. For example, if it is known that the demand for money, M_d, is related to the price level, P, to output Q, and to the mean prediction of next period's P, by

$$M_{dt} = \xi_t A_0 P_t^{a_1} Q_t^{a_2} (\text{antilog}\{E_t \log P_{t+1}\})^{-a_3} \qquad (7.8)$$

and that the money market clears,

$$M_{dt} = M_{st}, \qquad (7.9)$$

expectations of future price levels must recognize this fact. In (7.8), A_0 is a constant, and ξ_t represents a stochastic disturbance term, with a mean value of 1 and no serial correlation and stationarity. Writing (7.8) and (7.9) in logarithmic form, and using lower-case letters to denote this, we find that last period's expectation of the log of the current price level is

$$E_{t-1}p_t = -\frac{a_0}{a_1} + \frac{1}{a_1}E_{t-1}m_{st} - \frac{a_2}{a_1}E_{t-1}q_t + \frac{a_3}{a_1}E_{t-1}p_{t+1} \qquad (7.10)$$

since the expected value of u_t is zero. Successive iteration for $E_{t-1}p_{t+1}$, $E_{t-1}p_{t+2}$ and so on provides us with

$$E_{t-1}p_t = -\frac{a_0}{a_1 + a_3} + \frac{1}{a_1}E_{t-1}\sum_{i=0}^{\infty}\left(\frac{a_3}{a_1}\right)^i m_{st+i} - \frac{a_2}{a_1}E_{t-1}\sum_{i=0}^{\infty}\left(\frac{a_3}{a_1}\right)^i q_{t+i} \qquad (7.11)$$

(7.11) is an optimal predictor at $t-1$ of the logarithm of the price level at t. But it is hardly complete. For example, if

$$Q_t = \omega_t J_t K_t^{b_1} N_t^{b_2} \qquad (7.12)$$

the last term on the RHS of (7.11) is replaced by

$$-\frac{a_2}{a_1}E_{t-1}\sum_{i=0}^{\infty}\left(\frac{a_3}{a_1}\right)^i [j_t + b_1 k_2 + b_2 n_t]$$

if ω_t is a stochastic disturbance term with unit mean, stationarity, no serial correlation with ξ_t; and if

$$Q_t = T_t K_t^{b_1}(\text{antilog}\{p_t - E_{t-1}p_t\}$$

which reflects the possibility that current output and employment may be responsive to unexpected change in the price level,[34] the new final term on the

[34] This is the essence of the Lucas Surprise Supply Function. See Lucas (196).

RHS of (7.11) will reduce to

$$-\frac{a_2}{a_1} E_{t-1} \sum_{i=0}^{i} \left(\frac{a_3}{a_1}\right)^i [j_{t+i} + b_1 k_{t+i}].$$

This is so because $E_{t-1}(E_{t+i-1} p_{t+i})$ equals $E_{t-1} p_{t+i}$.[35]

In each of these cases, the price level forecast is much more sophisticated than the adaptive expectations hypothesis

$$E_{t-1} P_t = (1 - \mu) \sum_{i=0} \mu^i P_{t-1-i}, \tag{7.13}$$

which represents the integral of (7.6). If (7.8), (7.9), and (7.12) do provide a tolerably good description of reality, (7.13) is going to prove a good deal less lucky than (7.11) when (7.11) is modified to replace the endogenous q_{t+i} with technology, employment, and capital stock forecasts). Adaptive expectations may be optimal in meteorology, and acceptable for permanent income; they are not likely to work well for system-determined variables like the price level. But this still leaves the question of what this system is quite open. Take, for example, the tautology

$$\text{selling price} \equiv \frac{\text{mean money wage rate}}{\text{average product of labour}} (1 + \text{mark-up on labour costs}) \tag{7.14}$$

and write this $P \equiv (w/Z)(1 + m)$. There is a long Keynesian tradition that uses the dynamic equivalent of (7.14)

$$\hat{P} \equiv \hat{w} - \hat{Z} + \frac{\dot{m}}{1 + m} \tag{7.15}$$

not just to *describe* but actually to *explain* inflation. Certainly (7.15) imposes a restriction of consistency in expectations: if

$$E_s \log P_t = E_s \log w_t - E_s \log Z_t + E_s \log \frac{m_t}{1 + m_t}, \qquad s < t, \tag{7.16}$$

expectations will not be irrational. But this is not to say that (7.16) provides a complete foundation for inflation predictions. The general equilibrium theorist will declare that *if* all markets continuously clear, the neutrality result of section II will apply. The nominal values of P and w will exhibit trends whose common element is the trend in the money supply, and between which divergence is explained exclusively by 'real' factors, reflected here by Z and m. The predictions of $\hat{w}$, in other words, cannot possibly be dissociated from those of $\hat{M}$, the growth rate of the money supply. The monetarist will argue that one should 'look behind' $\hat{w}$, at $\hat{M}$; the Keynesian tradition asserts the opposite direction of causality. It is no less unthinkable that the evolution of the money supply responds to political and economic forces.[36] If so, forecasts of future values of the money supply will

---

[35] This says that your current expectations of what you will next year expect the price level to be in two years' time must equal your current expectations of the price level then.

[36] Goldthorpe (133) has a stimulating discussion of this point. See also Sargent and Wallace

be irrational unless estimates are made of how, when, and how powerfully these forces will operate. Even if the monetary authorities succumb to arguments in favour of a fixed growth rate of the money supply (considered below, in section VII), and publish a specific target growth rate, one should still speculate about when and how total their conversion will be, how long it will last, what could dislodge them from it, and so on. When a politician says 'I promise to do x' he may signal—wittingly or unwittingly—the impression that he thinks you do not believe him, and he is trying to reassure you. If so, the statement may have exactly the opposite effect to that intended, and may be treated like 'I am lying when I say this'. Interestingly, it seems likely that the proximity of expectations of future values of policy parameters to current announcements about these should depend on their observed proximity in the past. To that extent, adaptive expectations may be quite plausible. Indeed, both rational and adaptive expectations emphasize the importance of learning from experience; where they are likely to differ is in the breadth of experience considered relevant.

V: Disequilibrium (non-market-clearance) in the One-period Model

V: 1 *Repressed Inflation*

The macroeconomic theories of Keynes, and the econometric models built upon them, are far removed from the equilibrium model of the macroeconomy that we have considered up to now. Economists have long been puzzled by exactly what it is that separates Keynesian economic reasoning from traditional equilibrium analysis. The formal analysis of disequilibrium, of which Keynesian macroeconomics forms an important part, begins with Clower (60). Notable contributions after Clower include those by Barro and Grossman (26, 27), Benassy (38), Malinvaud (204, 205), and Muellbauer and Portes (226). The type of disequilibrium studied in these models is non-market-clearance. Somewhat confusingly, they are sometimes referred to as models of 'temporary equilibrium'.

We begin our study of disequilibrium by returning to the miniature model and asking what happens if the money supply is raised, but the price of goods and the money wage rate are both held rigid. The answer is that we enter a regime of repressed inflation.

An increase in the money supply, we saw in section II and Figure 7.2, raised the demand for bread (the product), and reduced the household's supply of labour. In Figure 7.5, the first effect is registered in the move from b_0 to b^*, the latter by that from N_s^0 to N_s^*. Notional excess demands emerge in the two markets: A_3A_1 for bread, C_0C_1 for labour. Ordinarily, one would anticipate a rise in w and P following such an event; certainly their equilibrium values do rise. But here, we are freezing w and P at their low initial values.

These notional excess demands interact. Households are likely to respond to rationing in the goods market (where supply is restricted to A_3) by reducing their

(281): in their study of hyperinflation, inflation may cause subsequent monetary expansion because of the budgetary revenue losses. There are many other variables to which monetary aggregates may respond. See chapter 6.

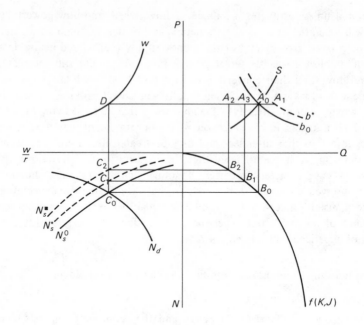

FIG. 7.5. Repressed inflation in the miniature model.

labour supply, as we saw in chapter 1. Labour supply falls, if it falls, because the 'virtual' price of goods, i.e. that which would have induced households to reduce their purchases of bread to A_3 voluntarily,[37] has risen. Labour supply is reduced from N_s^* to N_s, where a multiplier process of reduced-goods-supply interacting with reduced-labour-supply is assumed to stop. This multiplier, known as the 'supply-supply multiplier',[38] was discovered by Barro and Grossman (27). Output and employment collapse to a new low-level equilibrium, $C_2B_2A_2D$.

---

[37] See Neary and Roberts (233).

[38] The supply–supply multiplier is the vicious or virtuous circle that can arise under conditions of excess demand for labour and goods. The essential notion is that (i) output cannot be chosen freely by producers, since they cannot obtain the labour supplies that they wish; (ii) output is governed by, and varies positively with, the supply of labour freely chosen by households; but (iii) households' labour supply is affected by, and probably reduced as a result of, the excess demand in the goods market. Of these, (i) and (ii) are straightforward, but (iii) is not. The fact that a particular good is in excess demand—so that households cannot acquire as much of it as they would wish under conditions of full equilibrium—may affect the supply of labour in three ways.

First, the marginal rates of substitution between leisure and other goods over which the households can exercise choice may change. This effect can work either way. A shortage of fishing rods (complementary with leisure) should raise the labour supply; in other cases, it could fall. Secondly, household income and financial resources must now be concentrated on *fewer* goods on which discretion can be exercised, than would have been the case in full equilibrium. This diversion of 'spending' can only reduce the supply of labour, if leisure is assumed to be a normal good. Thirdly, the fact that the output of the good in question will be lower than in the extent that it does—and *some* households' incomes must be affected this way—labour supply should rise.

To see this in operation, suppose we consider the effects of a rise in government spending,

At this position, increases in output and employment will follow if the capital stock, or parameters reflecting technology, are raised. The constraints on households in the goods market, and on producers in the labour market, are both released. If repressed inflation is introduced into the version of the miniature model that incorporates a government, further results follow: a fall in government spending will raise output and employment, as will an increase in lump-sum taxation.

The reader may consider that repressed inflation is a fiction; surely, he may think, excess demand provokes price increases, more quickly and more reliably perhaps than excess supply provokes the opposite. The macroeconomic experiences of the Polish economy in the 1970s provide a clear example of repressed inflation, however. Its symptoms will be queues in the commodity market, a weak trade balance (unless exporters sell overseas to obviate domestic price controls), and shortages of labour. The UK in the period 1972-3 may constitute a more subtle instance: increases in monetary aggregates ranging from 15 per cent per year for M1 and 28 per cent per year for M3, in a period (from November 1972) when wage rates and prices were subject to strictly enforced ceilings. The perils of the supply-supply multiplier act as a warning against the combination of wage and price controls with highly inflationary demand management policy.

V: 2 *Classical unemployment*

In repressed inflation, buyers were rationed in both markets: firms could not buy the labour they would wish, nor households the goods. In classical unemployment, we continue to bserve excess demand in the goods market. The labour market, however, is in excess supply. There is unemployment, or insufficient hours of work, from labour's standpoint. Producers are in equilibrium in both goods and labour markets; they choose their trades without any rationing.

Figure 7.6 illustrates the consequences of increasing the money wage rate from its equilibrium value, w_0 to w^*. The money supply and the price level of goods are kept at previous equilibrium values. The product supply curve moves leftwards. Output falls; in the labour market, the demand for labour falls following the increase in the real wage rate. The new low-level equilibrium is $A^*B^*C^*D^*$.

In these circumstances, a rise in the supply of money, or a fall in lump-sum

under conditions of repressed inflation. For a given output level of the good on which government is spending more, there must now be less available for households to consume. The first and second of our three effects are now set to work. The second must tend to reduce the supply of labour, while the first could go either way. On balance, one should probably expect labour supply to *fall*. If it does, output will be lowered by all firms experiencing excess demand for labour. This must entail a further fall in what is available for households to buy. This will in turn affect households' choices about how much labour to supply. This time, all three effects will operate. The second will tend to lower labour supply further, the third to raise it, and the first could go either way. The second will overpower the third under various conditions—if part of the reduced value of producers' output is syphoned off in lower tax payments to the government; or if households' loss of profit income is delayed or incompletely perceived. In this case, there should be a *further* fall in labour supply. But this in turn will reduce still further the availability of goods for households, with a third round of repercussions on labour supply. The supply–supply multiplier is derived by summing the series of these effects on the goods market.

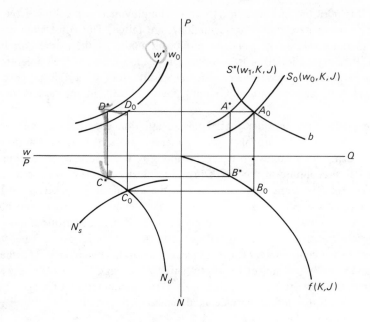

FIG. 7.6. Classical unemployment in the miniature model.

taxation, or an increase in government spending, will have no effects.[39] They will affect the notional demand for goods and the notional supply of labour, but since output is supply-determined and employment demand-determined, output and employment remain locked. Increases in output and employment will follow, however, if the capital stock is increased, or if the level of technology is raised,[40] or indeed if employment subsidies or income-tax changes lower the employer's perception of the real wage rate he pays for labour.

Whether classical unemployment is termed voluntary or involuntary may be a semantic matter. One possible explanation for 'excessive' real wage rates could be monopolistic behaviour on the part of trade unions. Majoritarian tyranny may be exercised by the large group of employees who raise their incomes with a real wage increase, on the minority—typically, those most recently hired, those about to retire, and other marginal groups—who lose their jobs as a result. Another possible cause is legislation that enforces a minimum real wage rate above equilibrium; in this case, unemployment will be enforced on those whose abilities, as perceived by employers, are too low for them to be profitable to hire at the minimum set.

VI: 3 *Keynesian Unemployment: A First Glimpse*

Keynesian unemployment is characterized by generalized excess supply, in both product and labour markets. It is the exact opposite of repressed inflation in this

[39] Assuming that they are insufficiently large to provoke a switch of regime, into repressed inflation.

[40] Except if technical progress is labour-augmenting when the profit share exceeds the substitution elasticity.

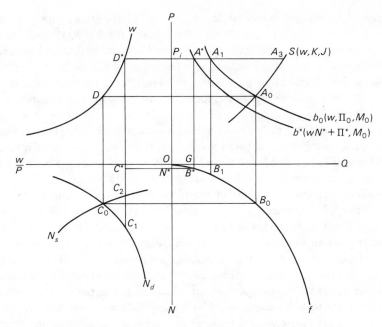

FIG. 7.7. Keynesian unemployment in the miniature model.

regard. Again households are rationed, but this time in the labour market; firms are rationed in the product market.

Keynesian unemployment can be reached by departing from the initial equilibrium constellation by raising the price level, and freezing the money wage rate, and the money supply and other parameters. Figure 7.7 illustrates. The price level increase causes notional excess supply in the product market, and, since the real wage rate has fallen, notional excess demand for labour. In this respect, Keynesian unemployment seems to be the opposite of classical unemployment. But the excess demand for labour is only notional. The fact that producers cannot sell the output they wish forces them to a constrained demand for labour which falls beneath the labour supply. The reduction in employment then causes a spillover effect in the product market. Household income is out below its preferred level, as a result of the rationing in the labour market; in consequence, the constrained demand for goods is lower than it would otherwise be. This interacts perversely with the demand for labour. A demand-for-goods demand-for-labour multiplier[41] applies. Like the supply–supply multiplier, the demand–demand multiplier arises from a positive feedback interaction between the product and labour markets. Again, like the supply–supply multiplier, it generates a low-level equilibrium where both output and employment are still below their full equilibrium values. But this is where the similarity between repressed inflation and Keynesian unemployment ends. Policy implications, and the effects of parameter disturbances, are often diametrically opposed in the two disequilibrium regimes.

[41] Invented by Kahn (177).

In Figure 7.7, notional disequilibria with P_1 are A_1A_3 excess supply in the product market and C_1C_3 excess demand for labour. The low-level constrained equilibrium, once the repercussions[42] of the demand–demand multiplier have been fully incorporated, is seen at A^* in the goods market and C^* in the labour market. The pitifully low level of employment, N^*, generates household income of $wN^* + \pi^*$ in nominal terms, which supports the constrained goods-demand curve b^*. Employers are in a constrained equilibrium at B^*, where labour input is minimized consistent with the exogenously imposed output level OG. The real wage rate is exceeded by the marginal product of labour at B^*, but the marginal revenue product of labour is undefined: the typical firm faces a rectangular average revenue curve, with marginal revenue defined only along its horizontal section.

The low-level equilibrium will be improved by expansionary monetary policy. This will move b^* rightwards in the product market, while its labour-supply-reducing effect will be irrelevant since employment is determined by the demand for labour. If government spending and taxation are introduced, a rise in the former must also raise output and employment. A reduction in taxes is also likely to do so, but the fact that this will raise the demand for money could conceivably neutralize or even offset its favourable product market effects. A rise in the stock of capital, or an improvement in technology, would necessarily reduce employment. A fall in the price level would increase real balances and increase the demand for goods, thereby raising the demand for labour. The magnitude and reliability of this real balance effect have, however, frequently been called into question; we shall return to these objections below (section VI: 3). An increase in the money wage rate would tend to add to output and employment in Keynesian unemployment if wage income is subject to a higher marginal propensity to consume, or conducive to earlier expenditure, than profit income.[43]

V: 4 *Further Observations on Disequilibrium in the Miniature Model*

In the context of our miniature one-period model, where there are only one product and one labour market, different types of equilibrium and disequilibrium might be categorized as in Table 7.1. In this section, we have been considering variants of the equilibrium model that all fall into category A. In section II, we were examining category E. There are other possibilities: one might describe B as the 'Bretton Woods' model, where individual countries' price levels, at least in terms of tradable goods, were bound together by the fixed exchange rate regime and the international commodity arbitrage mechanism of the kind considered in chapter 4. In categories C and D, the goods market will be equilibrated, perhaps in some restricted sense, as a result of the perfect flexibility of the price level; the economy will lie at the boundary between classical and Keynesian unemployment, or else (by fluke) at the full general equilibrium.

Figure 7.8 illustrates the case of a fixed money wage rate with a flexible price

---

[42] See section VI: 3 for an example of this. The demand–demand multiplier there is $[1 - E_1 + (E_2/L_2)L_1]^{-1}$.

[43] If neither of these conditions is true, so that household demand for goods is based simply on $wN^* + \pi^*$, a change in w^* has no effect, since it involves a mere relabelling of the components of a given total level of income.

Table 7.1. *Different categories of equilibrium and disequilibrium*

		Wage rate		
		Locked in money	Locked in real terms	Perfectly free
Price level	Locked	A		B
	Perfectly free	C	D	E

level (category *C*). As usual, $A_0 B_0 C_0 D_0$ denotes full equilibrium; this occurs (for $M = M_0$) with w_0 and P_0. Now suppose the money wage rate is locked above w_0, at w^*. Producers (who are in full equilibrium at all times in this model if we rule out excess demand for labour) will restrict their profit maximizing output level in response to this from S_0 to S^*. Output and employment settle down at Q^* and N^*, where the adverse repercussions of the fall in employment and output on consumer demand (and hence back on employment) have been fully incorporated: the demand for goods shifts inwards from b_0 to b^*.

In Figure 7.8, one solution to the excessive nominal wage rate is to expand the nominal money stock; for it is really the ratio of the former to the latter that has

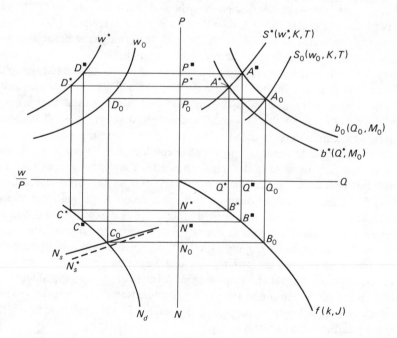

FIG. 7.8. The fix-wage flex-price version of the miniature model in equilibrium and disequilibrium: money wage rate locked.

risen too high. The effects of this will be to increase the demand for goods (shown for simplicity as a return from D^* to D_0, the old demand curve which applied when output was Q_0 and the money supply M_0). With the money wage rate locked at w^*, output increases along the supply curve S^*; and price rises too. Their new levels are P and Q. The ratio of output increase to price increase, in proportionate terms, is the elasticity of supply; as we saw in chapter 2, this is simply the ratio of wages to profits, multiplied by the elasticity of substitution between capital and labour in the production function. The real wage is cut, and this is consistent with the output and employment increases from Q^* and N^* to Q and N along f; the marginal product of labour $\partial f/\partial N$ is correspondingly lower at B than B^*.

A fiscal stimulus to aggregate demand would also (generally: see section VI: 3 below) increase employment, output, and the price level, no matter whether this took the form of a rise in government spending or a fall in taxes. An increase in the stock of capital, a fall in the money wage rate and technical progress would all have broadly similar effects on output (up) and the price level (down), as a result of a rightward shift of the supply curve. While the other two would clearly raise employment, technical progress has ambiguous effects on N; broadly speaking, the more elastic the demand curve, the likelier N is to rise.[44]

The favourable effect of monetary expansion on employment in Figure 7.8 is in stark contrast with the miniature equilibrium model with perfect price and wage flexibility, where the neutrality result ensured that real variables (of which N is one) were independent of the money supply. It also conflicts with models derived from fixing the *real* wage rate rather than the nominal wage rate, when the price level is perfectly flexible. These are portrayed in Figures 7.9 and 7.10. In Figure 7.9, the real wage rate is locked above its equilibrium value, in circumstances of classical unemployment where producers are in equilibrium in goods and labour markets. With the real wage rate frozen at w^*/P^*, above its full equilibrium value w_0/P_0, employment and output are held down to N^* and Q^*. The low real income level generates a reduced level of demand (b^*, not b_0); the commodity market clears at price P^*, where the exogenously determined output rate Q^* interesects the shrunken commodity demand curve b^*. This time, the consequences of monetary expansion do nothing for output or employment. Since the supply curve is now vertical, any increase in demand—shown for simplicity again as a return to the old, full equilibrium demand curve—simply bids up the price level from P^* to P. There is an equiproportionate jump in the money wage rate to w: the real wage rate remains unchanged *ex hypothesi* at w^*/P^*. Fiscal expansion will also have no real effects, unless it succeeds in altering the producers' production function, f, or the real wage rate paid by employers, w^*/P^*. An employment subsidy or income tax cut that *does* succeed in lowering the real wage rate perceived by employers will necessarily raise output and employment. A rise in government spending which exerts a favourable impact upon the production function f will certainly raise output. It may raise or lower employment, depending on the direction in which it moves the demand curve for labour, N_d.

[44] See Heffernan (157) and Sinclair (301) for a detailed analysis of this point. Model III in (301) is what is portrayed in Figure 7.8; Figure 7.9 depicts Model II.

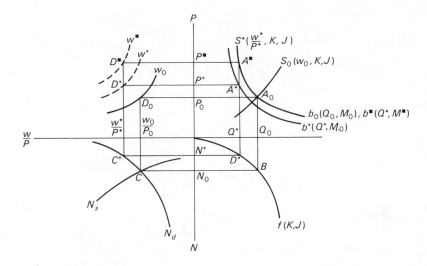

FIG. 7.9. The fix-wage flex-price version of the miniature model in equilibrium and disequilibrium: real wage rate locked above equilibrium.

The notion of rigidity in the real wage rate received after tax by households has received wide attention.[45] Real wage rigidity is more appealing than rigidity in nominal wage rates, because the latter can only be explained by money illusion, at least, if it is observed over long periods.[46] But a rigid real wage rate when the price level is flexible does not necessarily imply a regime of classical unemployment. If it is locked beneath its full equilibrium value, as in Figure 7.10, another kind of low-level equilibrium emerges. This time, output and employment are constrained by an inadequate *supply* of labour, rather than inadequate demand for it (as in Figure 7.9). If the real wage rate is locked at w^*/P^* below w_0/P_0, employment is cut below N_0, and output below Q_0. The market price of goods, which is flexible, rises to equilibrate the goods market; this reduces real balances (if the nominal money supply is given), stimulating a rise in labour supply. The low-level equilibrium is assumed to reach a state of rest at $A^*B^*C^*D^*$.

Finally, it should be noted that these 'fix-price' models of temporary equilibrium, where the price level and the money wage rate are held constant, can be transplanted straightforwardly into a world where inflation is occurring. Provided that the price level, the money wage rate, and the money supply all change in unison by equal proportions, and all parameters are given in real terms, the real disequilibria will not be affected.[47]

In Figure 7.10, the real wage rate is distinctly lower than the marginal product of labour, as measured by $\partial f/\partial N$ at B^*. Employment is supply constrained.

[45] See, for example, Bacon and Eltis (19), Sargan (277) and (278), and Henry, Sawyer, and Smith (158). It is also the basis of arguments for tax-based income policies: see Perry (250), Seidman (288) and Slitor (303). A general survey of arguments on this is found in Corden (67).

[46] A short-term rigidity in nominal wage rates will be observed if there is discontinuous negotiation of nominal wage rates.   [47] See also Corden (65).

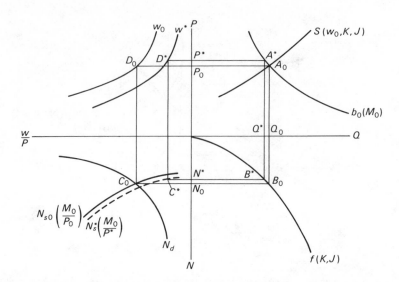

FIG. 7.10. The fix-wage flex-price version of the miniature model in equilibrium and disequilibrium: real wage rate locked below equilibrium.

The last of the five categories, cell E in Table 7.1, corredsponds of course with
the miniature general equilibrium model. Here, perfect wage and price flexibility
ensure that both labour and goods markets clear. The contrast between B and E
can be illustrated in an open economy, by the difference between fixed and floating
exchange rates. In cell B, the labour market clears; the goods and money markets
do not necessarily clear in the short run. An excess supply of money is decumulated
by running an external payments deficit, and is balanced by an excess demand for
goods. An excess demand for money accompanied by an excess supply of goods
leads to an accumulation of reserves. This is the essence of the monetary approach
to the balance of payments, under fixed exchange rates. Under floating, the
exchange rate equilibrates the domestic (and foreign) money market. An incipient
excess demand (supply) for money is cancelled by appreciation (depreciation)
relative to the rest of the world.[48] On a fixed exchange rate, however, an excess
supply of goods can be sold overseas. This suggests that a small open economy,
which is a price-taker in world markets, may never suffer from Keynesian
unemployment. This view is propounded by Dixit (88). It is possible, however, that
there could be an excess supply of *non-traded* goods;[49] and a small open economy's
exporters could also experience world-wide excess supply of their goods, with a
consequent rationing constraint upon their export levels.

Returning to category A, we may note that departures from a full, 'Walrasian'
equilibrium led sometimes to classical unemployment, sometimes to Keynesian
unemployment and sometimes to repressed inflation. Repressed inflation (RI)
emerged when both w and P were cut equiproportionately; Keynesian unemployment (KU), when P was raised; classical unemployment (CU), when w was raised.

[48] See chapter 4, section III: 3.   [49] See Neary (231) for a detailed analysis of this.

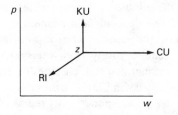

FIG. 7.11. Departures from Walrasian equilibrium.

Figure 7.11 illustrates this. Point Z is the point of Walrasian equilibrium, where markets for goods labour and money all clear. If w or P fails to equal its Walrasian equilibrium value, some form of disequilibrium and rationing must ensue. The analysis of this section has been conducted n the basis of the 'Short Side Principle'. This states that the actual quantity traded in any market i, q_i, will be minimum of quantity demanded and quantity supplied:

$$q_i = \min(q_{di}, q_{si}) \tag{7.17}$$

It is further assumed that if q_{di}, is the binding restraint, each and every seller is quantity-constrained; while each buyer is quantity-constrained if q_{si} is the binding restraint, which must occur when the market in question is in excess demand. In a model with just one kind of labour and one commodity, the variety of possible regimes is shown in Table 7.2. F_1 is Walrasian equilibrium, shown by point Z in

Table 7.2. *Possible Regimes in a 1 × 1 Model*

		Household rationed		
		Nowhere	Labour	Goods
Producer rationed	Nowhere	F_1	F_2	
	Labour	F_3		F_4
	Goods		F_5	

Figure 7.11. This is possible, but occurs only as a fluke. F_2 corresponds to classical unemployment, where the labour market is in excess supply and the goods market is in excess demand. Households are rationed in both markets, producers in neither. The opposite to this has been called 'Underconsumption';[50] households are not constrained in either market, but firms have an excess demand for labour and an excess supply of output. In a static one-period, underconsumption cannot rise. Either the firm cuts back its labour demand to consistency with the exogenously imposed demand limit on output in the goods market—and this will provoke Keynesian unemployment—or else the excess demand for labour must be reflected

[50] See Muellbauer and Portes (226).

in an excess demand for the producers' output (repressed inflation). The spillover effects will constrain effective demands and supplies to F_4 or F_5. In a dynamic setting, however, F_3 is perfectly possible; we shall illustrate it in section V below.

No market can suffer simultaneously from excess demand *and* excess supply (although an aggregate of distinct markets, e.g. for different kinds of labour, easily could). Consequently, the middle and lower right cells of the matrix in Table 7.2 are empty. It is clear that F_4 corresponds with repressed inflation, and F_5 with Keynesian unemployment.

One question that is provoked by both Table 7.3 and Figure 7.11 is the relative *probabilities* of the different regimes. This raises two issues: first, what are the relative sizes of the three disequilibrium regimes, F_2, F_4 and F_5; and second, is there any reason for expecting deviations from Walrasian equilibrium to be any likelier in one direction than another. The first question requires us to identify the position of the boundaries between the regimes. These vary with the type of utility and production functions assumed. Suppose both are Cobb–Douglas functions

$$U = \left(\frac{M}{P}\right)^{\beta}(h-N)^{\gamma}b^{\delta}, \qquad \text{where } \delta = 1 - \beta - \gamma, \qquad (7.18)$$

$$b = ZN^{\alpha}, \qquad (7.19)$$

where N denotes employment, b output and demand in the product market, M the nominal money demanded, and h the endowment of hours available to the household.

The boundary between CU and KU is found by imposing clearance on the goods market, but excess supply of labour; for households, N is exogenous ($\bar{N}$). Households maximize U subject to $\bar{M} + w\bar{N} + \bar{\pi} - Pb - M$ with respect to money holdings and quantity of the good bread alone. First-order conditions for this imply

$$\bar{M} = \frac{\beta}{\delta}Pb, \qquad (7.20)$$

which is a rectangular hyperbolic demand curve: the velocity of circulation of money is δ/β. Profit maximization by price-taking producers implies that

$$N = \left(\frac{\alpha Z}{w}\right)^{1/(1-\alpha)}$$

and hence, from (7.19),

$$b = (PZ)^{1/(1-\alpha)}\left(\frac{\alpha}{w}\right)^{\alpha/(1-\alpha)}. \qquad (7.21)$$

Inserting (7.21) into (7.20) to eliminate b, we derive the equation for P:

$$P = \left(\frac{w}{\alpha}\right)^{\alpha}\frac{N}{Z}\left(\frac{\delta\bar{M}}{P}\right)^{1-\alpha}. \qquad (7.22)$$

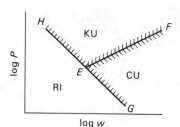

FIG. 7.12. The regime boundaries with Cobb–Douglas utility and production functions, and various parameter estimates.

(7.22) reveals that the elasticity of P to w equals the wage share of income, α. The KU/CU boundary has a gradient, therefore, equal to the wage share, if P and w are replaced by $\log P$ and $\log w$, as in Figure 7.12. The KU/RI border is found by suspending the equilibrium conditions of firms, and instead utilizing those for the household. Maximizing (7.18) subject to $\bar{M} + \bar{w}N + \bar{\pi} - \bar{P}b - M$ with respect to M, b, and N implies

$$N = h - \frac{\gamma}{\beta + \delta} \frac{\bar{M} + Pb}{w} \tag{7.23}$$

in addition to (7.20). Combining (7.20) and (7.23) with (7.19) permits us to solve for P in terms of w, $\bar{M}$ and other parameters alone:

$$P = \frac{\delta}{\beta} \frac{\bar{M}}{Z} \left[h - \frac{\bar{M}\gamma}{w\beta} \right]^{-1/\alpha}. \tag{7.24}$$

Differentiating $\log P$ w.r.t. $\log w$ from (7.24) establishes

$$\frac{\partial P/P}{\partial w/w} = -\frac{h - N}{\alpha N} = -\frac{\text{leisure time}}{\text{work time} \cdot \text{wage share}}. \tag{7.25}$$

Just as (7.22) gave us the gradient of the line EF in Figure 7.12, (7.25) is the gradient of EH.

The CU/RI border is characterized by labour market clearance in *effective* terms, and excess demand in the product market. This time, producers are in equilibrium; households are rationed in the product market, and hence supply an altered amount of labour, in our case less than they otherwise would in Walrasian equilibrium. Households' decisions emerge from maximizing (7.18) subject to $\bar{M} + \bar{w}N + \bar{\pi} - \bar{P}b - M$ with respect to their two free choice variables, M and N:

$$\bar{M} = M = w \frac{\beta}{\gamma}(h - N) \tag{7.26}$$

combining (7.26) with (7.21) and an expression for $\bar{\pi}$ (which equals

$$(1 - \alpha)(PZ)^{1/(1-\alpha)} \left(\frac{\alpha}{w}\right)^{\alpha/(1-\alpha)}$$

since producers are in equilibrium with the real wage equal to labour's marginal product) yields this solution for P in terms of w, $\bar{M}$ and the other parameters:

$$P = \frac{w}{\alpha Z}\left[h - \frac{\gamma \bar{M}}{\beta\ w}\right]^{(1-\alpha)}. \tag{7.27}$$

Differentiating (7.27) w.r.t. w, and substituting (7.26) to eliminate $\bar{M}$ reveals

$$\frac{\partial P/P}{\partial w/w} = -\left[\alpha + (1-\alpha)\frac{h}{N}\right] = -\left[\text{wage share} + \text{profit share} \cdot \frac{\text{time endowment}}{\text{work time}}\right]. \tag{7.28}$$

(7.28) is the gradient of EG in Figure 7.12. If we take α to equal $\frac{3}{4}$, and the ratio of N to h to be $\frac{1}{3}$,[51] the gradient of both EG and EH is $-\frac{3}{2}$, while that of EF is $+\frac{3}{4}$. These figures suggest that the sizes of the three regions can be ranked in descending order BI, KU, CU. It must be emphasized, however, that the ranking is highly sensitive to the initial assumptions made about the character of the utility and production functions, factor shares and the N/h ratio. For example, if (7.18) and (7.19) are generalized to being merely linear homogeneous functions,[52] the gradient of the crucial CU/KU boundary will be

$$\left(1 + \frac{\sigma_u}{\sigma_Q wN/\pi}\right)^{-1} = \left(1 + \frac{\text{utility-elasticity of substitution between } M/P \text{ and } Q}{(\text{wage bill/profits}) \cdot \text{elasticity of substitution in production}}\right)^{-1}, \tag{7.29}$$

where σ_u is the substitution elasticity in utility and σ_Q that in production. This can be seen by inspecting Figure 7.13. The elasticity of P to w equals

$$\frac{AB}{AC} = \frac{AB/BD}{AB/BD + BC/BD} = \left[1 + \frac{BC/BD}{AB/BD}\right]^{-1}$$

since AC represents the proportionate increase in the money wage rate. Now BC/BD is the reciprocal of the elasticity of supply; this elasticity equals $(wN/\pi)\cdot\sigma_Q$ when capital and the money wage rate are exogenous and producers are in

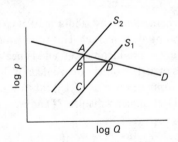

FIG. 7.13. Illustrating the Keynesian unemployment–Classical unemployment boundary gradient.

[51] This figure is suggested by the phenomenon of the eight-hour working day; if weekends, vacations, retirement leisure, unemployment, and other forms of non-participation in the labour market point to a lower ratio, subtracting sleeping time from h points to a higher one.

[52] The production function is assumed to be linear homogeneous in capital and employment, with the former exogenous.

competitive equilibrium.[53] *AB/BD* is the elasticity of demand, which equals one in the Cobb–Douglas case and σ_u in the more general case of homothetic preferences. Interestingly, (7.29) must lie between 0 and +1.

The second question provoked by considering the relative likelihoods of the three disequilibrium regimes was whether deviations from Walrasian equilibrium were likelier in one direction than another. The Keynesian macroeconomic tradition maintains two asymmetries which are relevant to this: the notion that goods markets clear faster than labour markets, and the hypothesis that price rises in markets with excess demand are faster than price falls in those with excess supply. Figure 7.14 depicts these ideas. The vertical axis shows the proportionate rate of change of money wage rates and prices over time, the horizontal the level of excess

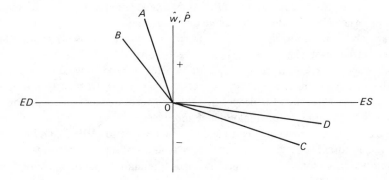

FIG. 7.14. The two Keynesian asymmetries in disequilibrium adjustments.

supply. Walras's *tâtonnement* hypothesis states that markets grope towards equilibrium by making the price of any good or factor move in the direction of excess demand for it:[54] excess supply provokes a fall, excess demand a rise. If the two Keynesian assymmetries are correct, *AOC* could represent the goods market *tâtonnement* equation, and the flatter kinked line *BOD* that for the labour market. In terms of Figure 7.12, this would imply that stochastic shocks that led to departures from Walrasian equilibrium at *E* into the repressed inflation regime would be self-correcting much more *quickly* than those which led to Keynesian unemployment. Classical unemployment (where the goods market is in excess demand) would also tend to disappear rather faster than Keynesian unemployment. Figure 7.15 illustrates the Keynesian asymmetries of Figure 7.14 by arrows of different length, superimposed on the disequilibrium regimes shown in Figure 7.12. If *OD* in Figure 7.14 is horizontal—so that money wage rates cannot fall, no matter how high the excess supply of labour—the economy will always be tending to the line *HEF* in Figure 7.15, until or unless dislodged by shocks.[55]

[53] See chapter 2, section II: 3.
[54] See Varian (327) and Arrow and Hahn (11) for detailed analysis.
[55] This provokes the interesting question of what happens if the economy is somewhere on *HE*. Strictly speaking, line *HE* is an 'underconsumption' region (see below), where there is a notional excess demand for labour and a notional excess supply of goods. If wage and price

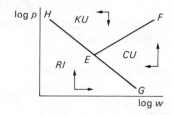

FIG. 17.15. Disequilibrium regimes and the two Keynesian asymmetries.

The foregoing arguments imply that Keynesian unemployment could well be the commonest type of disequilibrium. The economy is perhaps likelier to spend more time slightly above the line *HEF* than anywhere else, Figure 7.15 suggests. But this conclusion should be accepted very cautiously. If our economy is subject to wage and price controls *and* expansionary monetary (or fiscal) policy, the repressed inflation regime does become highly probable. Evidence that rises in money wage rates lead price rises at least as often as not[56]—whatever the reason for the finding—suggests that the economy may quite frequently move, temporarily at least, towards (or deeper into) the classical unemployment region. The classical explanations of unemployment, moreover, are numerous, subtle, and in some cases rather convincing, as we shall see below (section VII: 5). Our next task, however, is to examine disequilibrium regimes in a multi-period framework; use of the *tâtonnement* equations has already made the simple one-period model more than a little surreal.

VI: Disequilibria in a Multi-period Framework

VI: 1 *Underconsumption*

In this type of disequilibrium,[57] households can buy the goods and sell the labour they wish. First, in contrast, are rationed in both these markets. This cannot arise, as we saw, in a one-period model. In the two-period framework of section III: 3, it can occur. Figure 7.16 illustrates an underconsumption 'point of rest'. *ABCD* represents a full (Walrasian) equilibrium. The labour market clears at *C*, when the

changes respond to *notional* disequilibria in the manner shown in Figure 7.15, the economy would converge upon *E* from any point on *HE*. But if Figure 7.15 relates to *actual*, not notional disequilibria, there will be no tendency to slide down *HE* towards *E*. Along *HE*, firmst are presented with a high ratio of the virtual wage rate to the virtual price level, even although the actual real wage is low.

Notional excess demands and supplies are found by allowing everyone to optimize for a given set of prices, *on the assumption that no one is rationed as a result of disequilibria.* Actual, or 'effective' disequilibria are found by taking full account of the rationing constraints imposed upon agents. Both notional and effective disequilibria vanish when all markets clear. But effective disequilibria can vanish when notional disequilibria are present: the line *HE* is a case in point.

[56] See, for example, Eckstein and Girola (96).

[57] An underconsumption 'point of rest' is an equilibrium in one sense, precisely because it is a point of rest. But because notional excess demands for goods, and labour, do not vanish, it is a disequilibrium in a second sense; it is not a position of full market clearing.

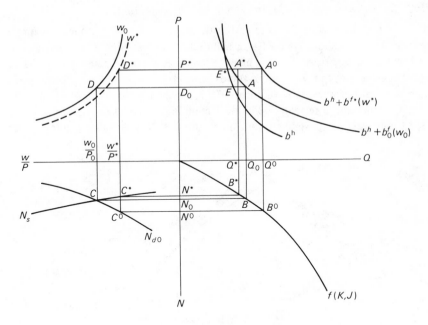

FIG. 7.16. Underconsumption.

demand for labour is that given by N_{d0}. Point A shows the goods market in equilibrium, with firms adding AE of output to their stock of capital. This 'point of rest' corresponds to w_0 and P_0.

Now suppose the money wage rate is lowered to w^*, and the price of goods raised to P^*. The drop in the real wage rate will, under our assumptions, reduce the supply of labour. It will also generate a notional excess demand for labour, equal to the distance $C^*C^\bullet$. Producers respond to the real wage rate fall by attempts not simply to add to employment and output for sale to households, but also by adding to their investment demand. The profitability of investment will certainly have risen if the fall in w is thought to be temporary: firms will attempt to substitute present employment for (now relatively dearer) future employment. This is reflected in the upper right panel by a higher investment demand D^f: total demand for output increases from $b^h + b_0^f$ to $b^h + b^{f*}$. At P^*, this implies total demand of $A^\bullet$. Unfortunately, however, output at $Q^\bullet$ is impossible. The labour supply constraint ($N = N^*$) holds output down to A^*. Household demand is reduced to E^*, as opposed to the higher level E at Walrasian equilibrium. It is in this sense that there is underconsumption at E^*. Households are assumed to buy all they want out of the production level Q^*. The residue A^*B^* is added to the stock of capital. A^*E^* is in fact less than the producers' preferred investment level, $E^*A^\bullet$; but from the standpoint of household purchases from the corporate sector *as a whole*, the goods market is in excess supply.

VI: 2 *The Keynesian Notion of Intertemporal Disequilibrium*

Intertemporal analysis is the core of the traditional Keynesian model. Unemployment in today's labour market is attributed to excess supply in today's goods market; this in turn arises because plans to save would exceed plans to invest at any higher aggregate output rate, given the existing constellation of wage rates, prices, interest rates and expectations. Figure 7.17 shows how this state of affairs could arise. Consider the intertemporal general equilibrium model of chapter 2, section VII: 3 illustrated in its simplest form in Figure 2.3. Now imagine a sudden switch

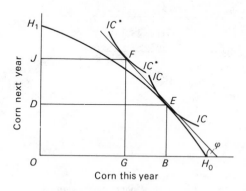

FIG. 7.17. Keynesian intertemporal disequilibrium.

in tastes. Social indifference curve IC shifts to IC^*. Imagine that the price ratio between current corn and next year's corn is locked. Producers will aim for a production programme at E. This is so, since, in equilibrium, plans to sell OB units of corn to households now, to retain BH_0 units now for investment, and to sell OD units of corn next period will maximize the value of their total sales (and hence profits, since costs are assumed predetermined). If production at E were feasible, and the resulting sum of present and expected future sales revenue were transferred to households to spend, households would maximize utility by planning to consume at F. But E and F are distinct points. There is disequilibrium. There is an excess demand for next year's corn, equal to DJ; and corresponding to it, and equal in value, an excess supply of this year's corn of BG. The Keynesian argument now runs as follows. The horizontal distance BG is perceived by producers; but the vertical distance DJ is not. The excess demand for future goods is hidden from view. There is no market now for future output. Instead, savers accumulate money, or claims to future money (bonds). Now if the switch in the preferred dates of consumption spending, illustrated by the indifference curve shift from IC to IC^*, fails to reduce the rate of interest on bonds, this year's investment will not increase above BH_0. The all-too-visible excess supply of current goods will induce producers to react as if workers had raised the preference for current leisure relative to current consumption, assuming that the money wage rate is given. Extra leisure will be provided, unwanted and unfairly, in the form of involuntary unemployment. Worse still, newly unemployed workers will be forced to reduce their expenditure, so current consumption will decline. In this climate, investment demand will also be vulnerable to increased expectations of inability to sell their output on the part of producers. The multiplier (very possibly exacerbated by an investment accelerator) generates a contractionary process, the end result of which is a low-level equilibrium volume of current output well below $OB + BH_0$.

Let us examine the steps in this Keynesian argument. The absence (or rarity) of commodity future markets is neither necessary nor sufficient for the catastrophe that ensued. If there were a comprehensive set of commodity forward markets, they too could be infected by non-equilibrating expectations of future spot prices, held with confidence, which could prevent the excess demand for future goods being registered in an appreciation in their current forward price. Claims to future goods might be sold in virtually limitless amounts by speculators convinced— wrongly convinced, perhaps—that their future spot prices would remain at a low level. Forward commodity markets could suffer from a liquidity trap, which had the same effect as interest-rate rigidity in preventing angle θ from falling. The absence of forward commodity markets is not sufficient, either: it could be that the set of forward *money* markets that in practice takes their place might, with much luck, succeed in removing intertemporal disequilibria entirely. What is needed in Figure 7.17, of course, is a drop in the rate of interest, so that $\tan \theta$ can fall directly. This raises planned investment above BH_0 and raises planned consumption above OG. In practice, the drop in interest rates may be too modest or too slow to prevent the contractionary process; but it must help to some degree to reduce the scale of the contraction. Behind the later stages of the argument lay the assumption that money wage rates and current prices were rigid, or at least only partly or gradually flexible downwards; and this implied that the positive feedback spillover effects noted in our previous analysis of Keynesian unemployment were given free rein. These points need to be developed more formally; it is to this that we now turn.

VI: 3 *Keynesian Aggregate Models*

We begin with the simplest Keynesian model: the INCEX or income-expenditure model. All prices and wage rates are locked, both here, and unless otherwise specified, below as well. Rates of interest are also assumed locked, as in Figure 7.17. Aggregation therefore proceeds without difficulty. Real total expenditure on current output, E, must equal real output of current goods, Q, for aggregate demand to be consistent with itself (involuntary inventory accumulation may be defined as part of E). Secondly, E is an increasing function of Q. This reflects the dependence of households' current consumption spending upon their current income receipts, probably because current income partly proxies permanent income (pp. 47–51), or perhaps because capital markets enforce this dependence (pp. 36–7). Household durable purchases should be positively associated with current income (pp. 29–30). The arguments for linking investment to profits (chapter 2, pp. 77–8) and profits with output (pp. 60 *et ff.*) may be invoked to hypothesize a positive dependence of investment demand upon Q, as well. With the capital stock and the level of technology given, employment is found by inverting the production function. Hence

$$E = Q, \tag{7.30}$$

$$E = E(Q), \qquad \text{where } 1 > E' > 0 \text{ for stability}, \tag{7.31}$$

$$N = f^{-1}(Q), \qquad f' > 0 \geqslant f'' \tag{7.32}$$

The Keynesian multiplier is $(1 - E')^{-1}$.

The system (7.30)–(7.32) is shown in Figure 7.18. N_0 and Q_0 are full employment levels of employment and output. They are not reached because at Q_0 there is a notional excess of current output A^0A^*. Aggregate demand consistency is secured at A, where output and employment levels are Q^* and N^*.

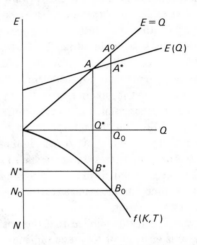

FIG. 7.18. The INCEX model.

The INCEX model imposes an exogenous, fixed rate of interest. The ISLM model (Figures 7.19 and 7.20) generalizes beyond this, and can therefore supply a richer set of answers to the questions raised by Figure 7.17. Function (7.31) is replaced by a broader function

$$E = E(Q, R_N, W, M, P, K, \&(\,.\,), G_1, G_2, t) \tag{7.33}$$

where R_N is the nominal rate of interest, and other variables denote, in sequence, nominal wealth, nominal money supply, price level, stock of capital, expectations of all future variables and events, nominal government spending on public goods, nominal government transfer payments, and income tax rate. Negative dependence of the optimum stock of capital (K^*) upon the cost of capital (pp. 66–7), and positive dependence of investment on $K^* - K$ may be invoked to suggest $\partial E/\partial R_N < 0$ when expectations of inflation are given; many arguments in chapter 1 suggested $\partial E/\partial w$, $\partial E/\partial M > 0 > \partial E/\partial P$; replacement demand aside, the theory of investment suggests $\partial E/\partial K < 0$; at least for direct effects, we should expect $\partial E/\partial G_1$, $\partial E/\partial G_2 > 0 > \partial E/\partial t$. The upper panel of Figure 7.19 illustrates (7.30) and (7.31), with all but Q and R as arguments of (7.33) suppressed. The middle panel

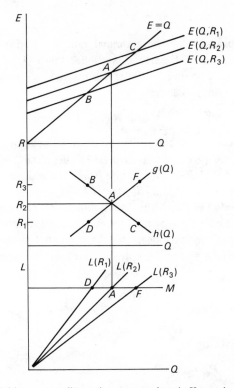

FIG. 7.19. Linking commodity and money markets in Keynesian disequilibrium.

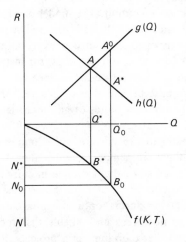

FIG. 7.20. The ISLM model.

shows the function $R_N = h(Q)$ which is found by solving (7.30) and (7.33) for R_N (assuming invertibility):

$$R_N = h(Q, \ldots) \qquad \text{'IS curve'.} \qquad (7.34)$$

In (7.34), $h' < 0$ because a higher nominal rate of interest entails lower real expenditure and hence, by the Keynesian multiplier, lower Q.

The lower panel of Figure 7.20 illustrates the money market. L denotes the nominal demand for money: assume

$$L = L(Q, R_N, \ldots), \qquad (7.35)$$

where L depends upon the same varaibles as appeared as arguments of E in (7.33). Many arguments in chapter 5 (and chapter 1) suggest $\partial L/\partial Q$, $\partial L/\partial W$, $\partial L/\partial P$, $\partial L/\partial G_2 > 0$ and $0 > \partial L/\partial R_N$; $\partial L/\partial G_1$ and $\partial L/\partial t$ are ambiguous, $\partial L/\partial K$ positive although already included within $\partial L/\partial W$; $\partial L/\partial M$ discountable. Amongst the expectational elements, perhaps the most important are that L should vary positively with expected values of the interest rate, and negatively with expected inflation (although this may have been fully incorporated already in R_N). Linking (7.35) with an exogenous nominal supply of money and a money market clearance condition

$$M = \bar{M}, \qquad (7.36)$$

$$L = M, \qquad (7.37)$$

generates (assuming invertibility)

$$R_N = g(Q, \ldots), \qquad \text{'LM curve'.} \qquad (7.38)$$

Now $g' > 0$ since a rise in real income raises the demand for money, which implies a higher interest rate ast he supply of money is given. In Figure 7.20, this system (7.32), (7.34), and (7.38) is illustrated. Once again, there is unemployment of labour and underproduction of output. The model points to a number of ways in which the government might remove these. There are five in all.

First, the authorities may operate directly on expectations $\&$ $(..)$. Persuading the market to expect lower long-term interest rates, for instance, will tend to reduce the demand for more liquid assets, since the prospective return on long-term bonds rises with the greater promise of capital gain. In a very simple model of Keynes's type, which aggregates boldly over bonds of all maturities, the demand for money will fall, reducing 'the' current rate of interest, which in turn will stimulate new durable buying and investment expenditure. The stimulus may not be large or long-lasting, but it will be there. In a more complex model with bonds of differing maturities, we should expect some slight decline in current long interest rates, and perhaps also some rise in current short rates. Since this change was unexpected by assumption, it will alter producers' optimal capital stock, employment and output programmes. It is by no means unthinkable that the current level of capital formation could rise, particularly on long-term projects. Reducing expectations of future income-tax rates, to take another example, should raise current consumption spending (chapter 1). This will shift $h(Q)$ rightwards. On the other hand, it should raise the current demand for money (chapter 1, again), and consequently shift $g(Q)$ leftwards. It will also alter producer programmes. The direction of the net effect on current Q is ambiguous. But that is not to say it is zero. In the long run, however, the authorities will find it hard to influence expectations by policy intentions unless their predictions about their own actions (and other events) are reasonably accurate.

Second, the authorities could increase the money supply $\bar{M}$, employing any one of the techniques mentioned in chapter 6. Differentiating (7.32), (7.34), and (7.38) reveals that

$$\frac{dQ}{dM} = \left[1 - E_1 + \frac{E_2}{L_2} L_1 \right]^{-1} \left\{ E_4 + \frac{E_2}{L_2} + \sum_j L_{\eta j} \phi_{Mj} + \sum_j E_{\eta j} \phi_{Mj} \right\} \qquad (7.39)$$

where E_i and L_i represent the partial derivatives of E and L with respect to their ith argument in the list $(Q, R_N, W, \ldots)$, ϕ_{Mj} is the effect of a change in the money supply upon the jth element in the set of expectations, and $L_{\eta j}$ and $E_{\eta j}$ represent the impact upon the demand for money and the demand for goods of a rise in the jth element of the set of expectations. Equation (7.39) is rather forbidding. It needs to be explained. The term $[1 - E_1 + (E_2/L_2)L_1]^{-1}$ is the Keynesian multiplier, cut down in size below its value in the INCEX model, $(1 - E_1)^{-1}$, to incorporate the monetary feedback effect via interest rates. An increase in Q tends to raise R_N, when the money market is in equilibrium; this cuts back the increase in Q, since certain expenditures, particularly on investment goods, are likely to be curtailed as a result. The expression $(E_2/L_2)L_1$ equals, by virtue of (7.30),

$$\frac{\text{interest-elasticity of demand for goods}}{\text{interest-elasticity of demand for money}} \cdot \text{income elasticity of demand for money}$$

This multiplier is common to *all* changes in Q engineered by demand management policy. It has no bearing on the relative potency of different instruments. Inside the brackets $\{\ldots\}$ on the RHS of (7.39), the first term E_4 is the direct effect on expenditure from a rise in the money supply. It is the real balance effect. E_4 should be very small when capital markets are perfect: a rise in money holdings is presumably likely to be treated as a windfall capital gain, raising permanent income by only the product of the real rate of interest and $\Delta \bar{M}$. Durable buying, and, if capital markets are imperfect enough to have restrained current consumption purchases below preferred levels, non-durable purchases as well, should register some increase. (It is a curious paradox that many monetarists who assert a large, quick effect of money supply changes on consumer spending often claim that capital markets are efficient; yet the old Keynesian tradition makes much of capital market imperfections and the multiplier $[1 - E_1 + (E_2/L_2)L_1]^{-1}$ while belittling the role of money.) As for the ratio E_2/L_2,

$$\frac{E_2}{L_2} \equiv \left(\frac{\text{money supply}}{\text{income}} \right) \left(\frac{\text{interest-elasticity of demand for goods}}{\text{interest-elasticity of demand for money}} \right). \qquad (7.40)$$

(7.40) vanishes if L_2 tends to minus infinity (the 'liquidity trap' case, depicted in Figure 7.17 and the INCEX model), or alternatively if E_2 vanishes, so that the rate of interest has no effect upon expenditure. In the former case, $h(Q)$ is horizontal; in the latter, $g(Q)$ is vertical. At the opposite extreme, (7.40) tends to infinity if $h(Q)$ is vertical—and the demand for money is completely insensitive to the rate of interest—or if $g(Q)$ is horizontal, betokening an infinitely great sensitivity of expenditure to the rate of interest. When (7.40) is very large, the Keynesian multiplier $(1 - E_1 + (E_2/L_2)L_1)^{-1}$ shrivels up to nothing. This does not, however, imply that a change in the money supply has no effect on Q: E_2/L_2 appears on the numerator of dQ/dM in (7.39) as well as on the denominator. If the interest-elasticity of the demand for money can confidently be treated as negligible (and E_2 not), so that E_2/L_2 is enormous, (7.39) tells us that

$$\frac{dQ}{dM} \rightarrow L_1^{-1}.$$

Equivalently, the elasticity of Q to M is simply the income-elasticity of the demand for money. In practice both the interest-elasticities in (7.40) appear to be small negative numbers, highly sensitive to how they are measured and defined.

The last two terms in the $\{...\}$ expression in (7.39) might be exemplified best by the impact that the monetary expansion had upon inflation expectations, and by the effect this in turn had on the demand for money (a-fall, probably, moving $g(Q)$ rightwards) and on the demand for goods (unclear on its effects on $h(Q)$— see chapter 1).

The other three ways of raising Q and N in the ISLM model are to alter public goods spending, G_1; to alter transfers, G_2; and to change the vector of tax rates (which for simplicity's sake is collapsed into the single parameter t). We may derive

$$\left[1 - E + \frac{E_2}{L_2}L_1\right]dQ = \left[E_8 + \sum_j E_{7j}\phi_{8j} - \frac{E_2}{L_2}\left(L_8 + \sum_j L_{7j}\phi_{8j}\right)\right]dG_1 \qquad (7.41)$$

$$+ \left[E_9 + \sum_j E_{7j}\phi_{9j} - \frac{E_2}{L_2}\left(L_9 + \sum_j L_{7j}\phi_{9j}\right)\right]dG_2 \qquad (7.42)$$

$$+ \left[E_{10} + \sum_j E_{7j}\phi_{10j} - \frac{E_2}{L_2}\left(L_{10} + \sum_j L_{7j}\phi_{10j}\right)\right]dt. \qquad (7.43)$$

There are two types of case when fiscal policy parameters are powerless to affect aggregate demand. First, dQ/dG_1, dQ/dG_2, and dQ/dt all vanish if $E_2/L_2 \rightarrow \infty$. This occurs when the *IS* curve, h, is infinitely less steep than the *LM* curve, g. The interest-rate then adjusts to neutralize the aggregate demand effect of any change in government spending or taxing, or indeed any change in planned saving or investment by the private sector. There is complete crowding out. When $E_2/L_2 \rightarrow \infty$, (7.4) tells us that dQ vanishes, assuming that the RHS is finite. The second case of impotence is encountered when the RHS of (7.41), (7.42), or (7.43) vanishes. On p. 212, we already mentioned one example of this: when the government increases transfer income now, and engenders expectations of offsetting lump-sum taxes later, in a world of perfect capital markets. This would make

$$E_9 = - \sum_j E_{7j} \phi_{9j}$$

and

$$L_9 = - \sum_j L_{7j} \phi_{9j},$$

so that dQ/dG_2 vanished. (7.41) and (7.43) can vanish without the aid of expectational changes. By fluke, it might be that the expenditure-reducing effect of a higher income-tax rate was offset by its negative effect on the demand for money (see chapters 1 and 5). In Figures 7.19 and 7.20, $g(Q)$ moves leftward *and* $h(Q)$ moves leftward; if the relative gradients happen to be just right, Q will be undisturbed. The same result would follow for public goods spending if that, too, raised the demand for money sufficiently so that $E_8/L_8 = E_2/L_2$, and the expectational terms also cancelled.

We should not conclude from all this, however, that fiscal policy is likely to be powerless, except in certain defined circumstances. It is not the case that L_2/E_2 appears to be vanishingly small in practice. The chance of a perverse response to income-tax changes is worth considering seriously, but there seems no reason for expecting a sizeable, direct, positive effect of public goods spending upon the demand for money. In (7.41), E_8 should be unity, or thereabouts, and L_8 a very small number of uncertain sign. Although (7.42) might be zero and (7.43) could even be negative, (7.41) should be positive. In a world with fixed prices and wage rates, with excess supply in labour and goods markets, direct government spending should be a powerful instrument for lowering unemployment. This is not to say, of course, that monetary expansion is less advantageous in these circumstances.

Two further points arise here. In a world with many goods and labour markets, the composition of government spending matters. Additional G_1 should be tilted towards those markets which suffer most acutely from excess supply. Any shortages of capital equipment, fuel, or indirect inputs, as well as labour, could imperil increases in employment, even if these shortages arise in other sectors. Similarly, if the government can identify groups whose marginal propensities to consume differ, redistribution could affect Q. Secondly, the size of the budget deficit. We examined the significance of this in the miniature general equilibrium model (section III: 4). How far do those results need to be modified in a Keynesian model? One way of showing the effects of a bond-financed budget deficit is to assert (i) that bonds are wealth to their holders; (ii) that a rising supply of bonds will imply a rising level of social wealth; and (iii) that this will move h steadily rightwards, since $L_3 > 0$, and g steadily rightwards since $E_3 > 0$. If both g and h move rightwards, R must rise. Q will fall (rise) if $(E_2/L_2)(L_3/E_3) > 1$ (<1). This is vulnerable to three objections. First, (ii) does not follow from (i): to all members of the community except the bond holder, the bond is a tax threat, or a public goods threat, or both. Secondly, a rising volume of bonds does not imply a rising value, if interest rates have to rise, as we saw in section III: 4. Thirdly, the argument ignores the fact that a rise in Q brought about by fiscal expansion—and this is of course defined by a *rise* in the level of G_1 or G_2 or a fall in t, and *not* measured by the *level* of the deficit—should stimulate additional savings, and thereby raise the demand for bonds. It is no more legitimate to argue from social accounting identities such as (7.3) and (7.4) that the government's budget must put up interest rates by raising the stock of bonds, than to state that the private and foreign sectors' net acquisition of financial assets must lower them by raising the demand for bonds.[58]

VI: 4 *Some Extensions to Keynesian Aggregate Models*

VI: 4 (i) *Variable money supply*   The nominal money supply may not be rigid. Instead, it may be the nominal rate of interest that is fixed. The relative merits of the two were considered in chapter 6. At this point, we need to see how the system (7.32), (7.34), and (7.38) needs to be amended to allow for this, and other possibilities. (7.36) is replaced by

$$M = M(Q, R_N, W, M, P, K, \&(. .), G_1, G_2, t). \tag{7.44}$$

In (7.44), $M_1 (\equiv \partial M/\partial Q)$ could be negative if the authorities typically reacted to a rise in unemployment by increasing the money supply. The case of an interest rate policy parameter would imply $M_2 = \infty$. Some lower, but still positive, value would be observed if the monetary authorities tried to smooth fluctuations in bond markets. Of the other M_i, M_3, M_4, and M_6 are uninteresting, but M_5 is likely to be positive, and to have important implications we shall observe below. M_8, M_9, and M_{10} may well be non-zero, given the tendency for ΔM to vary positively with the size of the budget deficit.[59]

If $M_2 = \infty$, $g(Q)$ is horizontal in Figs. 7.19 and 7.20; the Keynesian multiplier is augmented to $(1 - E_1)^{-1}$—these results follow, at least, on the assumption that other M_i are sufficiently small. One argument against expecting M_2 to be infinite, however, is that a nominal interest rate policy parameter can be dynamically unstable. As was observed in chapter 6, it can be maintained that nominal interest rates have more than quintupled in the US and the UK since the Second World War *precisely because*—not despite the fact that—the authorities tried to hold them down. Holding nominal rates below equilibrium usually implies open market bond purchases, monetary expansion, inflation, expected inflation, and, hence, in the end, high equilibrium nominal interest rates.

The exact shape of (7.44) will be of prime importance when the private sector is trying to ascertain how the government will react to events in framing future monetary policy.

---

[58] See Sargent (280) for a strong defence of this position, pp. 107–11.
[59] See Tobin (322).

VI: 4 (ii) *The open economy*   When the economy is opened to international trade, (7.30) is replaced by the condition

$$E - Q = \text{current account deficit on external payments} \qquad (7.45)$$

and the money market clearance condition (7.37) is—or should be—removed in favour of some change-in-reserves function,

$$\text{Reserves} = \Psi(L - M) \qquad \Psi' > 0, \Psi(0) = 0. \qquad (7.46)$$

The simplest models abstract from international capital movements by asserting that the RHS of (7.46) equals the LHS of (7.45).

Chapter 4 has already examined equilibrium and disequilibrium models of trade and payments. The significance of exports as a possible destination for unsold home-produced goods (which might thereby avoid Keynesian unemployment) has been considered above, in section V: 4.

VI: 4 (iii) *The trade cycle*   Traditional Keynesian cycle models start with Harrod (147) and Samuelson (267). They generalize the INCEX model (equations (7.30), (7.31), and (7.39)) by hypothesizing some variant upon

$$Q_t = u_t - u_{t-1} + a_1 Q_{t-1} + a_2 Q_{t-2} + a_0; a_0, a_1 > 0 < a_2. \qquad (7.47)$$

The simplest models constrain the stochastic terms by setting $u_{t-1} = 0$, and

$$u_{t+i} = 0 \qquad \text{for all } i < 0,$$
$$= \bar{b} > 0 \text{ for all } i \geq 0.$$

These restrictions imply that until date t, Q was stationary at $a_0/(1 - a_1 - a_2)$. Its new equilibrium value, Q^*, is $(a_0 + \bar{b})/(1 - a_1 - a_2)$. Stability[60] requires that $1 > a_1 + a_2$, otherwise Q^* is infinite. But will Q converge on Q^*? Will there be cycles? The answers to these questions depend on the values of a_1 and a_2. Convergence occurs if $a_2 > -1$, divergence if $a_2 < -1$. In the special case $a_2 = -1$, regular amplitude self-repeating cycles occur. Cyclical fluctuations will occur generally if a_1 is sufficiently small, and $a_2 < -4$; they will be impossible if $a_2 = 0$.[61]

Other models[62] postulate a more complex interaction of Q_t with both actual and desired levels of the stock of capital. Investment is high when the desired stock outstrips its actual level. But high investment implies a rising stock of capital, and a high (but trendless) level of output. If the latter governs the desired stock of capital, eventually equality between the two capital stocks will be reached. At this stage, investment will crumble, falling away to replacement levels. This will in turn drag down output, and with it, the desired stock of capital. Successive periods of disinvestment will occur. Harrod's growth model contains important elements of this story, as we shall see in chapter 9.

Further explanations for the phenomenon of the trade cycle include alternating phases of implementing, and storing up, changes in technology (Schumpeter (284)),

---

[60] In the sense of Samuelson's *Correspondence Principle*. See Samuelson (268).
[61] See Hicks (163) and Allen (3) for more detailed analysis.
[62] Hicks (163) and Goodwin (135) are examples.

alternating phases of monetary growth and contraction (Hawtrey (154)), and manipulation of demand management and other instruments by governments attempting
to win elections (Nordhaus (242), Frey and Schneider (117)). The phenomenon
itself is liable to change; the nine-to-ten year pattern of fluctuations before 1900,
and between 1920 and 1939, gave way to mild, brief fluctuations after 1945.
In the US the average periodicity has been three years, and the pattern highly
irregular; in the UK, a regular fifty-four month cycle has been observed, at least
until very recently. The majority of research devoted to the cycle in the 1960s and
1970s has centred on the role of money in the process. Amongst the issues considered have been whether money leads or follows Q,[63] what inferences can be
drawn from the answer to this,[64] whether the money supply is a good predictor of
subsequent (as against previous) real or nominal national income,[65] and whether
there is any association between real variables, such as Q or unemployment, and
nominal variables.[66] The consensus appears to be that money has a short lead; that
this may be consistent with some form of endogeneity as described by (7.44);
that it probably predicts subsequent prices much better than previous prices;[67] and
that there *is* some unmistakable, probably short-run relation between real variables
and the level of the nominal money supply.[68]

VI: 4 (iv) *Variable price level*   So far, the Keynesian aggregate models have
assumed fixed levels of prices and money wage rates. Introducing a perfectly
flexible price level is not a complicated extension. Since $E_5 < 0$ in (7.33) and
$L_5 > 0$ in (7.35), a rise in the price level will reduce the level of aggregate demand.
Linking $g(Q)$ and $h(Q)$ to eliminate R, we may derive (from (7.34) and (7.38))
an aggregate demand equation

$$Q = \chi(W, M, P, K, \&(..), G_1, G_2, t) \tag{7.48}$$

where $\chi_2 > 0 > \chi_3$, χ_4; $\chi_6 > 0$; and the other partial derivatives are ambiguous
for reasons already noted. If, in addition, an aggregate production function, such as
(7.2), can be employed, if technology and capital are parametric, and producers
are in competitive equilibrium, we may argue:

$$Q = f(N), \qquad \text{inverting (7.32),} \tag{7.49}$$

$$\frac{w}{P} = f'(N), \tag{7.50}$$

$$\therefore Q = f\left(f'^{-1}\left(\frac{w}{P}\right)\right). \tag{7.51}$$

---

[63] Friedman and Schwarz (128) and Friedman and Meiselman (127).   [64] Tobin (322).
[65] Sims (298) and Feige and Pearce (103).   [66] Sims (299).
[67] In the US, this appears to be true of real income, too (Sims (298)); in the UK, not (Goodhart, Gowland, and Williams (134)).
[68] This conflicts with the neutrality hypothesis. See Sims (299). It also provides support for
the Lucas Surprise Supply Function, discussed below (p. 246). See also Mishkin for further
corroboration of Sims's finding (219).

Now (7.51) may be rewritten

$$Q = F\left(\frac{w}{P}, K, J\right). \tag{7.52}$$

Linking (7.48) and (7.52) determines output, the price level, and the employment level, for given values of: wealth, capital stock, technology parameters (these are predetermined); the nominal wage rate, w; the demand management instruments M, G_1, G_2 and t; and the set of expectations. This is a full version of the model presented in Figure 7.8.

Many of the controversies between monetarists and Keynesian are powerfully and graphically illuminated by (7.48) and (7.52). The extreme Keynesian tradition maintains that χ_2 and χ_3 are negligible, and that it is the last five arguments of χ that really 'drive' Q. The argument depends upon (i) a negligible real balance effect, E_4; (ii) a vanishingly small ratio (E_2/L_2) of gradient of h to gradient of g; and (iii) fiscal policy being framed in 'real terms' $(G_1/P$ and $G_2/P)$.[69] This means that a fall in the price level will have no direct effect on expenditure, and also that interest rates will either fail to fall in the wake of the drop in the transactions demand for money, or any fall in interest rates will leave expenditure unchanged. Alternatively, the nominal interest may be fixed by policy $(M_2 = \infty)$. On the supply side, the hypothesis that $f'' = 0$ in (7.50) implies a horizontal supply curve, (7.52), which is defined up to the full employment output level. The extreme Keynesian view permits a complete separability of inflation from output changes. Output changes are caused exclusively by changes in demand. On the other hand, following the spirit of (7.14), price rises are caused exclusively by (i) increases in money wage rates, unmatched by productivity increases; or (ii) falls in the labour share of output. Fiscal expansion or suitable expectations will determine growth; inflation control calls for incomes policy, faster productivity increases, or controls on profits or rents.

The monetarist view can be described by the addition of a labour supply equation

$$N_s = N_s\left(\frac{w}{P}, \frac{M}{P}, \frac{\pi}{P}, \&(..), \frac{G_1}{P}, \frac{G_2}{P}, t\right) \tag{7.53}$$

and a labour market clearance condition

$$N_s = N$$

(where N denotes the *demand* for labour). Aggregate *supply* is now vertical, not aggregate demand; aggregate demand is, by contrast, an approximately unit-elastic function governed largely if not wholly by the demand and supply of money (7.35), (7.36) and (7.37). Growth is dependent on increases in factor supplies, or technology; inflation occurs if monetary expansion proceeds too fast (probably if it exceeds the rate of growth of real output).

---

[69] (iii) could be defined on the ground that government does not, or should not, suffer from money illusion. In the 1970s, however, there has been a pronounced shift towards setting nominal targets for G_1 and G_2: witness the programme of 'cash limits' in the UK that began in April 1976.

An interesting compromise between the two extreme views of supply is the 'Surprise Supply Function' proposed by Lucas (196). The notion here is that an *unexpectedly* high present price level will provoke an increase in output and employment. Firms and workers respond to an unexpectedly high present price as a favourable movement in their 'terms of trade'. Workers plan to work more hours in this period, and less later when their expected real wage rate comes down again. Firms run down inventories and add to current output, in order to make the most of what their managers consider to be a temporary rise in the relative price of their product, in terms of other products and factors. Alas, the increased employment and output are based on an illusion. A neutral increase in all goods and factor prices will soon reveal itself as just that, and if all supplies are homogeneous of degree zero in current and expected prices, output and employment levels will sink back to 'natural' levels. The Lucas model imposes continuous labour and goods markets clearance, but introduces imperfect information about current prices. All you see is the price of the good you sell; your impressions of prices of other goods are unreliable, and/or out of date. Consequently, when all current prices are unexpectedly increased in equal proportion, as a result of an unexpected rise in the money supply for example, economic agents will find it impossible to distinguish accurately between the neutral increase in the absolute price level that has occurred, and any random shifts in relative prices which may be occurring. They will be deluded into thinking that relative prices have changed much more than they actually have. Producers will reschedule input and production programmes; and households will alter their labour supply and commodity demand programmes, along the lines explored in chapter I and considered by Lucas and Rapping (200).

These output and employment effects will not be permanent, however, since everyone will soon observe that his or her impressions of relative price changes were erroneous.

VI: Unemployment Inflation and Macroeconomic Policy

VII: 1 *The Traditional View*

Irving Fisher (109) can be credited with the first empirically based claim that the level of unemployment and the rate of increase of prices were linked. Further analysis of the relationship was undertaken by Tinbergen (317) and Brown (47). It was the startling evidence on the robustness of the relation provided by Phillips (256) that made him its eponymous hero. With the exception of a group of inter-war years characterized by enormous unemployment or huge rises or falls in money wage rates, almost a century of peacetime British experience conformed closely to a negative convex redlationship between the rate of change of money wage rates ($\dot{w}$) and the level of unemployment. The rate of change of unemployment was an additional, but weaker influence on $\dot{w}$ (this time, negative).

The 'theory' to explain the Phillips curve is essentially Walras's *tâtonnement* principle:[70] price moves in the direction of excess demand. The difference between

[70] It should be emphasized, however, that Walras's *tâtonnement* hypothesis specifically precludes trading until the equilibrium price vector is attained; and it is also a timeless concept,

unemployment and recorded vacancies is a measure of excess supply (excess demand when negative), Lipsey argued (194). If this is so, Walras's hypothesis should lead from a negative relation such as *BOD* in Figure 7.14 (possibly linear, possibly curved) to a negative relation between $\hat{w}$ and the level of unemployment. The latter might, however, prove unreliable, particularly if vacancies were highly volatile. Although Walras's *tâtonnement* process relates to a hypothetical competitive economy, the results of and the explanation for the Phillips curve were quite consistent with the view that the impetus for wage rises sprang from the trade unions, whose willingness and ability to press for them were greater when unemployment was very low.

No less striking than the negative association between $\hat{w}$ and U for the period in question—amply confirmed on US data[71]—was its convexity. The years 1921-3 aside, there were virtually no cases of *falling* money wage rates, even with unemployment up to and above 10 per cent. Price increases were considered to be based on wage rises, minus productivity increases, by a simple mark-up equation.

The policy implications drawn from Phillips' and others' evidence were that the authorities should control aggregate demand in the goods market so as to engineer an optimal trade-off between the social ills of unemployment and inflation. Occasionally, wage–price controls were advocated on the ground that they could allow the authorities to improve upon the Phillips curve. Lower levels of unemployment could be attained by expansionary demand management policy, and inflation could be held in check by legal limits.

VII: 2 *The Phelps–Friedman View*

Belief in a predictable negative relation between inflation and unemployment was undermined by evidence that both seemed to be rising from the mid-1960s. It was also shaken by theoretical developments. Phelps (252) and Friedman (123) argued that unemployment should be independent of the rate of inflation in the long run.[72] For Friedman, the Phillips curve should describe changes in actual or expected *real* wage rates; its empirical success in earlier periods lay in the accident that the trends in actual and (presumably) in expected prices were negligible then. Phelps and Friedman both argued that attempts to hold unemployment below its natural level would lead not to inflation, but to accelerating inflation, since they could only be successful by engendering unexpectedly rapid inflation. Unexpectedly slow inflation was the consequence of unemployment above its natural rate; given time, unexpectedly slow inflation would lower expectations of its future level. At the core of these arguments was the hypothesis of adaptive expectations. In the linear case,

$$E_t x_{t-1} - E_{t-1} x_t = (1 - \mu)(x_t - E_{t-1} x_t). \tag{7.54}$$

unlike the Phillips curve which relates the state of unemployment to the speed with which money wage rates change. This said, however, there is a close resemblance between the concepts. Recall Figure 7.14.

[71] See Samuelson and Solow (275) for an early example.
[72] See also Lucas (197) for a celebrated article with theoretical and empirical support for this view, and Gordon (136).

In the Phelps–Friedman view, x_t stands for the *rate of inflation* at date t (in discrete time, $(P_t - P_{t-1})/P_{t-1}$, and not the level of prices then.

To the basic Phillips curve relation

$$\frac{w_t - w_{t-1}}{w_{t-1}} = H\left(\frac{U_t}{U_{Nt}}\right) + \epsilon_t \tag{7.55}$$

(where U_t and U_{Nt} denote the actual and 'natural' rates of unemployment at date t, $H(\ )$ and $U_t - U_{Nt}$ have opposite signs, and ϵ_t is a disturbance term with mean value zero), Phelps and Friedman added a term in the expected rate of inflation

$$\frac{w_t - w_{t-1}}{w_{t-1}} = H\left(\frac{U_t}{U_{Nt}}\right) + a\,\frac{E_{t-i-1}P_{t-i} - P_{t-i-1}}{P_{t-i-1}} + \epsilon_t. \tag{7.56}$$

In (7.56), i could be zero (so that participants in today's labour market set today's wage rates given their previous expectations of today's—as yet unknown—level of prices); or it might be $+1$ (so that it is today's expectation of *next* period's price level that influence today's wage bargaining); or it could be a mixture of the two. Phelps and Friedman both argued strongly that a should be large, and most probably unitary. The simplest price-setting equation to combine with (7.56) would be

$$\frac{P_t - P_{t-1}}{P_{t-1}} = \frac{w_t - w_{t-1}}{w_{t-1}} - \frac{Z_t - Z_{t-1}}{Z_{t-1}} + v_t, \tag{7.57}$$

where Z denotes (as before, in (7.14)) the average product of labour, and v_t is a stochastic term with zero mean. (7.57) is convenient but crude: it reflects assumptions that labour's share in output is trendless, that changes in prices and wage rates are perfectly synchronized, that the prices of all factors other than labour more equiproportionate in step with wage rates; and that excess demands or supplies in the product market(s) are either insignificant or negligible.

Now (7.13) has an integral

$$\frac{E_{t-1}P_t - P_{t-1}}{P_{t-1}} = (1 - \mu) \sum_{i=0}^{\infty} \mu^i\,\frac{(P_{t-i-1} - P_{t-i-2})}{P_{t-i-2}}. \tag{7.58}$$

If we set $i = 0$ in (7.56), we may derive an inflation equation from (7.56), (7.57), and (7.58):

$$\frac{P_t - P_{t-1}}{P_{t-1}} = \epsilon_t + v_t - \frac{Z_t - Z_{t-1}}{Z_{t-1}} + H\left(\frac{U_t}{U_{Nt}}\right) + a(1 - \mu) \sum_{i=0}^{\infty} \mu^i\,\frac{P_{t-i-1} - P_{t-i-2}}{P_{t-i-2}}. \tag{7.59}$$

(7.59) states that current inflation is explained by the difference between actual and natural unemployment rates, and labour productivity movements, not just in the current period but, with diminishing importance as time goes back, in all past periods, too. Demand management policy that engineers excess demand for labour in the current period will carry on raising prices in future periods, not just now. Repeated substitution reveals that

$$\frac{P_t - P_{t-1}}{P_{t-1}} = \sum_{h=0}^{\infty} a^h (1-\mu)^h y_h, \tag{7.60}$$

where

$$y_h = \underbrace{\sum_{i=h-1}^{\infty} \mu^i, \sum_{j=i-1}^{\infty} \mu^j, \dots, \sum_{n=m-1}^{\infty} \mu^h}_{h} \left[\epsilon_{t-h} + v_{t-h} - \frac{Z_{t-h} - Z_{t-h-1}}{Z_{t-h}} + H\left(\frac{U_{t-h}}{U_{Nt-h}}\right) \right].$$

(7.60) implies that a decision taken by the authorities to hold unemployment at a level below equilibrium over a long period will generate accelerating inflation. There is no long-run trade-off between the level of unemployment and the rate of inflation, Friedman concluded; in Phelps's view the long-run Phillips curve might not be vertical, but it was certainly much steeper than the short-run relationship.

What role does the money supply play in the traditional and Phelps–Friedman views of inflation? In the traditional view, an increase in the money supply moved the *IS* curve, $h(Q)$ in Figure 7.19, somewhat to the right, unless—as was often assumed—real balance effects in spending could be ignored. It also moved the *LM* curve, $g(Q)$ in Fig. 7.19, somewhat to the right, leading to downward pressure on interest rates and some increase in the prices of nominal and real[73] assets, unless —as was sometimes suggested—fixed expectations of future asset prices kept their spot prices down. Whether as a result of real balance effects or asset price changes, there would be some (possibly very gradual) expansionary effect on investment and consumption spending. Perhaps after a further dealy, unemployment would drop. This would raise the *rate of increase* of money wage rates, especially if unemployment was already low; in turn, the rate of inflation would increase from (7.57), although even this could be doubted if the fillip to aggregate demand and output raised the growth rate of labour productivity temporarily, with previously hoarded labour now costing less per unit of output.[74] In short, a complicated, tenuous relationship existed between the *level* of the money supply and the *rate of change* of prices, which was subject to several qualifications, delays, and the possibility of a perverse response. If prices rose when the money supply was held fixed in nominal terms, unemployment would rise eventually, all else equal; but the velocity of circulation might be pushed upwards quite far, before negative pressure on inflation became at all substantial. At best, moreover, wage rates would only come to rise more slowly. Keynesian asymmetries could be invoked to prevent them from falling.

The Phelps–Friedman view represents a large shift towards the miniature equilibrium model of section II and the monetarist model identified in section VI. If deviations of unemployment from its natural rate have next to no connection with the *level* of inflation in the long run, employment and output aggregates may also be treated as (approximately) independent of aggregate demand. With supply

---

[73] It was Friedman (125) and Tobin (319) who integrated real assets into a transmission mechanism originally stated by Keynes in terms of bonds.

[74] See Matthews (250) for an account of this phenomenon in the UK.

exogenous, the rate of inflation equals the increase in aggregate nominal demand minus the growth rate of output. If empirical evidence suggests that the supply of money is very closely linked to aggregate nominal demand, as Friedman consistently claimed, there will be an approximately one-to-one link between the growth rate of the money supply, and the rate of inflation.

VII: 3 Why the Phillips Curve Could be Vertical in the Short Run

The Phelps-Friedman view was built on adaptive expectations. Adaptive expectations are rational if, and only if, they are evidently optimal predictors. (7.13) and (7.58) are rational if and only if *in practice*

$$\frac{P_t - P_{t-1}}{P_{t-1}} = \frac{P_{t-1} - P_{t-2}}{P_{t-2}} + u_t - \mu u_{t-1} \tag{7.61}$$

has been observed to explain prices in the past. In (7.61) u_t and u_{t-1} are serially uncorrelated, zero mean disturbance terms. The inertia coefficient μ, which is otherwise an *ad hoc* construct, is then rationally based in the observed serial correlation pattern of inflation. Could (7.59) and (7.61) be consistent? This is an important question: if the answer is negative, the Phelps-Friedman view is built upon the quicksands of irrationality, which is surely no firmer base than the money illusion foundation for many Keynesian constructions.[75]

For (7.59) and (7.61) to be consistent when $a = 1$, it is sufficient that

$$\frac{Z_{t-1} - Z_{t-i-1}}{Z_{t-i-1}} \quad \text{and} \quad H\left(\frac{U_{t-i}}{U_{Nt-i}}\right)$$

both be serially uncorrelated random disturbance terms with zero mean, and that

$$u_t - \mu u_{t-1} = \epsilon_t + v_t - \mu \epsilon_{t-1} - \mu v_{t-1} - \frac{Z_t - Z_{t-1}}{Z_{t-1}} + \mu \frac{Z_{t-1} - Z_{t-2}}{Z_{t-2}}$$

$$+ H\left(\frac{U_t}{U_{Nt}}\right) - \mu H\left(\frac{U_{t-1}}{U_{Nt-1}}\right). \tag{7.62}$$

We reach (7.62) by differencing (7.59).

The least satisfactory element in (7.62) is the presence of the endogenous variables U_t and U_{t-1} on the RHS. In the short run, Phelps and Friedman argue that U_t can be, and is, affected by policy variables such as the money supply. Worse still, we saw that the *long run* exogeneity (or near exogeneity) of unemployment and output from the rate of inflation in the Phelps-Friedman models implied a very close link between inflation and the growth of the money supply. Suppose for simplicity's sake we can collapse equations for the demand for money, the supply of

---

[75] See, for example, Figure 7.7. Here, an expansion of the money supply can raise output and employment because the *nominal* wage rate is locked and the real wage can be reduced by price increases.

money (M) and money market clearance into the rate-of-change aggregate demand equation (where lower case letters denote logarithms)

$$p_t - p_{t-1} = m_t - m_{t-1} - \alpha(q_t - q_{t-1}). \tag{7.63}$$

Granted this, it will only be by fluke that (7.59) and (7.61) are consistent: (7.62) places very tight limits on the time-path of M_t, the variable which must really be driving the inflation rate. Now (7.61) and (7.63) are consistent if history reveals that M_t has evolved according to the process

$$m_t = m_{t-1} + \alpha(q_t - q_{t-1}) + u_t - \mu u_{t-1}. \tag{7.64}$$

If there is information available about the authorities' intentions about M_{t+1}, or about other variables that may influence M_{t+1}, rational expectations of future price levels will surely allow for this information. There is no reason whatsoever why the money supply should follow an autoregressive path like (7.64). Stock market participants, company treasurers, trade-union officials, and others concerned with predicting inflation should often be able to guess the growth of the money supply in the near future more successfully by using economic theory and economic information, than by employing a mechanical weighted average of past increases in the money supply.

It is possible that the Phillips curve is vertical in the short run. If so, the authorities will be unable to employ demand management instruments to exert a systematic effect upon unemployment over any length of time. To simplify, make the average product of labour, Z_t, stationary, set v_t in (7.57) to zero, set the expectational coefficient a in (7.54) to unity and the lag i in (7.56) to zero, and linearize the relation between wage increases and unemployment. Consequently, (7.56) and (7.57) imply:

$$p_t - p_{t-1} - (E_{t-1}p_t - p_{t-1}) = \beta[U_{Nt} - U_t] + \epsilon_t. \tag{7.65}$$

Now suppose that the growth of the money supply has three elements: (i) a fixed growth rate, k: (ii) a feedback rule that relates $(m_t - m_{t-1})$ positively to $U_{t-1} - U_{Nt-1}$; and (iii) a random term with zero mean, η_t:

$$m_t - m_{t-1} = k + \zeta(U_{t-1} - U_{Nt-1}) + \eta_t. \tag{7.66}$$

Suppose q_t and U_t are linked by

$$q_t = \delta - \gamma U_t \tag{7.67}$$

continue to assume that aggregate demand is modelled by (7.63) and consider the natural rate of unemployment, U_{Nt}, to be an exogenous constant, n, known to everyone.

Our question is, is the expected level of unemployment affected by k or ζ, the systematic influences on the evolution of the money supply? Consider (7.65). The LHS equals

$$m_t - m_{t-1} - \alpha(q_t - q_{t-1}) - (E_{t-1}p_t - p_{t-1})$$

from (7.63); using (7.67) and (7.66) this reduces to

$$k + \zeta(U_{t-1} - n) + \eta_t + \alpha\gamma(U_t - U_{t-1}) - (E_{t-1}p_t - p_{t-1}).$$

This suggests that U_t will be affected by the growth rate of the money supply, k, and other parameters:

$$U_t(\beta + \alpha\gamma) = -\zeta U_{t-1} - k\eta_t + n(\beta + \zeta) + \epsilon_t + (E_{t-1}p_t - p_{t-1}). \qquad (7.68)$$

(7.68) points to a positive association between unemployment and expected inflation. If expectation of inflation is given unemployment is negatively related to the constant element k in the growth rate of the money supply, and to the size of the feedback coefficient ζ.

(7.68) achieves its implications, however, by exogenizing expectations. What difference does endogenizing $(E_{t-1}p_t - p_{t-1})$ make? Suppose everyone knows (7.63), (7.65), and (7.67). Imagine that the monetary authorities had obeyed the feedback rule (7.66) long enough for everyone to have deciphered it from their actions. If so, we may replace

$$E_{t-1}p_t - p_{t-1} \quad \text{by} \quad E_{t-1}m_t - m_{t-1} - \alpha\delta(U_t - U_{t-1}).$$

Now expected monetary growth equals simply $k + \zeta(U_{t-1} - n)$ since the mean expected value of η_t, the random element in monetary growth, is zero. Further, $E_{t-1}U_t$ equals n, since there can be no non-zero forecast of the discrepancy between current expectations of inflation and actual inflation, and the expected value of ϵ_t is zero. From this, we can infer that (7.68) simplifies drastically:

$$(\beta + \alpha\gamma)(U_t - n) = \epsilon_t - \eta_t. \qquad (7.69)$$

(7.69) is a powerful result. The difference between actual unemployment and its natural rate is a random forecast error which the authorities cannot alter by systematic action. There is *no* trade-off between inflation and unemployment, not even in the short run, once economic agents have been able to identify all the systematic influences on monetary policy. Only innovations in monetary policy can exert real effects. But policy innovations have disadvantages. If repeated, they cease to be novel and resistance to their effects is built up. The private sector wastes real resources on trying to decipher the logic, if any, behind the innovations. Worse still, it can be shown that if the authorities have no informational advantage and attempt to use monetary policy to contain future deviations of actual from natural unemployment that they anticipate, all they will succeed in doing on average is to amplify disturbances. The conclusion to which this line of reasoning tends is unmistakable: 'Patient, heal thyself'. In section VII: 6, we shall attempt an adjudication between this conclusion and interventionist arguments.

VII: 4 *Why the Phillips Curve May Not Be Vertical in the Long Run*

There are numerous arguments for thinking that inflation and unemployment *are* related in the long run, no matter what their short-run association.

Inflation is a tax on real balances. Chapter 8 will explore this point in detail. It is enough to notice now that there is likely to be some budget-imposed link between the rate(s) of income tax and the total yield of inflation tax. This link will presumably be negative. The yield of inflation tax will at first rise with the rate of inflation; and it may start to fall away, however, when inflation reaches a sufficiently rapid pace. The higher the rate of income tax, the greater the incentive to continue searching for new employment in a state of temporary joblessness, rather than take a probably less lucrative job sooner. This will be particularly strong if rates of income tax are expected to drop back. Furthermore, if the proceeds of taxation are partly passed back to households as transfer incomes, there may well be a small, but discernible link between inflation tax revenue and the size of the transfer. To the extent that leisure is a normal good, the higher the transfer, the greater the incentive for leisure. In Mirrlees's model, for example, there is a clear positive association between the proportion of the population who do not work and the rate of transfer; to this extent, if higher inflation permits an increase in the transfer, it will raise unemployment. On the other hand, if it permits a cut in the rates of income tax, the opposite effect could occur.

Another inflation–unemployment link arising from the fiscal effects of inflation occurs if there is some rigidity in the real after-tax wage rate paid to households. Any reduction in income-tax rates that higher inflation allows will then be expected to raise employers' demand for labour. Classical unemployment would fall in these conditions. A further effect arises if, following Schramm (283), we postulate that output is a twice-differentiable well-behaved function of labour services, capital services, and the liquidity services provided by stocks of real balances (and perhaps other inventories). The lower the rate of inflation, this time, the lower the cost of real balances, the greater the stock of real balances, and the higher—for a given real wage rate—the demand for labour. In classical unemployment conditions, this effect will be translated into lower unemployment. It is fair to admit, however, that the size of this effect may be miniscule.

There are other possible links, as well. The higher the rate of inflation, the more quickly contracts will be renegotiated in labour and goods markets. Frequent contract renegotiation spells high costs, strike threats, and other nuisances; but it also implies a speedier response to technological and other shocks that would otherwise bring labour market disequilibrium while wage relativities are locked. This points to a negative link between inflation and unemployment. So could Keynesian asymmetries, if inflation allowed relative wage rates and real wage rates to sink faster in labour markets characterized by excess supply than could occur without it: downwards rigidity of nominal wage rates is bypassed by inflation. It is by no means inconceivable that unemployment exacerbates inflation: unemployment benefits insulate aggregate demand from the effects of unemployment, while restraining aggregate supply; the higher the level of unemployment, the lower the receipts of taxation on earnings and profits and the higher the transfer payments, with (in consequence) some danger of a faster growth of the money supply. Finally, it may be observed that what is worst about inflation may be the distortions created by governments when they try to stop it: wage and price controls perhaps, which suppress excess demands and induce the kind of contractions in output that occur under repressed inflation; or exceptionally harsh credit policies, with their trail of often unjustified bankruptcies. The faster the rate of inflation, the greater the probability of such policies, and the greater the uncertainties to which they give rise. Increased unemployment is a probable outcome.

VII: 5 *Unemployment: Concluding Comments on its Causes and Cure*

We may distinguish between equilibrium and disequeilibrium unemployment. Examples of the former include voluntary unemployment caused by unearned and unconditional income, whether provided by inherited wealth or transfer incomes from the State; voluntary unemployment attributable to unemployment benefits; and forms of unemployment and underproduction attributable to allocative inefficiency or poverty of information. Disequilibrium unemployment and underproduction emerge because of inflexibility of wages and prices.

Chapter 1 explored the first kind of equilibrium unemployment (section II: 3), and chapter 4 provided a more detailed explanation of joblessness as an inevitable by-product of certain kinds of fiscal redistribution. Unemployment benefits as a possible cause of unemployment were also considered in chapter 1. Evidence on their quantitative importance is conflicting;[76] their contribution to rising unemployment in the 1970s appears to have been positive but possibly quite modest.[77] Allocative inefficiency and informational poverty deserve some discussion as causes of unemployment.

We saw in chapter 2 that a profit-maximizing producer's output and employment levels were related negatively to the elasticity of demand for his product. This relationship can generate equilibrium unemployment in an economy with monopoly in production. Figure 7.21 presents a simple partial equilibrium analysis that depicts some of the issues raised by a related phenomenon: bilateral monopoly between a monopoly producer and a monopoly trade union. The curve CC represents the value of labour's marginal product, DD its marginal revenue product. DD lies below CC to reflect product market monopoly. If the employer faces an exogenous wage rate w_n, his profit maximizing employment level will be N_A, where the highest attainable isoprofit function ϕ_A is tangent to $w_A AG$.

The wage rate may be exogenous for two reasons. It could be imposed by perfect competition in the labour market with the employer deprived of any monopsony power. Alternatively, it may be imposed by a trade union, which maximizes its own utility by selecting point A on the choice frontier DD. λ_A is

[76] See Andrews and Nickell (338), Atkinson and Flemming (14), Nickell (240) and (359), Cubbin and Foley (72), and Maki and Spindler (203). For the effect of unemployment benefits on unemployment in inter-war Great Britain, see Benjamin and Kochin (39), and Dimsdale (84).

[77] Nickell estimates the elasticity of unemployment to the marginal replacement ratio (benefit to taxed wage income, corrected for tax repayments) at about 0.6.

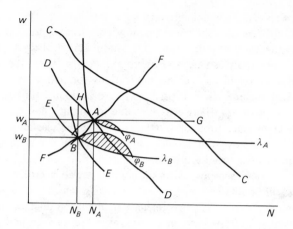

FIG. 7.21. Inefficient employment-reducing equilibrium under bilateral monopoly.

a trade-union indifference curve between its two 'goods', wage rate and employment level (see Sinclair (300) for further exploration of this theme). In the latter case, some combinations of wage cut and employment increase would bring rises in the producer's profits *and* the union's utility. These combinations are illustrated by the striped lozenge-shaped area east-south-east of point A. Point A illustrates a Stackelberg equilibrium; union leads by setting w_A in cognizance of the firm's reaction function DD; employer follows by setting N_A to maximize profits, treating w_A as exogenous. Optimization by both parties acting in this fashion—as they see it, in their own best interest—fails to maximize their joint interest, still less (by any definition) the social interest.

If the employer learns by experiment, or experience of disequilibrium, that w_A is *not* exogenous, he may observe that the union's 'Engel curve' of optimal w, N combinations is FF. Curve FF will not, of course, be unique, unless (as we assume here) the employer experiments in a particular fashion, e.g. by equiproportionate changes in employment at any wage rate. The mantle of leadership now falls on the employer, who maximizes profits subject to the restraint FF. This leads to the wage-rate-employment pair w_B, N_B: FF is tangent to the employer's highest attainable isoprofit curve ϕ_B at B. Union utility is reduced to λ_B; the union is now deceived into thinking that the employer's reaction function is EE, not DD. The marginal revenue product of labour, given by DD, now exceeds the wage rate; but the former (at H) equals the firm's perception of the *marginal* cost of labour. The employer has cut back employment because he has learnt that raising employment drives up the wage rate. FF need not slope up; if the λ_i were Cobb–Douglas, it would be horizontal (if DD were linear and disturbed in the fashion assumed); with a higher elasticity of substitution between w and N in the union's utility function, it would have negative gradient. But if FF does slope upward, round 2 in the Stackelberg wage-rate war will lead to a cut in w and N, at point B. Point B is even less efficient from the standpoint of the employer's and the union's interests: the set of w and N pairs that will be preferred by both to B expands to the larger striped area east of B.

Point *B* in Figure 7.21 is not likely to be a final resting place. Threats, retaliation, attempts at deception and quite possibly collusive negotiation may ensue to
move *w* and *N* in almost any direction. But what Figure 7.21 does establish clearly
is that bilateral monopoly can give rise to grotesquely inefficient trades. Unemployment is an all-too-probable outcome. Implications for policy that may be drawn
from Figure 7.21 include: (i) anti-trust policy to prohibit collusion among oligopolists may narrow the gap between the value of labour's marginal product (*CC*)
and its marginal revenue product (*DD*), by raising the elasticity of each firm's
average revenue, thereby stimulating employment; (ii) the abolition of import
quotas for commodities produced by one domestic firm (or a small group of firms)
may raise employment sharply, as its monopoly power is broken: protection, if
required, may still be retained in the form of tariffs, which (unlike quotas) do not
confer monopoly power; (iii) price regulation in the product market could also
secure the advantages of (i), as could a more general set of wage and price controls,
although either carry the grave danger of creating disequilibrium; (iv) legislative
or other reforms of the labour market, which might include profit-sharing, worker-
directors, or curbs on trade union power.[78] It could be wrong to infer that government could achieve much in Figure 7.21 by raising the money supply; if producer
and union utility functions are homogeneous of degree zero in all prices, the distortions will simply reappear at higher nominal values of wage rates and prices.

Poverty of information has long been recognized as a cause of unemployment.
Employers take time to hire, and workers take time to search. In both cases there
are substantial costs of gathering information about potential applicants for jobs,
or potential jobs for which to apply. Phelps's search theory of unemployment
explains why workers sometimes stay unemployed and turn down offers of jobs:
they expect more attractive job offers later. Their reservation price exceeds the
wage rates most recently offered. They aim to stay out of the labour market
temporarily, just like Keynes's wealthholders who sell bonds when they anticipate
increases in interest rates. Workers see a speculative return from unemployment.
The average duration of unemployment is a most important variable, since total
unemployment at any moment is the product of average duration and the number
of job seekers in a given interval of time. The original theory has been developed
further by Lucas and Prescott (199). It can also be applied to the hirer of labour:
this time, it must be expectations that future wage rates will be lower, or future
labour quality higher, that make the employer shy away from offering jobs now.

The search theory has undoubted appeal. But it is open to objections. Quits are
less common than lay-offs, so that at least the initial decision to become unemployed usually does not lie with the worker, although how long he remains
unemployed, of course, may. Many people search for new jobs before leaving their
old one. Furthermore, a spell of joblessness on the applicant's *curriculum vitae*
may do more damage to his earnings prospects than evidence of having taken up
low-paid employment for a while. Moreover, workers are usually free to leave jobs
if new opportunities arise, and are rarely less able to perceive such opportunities

---

[78] For detailed economic analysis of the theory of profit-sharing and labour management,
see Drèze (94), Furubotn (129) and Meade (212); also Brown and Medoff (48).

than the unemployed. From the employee's position, a wage contract is more flexible than a long-term bond. Then there is the problem that the imperfect-capital-markets explanation of consumption falls in recessions accords ill with the search theory of unemployment: imperfect capital markets will goad the searcher into accepting job offers quickly. The policy implications of the search theory point clearly to the role of unemployment benefits in lengthening search;[79] the current rate of income tax also has the same effect; and government might assist by subsidizing job advertisements, removing legal restrictions on both parties to short-term, flexible wage contracts, and extending information about job offers and wage rates. Diamond (345) extends these ideas further.

Informational poverty is serious; more serious still, perhaps, is asymmetry in information. In chapter 1, we saw the relevance of Akerlof's model of quality-uncertainty (1) to markets for used consumer durables. The 'used labour' market may be even more of a problem. A worker who pleads for a job, and offers his services cheaply to undercut rivals, may emit a 'low-quality' signal[80] to the prospective employer. The more desperate he is for work, the more he bids the wage rate down; but the employer's reaction may be very unfavourable. A spell of unemployment, we have already seen, looks bad on a *curriculum vitae*. It may also sap a man's self-confidence, shake his ability to concentrate at work, and corrode his skills. Alas, the employer knows this too. For the miserable few, unemployment may be a vicious trap of falling earnings prospects, falling ability, and ever-lengthening bouts of demoralizing joblessness.

The 'lemons' argument can be adduced to explain why excess supply in the labour market may be slow to clear. Firms are reluctant to provoke a fall in the quality of their job applicants, and perhaps their existing employees as well, by reducing wage rates unilaterally, and they will suspect low wage offers. Just as worrying, it can explain why excess demand persists in credit markets. You do *not* raise the probability of getting a bank loan by raising the rate of interest at which you say you are willing to borrow; this merely raises the probability of your going bust, and signals to the banker that you are a bad risk. Excess demand for credit and excess supply of labour are intertwined, above all in Keynesian unemployment. At this point we have exhausted equilibrium explanations of unemployment, and turn to consider disequilibrium explanations. The borderline between the two is perhaps as arbitrary as that between voluntary and involuntary unemployment; the two are closely linked.

In Keynesian unemployment, cause and cure are simple: aggregate demand for goods is too low, and should be raised by government spending increases, tax cuts or monetary expansion. In repressed inflation, employment is raised by doing the

---

[79] It does *not* follow, however, that the optimal rate of unemployment benefit is zero. For one thing, there is a social gain in efficiency if a better match between people and jobs is achieved, and the deprivation of unemployment benefits would goad people into accepting the job offers too early from the standpoint of social efficiency. Optimal unemployment benefit rates have been derived by Diamond (82) that capture the effect of externalities, and Flemming (114) on the assumption that workers are averse to risk. (Risk aversion can also lead to insufficient search in the absence of unemployment benefits.)

[80] See Spence (307) for a seminal paper on signalling in the labour market.

exact opposite. In classical unemployment, all three are irrelevant, except in so far as they alter the real wage rates perceived by firms or their production functions. In a world with more than one kind of labour and more than one kind of product, disequilibria are likely to be mixed. Excess demand for plumbers and oil, excess supply for wheat and schoolteachers. Can we draw any specific conclusions about how government policy should be framed?

In our final section in this chapter, we shall attempt to adjudicate generally between the arguments for and against active stabilization policies. At this juncture, there are some detailed points which need to be made. Disequilibria arise primarily for two reasons: an unforeseen event disturbs the equilibrium; and time must elapse before the structure of prices fully reacts to the shock. Before adaptation is complete, prices will be out of line. Disequilibrium will occur in the market in question; it also has complex, sometimes quite dramatic knock-on or spill-over effects on other markets.

Consider the market for labour employed by a large group of competitive firms, illustrated in Figure 7.22. Suppose that these firms negotiate the wage rate with a single union representing the labour. Neither union nor employers know how labour supply or product demand conditions will alter over the life of the contract period. When the latter are mapped into employment : wage rate space, the range of possibilities is depicted in Figure 7.22. Let us suppose that the union would have selected point B on the mean expected demand curve, $E(D)$, as being the most desirable wage-rate–employment trade-off available, had there been no uncertainty; and assume too that point B is also agreed upon under uncertainty as well, as a mean expectation.

Given the possibility of shocks affecting the supply of job applicants (S) and the demand for labour (D), the union and the employers must choose how to react. Should they contract to fix the number of jobs at $\bar{N}$, and let the wage rate float between E and F, depending on what happens to demand? Or should they lock the

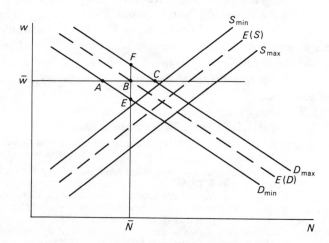

FIG. 7.22. Uncertainty and the wage-employment contract.

wage rate at $\bar{w}$ over the life of the contract, and let the number of jobs take the strain of the disequilibrium? Or some mixture? Some arguments point to the 'fix-$\bar{w}$' policy: particularly, the fact that for at least a majority of workers, A will be preferable to E in the low demand case, especially if a fall in N means a fall in jobs, not the introduction of shorter hours for all, and the government sustains the incomes of the unemployed by benefits.

We assumed above that B is an equilibrium position for the union both under certainty and uncertainty about D and S. This may not be so. Suppose the range of possible shifts in D and S widens. From the union's standpoint, high employment is good, because it raises membership dues, union power, and the utility of the individuals concerned (if they are worried about unemployment); and a high wage rate is good for similar reasons. If the wage rate turns out to have been pitched too high (D is at D min), at least there is the consolation of a high wage rate to compensate, to some extent, for the low employment level. But if events take a different course and the wage rate turns out to be below a market equilibrium rate (D is at D_{max}, S at S_{min}, and a value of w set initially below $\bar{w}$) the union suffers from *both* low employment and *low* w. It is better to err on the side of a high wage rate; increased uncertainty could make the optimal wage rate still higher.

Azariadis (17) has argued that risk-averse workers would gain by entering implicit contracts with risk-neutral firms, which made employment, not the wage rate, bear the strain of random movement in the demand for labour. In a bad state, idle workers can be compensated by extra leisure and 'stand-by' wages. So a fix-w contract that gives the worker the same expected utility as a fix-N contract should offer the firm higher expected profits. Azariadis' argument has been extended by Gordon (136) and Loewenstein (357), among others. Asymmetric information has recently been perceived as an important issue: a fix-N contract would tempt the firm to pretend that D in Fig. 7.22 was lower than it was (see Hart (353)). Goods markets, too, may exhibit similar advantages for fixing prices (rather than quantities or in their own right). Infrequent price changes build customer loyalty. Unilateral price rises provoke existing customers into search and brand-switching; unilateral price cuts persuade existing customers to increase purchases, perhaps, but fail to attract many new customers frequently in markets characterized by imperfect information.[81] Even under competitive assumptions, prices may rest out of market-clearing equilibrium if individual traders conjecture that attempts to sell more of goods in excess supply will provoke a new set of prices that promises the lower utility.[82]

However we explain temporary rigidity in prices or wage rates, how can government act to alleviate the consequences of the unforeseen events that turn them from efficient arrangements into job threats? Perhaps the most attractive instrument is the employment subsidy.[83] Involuntary unemployment implies that the social opportunity cost of employment lies below the current wage rate paid by

[81] Negishi (236) provides an illuminating interpretation of Keynesian unemployment which is partly based on this idea.

[82] See Hahn (143) for an original account of non-Walrasian conjectural equilibria.

[83] See Kaldor (178) for a pioneering analysis of this instrument of policy. Layard and Nickell (191) have an interesting proposal for incremental employment subsidies.

firms. The 'virtual price'[84] of labour paid to households rationed by disequilibrium in the labour market is beneath the price of labour perceived by their employers. Disequilibrium in this context acts just like a tax on employment. *Ergo*, the correct solution to the distortion is to alleviate the implicit tax by subsidiary employment.

The employment subsidy helps in both Keynesian *and* classical unemployment. In the former case it boosts employers' profits or, if passed on in higher wage rates, workers' consumption; this raises aggregate demand. In the latter, unless fully passed on to households,[85] it must lower the real cost of hiring labour perceived by employers; employment will increase directly. What are its drawbacks? Primarily, the exchequer costs, borne by the State (and hence the tax payer). But these may be slight—even negative—given the high financial cost of unemployment, in the form of benefits, social security payments, and lost tax receipts. If, as Layard and Nickell suggest (191), subsidies are restricted to *additional* employees, the financial cost of the measure will be minimized; for employers will receive no rent on intra-marginal employees. Against this, additional employees this year become next year's intramarginal employees. Employers who believe 'if he's good, he'll go; if he isn't, he'll be with you for ever' will look askance at a measure that makes such a modest dent in the discounted present value of life-time wage costs. Perhaps the ideal policy if unemployment is unexpectedly high, is to combine temporary employment subsidies on additional employees, with legislative and other measures to reduce the apparent irreversibility of the hiring decision in the eyes of the hirer.

Government investment is another attractive measure. If it alters producers' production conditions favourably, it will raise output—and very probably employment[86]—in classical unemployment. These effects will be enduring, if the real wage rate remains fixed. In Keynesian unemployment, it will strengthen aggregate demand while it is actually taking place, provided that private sector expenditure is less than fully 'crowded out' as a result of interest rate changes (see section VI: 3). Private sector investment subsidies will have similar effects, unambiguously raising the demand the demand for labour for a given real wage rate as the stock of capital is built up (classical unemployment), or boosting aggregate demand unless $g(Q)$ is vertical in Figure 7.19 (Keynesian unemployment). The disadvantage with both is the long lead time required. The government needs instruments that react swiftly to disequilibria. This is not really because the the rate of the preference biases choices in favour of earlier benefits—the point is that such tendencies as there are for wages and prices to move towards equilibrium make disequilibrium a *short-run* problem; and it is ludicrous to think that authorities have lengthy advance warning of the date and character of the stochastic shocks that create the disequilibria. To the extent that investment expenditures *can* be rephased, however, there is much to be said in favour of an investment subsidy which is announced as being temporary at the start.

---

[84] See Neary and Roberts (233). The virtual price here is the marginal real wage rate which would make the households *opt* for the labour supply they are constrained to provide.

[85] This might eventually prove an important qualification.

[86] Assuming that it is analogous to private capital formation or technical progress. See section V: 2.

We have considered measures which might succeed in lowering unemployment in both its classical and Keynesian forms. Other devices, such as softening minimum wage legislation or expanding the supply of money, will achieve this desired effect (if at all) in only *one* of the two regimes. Sometimes they will exert contrary effects in the two cases. Reducing minimum wage rates will unquestionably alleviate unemployment in the classical case. In the Keynesian unemployment model, it will have no effect if consumer spending is unaffected by the distribution of income between wages and profits, and the level of investment spending is unchanged. If, however, profit incomes accrue after a delay, or are not fully perceived as income by the households that receive them, or are more liable to be saved rather than spent for some other reason, any contraction in wage rates will damage consumer expenditure at the existing employment level. Unless there is a compensating increase in investment expenditure, equilibrium employment will sink.[87] It therefore seems most important that the authorities should be able to decide whether a sudden increase in unemployment is predominantly due to Keynesian or classical forces, before considering how best to respond to it. Can they?

In certain circumstances, they can. If real wage rates have risen steeply in the recent past, for whatever reason, a rise in unemployment is rather likely to be classical. Producers respond to dearer labour by dismissals, refusals to hire new labour, and bankruptcies. The absence of any rise in real wage rates is indicative of Keynesian unemployment. Another litmus paper is provided by evidence of disequilibrium in the goods market. High import levels point to classical unemployment, low to Keynesian. Questionnaire evidence that producers would (or would not) increase production if the cost of labour or materials were cheaper points to classical (Keynesian) unemployment. Then there are inventory statistics: sudden decumulation may (but need not) point to excess demand in the goods market. Yet, in practice, the two types of unemployment will be hard to tell apart. This is partly because they may both be present, with some goods in excess demand and others in excess supply; and partly because the relative flexibility of many commodity prices moves the economy rather swiftly towards the boundary between them, confirming the model depicted in Figure 7.7.

VII: 6 *The Arguments For and Against an Active Stabilization Policy*[88]

In section VII: 2, we set up a model where the authorities could not even exploit a temporary trade-off between inflation and unemployment. Any systematic monetary policy would be discovered and neutralized by anticipations of its effects. Random elements in monetary policy could secure real effects temporarily, but on average they would succeed in raising the variance of unemployment about its natural rate, while leaving its mean value unaffected. If this model is a reasonably

---

[87] See Keynes (182), ch. 19, for detailed analysis of why in his view wage cuts *could* lower employment, and Brown *et al.* (342) for the effects of a minimum wage.

[88] Important papers in this debate include Barro (24), Sargent and Wallace (282), and Weiss (330). Grossman (138) has a valuable survey of the reasoning underlying rational expectations equilibria, and their implications; these are issues central to the debate. For a recent statement of arguments against Keynesian stabilization policy, see Beenstock (36), while Buiter (343) provides a powerful and imperfect counter-attack. See also Begg (339).

reliable description of reality, the case for an active stabilization policy is destroyed. In this model, the authorities could affect the mean values of output and unemployment *if and only if* expectations were for some reason partly exogenous or predetermined. Rational expectations rendered monetary policy impotent. Much depends, therefore, upon the validity of the assumptions that underlay this model.

Before assessing this, however, we should first decide what is meant by an 'active' stabilization policy. The simplest form of passive policy is for governments to do nothing. This means, for example, fixing the growth rate of the money supply to the constant number k in equation (7.66), as recommended long ago by Milton Friedman (120).

Active policy, therefore, falls into two types. First, there is the regular, planned response to the unpredictable. This is captured by $(U_{t-1} - U_{Nt-1})$ in (7.66). When unemployment exceeds its natural rate, the money supply growth rate should be stepped up in the next period. Before date $t - 1$, the sign and size of $U_{t-1} - U_{Nt-1}$ could not properly be forecast by anyone, not even the authorities themselves. But once they can observe it, they react by an automatic feedback rule. Secondly, there is the still more active policy of *attempting to forecast* $U_{t-1} - U_{Nt-1}$ despite the difficulties before date $t - 1$, and altering the set of policy instruments accordingly so as to maximize some function for expected inter-temporal social welfare. Formally, this is often set up as the problem of minimizing a loss function which is quadratic in deviations of variables (such as real consumption per head, unemployment and inflation) from their predetermined optimal values. This framework is also applied to the somewhat less ambitious task of devising an optimal set of feedback rules (by which experience of actual stochastic disturbances is then translated into particular pre-specified responses).[89] Buiter (343) argues strongly for such rules.

One argument in favour of both kinds of active policy is based on the hypothesis that the authorities have an informational advantage over the rest of the community. Sampling theory suggests that there are pronounced economies of scale: individual households or companies will find it prohibitively expensive to discover statistically significant samples of information on the movement of aggregate price and output indices for the whole economy, but governments are well placed to exploit the law of large numbers and obtain this information relatively cheaply.

Information, therefore, has much of the character of a public good. But should the government withhold the information it has gathered? Doing so would mean that individual agents would engage in costless, avoidable, information-gathering activity of their own. The precepts of allocative efficiency prescribe that the authorities' information be published. Military and diplomatic secrets, and potentially damaging information relating to identifiable companies or individuals, are the only exceptions to this. Samuelson once argued (274, p. 361) that Keynesian economics in a sense destroyed itself: a 'neoclassical synthesis' could be imagined,

---

[89] See Phillips (255), Turnovsky (326), and Nagatani (229), ch. 9, for an account of macro-economic applications theory, and Intriligator (169) for an outline of its mathematical properties. The Ball Committee Report on Policy Optimization, Cmnd. 7148 (1978) can be recommended for its detailed scrutiny of the arguments for and against the application of control theory to stabilization policy. See also Johansen (170), Shupp (296), and Modigliani (220).

whereby successful use of Keynesian instruments to cure the Keynesian problem of deficient aggregate demand disposed of the Keynesian phenomenon. If the authorities follow the precepts of allocative efficiency, Keynesian economics is self-destroying in a second sense. The authorities should denude themselves of their informational advantage. Once they are no better at predicting the future than the private citizen, they are powerless to affect his behaviour for the better by monetary means.

It can be argued that Keynesianism is not the only self-negating doctrine in economics. Perhaps monetarism and the New Classical Macroeconomics will prove to suffer the same fate. The New Classical Monetary Economics rests upon the assumptions that markets clear, that expectations are formed optimally, and that money is neutral. Experience of the Great Boom from 1945 until 1973 tends to confirm these assumptions, and the predictions of models built upon them. The gradual climb of inflation in many countries mirrored the monetary growth data quite closely. In most countries unemployment was usually very low by historical standards. Expenditure was subject to considerable inertia. The Keynesian phenomena of the 1930s—mass unemployment, sticky prices, ferocious fluctuations in expenditure—faded from memory.

Most professional economists and government policymakers are now at one in thinking that active stabilization policy is very unwise. Supply is exogenous, as far as monetary policy is concerned; monetary expansion simply raises prices. How ironic if the economies of the West start, once again, to obey the Keynesian laws of boom and slump, precisely because the authorities are convinced that such phenomena cannot occur! The steadiness and the low average level of unemployment between 1945 and 1973 may be ascribed more to belief that the authorities *would* intervene to stabilize real output and employment, than to their actual stabilization policies.[90] This safety net has now been removed. Price stability is the new objective. The New Classical Macroeconomics teaches that price stability is the only objective the authorities can sensibly pursue. As Figure 7.22 shows, one may have price stability or employment stability, but never both. Lucas has warned (198) against the dangers of extrapolating economic agents' behaviour across periods when policy has changed. Perhaps monetary policy is becoming capable of executing substantial real effects, at just the moment—and precisely because —those framing it have ceased to believe that it can.

Further qualifications on the nihilistic modern view on what can be achieved by active stabilization policy include:

(*a*)   the problem of the transition between rational expectations equilibria, which is at present only imperfectly understood, and typically has to follow a unique path towards a saddle point equilibrium in order to converge;

(*b*)   the related 'bilateral monopoly' problem of how the private sector, and the government, now react to each other in a state of affairs when everyone thinks the authorities have lost their ability to influence events because their original

[90] Most studies of the UK economy conclude that stabilization policies have on balance amplified the variations of real GDP about its trend. See Dow (93), Matthews (209), and Worswick and Matthews's contributions to Cairncross (53).

Keynesian feedback rules have become predictable but are now discarded;

(*c*) expectations formed *at* different dates: if some wage rates or prices for date 2 are set at date 0 in the light of expectations held then, monetary policy that reacts systematically to date 1's shocks *can* affect output in date 2;

(*d*) expectations formed *for* different dates: the impotence result also fails if date 2's output depends on date 1's expectations of the price level in date 2 *and date 3* (e.g. because this is related to nominal interest rates): predictions of prices at date 3 will be influenced by foreknowledge of how the authorities will react to date 2's shocks;

(*e*) if the authorities adopt an entirely passive macroeconomic policy, the fact that risk aversion, and the dangers of *real* disequilibria of a Keynesian nature, combine to alter the private sector's behaviour, in a manner likely to aggravate allocative inefficiency and distributive injustice; the likelihood of this may be related negatively to k;

(*f*) the phenomenon of positive serial correlation in output and unemployment:[91] if output is above trend at one date, the statistics reveal that it is likelier than not to remain above trend at the following date; hence $U_{t-1} - U_{Nt-1}$ may to *some* extent be predictable by the authorities once they know $U_{t-2} - U_{Nt-2}$, $U_{t-3} - U_{Nt-3}$ and so on; if for some reason other economic agents do not know that output and unemployment are serially correlated, monetary policy *can* expect effects on unemployment; on the other hand, if the authorities and other agents share the same information the neutrality results are reconfirmed;

(*g*) the authorities may well be able to alter the natural rate of unemployment, U_N, by fiscal policy parameters such as unemployment-benefit rates and marginal income-tax rates, by subsidizing the dissemination of information about jobs and job-seekers, *and* (given the arguments advanced in section VII: 4) by altering the growth rate of the money supply, k;

(*h*) the fact that rational expectations equilibria need not be optimal or unique (Grossman (138), Grossman and Stiglitz (139)) suggests a potential role for the government in selecting between different equilibria, subsidizing the provision of information or helping to compensate for any incompleteness in markets in other ways; indeed, if agents entertain 'rational conjectures' (conjectures about their present and future economic environment, which experience confirms as having been rational), it is perfectly possible for expectations to be self-fulfilling, thus confirming the idea that a Keynesian recession may develop spontaneously (Hahn (143));

(*i*) there will never be agreement among economists on what constitutes an optimal model of the economy; the best trade-off between detail and simplicity varies with the purpose the model is designed to fulfil; it is interesting to speculate on how differently the New Classical Macroeconomics would be would be regarded, had the Yom Kippur War of 1973 and the fall of the Shah

[91] Furthermore, positive serial correlation in output and unemployment *may* be explained by phenomena which do not impugn the classical neutrality result. Sargent (280) has demonstrated this by assuming that firms face increasing costs of adjusting employment quickly. See also Kydland and Prescott (356).

of Iran in 1978–9—two events that indirectly led to massive increases in oil prices—*not* happened to coincide with expansionary monetary policy in many Western countries;

(*j*) the fact that the impotency result for systematic monetary policy under rational expectations may not apply when non-linear macroeconomic relationships are introduced (Shiller (294));

(*k*) empirical tests of the natural rate–rational expectations–neutrality hypothesis are not fully confirmatory (e.g. Pesaran (360) and Hoffman and Schlagenhauf (354)).

Summary of Notation in Chapter 7

$\bar{B}$	the stock of interest bearing debt (bonds)
b	bread
b^f	investment demand
b^h	household demand
c	coupon attached to a bond
G	government expenditure
I	investment
J	a technology parameter
K	capital stock
M	money supply
$\bar{M}$	the stock of non-interest bearing debt
M/P	real money holdings
N	labour input
N_d	demand for labour
N_s	supply of labour
P	price
Q	output
q	the actual quantity traded in a market
S	retained profit
t	tax rate
t_c	corporation tax rate
U	unemployment rate
U_N	natural rate of unemployment
u	stochastic disturbance term
W	wealth
Z	the average product of labour
$(h-N)$	leisure retained
$\mathscr{E}$	the expectation of all future variables
π	profit
σ_U	the substitution elasticity in utility
σ_Q	the substitution elasticity in production

Chapter 8

Optimum Monetary Policy
in the Long Run

We begin, as usual, by constructing a model. It is not unlike that first posed by Friedman,[1] whose controversial paper has received wide attention.

Assume:

(A1) all real balances, z, are outside and fiat;[2]

(A2) the marginal cost of creating real balances, γ, is negligible;

(A3) the economy suffers from distortions in no market other than, perhaps, that for z;

(A4) the demand for z, $h\,(R_N)$, is decreasing in the nominal rate of interest, $R_N : h' < 0$;

(A5) satiation: $h(0) < \infty$;

(A6) the second Fisher Equation: $R_N - R_R = \dot{P}^e$ where $R_R =$ real rate, $\dot{P}^e =$ expected inflation;

(A7) $R_R = \bar{R}_R$, a parameter.

These assumptions generate implications as follows. Given A3, efficiency prescribes that money be priced at its marginal cost; this, given A2, is zero. A4 defines its marginal cost as the nominal rate of interest, which ought, therefore, itself to be zero. Given A5, this optimum level of z will be finite. A6 carries the argument further and shows that the sum of the real rate of interest and the rate of expected inflation should be zero. Given A7, policy must be directed, if at all possible, to making the rate of expected inflation equal minus the real rate of interest. Before we proceed to see how this might be done, a diagram may help to clinch understanding of the argument so far.

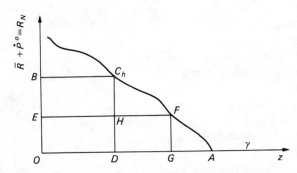

FIG. 8.1. The optimum quantity of money: money should be a free good.

[1] See Friedman (124); and also criticisms by Hahn (141) and extensions by Jovanovic (355).

[2] Fiat money is the non-interest-bearing liability of the State, or 'token' money, in the form of cash.

The horizontal axis is coextensive with the marginal cost function, γ. If the nominal rate of interest is positive (e.g. at B or E), the demand for real balances will be given by the function, h: it will be D when $R_N = B$, or G when $R_N = E$. The optimum provision of real balances occurs at A, where society is satiated (given A5). Money should, according to our model, be a free good. But this does *not* mean that its purchasing power in goods should be reduced to zero. Rather, it is the opportunity cost of holding money that should be eliminated. This opportunity cost is the nominal rate of interest; for it is this interest rate which is sacrificed by holding money, and not holding the other paper-denominated asset, unindexed bonds.

How, then, is point A reached? Not, emphatically not, by increasing the nominal money supply, even less by increasing its rate of growth. Why is this so?

Rapid monetary expension, if sustained, will lead to high expectations of inflation. Faster monetary expansion, if sustained, will lead to higher expectations of inflation. This, given A6 and A7, will mean a higher nominal rate of interest. A higher value of R_N will (given A4) cut z. We have an important, and unobvious result: the real value of the money supply is negatively related to the long-run growth rate of the nominal money supply.

So reducing the nominal interest rate means reducing the growth rate of the nominal supply of money. In the long run, this is only to be expected, given assumptions 4, 6, and 7. There are two ways of getting to the result by explicit assumptions:

either (A8a) expectations are rational;

or   (A8b) expectations of the future price level are adaptive and extrapolative;

      (A9) there is a positive association between the rate of inflation and the rate of growth of the nominal money supply.

A9, when coupled with A8b, establishes the point that lowering $\hat{P}^e$ means lowering the growth rate of the nominal money supply. A8a requires that expectations of inflation be formed on the basis of knowledge of A9, and hence of *expected* changes in the money supply (M). In the long run, $\hat{M}$ and $\hat{M}^e$ should converge, under both rational and adaptive expectations. Assumption A8b states that $d\hat{P}^e$ is increasing in the error, $\hat{P} - \hat{P}^e$, in forecasting inflation. We can derive the conclusion that, as a long-run general policy, the nominal money supply should be increased (if at all) only rather slowly. But how slowly?

Suppose we confine attention to balanced growth paths, along which the income-velocity of money, V, is stationary:

(A10)   growth is balanced so that $\dot{V} = 0$ $\left(V \equiv \dfrac{Y}{Z} \right)$.

A10 implies that $\hat{Y} = \hat{Z}$: the growth rate of income equals the growth rate of real balances. In other words, $\hat{P} = \hat{M} - \hat{Y}$. With balanced growth, there will be no difference between actual and expected inflation. Hence $\hat{P}^e = \hat{M} - \hat{Y}$. Now since optimality requires $\hat{P}^e + \bar{R}_R = 0$, we may infer

$$\hat{M} = \hat{Y} - \bar{R}_R. \tag{8.1}$$

The only policy-parameter in this equation is $\hat{M}$. We may conclude that the optimum long-run growth rate of the nominal money supply is the difference between the growth rate of income and the real rate of interest. The reason for this is that there is a one-for-one long-run link between the nominal rate of interest and the growth of the nominal money supply. In the interesting special case of the Golden Rule[3] (where the permanent value of consumption per head is maximized, in a simple one-sector growth model), $\hat{Y}$ must equal $\bar{R}_R$. So in the Golden Rule example, the optimum long-run growth rate of the nominal money simply is zero. The money supply should be stationary. Deference to the Keynes–Ramsey Rule (see pp. 303–5) in a one sector growth model gives rise to a saddle point that is a defined optimum, superior to the Golden Rule position, so long as $\bar{R}_R > \hat{Y}$. This would, in our context, point to a policy of long-run monetary contraction ($\hat{M} < 0$) as being best.

Let us summarize the argument so far. Efficiency dictates that money be provided up to the point where its marginal benefit equals its marginal cost. If the latter is zero and the former is given by the nominal rate of interest, we must somehow ensure that this interest rate is brought down to zero. What this will do is to give the holders of money the same respective rate of return in real terms as is available on every other asset. Money holders expect to get a positive return, because they expect prices to drop—ideally at the speed of the real rate of interest. But expectations must conform with reality in the long run. So prices must *actually* drop at this rate. So rapid increases in the nominal supply must be avoided; all they will do is generate inflation; inflating expectations, and a quite unnecessary and indeed damaging rise in the velocity of circulation. But how damaging?

Let us return to Figure 8.1. Suppose a faster, sustained, value of $\hat{P}$ raises R_N from E to B. This will cut z from G to D. What does society lose as a result of this? To answer this question precisely, we need to make further assumptions. The simplest set of assumptions is:

(A11) the marginal utility of wealth is constant and equal for all agents;

(A12) social welfare is the sum of all agents' utilities;

(A13) the utility functions (of each producer for whom real balances are a factor of production, and each consumer for whom they are an ideally appreciating good, yielding a stream of services) are additiviely separable in the utility gained from money;

(A14) the State can tax by lump sums without cost.

What is lost by raising R_N from E to B is the area $CFGD$. Money-holders' surplus gets chopped down by $BCFE$, while the State's yield from inflation tax changes from $OGFE$ to $ODCB$. Our assumptions allow us to deal with money as a separate good from the rest of the economy (A14, and A3 to silence any objection raised on the basis of the Second Best Theorem); to pay no attention to the distribution of income (A11 and A12); and to treat changes in government revenue with indifference (A14). The concept of 'inflation-tax' needs explanation.[4] When $R_N = B$,

---

[3] See chapter 9 for a detailed treatment.
[4] See Barro (21) and Cagan (52).

the government has monetary non-interest-bearing obligations of *OD*, measured in real terms. In all probability it will have interest-bearing obligations, too; if these take the form (as they usually do) of unindexed bonds, the government will have to pay a nominal interest rate of *B* upon them.[5] The rectangle *OBCD* therefore represents the debt-servicing charges that the government escapes by having *OD* of its debts out in the form of outside fiat money.

Given these assumptions, society's gain from cutting R_N from *B* to *O* will be an area *CAD*. The size of the gain depends chiefly on the interest-elasticity of *h*. Given that *h* sums up producers' and consumers' demand for money, we need to reflect upon what area *CAD* might refer to, in practice. For the producer, it will include the increase in the value of output which follows a rise in the inventory of money.

Trips to the market to convert temporary cash surpluses into commodities will be much less frequent than, for instance, under really rapid inflation. Inventories of cash can replace some of the inventories of raw materials, saving space and other real resources. From the household's point of view, shopping expeditions may be less frequent, and stocks of commodities less large: hyperinflation would force people to spend cash frantically as soon as they received it for fear of suffering from its continuing steep fall in value; and it could also encourage them to pre-empt and hoard commodities, instead of holding cash. A mild rate of price decline, as soon as it came to be expected, would put an end to such time-wasting, resource-wasting, and space-wasting activities. Another likely advantage of the negligible nominal interest rate would be a saving in the frequency and costs of transactions in alternative assets. Fears of more rapid inflation will be reflected in higher nominal interest rates; optimal cash management will probably lead to a fall in average cash balances in favour of holdings of interest-bearing deposits and bonds (as well as of the commodity stocks already considered). This will spell increased costs in shoe leather, telephone calls, dealer's commissions, and the like. All have a social implication: additional real resources are used up. Bringing R_N down would put this process into reverse.

These, then, are what is gained by cutting equilibrium inflation. They therefore constitute a powerful argument against inflation. The optimum rate of inflation is slightly negative, so that prices can be expected to decline at a rate equal to the real rate of interest. The other argument against equilibrium inflation relates to the costs of price changes. It implies that the optimum rate of equilibrium inflation is zero, not slightly negative. This second argument is very simple.

Changing prices is expensive. Machinery monitoring telephone calls has to be recalibrated when the unit-time charge is altered. Vending machines, or the size of the objects they purvey, have to be changed. Brochures, price lists, menu cards have to be amended. Furthermore, consumers' memories of particular prices become misleading unless qualified by date subscripts, which are hard to recall; information gleaned from past searches and shopping expeditions gets out of date. The costs of changing price mean that price changes are discontinuous: the goods in question become 'fix-price' for some interval of time (a week, say, or a year).

---

[5] They will pay this rate on any indexed bonds, too, if we assume that actual inflation is correctly forecast: indexed bonds will give a nominal yield of $\bar{R}_R + \dot{P}$, unindexed $R_R + \dot{P}^e$.

Inflation does two things: it cuts the fix-price interval (leading to higher costs directly, because of the greater number of price changes); and because price changes are not synchronized, it tends to disturb the time path of relative prices, increasing their absolute deviation from their norms. If the mean values around which relative prices gyrate are both stationary and optimal, there is a strong presumption that inflation exacerbates disequilibria and reduces potential and actual welfare. In addition, it forces households to remember more information (price-and-date information as well as just prices), or to search and shop more, or both. So the best 'background' rate of inflation is zero. Rotemberg (362) provides a model for this.

Both arguments (our monetary case for slightly negative inflation, and this second argument for zero inflation) are to be distinguished sharply from arguments for and against 'disequilibrium' inflation. The simplest of these is the 'Mohammed-and-the-mountain' argument.

Walras's adjustment hypothesis for disequilibrium is that price turns in the direction of excess demand. As we saw in chapter 7, one might wish to qualify this by stressing its possible asymmetry: price rises faster in excess demand than it falls in excess supply. If so, disequilibria may be removed more equickly if you have rapid inflation. Suppose the price of chalk is 50 per cent higher than it should be, and the price of cheese, 50 per cent too low. So the relative price of chalk to cheese is three times as high as it ought to be. Without inflation, the price of chalk would stay too high for ages. General inflation drives up the shadow price of chalk (Mohammed) directly, towards the sticky actual price (the mountain). Now relabel cheese as corn, and chalk as labour. The significance of the old Keynesian nostrum that excess demand looks after itself, but excess supply does not, now comes clear. Inflation now seems to be a useful device for cutting real wages, and raising output and employment. This thought was central to orthodox macroeconomic policy for much of the post-war period. At the time of writing, it has recently become unfashionable in official circles.

A retort to the 'Mohammed-and-the-mountain' argument is that it may not work for long. One needs to ask what took the price of chalk (or labour) up so high in the first place. If it really was an accident, all well and good. But can one be sure? If it is not accidental, it will recur, and the human impulses behind it will sooner or later be inured to inflation. To put it crudely, if unemployment is the outcome of a trade union's attempt to corner the market, the notion that inflation can restore employment is a confidence trick. Only *unexpected* inflation can deceive. Expectations adjust.

One compelling argument against unexpected inflation is that it redistributes wealth arbitrarily, and therefore, for a risk-averse community, frighteningly. Typically, borrower gains from lender. Often it is the old who suffer most. Their reserves of human capital have been drained, and their slender holdings property are looted unless protected by indexation. A temporary gain from unexpected inflation will probably be recorded by a young, male, unionized houseowner.

These social effects of inflation have been identified empirically in several studies.[6] But within the confines of A11 and A12 of our model, they fade into

[6] See Birati and Cukierman (40), Fischer and Modigliani (11), and Wolff (336).

insignificance, and A10 (which anyway rules out anything unexpected) probably prevents them in the first place. This reflection reminds us of the need to question and try to relax all our assumptions.

A1 is unreasonably restrictive. The kind of money we have considered is paper currency. Banks have not yet been given a role. It is probably much easier in a contemporary economy, where paper currency forms a tenth or less of the money supply according to conventional measures, to require that banks' assets and liabilities be indexed. Such a proposal would reduce the yearly private opportunity cost of holding money (in its most important form, at least) to a very small number. It would really be very much easier to implement, given an initial position where expectations of inflation are positive, than adopting a monetary programme that brought down $\hat{P}^e$ to minus the real rate of interest. Requiring the banks to pay the rate of inflation to all depositors would, no doubt, lead to an enormous increase in their outgoings. If they charged the rate of inflation on overdrafts (plus some surcharge to redflect costs and risk), and were paid the rate of inflation on their average vault cash (UK: 'till money') and balances with the central bank, their profits need not fall so much. What is more, banks in these circumstances would (and presumably should) charage realistic fees for services provided. The marginal cost of clearing a cheque is by no means negligible. To provide this service free, in lieu of inflation-compensatory interest on bank deposits, is to compound injustice with inefficiency. The argument that adding inflation to bank deposit interest may be preferable to getting rid of inflation expectations was first advanced by H. G. Johnson (171). Furthermore, if the quantity of inside (or bank-produced) money is not optimal, there can be no reason for expecting a zero nominal interest rate to curve that quantitatively larger problem too.

A2 is also open to objection. The marginal costs of creating real balances, it will be recalled, have nothing whatever to do with the cost of paper and printing ink. They are the costs of reducing expectations of inflation: this is the only way of cutting R_N and thereby raising z. One way of modelling these costs is to explore the implications of A8b with the rest of the model.

Suppose we assume that actual inflation is related to expected inflation and unemployment as in the Natural Rate Hypothesis:

$$\hat{P} = \hat{P}^e + g(U - \bar{U}) \tag{8.2}$$

where U = unemployment rate, $\bar{U}$ = natural unemployment rate, $g' < 0$. Total labour supply, $\bar{L}$ equals U plus actual employment, N. Now introduce an aggregate production function, $Y = f(N)$, and the adaptive-extrapolative expectations hypothesis for price expectations,

$$d\hat{P}^e = \beta[\hat{P} - \hat{P}^e] \qquad \text{(where } \beta > 0\text{).}$$

We may now infer

$$d\hat{P}^e = \beta g(\bar{L} - f^{-1}(N) - \bar{U}), \tag{8.3}$$

which gives us a simple measure of the welfare cost of cutting $\hat{P}^e$. For simplicity's sake, we abstract from population growth, technical change and capital formation.

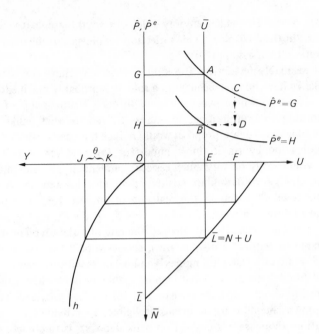

FIG. 8.2. The costs of reducing inflation under adaptive expectations.

The argument can be represented geometrically.[7] In the top-right quadrant, two short-run Phillips curves are drawn, each for stipulated rates of expected inflation; the vertical line $\bar{U}$ represents the natural rate of unemployment, which can be identified with Champernowne's 'basic rate' (55). The bottom-right quadrant measures actual employment (N) vertically downwards, against unemployment measured horizontally. The lower-left quadrant depicts a production function, with positive but diminishing marginal product of labour. Non-labour inputs, technology, and the size of the labour force are all given. We start at A, with actual and expected inflation equal at G. If we wish to measure the cost of cutting expected inflation, to H, we must consider the output loss this implies. Suppose that the least-cost path from A to a new equilibrium at B involves an immediate increase in unemployment from E to F, for t periods, and then, when actual inflation has fallen to H, an immediate reduction in unemployment. In terms of output lost, the cost of raising unemployment to F is θ, equal to JK in Figure 8.2. A very rough measure of total output lost would be $t\theta$. In present value terms, discounted at the real rate of interest, $\bar{R}_R$, this would equal

$$\theta \frac{1 + \bar{R}_R}{\bar{R}_R} [1 - (1 + \bar{R}_R)^{-t}].$$

These figures would, however, exaggerate the true cost of lowering expected inflation. The only redeeming aspect about having unemployment temporarily at a supernatural level of F is that extra leisure is created. This extra leisure is surely

---

[7] See Buiter and Miller (344) for an open-economy model of the costs of cutting inflation.

not valueless, if we are to take it that the private marginal utility of leisure is positive. In ideal conditions, the $\bar{U}$ line may be taken to illustrate the unemployment level where marginal rate of transforming leisure into income just equals the household's marginal rate of substitution between leisure and income. At F, however, marginal utility of leisure has fallen far below that of income, multiplied by the marginal rate of transforming leisure into income, at least for those unable to work as long as they would have in full equilibrium at E. The overall social loss will be highest when the burden of the fall in employment is concentrated on rather few workers (particularly if the social welfare function is strongly averse to inequality); when the workers affected cannot easily borrow or dissave; when returns to labour in the production function diminish only slowly; and when expectations of inflation are very sluggish and hard to dislodge.

The social loss from cutting $\hat{P}^e$ will, none the less, be only temporary. To set against it, we have the area of permanent gain: the increased money-holders' utility, the increased area under the demand function for real balances, h. Yet it is not at all clear that it is worth the cost, under assumption A8b, even when this last area is divided by $\bar{r}$ to express it as a present-value-stock. What about assumption A8a?

Under the most favourable conditions, A8a will allow us to bypass the pain of supernatural unemployment while $\hat{P}^e$ is being brought down. Suppose the authorities announce their intention of bringing the rate of growth of the nominal money supply down, steadily, each year, towards zero. If the public believes that this is their intention, and that they will succeed in being able to do so, the battle will be won; or won, at least, assuming that the public believes the Quantity Theory of Money, and forms expectations rationally, given that belief. But circumstances are unlikely to be so favourable. There is ample historical evidence that governments often prove incapable of fulfilling promises, for a variety of reasons. There is also statistical evidence against the hypothesis that $\hat{P}$ equals $\hat{M}$, minus a constant in each and every period,[8] in addition to the theoretical considerations which point to several factors that could temporarily upset the association.[9]

A3 is, as Hahn argues in a pugnacious review (141) of Friedman's original paper, a rather ironic assumption. The existence of money is explained by a combination of transactions costs and information costs. How odd, therefore, that the welfare economics of money should be conducted under an assumption that negates conditions necessary for its existence! This is a good debating point. But it is not clear *a priori* (given the Second Best Theorem) that the known imperfections of the world make this analysis any less legitimate than that of other applications of a traditional welfare-economic approach (for example, to bus journeys, or bananas).

A4 is unexceptionable. But how paradoxical it is that the only serious attempt to prove that the demand for money was independent of interest rates once emanated from Friedman![10] Yet the size of the welfare cost of inflation is directly

[8] Sims (299) for example finds that American macroeconomic data reject the hypothesis that real variables, such as real output and unemployment, are independent of the money supply.

[9] As was seen in chapter 7, (temporary) stickiness in prices and money wage rates can, for instance, imply that changes in the money supply exert powerful effects on real variables, depending on the type of non-market-clearing regime.

[10] Friedman (122). His claim to have found this was later disproved by Laidler (188).

related to (the modulus of) the interest-elasticity of the demand for money. So it is writers in the Keynesian tradition, with its insistence on a rather elastic h curve, who must take Friedman's Optimum Quantity of Money argument most seriously.

In this connection, A3 and A14 may be relaxed together to establish an important point. Suppose the government does not, or cannot, levey lump-sum taxation. Consider, too, what would happen if we introduce a strict public good. A3 would be violated. In general, the government must now intervene to provide the public good in sufficient quantities. This calls for taxation, which is (regrettably but now unavoidably) distorting. In these circumstances, the State should consider taxing labour income, property income, foreign trade, purchases of consumption goods and—pertinently—real balance holdings. If the vector of taxes on each is to be efficient, when tax is levied on each the marginal distortion cost of each tax should be equal. If the demand for real balances is rather inelastic to the nominal rate of interest, money must be an excellent candidate for taxation, on Ramseyite (optimal commodity taxation) grounds.[11] This is so, because a finite rise in R_N from zero will not cut z much, and should yield a large revenue to the State. To set against the original marginal-cost pricing argument for slight negative inflation, and the cost-of-price changes argument for zero inflation, we can now see there is a substantial public finance argument, which has to be taken seriously, for positive inflation. The public finance argument could be rather cogent if (as Friedman had argued earlier) the interest elasticity of the demand for money is trivial.

A5 is rather strong. If there is one producer for whom the marginal product of money is everywhere positive, or one household for whom its marginal utility as a consumer good is positive, A5 will fail. A5 is inconsistent with the concavity assumption so widely imposed on utility and production function in other contexts. If A5 were relaxed, the optimum quality of (real) money would be infinite.

A6 is a break-even condition for speculation in a perfect market. It is open to objections in the presence of taxation, transactions costs, risk-aversion, imperfect capital markets, or divergent expectations. A6 results from assuming the absence of these awkward but inescapable real-world phenomena.

A7 is central to the analysis. If the real rate $\bar{R}_R$ is not independent of expected inflation, a reduction in $\dot{P}^e$ need be neither sufficient nor necessary for a reduction in the nominal rate. Experience certainly suggests that the actual real rate $\bar{R}_R$, measured in retrospect, is brought down—often to a negative value—when actual inflation is rising. But whether the *expected* real rate (actual R_N less $\dot{P}^e$) is affected by *expected* inflation is less clear.[12]

The remaining assumptions call for less comment: most have been discussed in other chapters, or *en passant*; and they have a more tightly defined job (e.g. to

---

[11] See Atkinson and Stiglitz (15) for proof and discussion of Ramsey's result and summary of later work. See also Friedman (126), and Feldstein (106).

[12] Such an effect could occur even in the long run, if, for example, the community's average propensity to save varied with the nominal rate of interest, R_N, or the level of real balances. The reader is referred to Wan (329) for an excellent summary of models which do imply a long-run link between R_R and $\dot{M}$, such as the possible real balance effect on savings. In general, the effect of a change in $\dot{M}$ upon R_R may go either way. See also Tobin (363) and Ramanathan (361).

allow us to measure the costs of not being at the optimum, rather than just tell us where the optimum is). We turn now to a summary of the central points of this chapter.

Inflation has the drawback of dissuading people from holding money; for society, the marginal cost of these marginal holdings is negligible. This principle can be extended, under strict conditions, to a rule about how fast the money supply should be allowed to grow. The answer: very slowly, perhaps even not at all. Prices should keep dropping, in long run equilibrium, at a speed equal to the real rate of interest. At the least, the principle provides a case against inflation, other arguments against which are provided by the costs of changing prices, and (in the short run, if there is no indexation) by the fears of arbitrary redistribution. But inflation could be a relatively costless source of revenue to the State, and might even accelerate the removal of disequilibria; and requiring social efficiency in the provision of bank-supplied money would anyway call for other measures.

Summary of Notation in Chapter 8

L	labour supply
M	money stock
$\hat{M}$	the rate of growth in the money supply
N	actual employment
$\dot{p}^e$	the expected rate of inflation
R_N	the nominal rate of interest
R_R	the real rate of interest
U	unemployment
$\bar{U}$	natural unemployment rate
V	income velocity of money
z	real balances
γ	the marginal cost of creating real balances

Chapter 9

Growth

I: Introduction

This chapter explores long-run issues. Until now, we have assumed that society's stock of capital is exogenously given. This assumption has given us a very one-sided, static view of economic relationships. That view has proved illuminating, but it is now time to abandon it. Sections II, III, and IV of this chapter concentrate on the positive aspects of the theory of economic growth. Section II examines a model of growth for an economy in continuous equilibrium with just one product. In section III, the assumption of equilibrium is removed: we analyse a simple dynamic counterpart to the disequilibrium models studied in chapter 8. In section IV, attention moves to the multi-sector growth framework of Neumann and to a special case developed by Robinson and Sraffa. The chapter concludes with section V, which is devoted to a brief analysis of the normative issues raised by economic growth.

II: The Standard Growth Model with Equilibrium

Economic growth raises long-term issues. It is concerned, for instance, with changes in aggregate output, living standards, and the distribution of income over decades or even centuries. Economic growth is defined as an increase in a community's real aggregate income, over an interval of time. Usually this interval is taken to be very much longer than a month or even a year. In such a short period, whether real national income rises or falls will depend primarily upon whether there is a boom or a slump in aggregate demand, or upon random influences (stochastic shocks) affecting preferences, technology, or endowments. The longer the time span considered, the greater the chance that more systematic long-term supply-side influences will dominate the ebb and flow of the business cycle, and other short-term factors.

The natural starting point of any economic investigation is the concept of equilibrium. It may strike the reader as unrealistic and perhaps rather anaemic. But it is impossible to grasp the true character of disequilibria and other real world complexities, without a thorough understanding of equilibrium relationships in the simple abstract case.

Economic growth introduces a new concept of equilibrium: *balanced growth* (BG). An economy is in balanced growth when all growing variables grow at a common rate. Population, employment, output levels, and capital stocks all grow equiproportionately in BG. BG is distinct from that shorter-term concept of general economic equilibrium that we have met so often in earlier chapters of this book; namely, *market clearance* (MC). An economy could have one without the other. Markets for all goods, factors, and assets could be clearing continuously, and yet (for instance) the ratio of capital to labour might be rising in one or more industries.

That would be MC without BG. Also, the ratios of aggregate output to labour and to capital might be stationary (as in BG) with a large, and constant, rate of unemployment of labour: GB without MC.

The idea of equilibrium in economic contexts at once provokes four questions. Does it exist? Is it unique? Is it stable? Is it optimal? These questions arise with BG no less than with other equilibrium concepts. The existence question is, Is BG possible, given the assumptions of the model? The uniqueness question asks whether one, or more than one, set of values for the system's variables can be found, in which the system is in BG. The stability issue turns on whether a chance deviation from BG sets into motion forces tending to restore BG, or not. If a particular configuration BG is to be optimal, social welfare must not be higher at any alternative feasible configuration.

Our analysis of growth begins with a model first proposed by Solow (304) and Swan (314). Let us call it the Standard Growth Model, or SGM for short. The SGM strips down the theory of growth to its barest essentials. There is a single commodity, produced with unchanging, constant returns-to-scale technology from inputs of labour and man-made capital alone. Competitive equilibrium prevails in commodity and factor markets. Capital lasts forever, an exogenous share of each period's output is set aside for investment, and population grows at an exogenous rate.

Formally, and in slightly more detail, the SGM assumes:

(A1) one good is produced. The output rate at date t, $Q_t = f(K_t, N_t)$ where K_t and N_t represent the (homogeneous) capital stock and labour force at date t;

(A2) f has these properties: constant returns to scale; positive first partial and cross partial derivatives, and negative second partial derivatives;

(A3) perfectly competitive equilibrium in the commodity and factor markets;

(A4) no depreciation;

(A5) constant technology: f is constant over time;

(A6) the investment share of income (= $\dot{K}/Q$) is an exogenous parameter, s (> 0);

(A7) The proportionate growth of population (and hence of the labour force, assuming fixed hours of work and no demographic differences) is an exogenous parameter, n (> 0).

The only technical assumption, A2, stipulates that each factor's marginal product is defined everywhere, positive, and diminishing, and bolstered by an increase in the supply of the other factor. These conditions on the production fraction are often summarized by saying that the function is 'well-behaved'.

The fact that the economy is growing means that it would be hard to portray the function f, as was done for instance in chapter 7 for a single date when the stock of capital could be taken as fixed. But the constant returns to scale assumption (part of A2), together with the assumption of unchanging technology (A5), permits us to depict a constant technological relationship between the *average product of labour* and the *ratio of capital to labour*. Denote the average product of labour (Q_t/N_t) by q_t, and the capital–labour ratio (K_t/N_t) by k_t. Then, from A2 and A5,

$$Q = f(K, N) \tag{9.1}$$

may be written:

$$q = g(k). \tag{9.2}$$

The restrictions on the partial derivatives of f (A2) imply for 9.2 that $g' > 0 > g''$: the marginal effect on output per head of a rise in capital per head is positive but diminishing. Hence g is increasing and concave in k. The division of output and capital by labour turns the production function into 'intensive' or per caput form. In what follows, there is one further ratio of importance, that of q to k. This is the average product of capital. Denote this by A. Equation (9.2) is depicted in Figure 9.1.

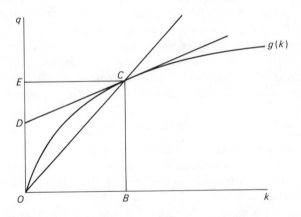

FIG. 9.1. The per caput production function in the Standard Growth Model.

A, the average product of capital, is the gradient of OC. The capital–labour ratio is given by OB. OE represents the average product of labour. The gradient of CD (the tangent to g at C) is the marginal product of capital. In perfect competition (A3), this equals the real rental on capital. In this one-good economy (A1) where capital does not depreciate (A4), the real rental on capital boils down to the real rate of profit or interest. The economic meaning of DE can be identified by noting that:

$$DE = CE \cdot \text{gradient of } CD = k \frac{\partial q}{\partial k}:$$

DE is the level of profit, or interest, per worker. Subtracting DE from labour's average product leaves the (real) wage rate, OD. The concavity of g implies that the wage rate increases with k, while the profit rate falls as k rises. The profit share of output ($= (k/q)(\partial q/\partial k)$, or the elasticity of q to k) is shown by the ratio of DE to OE, and the ratio of profits to wages is DE/OD. How DE/OD rises with k is ambiguous. A rise in k makes capital more plentiful and less dear. The first, or volume effect raises DE/OD; the second, or price effect cuts it. Which effect dominates—volume or price—depends on the elasticity of substitution between capital and labour (σ). When σ exceeds one, capital and labour are substitutes and extra capital can be accommodated (relative to labour) with only a slight fall in its reward per unit. So the profit share, and the profits/wages ratio, both go up. With σ less than one, increasing capital meets steeply diminishing returns, and the large fall in capital's marginal product outweighs the volume effect of extra capital. So both these ratios decline. For a short algebraic demonstration of this point, refer back to chapter 2, section II: 2.

So far, Figure 9.1 and the reasoning that accompanies it have been considered only in a static sensé. It is time to introduce BG explicitly. In BG we saw output, capital, and labour grow equiproportionately. Denoting the proportionate rate of change of a variable over time by a circumflex (so that $\hat{x} = (dx/x)/dt = \dot{x}/x$), BG entails,

$$\hat{Q} = \hat{K} = \hat{N}. \tag{9.3}$$

Now $\hat{K} = \dot{K}/K = \dot{K}/Q \cdot Q/K$ and AG, together with the definition $A \equiv q/k \equiv Q/K$, allow us to infer that,

$$\hat{K} = sA. \tag{9.4}$$

Now (9.4) is *always* true, in and out of balanced growth. The growth rate of capital equals the average product of capital, multiplied by the investment share of output (9.4) is a tautology, but a highly illuminating identity none the less.

Returning to the BG condition, (9.3) and A7, we note that capital and labour must grow in equal propportion. If they did not, k would not be stationary; in fact,

$$\hat{k} = \hat{K} - \hat{N} = sA - n = sg(k)/k - n, \tag{9.5}$$

and in BG, $\hat{k} \equiv \dot{k}/k = 0$. So BG implies that

$$sA = n. \tag{9.6}$$

Now (9.6) states that, in balanced growth, *the average product of capital equals the ratio of the population growth rate to the investment share of output*. Consequently, if the capital–labour ratio OB in Figure 9.1 is to be stationary, the gradient of OC must represent not just the average product of capital, but also the ratio of n to s. A balanced growth equilibrium occurs where a ray from the origin with gradient n/s cuts the curve g.

The existence of a BG equilibrium requires, then, that there be an intersection between g and the n/s ray. Now n and s are both positive. While s has an upper limit of unity, n has no upper limit. So the ratio of n to s could lie anywhere between plus infinity and zero. Consequently, for a BG equilibrium to exist, the curve g must be such that *any* positively-sloped ray from the origin cuts g somewhere. This requires that g have the following property: there must exist some k at which $g(k)/k$ can take on *any* positive value. (In BG, $n/s = A$, from 9.6, and $A = g(k)/k$.) Formally, this condition can be expressed,

$$\infty > gg' > 0 \qquad \text{for all } k : \infty > k > 0.$$

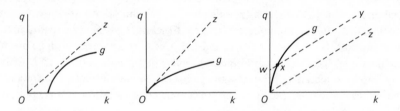

FIG. 9.2. Cases where the existence of balanced growth equilibrium is impossible.

It is weaker than, and implied by, the 'Inada' conditions

$$0 = g(0) = g'(\infty) = g(\infty)^{-1} = g'(0)^{-1}.$$

Figure 9.2 illustrates three cases of non-existence that the condition on gg' precludes. In the left-hand and middle panels, any n/s ray as steep as, or steeper than, OZ would 'miss' the curve g completely. In both cases, $gg' \leqslant 0$ for sufficiently small positive k. The right-hand panel shows the curve g lying above line WY at all points right of X. An n/s ray as flat as, or flatter than OZ (parallel to WY) would also miss the curve g. In this instance, gg' tends to $+\infty$ for sufficiently large k.

The condition $\infty > gg' > 0$ rules out non-uniqueness too, given that $g' > 0 > g''$. Non-uniqueness would require *either* that $g < 0$ for sufficiently low k (as in the left-hand panel of Figure 9.2, where a flat enough n/s ray would cut g twice) *or* that g had one or more points of inflexion, where g'' would of course vanish. The SGM goes on to give an affirmative answer to the stability question too. Two conditions suffice here, both of them already entailed by the model's assumptions. The concavity of g (A2), and the fact that the savings ratio is positive (A6). Figure 9.3 illustrates.

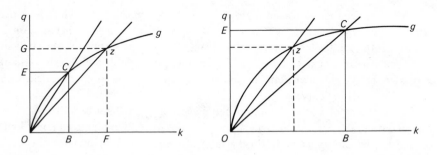

FIG. 9.3. The stability of balanced growth equilibrium.

In both panels of Figure 9.3, point B represents the initial current level of the capital–labour ratio, inherited from the past. In the short run, k is predetermined. In the long run, however, k can change, as given by equation (9.5). Now the gradient of OC is the initial current level of A (the average product of capital). OZ is a ray from the origin whose gradient equals n/s. In the left-hand panel, the initial value of k is *less* than the balanced growth value, at F; in the right-hand panel, greater. So, will the capital–labour ratio rise in the left-hand panel, and fall in the right-hand panel? The answer to this question must be 'Yes' for BG to be stable. Fortunately, the answer is Yes. In the left-hand panel, A exceeds n/s, hence sA exceeds n (recall that $s > 0$ from A6). Consequently, $\hat{K}$ (which must equal sA) exceeds n, and k rises. In the right-hand panel, the fact that n/s exceeds A and the assumption that $s > 0$ together imply that $n > sA$, whence k must fall. (Recall that $\dot{k} = k(sA - n)$.) The concavity of g, and the assumption that s cannot be negative, together guarantee that the BG equilibrium at Z is approached stably from both directions.

Figure 9.3 illustrates the qualitative inferences that may be drawn from comparative dynamics in BG. Take the left-hand panel, and suppose now that point C represents the 'old' intersection point between g and the 'old' n/s ray, while the 'new' BG configuration occurs at Z. To shift the BG equilibrium from C to Z, we must lower n/s: so the population growth rate must have dropped, or the savings ratio must have risen. At Z, the tangent to g is flatter than at C. So the rate of profit has to fall. This tangent's vertical intercept will be higher, so the new BG equilibrium will yield a higher wage rate. Labour's share will be higher in the new BG equilibrium if the substitution elasticity is less than one, and lower if above one. In addition to these income distribution effects, we can also infer that a fall in n or rise in s will raise the BG equilibrium values of output per head and capital per head, and reduce that of A, the average product of capital.

Thus far, a fall in n behaves just like a rise in s. But there are two very important variables which respond differently in these two cases. They are $\hat{Q}$, and consumption per head. A fall in n *lowers* the growth rate of output in balanced growth. Once the new BG equilibrium is reached, capital, labour, and output grow equiproportionately—and the fact that n has fallen means that $\hat{Q}$ will, sooner or later, have to drop, too. A rise in the savings ratio, on the other hand, leaves the growth rate of output $(\hat{Q})$ *unchanged* in BG equilibrium. This is because n has not changed. Ironically, the SGM is *not* a theory of the growth rate. The BG equilibrium growth rate is exogenous, by virtue of A7. The independence of $\hat{Q}$ from s in BG equilibrium should not be held to imply, however, that raising the investment share of income has no effect on the growth rate in the short run. Differentiating (9.1) totally, we find,

$$\hat{Q} = \theta_k \hat{K} + \theta_n \hat{N},$$

where θ_k and θ_n are the elasticities of Q to K and N respectively, and equal the profit and labour shares of output given A3; and this can be restated,

$$\hat{Q} = n + \theta_k(sA - n) \tag{9.7}$$

since $\hat{K} = As$ and $\theta_k + \theta_n = 1$. (9.7) shows clearly that a rising s *will* raise $\hat{Q}$ when the average product of capital (A) and the profit share (θ_k) can be taken to be (approximately) given. Eventually, however, the rise in s will lower A, until sA

returns to equality with n. How long this takes is an intriguing question: Atkinson (12) finds over a hundred years!

The other variable that responds differently to a rise in s and a fall in n is consumption per head. A fall in n raises q, and hence $q(1-s)$, which equals consumption per head. But a rise in s does not necessarily raise $q(1-s)$. This is so because consumption per head can be written,

$$q - nk$$

in BG, since BG implies $sA = n$, or $sq = nk$; and the effect of a rise in s upon $q - nk$

$$\frac{d[q-nk]}{ds} = \frac{\partial[q-nk]}{\partial k}\frac{\partial k}{\partial s} = (g'-n)\frac{\partial k}{\partial s}, \tag{9.8}$$

where $\partial k/\partial s > 0$ from earlier (a rise in the savings ratio must, we saw, increase the BG value of k). From (9.8), a rise in s must lower consumption per head in BG equilibrium if the rate of profit is below the growth rate. If g' exceeds n, however, a rise in s (or, at least, a small enough rise in s) must raise consumption per head. The reason for the sign-ambiguity of (9.8) is that increasing the investment share of income has two contrary effects on the BG value of consumption per head. Output per head will be raised, because of the larger capital per head that will have been built up; yet since a higher fraction of output per head is necessarily being devoted to investment, a smaller fraction is left to consumption. Which effect dominates depends on how large the capital–labour ratio, and the growth rate, are. The greater is k, the smaller the gain to q from raising k: there are diminishing returns to capital, as shown by $g'' < 0$. Provided that k is low enough for g' to exceed the growth rate, the first effect dominates. But if n is large, in BG, the capital stock must grow quickly, too. The sheer task of equipping the new workers with the same capital as their older colleagues will usurp a large share of available output. Raising k still further in such circumstances will lower the BG value of consumption per head, because the second effect will overwhelm the first.

When $g' = n$, (9.8) suggests that a tiny change in k (or s) will have no effect on consumption per head. Since

$$\frac{\partial}{\partial k}(g'-n) = g'' < 0 \text{ (from A2).}$$

Consumption per head will be at a maximum. When the growth rate of population (or capital, or labour, given BG) equals the competitive real rate of profit (or interest), therefore, the balanced growth value of consumption per head is maximized. This result is known as the *Golden Rule*: 'do unto others as you would have them do unto you.' If each generation bequeaths that ratio of capital to labour, the Golden Rule stipulates, which it would wish its predecessors to have left for it, the rate of interest should equal the growth rate. If intertemporal social welfare is maximized by achieving the largest permanent value of consumption per head, BG is optimal if and only if $g' = n$. The answers to the fourth 'equilibrium' question that BG poses, the optimality question, must therefore be: 'No, except by accident'.

There is only one value of k, and hence only one value of n/s, that maximizes consumption per head.

The Golden Rule stipulates that the growth rate should equal the rate of interest. One way of interpreting this is the 'biological interest-rate rule' for discounting the benefits and costs of social investment profjects. Net benefits should be discounted by the speed with which population grows. Another is to express the condition $n = g'$ in terms of the 'optimal' investment share of income. Dividing both sides by the average product of capital gives $(n/A) = \theta_k$ (since $\theta_k = (k/g)g'$); the BG condition $n = As$ therefore entails,

$$s = \frac{n}{A} = \theta_k. \qquad (9.9)$$

(9.9) implies that a society should invest all its profits and consume all its wages, if there is perfect competition.

We shall return to the optimality issue later (section V). It is worth recalling at this stage, however, that the Golden Rule rests on some highly restrictive assumptions. These include balanced growth, unchanging technology, independence of output from natural resources such as land or fossil fuels, and the absence of uncertainty.

Our next task is to widen the scope of the analysis of growth theory. This is best done by relaxing the assumptions of the Standard Growth Model. In the next section, we examine some of the effects of introducing *disequilibrium*. This relaxes the SGM's third assumption (perfectly competitive equilibrium). Then, we consider generalizations of the one-sector assumption (A1 in SGM) to an arbitrary large number of sectors, n. In the final section, we consider some further extensions: the Golden Rule is examined and contrasted with another approach to the optimality issue, the Keynes–Ramsey Rule. Before turning to these large questions, it is convenient for us now to see briefly what may happen when three other assumptions are relaxed. These three assumptions are A4 (no depreciation), A6 (exogenous investment share of income), and A7 (exogenous population growth).

Introducing depreciation raises a tricky question: does capital wear out over time, or because of use? The fact that used car prices vary negatively with both age and mileage suggests that both time and use take their toll. Fortunately in the SGM, capital is always fully employed. Since it is never idle, use-depreciation and time-depreciation behave alike. So we may assume that capital wears out over time; and the easiest assumption is that it depreciates at a given rate δ. Exponential depreciation implies that the quality of a capital good falls from its initial level, according to the formula $e^{-\delta t}$. It permits straightforward aggregation of capital goods of different vantages.

Depreciation enforces distinctions between gross and net output, and gross and net investment. In either case, depreciation equals the difference between the two. Using subscripts G and N to denote gross and net, respectively, we may reunite 9.1 and 9.2 as,

$$Q_G = \delta K + Q_N = f(K, N) \qquad (9.10)$$

$$q_G = \delta k + q_N = g(k). \qquad (9.11)$$

Now K equals *net* investment. If s is defined to be the ratio of net investment to net income, we have

$$\hat{k} = sA_N,$$

where A_N is the average net product of capital (Q_N/K). Balanced growth occurs where $sA_N = n$, or in terms of the average gross product of capital, $A_G(= Q_G/K)$, $n = s(A_G - \delta)$.

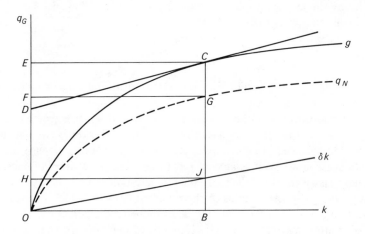

FIG. 9.4. The Standard Growth Model with exponential depreciation.

Diagrammatically, Figure 9.1 may be amended to show the consequences of allowing depreciation. The dashed curve in Figure 9.4 depicts net output per head, q_N, and the solid curve g refers to q_G. The vertical difference between these curves measures depreciation per head, which is also shown by the ray from the origin, labelled δk. If the capital labour ratio is B, BJ $(= OH = CG - EF)$ is depreciation per head. As before, OD is the wage rate. But DE, non-wage income per head, now has two components: depreciation (EF) and real interest (DF). The marginal product of capital (gradient of CD) now equals the real rate of interest plus δ.

The gradient of OC measures $A_G = A_n + \delta$. Point C is a balanced growth equilibrium if and only if $n = sA_N$ at C; i.e., if the gradient of OC happens to equal $\delta + n/s$. Answers to the existence, uniqueness, and stability questions remain affirmative. Optimality (in the sense of maximizing the balanced growth value of consumption per head) remains just as chancy: the optimality condition (9.8) becomes,

$$g' = n + \delta. \tag{9.12}$$

Manipulation of (9.12) implies that gross (net) investment should equal gross (net) profits. As before, a society should consume its wage bill, and not a penny more. But once again, the reader is cautioned against generalizing this result beyond the assumptions that yield it.

Endogenizing s and n (relaxing assumptions A6 and A7 of the SGM) throws light upon three ways in which these two variables might be interdependent. The Life Cycle Hypothesis of Consumption (see chapter 1) revealed a powerful, usually positive dependence of s upon the speed with which population grows. A society where population grows fast steadily will have a low average age, and few retired people in proportion to those of working age. To take a simple case where all income is earned as wages, the interest rate is negligible, wage rates are known to be stationary, there are no bequests, everyone aims to consume at a constant rate, dates of retirement and death are known and uniform, and population has grown steadily at the rate n, the savings ratio can be found to equal,

$$s = 1 - \frac{S}{T} \frac{1 - e^{-nT}}{1 - e^{-nS}}, \tag{9.13}$$

where S equals the duration of working career, and T the span of working career and retirement. Differentiation of (9.13) reveals that the elasticity of s to n is positive, and less than (but often close to) 1. Hence the Life Cycle Hypothesis, with its theory of how s is related to n, will often weaken—and may all but extinguish—the gloomy negative effect of higher population growth on long-run living standards.

The second way s may depend on n follows from the 'classical' savings hypothesis:

$$s = s_\pi \theta_K + s_w \theta_N = (s_\pi - s_w)\theta_K + s_w \tag{9.14}$$

examined in chapter 2. In (9.14), s_π and s_w are the savings propensities out of profits and wages. Assume them to be given average (and hence marginal) propensities. Now we have seen that capital's share of income, θ_K, generally varies with k (the capital–labour ratio) in the SGM. Only when the production fruition happens to be Cobb-Douglas is this not so. Furthermore, the balanced growth value of k was found to be related negatively to n. Combine these observations, and we have a line of thought that makes s vary with n:

$$s = (s_\pi - s_w)\phi(\psi(n)) + s_w, \tag{9.15}$$

where ϕ represents $\theta_K = \phi(k)$, and $k = \psi(n)$. Here, $\psi' < 0$ and the sign of ϕ' equals the sign of $\sigma - 1$. (These results were established on p. 62.)

Assuming that $s_\pi > s_w$, a rise in n increases s if capital and labour are complements ($\sigma < 1$), and reduces it if substitutes. One question that arises in this connection concerns stability: now that s may vary positively with k (namely, when $sn(\sigma - 1) = sn(s_\pi - s_w)$), might not $sA - n$ be an *increasing* function of k? If it were, $\dot{k} = k(sA - n)$ would explode, at least locally. Could capital per head keep rising, as income distribution keeps swinging in favour of profits (if $\sigma > 1$) and this boosted s (as $s_\pi > s_w$)? The answer, fortunately, is No. From

$$\hat{k} = sA - n,$$

we have

$$\hat{k} = (s_\pi - s_w)\theta_K A + s_w A - n = (s_\pi - s_w)g' + s_w A - n. \tag{9.16}$$

Since $g'' < 0$ and A varies negatively with k, an increase in k *lowers* $\hat{k}$.

The third and final possible link between n and s runs the other way. Malthus maintained that population varied positively with the excess of the current real wage over its subsistence level $(\bar{\bar{w}})$. Prosperity spelt early marriage and high fertility. If we make n vary positively with $w - \bar{\bar{w}}$, we create a new positive link between n and k, since a high k implies a high wage rate. The system remains stable however, since this link furnishes yet a further reason for having $\hat{k}$ vary negatively with k. This is evident from $\hat{k} = sA - n$.

III: The Standard Growth Model with Disequilibrium

It was Harrod who first explored this terrain (147, 148, 149, 150, 151). Indeed, the model he proposed was not an amendment to the SGM (since Solow and Swan developed their models some twenty years after Harrod started work on his), but rather a dynamic extension of Keynes's *General Theory*. What follows crystallizes Harrod's model in a new presentation which departs sharply from conventional accounts, but which facilitates comparison with both the SGM and the static disequilibrium analysis of chapter 7.

Formally, the disequilibrium version of the SGM (call this DSGM, for short) modifies the third assumption of the SGM, and adds a new one:

(A3*) The wage rate and the interest rate are locked at $\bar{w}$ and $\bar{r}$. Firms are identical and competitive and try to minimize costs.
(A8*) Firms attempt to invest an amount I_{t*} at date t.

Now A8* is an important novelty. The SGM contained no investment equation. Had it done so, it would have been overdetermined. The DSGM is not overdetermined, because a new unknown is introduced. This is the margin between actual output, and full capacity output. We encountered this point first in chapter 2, section VII: 1. Perfect price flexibility, entailed by A3, guaranteed that the problem of deficient aggregate demand simply did not arise in the SGM. Not so with the DSGM.

At any instant, firms may be in one of four possible positions:

State:	State 1	State 2	State 3	State 4
Name:	Full Equilibrium	Labour Market Constrained	Capital Market Constrained	Product Market Constrained

State 1 corresponds with momentary full equilibrium (not necessarily balanced growth) in the SGM. There is full employment of labour and capital.. In State 2, there is a notional excess demand for labour. Output, and the demand for capital, are both constrained as a result of the insufficiency of labour. It is capital that is in notional excess demand in State 3; the scarcity of capital constrains output and employment. In State 4, the demand for both capital and labour is held down because the demand for the product is insufficient. This is explained by the low level of I^*, attempted investment. From A7, aggregate demand equals I^*/s, where $1/s$ is the Keynesian multiplier.

Table 9.1. *Inputs, output, and average products in different disequilibrium regimes*

	State 2	State 3	State 4
K	$\bar{N}\left(\dfrac{a_2}{a_1}\right)^{\sigma/(\sigma-1)}[r^{\sigma-1}a_1^{-\sigma}-1]^{\sigma/(1-\sigma)}$	supply-constrained, $\bar{K}$	$\dfrac{I^*}{s}a_1^{\sigma/(1-\sigma)}[1+h]^{\sigma/(1-\sigma)}$
$A=Q/K$	$\left(\dfrac{r}{a_1}\right)^{\sigma}$	$a_1^{\sigma/(\sigma-1)}[1-w^{1-\sigma}a_2^{\sigma}]^{\sigma/(1-\sigma)}$	$a_1^{\sigma/(1-\sigma)}[1+h]^{\sigma/(1-\sigma)}$
N	supply-constrained, $\bar{N}$	$\bar{K}\left(\dfrac{a_1}{a_2}\right)^{\sigma/(\sigma-1)}[w^{\sigma-1}a_2^{-\sigma}-1]^{\sigma/(1-\sigma)}$	$\dfrac{I^*}{s}a_2^{\sigma/(1-\sigma)}\left[1+\dfrac{1}{h}\right]^{\sigma/(1-\sigma)}$
$q=Q/N$	$a_2^{\sigma/(\sigma-1)}[1-r^{1-\sigma}a_1^{\sigma}]^{\sigma/(1-\sigma)}$	$\left(\dfrac{w}{a_2}\right)^{\sigma}$	$a_2^{\sigma/(1-\sigma)}\left[1+\dfrac{1}{h}\right]^{\sigma/(1-\sigma)}$
Q	$\bar{N}a_2^{\sigma/(\sigma-1)}[1-r^{1-\sigma}a_1^{\sigma}]^{\sigma/(1-\sigma)}$	$\bar{K}a_1^{\sigma/(\sigma-1)}[1-w^{1-\sigma}a_2^{\sigma}]^{\sigma/(1-\sigma)}$	demand-constrained, I^*/s

Table 9.1 illustrates how several variables are governed, or constrained, at any instant, in the three disequilibrium states. The Constant Elasticity of Substitution production function,

$$Q = (a_1 K^{(\sigma-1)/\sigma} + a_2 N^{(\sigma-1)/\sigma})^{\sigma/(\sigma-1)} \qquad (9.17)$$

is chosen to provide concrete solutions.

In Table 9.1, h equals $(a_2/a_1)^\sigma (w/r)^{1-\sigma}$, the competitive ratio of wages to profits. Figure 9.5 presents a diagrammatic picture of these three disequilibrium regimes. Formally, Table 9.1 and Figure 9.5 illustrate solutions to the problem:

$$\underset{K,N}{\text{Max}}\ [Q(K, N) - wN - rK] \quad \text{subject to}$$

$$\text{(i)}\ N \leqslant \bar{N}$$

$$\text{(ii)}\ K \leqslant \bar{K}$$

$$\text{(iii)}\ Q \leqslant I^*/s \qquad (9.18)$$

with the form of Q given by (9.17). State 2 arises when the first constraint binds; it is the second constraint that binds in State 3; and the fourth state occurs when the last constraint binds. Point D in all panels of Figure 9.5 shows the constrained

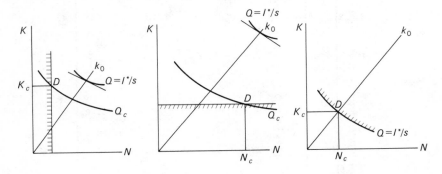

FIG. 9.5. Labour, capital and product market constraints in disequilibrium.

choices of the producer: K_c, N_c and Q_c (or rather two of these three) are the constrained values of the inputs and output. In the left-hand panel, the labour supply constraint binds, while State 3 is depicted in the middle panel. It is noteworthy that the producers will have more of the unconstrained factor (more capital in State 2, more labour in State 3) than implied by the 'optimal' capital–labour ratio, k_0. So, a supply constraint on one factor forces firms to substitute into another factor. On the other hand, Table 9.1 shows clearly that the demand for the unconstrained factor, and the output level, respond equiproportionately to an increase in the supply of the factor in excess demand.

This paradox is resolved by noting that the quantity constraint on one factor can be expressed as a pseudo-tax on its hiring price. There is an exact analogy here with the concept of 'virtual price' employed by Neary and Roberts (233) in the context of disequilibrium and rationing facing the consumer. This useful idea was encountered first in chapter 1, and again in chapter 7. In the left-hand panel, firms face a 'virtual tax' on labour; in the middle panel, on capital; in the right-hand panel, on their product, Q. In the first two cases, the disequilibrium constrains producers to a 'second-best' capital–labour ratio shown by the gradient of a ray from the origin to D. If the quantity restraint is relaxed, firms expand along this second-best ray. A large enough progressive relaxation of, say, the labour constraint in the left-hand panel of Figure 9.5 could transform the position of the firm into State 3, an excess demand for capital. There would be discontinuous jumps, first to the optimal capital–labour ratio k_0 (when both factor constraints bind) and then to the flat second-best ray from O to D in the middle panel. How far these second-best rays deviate from the first-best depends chiefly on the elasticity of substitution, σ.

In what amounts to a special case of our DSGM model studied by Malinvaud (205), σ is set to zero, and all rays converge. In this convenient case, (9.17) shrivels up to:

$$Q = \text{Min}\left[\frac{K}{a_1}, \frac{N}{a_2}\right],\tag{9.19}$$

and inclusion of our three possible disequilibrium regimes extends this to:

$$Q = \text{Min}\left[\frac{\bar{K}}{a_1}, \frac{\bar{N}}{a_2}, \frac{I^*}{s}\right],$$

$$K_c = \text{Min}\left[\bar{K}, \frac{a_1}{a_2}\bar{N}, a_1\frac{I^*}{s}\right],$$

$$N_c = \text{Min}\left[\frac{a_2}{a_1}\bar{K}, \bar{N}, a_2\frac{I^*}{s}\right].\tag{9.20}$$

(The reader will recall from Table 9.1 that $\bar{K}$ and $\bar{N}$ represent exogenous supply limits on the factors K and N, while K_c and N_c refer to the capital and labour actually employed.) (9.20) is in fact a special case of the data presented in Table 9.1.

If we compare the four states with the various equilibrium and disequilibrium regimes identified in chapter 7, State 1 is Walrasian equilibrium, while States 3 and 4 correspond with classical unemployment and Keynesian unemployment respectively. State 2 resembles Repressed Inflation, where both labour and goods are in excess demand. But the parallels are not quite exact, since the behaviour of the household sector, and the deviation of planned investment from optimization by producers, have not been modelled explicitly.

So much for static analysis. How do output, employment, and capital move over time? To answer this, we must first distinguish clearly between the short run and the long run. In the *short run*, output, employment, and utilized capital all grow *at the speed of the binding constraint*. In the *long run*, all grow *at the speed of the slowest-growing constraint*.

From A7 (the population growth assumption, inherited from the SGM) we know that the available labour force grows at an exogenous rate n. This Harrod called the *natural rate of growth*. When the economy is in State 2, the levels of output and utilized capital grow in proportion to each other, at the natural rate. In State 3, it is the capital constraint that binds. So output and employment grow in line with the supply of capital, which is fully utilized. From A6 (the savings ratio assumption of the SGM, carried over unamended) we know that the growth of the available stock of capital

$$\hat{K} = sA^*$$

(see (9.4) and the surrounding discussion). Here, A^* is defined as the ratio of actual output to the total available stock of capital, and not (as in Table 9.1) as the ratio of actual output to capital employed. For a reason that will soon be apparent, $\hat{K} = sA^*$ may be identified with Harrod's *warranted rate of growth*.

In State 4, the demand restraint on output binds. Output, capital employed, and labour employed must all grow at the rate $\hat{I}^*$, given the constancy of s. So far, $\hat{I}^*$ has been assumed exogenous, in both level and rate of change. But this is unreasonble. We must ask what could cause the growth of $\hat{I}^*$ to change, and when— if ever—it will *not* change. Harrod's answer was that $\hat{I}^*$ would be stationary if actual output grew at the warranted rate. Now the warranted growth rate was identified above with growth rate of the total capital stock available for use. So the stationarity of $\hat{I}^*$ requires the constancy of A^*. If output grows at the same speed as the total available stock of capital, there will be no incentive to raise or reduce the growth of planned investment.

If, on the other hand, output grew *faster* than the total available stock of capital, Harrod conjectured that firms would revise their investment plans upwards— strictly, $\hat{I}^*$ would increase. If actual growth fell short of its warranted rate, so that the ratio of output to available capital declined, $\hat{I}^*$ would be lowered. In qualitative terms, we have

$$\mathrm{sn}(\dot{\hat{I}}^*) = \mathrm{sn}[\hat{Q} - sA^*]. \tag{9.21}$$

(9.21) states this crisply: equality of the actual ($\hat{Q}$) and the warranted (sA^*) growth rates is necessary and sufficient for planned investment to grow steadily; while planned investment accelerates if actual exceeds warranted growth, and decelerates when actual growth falls below its warranted rate.

The stability of $\hat{Q}$ becomes dubious when the system is demand constrained, for then $\hat{Q} = \hat{I}^*$ (given that s is constant). In State 4, therefore, (9.21) tells us

$$\mathrm{sn}\,\dot{\hat{Q}} = \mathrm{sn}[\hat{Q} - sA^*],$$
$$\mathrm{sn}\,\dot{\hat{I}}^* = \mathrm{sn}[\hat{I}^* - sA^*], \tag{9.22}$$

which is patently unstable. (9.22) provide Harrod's famous and disturbing *knife-edge* result. So the dynamic dangers the economy faces are if anything even more alarming than the static ones. Not just the stability of actual growth, even the existence of balanced growth becomes virtually impossible: balanced growth requires that $n = sA$, but with all these three variables exogenous, equality can only occur by the merest chance. A7 exogenizes n, A6 exogenizes s, and (as Table 9.1 illustrates), the fixed factor prices assumption exogenizes the average product of capital employed, A.

Are Harrod's depressing results inevitable, or will amended assumptions restore the existence of balanced growth, and the stability of actual growth? Comparison with SGM reminds one that steady, balanced growth *is* possible under other assumptions. Restoring full price flexibility replaces Harrod's planned investment equation, A8*; this ensures that static disequilibria are impossible. States 2, 3, and 4 vanish. So, too, does the aggregate-demand instability problem revealed (in State 4) by (9.21) and (9.22). The existence of balanced growth is guaranteed provided that A can always adjust to bring $n = sA$. What is needed for this is sufficient substitutability between capital and labour along the production function. If $gg' > 0 > g''$ for all $\infty > k > 0$, the existence of balanced growth is guaranteed. If, to take an extreme case, there is no substitution, the production function f is as in 9.19, and g is portrayed in Figure 9.6. Along the ray OC, the capital constraint binds output, to the right of point C, it is the labour supply that binds as a constraint. If n and s are such that the ratio equals the gradient of the steep dotted line (n/s), balanced growth equilibrium is impossible. Labour keeps growing

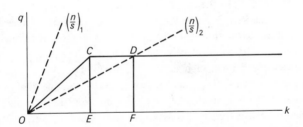

FIG. 9.6. The production function per caput when there is no substitution between capital and labour: the possible non-existence of balanced growth.

faster (at a rate n) than the available stock of capital (sA). But with n and s at different rates, so that n/s equals the gradient of OD, balanced growth is possible. The ratio of the available stock of capital to the labour force is F, while E shows the ratio of capital actually employed to the labour force. EF/FO is the proportion of the capital stock unused in balanced growth. Continuous full employment of both factors requires the ratio of n to s to equal the gradient of OC. This will, of course, only happen by accident.

Allowing n or s to vary endogenously would introduce another possible way of achieving balanced growth, even when the average product of capital was inflexible. The stability of the actual growth process may be restored by a variety of routes. In addition to price flexibility, appropriate assumptions on how expectations of output growth are formed and react to forecast errors (Sen (289), and time lags in the investment equation (Samuelson (267), Hicks (163)), may at least limit the extent of instability. The time-lags and expectations approaches are in fact related. The time-lags approach has proved important in the development of business cycle theory. Consider a static version of the concepts underlying (9.20), (9.21), and (9.22):

$$I_t^* = V[Y_{t-1} - Y_{t-2}] \tag{9.23}$$

$$Y_t = \text{Min}\left[I_t^* + C + (1-s)Y_t, \frac{K_t}{a_1}, \frac{N_t}{a_2}\right], \tag{9.24}$$

where C represents 'autonomous' expenditure, and $(1-s)Y_t$ 'induced' consumption expenditure. If the aggregate demand constraint upon output Y_t binds, we have

$$Y_t = \frac{1}{s}[C + V(Y_{t-1} - Y_{t-2})]. \tag{9.25}$$

Now (9.25) yields two stationary solutions for income. Y can be stationary in *level* at C/s, or stationary in *rate of change* when autonomous consumption is zero, at the growth rate (defined as $(Y_t - Y_{t-1})/Y_t$) of $s/(V - s)$. Scrutiny of the stationary level solution $Y = C/s$ shows that Y_t may or may not converge on its new equilibrium value if, for example, the parameter C is disturbed; once and for all, and it may converge or diverge with or without oscillations. Everything depends on the values of s and V. In the special case of $V = 1$, self-repeating oscillations are set up. For $V < 1$ and sufficiently large s, there is oscillatory convergence. If the time lags are removed, on the other hand, there is non-oscillatory divergence— complete instability—for all positive values of s and V. The level of output must be bounded by other conditions, such as the capacity ($a_1 Y_t \leqslant K_t$) or full employment ($a_2 Y_t \leqslant N_t$) constraints of (9.24), at the lower level a non-negativity condition for gross investment in (9.23), so that $Y_t \geqslant C/s$. Note, too, that the stability worries can be banished if perfect foresight is assumed: see chapter 2, section VII: 3.

For Harrod, it was extremely unlikely that growth would be steady and balanced with continuous full utilization of capital and labour. The overriding reason for his pessimism was the assumption of sticky factor prices. Solow demonstrated that perfect price flexibility, coupled with a sufficient set of technological opportunities to substitute capital for labour, could guarantee continuous full use of both factors and a long-run tendency to balanced growth. The major issue separating the two models (DSGM and SGM) is the extent of price flexibility. In practice, prices *do* tend to respond to disequilibrium, but at finite and varying speeds. In asset markets, faster than in goods markets; in goods markets, often faster than in labour markets; and in all markets, often more quickly in excess demand than in excess supply. This suggests that DSGM has a comparative advantage as a *short-run* theory of the dynamics of national income, and SGM as a longer-run theory. Furthermore, markets tend to clear more quickly and more effectively—thus validating the SGM —when governments behave as if they malfunction. Witness the 1950s and 1960s, and the battery of interventionist demand management policies, and stabilization schemes (e.g., unemployment and deposit insurance, and progressive taxes). These were years of nearly continuous full employment of labour and capital in the advanced industrial countries. They are much better described by the SGM than the DSGM. But when governments are convinced that markets do work efficiently, as in the early 1930s and early 1980s, disequilibria are apt to be grave and persistent. Perhaps, therefore, the dynamic adjustment of the economy in any period is better described by theories out of fashion in the government circles of the day.

IV: The Many Sector Growth Model: Neumann and Cambridge

In this section, additional sectors are introduced. We describe briefly a many sector growth model proposed by John von Neumann, and a special case of this known as the 'Cambridge' model.

The Neumann model is intricate and revolutionary. Although first published in English in 1945 (237), it had been developed many years earlier. The essence of Neumann's model is that goods produce goods over time. Production 'activities' require inputs of goods at one point in time. They mature into a set of outputs at the end of the production period. These outputs include every kind of capital, materials, and equipment. Then they form the inputs, in turn, for the next production period. Labour plays the role of farm animal in Neumann's model. Labour is itself a part of the productive process. The inputs into a particular productive process could consist of the food, shelter, and clothing needed to support labour at work, plus (say) coal, copper, steel, and telephones as direct material inputs. Natural resources are assumed to be in unlimited supply, or else not used as inputs. The set of possible technological relationships does not vary over time.

There are two economic conditions imposed upon this elaborate network of possible technological relationships: *equilibrium* and *competition*. Equilibrium imposes the condition that the value in current prices of current output maturing equal the current-prices value of next period's inputs. This implies that there is no good in excess demand (for which output from the production period just ending is less than input requirement for the period just about to start). It also implies that any good in excess supply must be free. Formally, where P_s and X_s are vectors for goods prices and activity levels N at date s, and A and B represent input-activity and output-activity matrices,

$$A = \begin{bmatrix} a_{11} & a_{12} & \cdots & a_{1m} \\ \vdots & \vdots & & \vdots \\ a_{n1} & a_{n2} & \cdots & a_{nm} \end{bmatrix} \quad \text{and} \quad B = \begin{bmatrix} b_{11} & b_{12} & \cdots & b_{1m} \\ \vdots & \vdots & & \vdots \\ b_{n1} & b_{n2} & \cdots & b_{1m} \end{bmatrix}$$

(so that a_{ij} is the input of good i, and b_{ij} the output of good j, in each case per unit of activity j; and $i = 1, \ldots, n$, and $k = 1, \ldots, m$) we can express the equilibrium condition as:

$$P_t BX_t = P_t AX_{t+1} \tag{9.26}$$

Competition ensures that, for every activity undertaken, the current value of all inputs into current production must equal the value of outputs of current production valued at the prices ruling when outputs mature. Any activity for which the former exceeded the latter would not be undertaken. Any activity for which the latter exceeded the former would infringe the competitive condition that (supernormal, 'surplus') profits must not be positive. The competitive condition requires that,

$$P_t AX_t = P_{t+1} BX_t. \tag{9.27}$$

Now the pre-emption of goods is costly. If R is a unique, time-independent rate of interest for a loan of duration equal to the production period, the length of time between dates, then

$$P_{i,t} = P_{i,t+1}(1 + R) \tag{9.28}$$

will be a condition of equilibrium. Further, suppose that the system is in balanced growth at the rate G; so that for each activity

$$X_{j,t+1} = (1 + G)X_{j,t}. \tag{9.29}$$

Neumann proves that there will exist, for date t, a set of prices P_t^* and activity levels X_t^* such that

$$\frac{P_t^* BX_t^*}{P_t^* AX_t^*} = \frac{\text{Current output maturing, valued at current prices}}{\text{Previous inputs, valued at current prices}} = 1 + R^* = 1 + G^*. \tag{9.30}$$

(9.30) describes a balanced growth equilibrium, at which the growth rate is maximized (G^*) and equal to the lowest possible interest rate (R^*). (9.30) can be seen to follow from (9.26)–(9.29): insert a generalized form of (9.29) for all j into (9.26), and of (9.28) into (9.27), and derive,

$$P_t BX_t = \frac{1 + G}{1 + R}P_t BX_t \tag{9.31}$$

from which the equality of the growth rate and the interest rate follows at once. For the briefest rigorous proof of the existence of G^*, the reader is referred to Bliss (42), p. 263.

The Neumann solution of maximal balanced growth obeys the Golden Rule. The rates of interest and growth are equal. Profits equal savings. Profits in this context equal the interest costs of the productive process; 'supernormal' profits, in the sense of a surplus payment to the entrepreneur, are zero (from (9.27)). Neumann's maximal growth rate will equal Harrod's natural growth rate n either by happy accident or if a Malthusian assumption is brought in—that population adjusts to keep labour's wage at a subsistence level. Otherwise, n might exceed G^*, in which case there will be growing unemployment, and Neumann's growth equilibrium will be balanced only for goods in relation to each other, and not between goods and labour as a whole.

It should not surprise one that G and R turn out to be equal when all profits are saved. In balanced growth, the rate of output growth (common, in Neumann's model, to all activities) will equal the ratio of investment to capital; and this ratio can be defined:

$$\frac{I}{K} = \frac{\pi}{K} \times \frac{I}{\pi}.$$ (9.32)

In (9.32), π/K is the rate of profit, which we can identify with R, and I/π is the savings/profits ratio, seen to be unity. (9.32) merely multiplies the investment/capital ratio by the ratio of profits to itself, just as (9.4) could be derived by multiplying I/K by the ratio of output to itself. One interpretation of (9.32) is to exogenize I/K, by assuming balanced growth at an exogenous rate n, and to fix I/π by assumption. The (9.32) 'determines' the rate of interest π/K.

The use of identity to (9.32) to fix π/K when I/K and I/π are taken to be given is a crucial step in a 'Cambridge' growth model. This has developed independently from Neumann's model, but turns out on inspection to be a special case of it. The roots of the Cambridge model lie in Ricardo and Marx. The simplified Cambridge model presented here spotlights some key elements common to Robinson (264) and Sraffa (308). But the reader is warned that space forbids more than the briefest of treatments of a diverse and voluminous literature, just as it did when one of the model's intellectual ancestors, the Marxian Theory of Prices, was summarized in chapter 2.

Our simplified Cambridge model starts with the following assumptions:

(A1**) The economy produces n goods, with no joint production. Output matures one period after the inputs of labour, other goods, and (possibly) durable capital goods. All primary inputs are used equiproportionately in every industry;

(A2**) constant returns to scale in every sector;

(A3) perfectly competitive equilibrium in the commodity and factor markets;

(A4**) any depreciating durable capital goods keep working in the same sector throughout their working lives;

(A5) constant technology;

(A6**) an exogenous ratio of investment to profits (call this λ);

(A7) population (and, given balanced growth, every input and output) grows at an exogenous rate, n.

The third, fifth, and seventh assumptions carry over unchanged from the SGM. The first and second assumptions embody the foundations of the Non-Substitution Theorem (chapter 4). This states that if there are constant returns everywhere, only one primary factor, and no joint production, competitive relative prices are governed exclusively by technology and independently of the pattern of demand. A4** rules out a subtle type of joint production between, say, beer and strawberries that would arise if breweries sold their used trucks to strawberry farmers. A6** is already familiar.

Together, these seven assumptions allow us to strip down the Neumann network to a set of simple relations:

$$P_i = \left(1 + \frac{n}{\lambda}\right)\left[wa_{iL} + \sum_k a_{ik}P_k\right],$$ (9.33)

where a_{iL} is the labour input per unit of activity i; a_{ik} the input of good k into activity i; each activity i produces one and only one good, good i, one unit per unit; and P_i is the price of good i. wa_{iL} is the *direct* labour cost of production, measured at the date of input, one period ahead of output. When valued at the date of output, when the good is sold, wa_{iL} is multiplied by $1 + (n/\lambda)$, since, from A6**, A7, and the identity (9.32), n/λ is the rate of interest.

$$\left(1 + \frac{n}{\lambda}\right) \sum_{k}^{n} a_{ik} P_{ik}$$

measures the cost of material inputs into one unit of good i, again carried forward to the date at which the good is ready for sale. Now since it is a set of n linear equations, one for each produced good (9.33) may be solved for the price vector $\mathbf{P}$ (assuming there is no linear dependence). This means that for each good,

$$\left(1 + \frac{n}{\lambda}\right) \sum_{k}^{n} a_{ik} P_{ik}$$

can be reduced ultimately to current *indirect* labour costs. (9.33) may then be expressed as,

$$P_i/w = \sum_{\tau=1}^{\infty} C_{i\tau} \left(1 + \frac{n}{\lambda}\right)^{\tau}, \tag{9.34}$$

where $C_{i\tau}$ is the amount of labour, direct or indirect, 'stored up' τ periods ago in one unit of good i now.

Two important inferences may be drawn from (9.34). One is a positive point which emerges from the assumptions A1**–A7, but is drowned in a sea of indeterminacy as soon as the *slightest* change is made in any of them. This is that prices in this model are independent of the pattern of demand. Prices are costs, and costs are governed here exclusively by technology, the wage rate, and the interest rate n/λ. The smallest relaxation of the assumptions, however, restores Marshall's dictum that, in the determination of prices, 'both blades of the scissors' (demand *and* supply) 'do the cutting'.

The second inference from (9.34) is negative. One might hope to find that the set of cost-minimizing production techniques the economy employs changes, if at all, *monotonically* with the rate of interest n/λ: that when n/λ were very large, everyone would want to go for a 'last minute' production process, and that as n/λ dropped, producers would switch into progressively more and more 'roundabout' processes where the indirect labour bulked more and more heavily. Alas, this hope cannot be fulfilled, save by happy accident. Compare two production processes, A and B, for good i. From (9.34),

$$\text{under } A, \quad P_{iA}/w = \sum_{\tau=1}^{\infty} C_{i\tau A} \left(1 + \frac{n}{\lambda}\right)^{\tau};$$

and

$$\text{under } B, \quad P_{iB}/w = \sum_{\tau=1}^{\infty} C_{i\tau B} \left(1 + \frac{n}{\lambda}\right)^{\tau}.$$

Hence,

$$\frac{P_{iA} - P_{iB}}{w} = \sum_{\tau=1}^{\infty} (C_{i\tau A} - C_{i\tau B}) \left(1 + \frac{n}{\lambda}\right)^{\tau}. \tag{9.35}$$

The point is that (9.35) does *not* necessarily only switch sign once as n/λ varies from ∞ to zero. If it did, for instance from positive to negative at $(n/\lambda)^*$, one could infer that process A would be preferred for $n/\lambda > (n/\lambda)^*$ and process B when $n/\lambda < (n/\lambda)^*$. $(n/\lambda)^*$ would be the critical, or 'switch-point' interest rate. But unfortunately (9.35) may switch sign at numerous values of n/λ. An example: suppose the stored-up labour coefficients in the two processes are,

	$\tau = 1$	$\tau = 2$	$\tau = 3$	$\tau = 4$
$C_{i\tau A}$	50	100	100	0
$C_{i\tau B}$	100	$12.\overline{87}$	$137.\overline{87}$	0

Both processes give the same value to P_i/w when $n/\lambda = 10$ per cent and $n/\lambda = 20$ per cent. Process B gives a lower value to P_i/w when the interest rate is below 10 per cent, or above 20 per cent. Process A gives a lower P_i/w—and will therefore be preferred by cost-minimizing producers—when the interest rate is anywhere between 10 per cent and 20 per cent. This phenomenon is known as 'reswitching', or 'double-switching'.

Figure 9.7 illustrates the problem. The horizontal axis measures time (t). The origin is the present ($t = 0$), and points to the left of the origin refer to the past: the further to the left, the longer ago. The vertical axis measures the present value of labour inputs applied at previous dates under two processes 1 and 2. For simplicity, time is now assumed continuous, not discrete. The *present* value of the direct and indirect labour costs in project j becomes:

$$w \int_{-\infty}^{0} C_j(t) e^{-nt/\lambda} \, dt.$$

Figure 9.7 assumes $w = 1$, without loss of generality. The top row shows process 1, which involves a modest labour input in the very recent past (in the period running from F to G) and a larger input for quite a long period before that (from E to F). A second process, labelled 2, is illustrated in the middle row. Process 2 has a much greater labour input than 1 in the immediate past (period H to J, which is concurrent with period F to G). Process 2 also has a smaller labour input before that *but over a longer time period*. Which of the two processes is more roundabout, more capital intensive, on average longer in gestation between inputs and outputs? We cannot readily say. A comparison of the two processes highlights the two

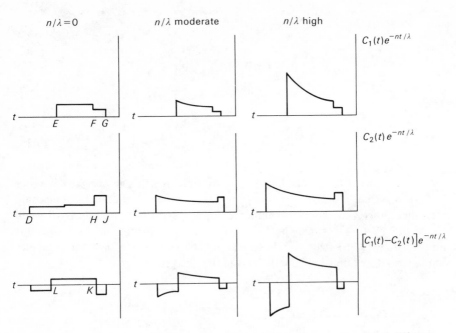

FIG. 9.7. A comparison of different labour input date-profiles compounded at different interest rates.

dimensions of capital—*volume* and *antiquity*. By the volume dimension, process 1 is much the more capital intensive, viewed at least from the period when the last labour input is applied: very little labour is needed at this final stage, in period H to J. Process 2 uses much more labour at this period. But process 2 starts earlier, at D rather than E. So, process 1 is less capital-intensive on the antiquity criterion, if we compare commencement dates.

The third row shows the difference between the two processes' labour input profiles. This is negative in the initial and final stages, and positive in between. Now in a competitive system, firms will opt for the process with the smaller cumulated cost stream. If the area above the line is smaller than that below, process 1 is preferred to 2; and conversely. Which process wins on this score depends on the rate of interest, n/λ. In the left-hand column, n/λ is set to zero. It is moderate in the middle column, and high on the right. As drawn, process 2 wins in the middle column, and process 1 when the rate of interest is zero or high. Because of compounding a positive rate of interest blows up the current value of labour inputs in the distant, much more than in the recent past; and when the interest rate jumps, this skewed blow-up effect gets even more pronounced. Had the cost difference stream in the bottom row crossed the origin just once, say at K, reswitching could not arise. If it were above the origin at all earlier dates and below it for all later dates, project 1 would always be preferable with a sufficiently low rate of interest, and project 2 at a sufficiently high one. There would be one and only one switch point. But, if the cost difference stream crosses the axis more than once, there are likely to be two—or more than two—interest rates at which the cumulated cost difference stream vanishes:

$$\int_{-\infty}^{0} [C_1(t) - C_2(t)] e^{-nt/\lambda} dt = 0. \tag{9.36}$$

Double-switching, or indeed multiple-switching, is inevitable when this term vanishes at more than one value of n/λ.

Figure 9.7 illustrates double-switching when the stream of production costs is stripped down to labour costs, and valued retrospectively at the point when the good produced is ready for sale. But the phenomenon is not confined to this case. The concept of cost could be broadened beyond labour to cover any inputs, primary or otherwise. Incidentally, the Neumann model restores respect to the Malthusian view of labour as a produced, not a primary, factor. Whether it is labour or goods that are primary may be as futile to dispute as the chicken-and-egg problem. Furthermore, the date at which the cost stream is valued is irrelevant. The sign of the integral (9.36) is unaffected by multiplying it by

$$e^{nt/\lambda},$$

which values the cost difference stream at date s, instead of date 0.

The simplified Cambridge model has derived prices from labour costs and the rate of interest. (9.34) testifies to that. The distribution of aggregate income between labour and capital, however, awaits the imposition of demand conditions. It is demand that governs the composition of total output, q, and hence total current labour costs, which (9.33) shows to be

$$(1 + n)w \sum_{i}^{n} a_{iL} q_i. \tag{9.37}$$

Note that (9.37) is the value of current direct labour inputs into next year's production, which will be $(1 + n)$ times higher than this year's.

The nominal value of current aggregate profits can be found by subtracting (9.37) from the value of current output:

$$\frac{n}{\lambda} V = \sum_{i}^{n} q_i \{ P_i - w(1 + n) a_{iL} \}. \tag{9.38}$$

Full employment of labour requires that N, the current labour force, equal

$$\sum_{i}^{n} a_{iL} q_i.$$

In (9.38), V is the current nominal value of capital. This equation shows V to be dependent upon prices, and hence on the wage rate, technological coefficients, the growth rate and the investment-profits ratio λ, and also upon economic agents' tastes since these shape the aggregate composition of output.

It must be stressed that any relaxation of assumptions A1** to A7 destroys much, or all, of the set of simple one-way 'causal' links in the Cambridge model. These links run on from n and λ to R; from R, w, and the technology matrix to the price vector $\mathbf{P}$; from $\mathbf{P}$ and tastes to $\mathbf{q}$; and thence to aggregate profits. In general, these variables are (for the most part) co-determined.

One example: joint production, diminishing returns, or a second primary factor land, or heterogeneity in the labour force would certainly, or almost certainly,[1] make prices depend upon demand as well as costs. Another example: the pattern of demand is in practice highly likely to vary with factor shares, so that $\mathbf{q}$ and $(n/\lambda)V/\Sigma_i P_i q_i$ are linked two ways. More important, it is extremely restrictive to assume an exogenous ratio of investment to profits (A6**), which is fixed independently of relative prices, $\mathbf{q}$ and the factoral distribution of income.

Compared with the Cambridge edifice, Neumann's model is a towering construction of generality. The Cambridge model may be thought of as a special case of, or a rather minor footnote upon, the Neumann framework. The SGM and DSGM if anything merit such epithets even more. On the other hand, these three special cases all achieve a high degree of simplicity. This makes them colourful, easily grasped, straightforward to apply—yet, unfortunately, also apt to mislead. Two fallacious beliefs that surfaced in the heated debates on capital theory in the 1960s show that even experts could be misled. One is the old (Cambridge) claim that there is a logical flaw, or *meretricious* circularity, in the neoclassical model that identifies the rate of interest with marginal products of capital, in a competitive model without price changes or depreciation. This claim is false. Those who made it were blinkered by the special assumptions and the artificial reasoning that led up to (9.38), into forgetting that a two-way connection between R and V was perfectly possible under other conditions. The other was the hint, rarely made explicit, but all too easily drawn by a hurried reader of rival 'neoclassical' writings, that those (Cambridge economists) who questioned the robustness of a trustworthy, negative relationship between the rate of profit and some aggregate index of the capital stock in a multi-sector model were fussing about a weird pathological special case. They were not. Double-switching shows up the relationship between interest rates and capital-intensity in its true colours—intricate and treacherous. To deny this is to remain blinkered to a one-good assumption, overt or in disguise.

We conclude this section with a summarized comparison of the key aspects of the three 'simple' theories of growth: the SGM of Solow (and Swan), the DSGM of Harrod (and Domar[2]), and a 'Cambridge' model distilled from Robinson (264) and Sraffa (308). This is presented in Table 9.2.

---

[1] Certainly, if industries differed in the proportions with which these two (or more) primary factors were employed.

[2] Several years after Harrod's early publications on his growth model, E. Domar (90) developed a related but distinct growth model. For an excellent account of the differences between Domar's views and Harrod's, see Wan (329), ch. 1.

Table 9.2. *Summarized comparison of the three 'simple' growth models*

Variable	Model		
	SGM (Solow–Swan)	DSGM (Harrod)	Cambridge (Robinson, Sraffa, *et al.*)
Interest rate, R	Perfectly flexible; equals marginal product of capital (minus depreciation rate, if any); positive, and decreasing with k (the capital–labour ratio); *should* equal the growth rate, if balanced growth consumption per head is to be maximized.	May be inflexible	Exogenous, given the assumption of an exogenous ratio of investment to profits; in balanced growth, equals $n =$ profits/investment
Wage rate, w	Perfectly flexible; equals output per head minus Rk; increases with k.	May be inflexible	Numeraire (cf. Keynes's 'wage-units')
Prices of goods	Perfectly flexible; no relative prices, since only one good.	May be inflexible; no relative prices, since only one good.	Cost-determined by R, w and technology (Non-Substitution Theorem)
Technology	Continuously flexible.	May be inflexible (or k may be fixed because w and R are fixed)	Discontinuously switchable, with possible 'double-switching' of processes
Growth rate in short run	$n +$ Profit Share $(sA - n)$ (where $s =$ exogenous investment share in income, and $A =$ momentarily determined average product of capital).	Growth rate of binding constraint; labour supply, available stock of capital, or aggregate demand.	In balanced growth, n
Growth rate in long run	n (system converges eventually on balanced growth, where $sA = n$).	Slowest growing of: labour supply, available stock of capital, or aggregate demand.	In balanced growth, n

V: Optimum Saving

There are two rules that try to answer the critical question, how much of its income should a society save? These are the Golden Rule (GR)[3] and the Keynes–Ramsey Rule (KRR).[4]

V: 1 *The Golden Rule* (GR)

Assume:

(B1) output per head, q, is increasing and concave in capital per head, k;

(B2) q and consumption per head, z, are stationary;

(B3) the maximand is z.

---

[3] See Phelps (251).   [4] See Ramsey (260). Dixit (86) contains a detailed account.

These assumptions imply:

(a) the marginal product of capital should equal the (common) growth rate of capital, output, and labour;
(b) all investment projects should be discounted by the population growth rate, n;
(c) the investment share in output should equal the elasticity of output to capital (equivalently, the competitive profit share).

Proof:

$$z = q(k) - nk = x(k) - \hat{K}k, \tag{9.39}$$

where $\hat{K}$ = the growth rate of capital.

A maximum for z implies

$$\frac{\partial z}{\partial k} = 0 > \frac{\partial^2 z}{\partial k^2},$$

and, given (9.39),

$$\frac{\partial x}{\partial k} - \hat{K} = 0 > \frac{\partial^2 x}{\partial k^2}. \tag{9.40}$$

Now by the first-order condition, $\partial q/\partial k = \hat{K}$ yields (a) directly. By assumption B2, $\hat{K} = n = \hat{Q}$ (where Q = total output), so that $\partial q/\partial k = n$, which yields (b). To obtain (c), multiply both sides of the first-order condition $\partial q/\partial k = \hat{K}$ by k/q to get: $\partial \log q/\partial \log k$ (which is definitionally equal to the elasticity of output to capital, and the competitive profit share) equals $\dot{k}/Q$ (which equals the investment share in output).

The Golden Rule results relate exclusively to balanced growth. They do not generalize. There are two problems in particular with this. First, society inherits a particular ratio of capital to labour from the past. It is only by chance that this will equal the unique Golden Rule ratio, k^*, at which n equals the marginal product of capital. If k differs from k^*, the Golden Rule can offer no advice. All its says is that history has been unkind. Secondly, assumption B2 is narrow. Since $\dot{k} = 0$, the ratio of n to s must be rigid. In practice, q is subject to two contrary influences that operate over time. There is technical progress, which tends to raise q. In general, technical progress will justify less saving, since it implies that posterity will be better equipped to meet its own needs from superior technology. On the other hand, there are natural resource constraints. Land is finite and many natural resources, worse still, are depletable. This implies that q will tend to fall over time, especially if n is high. The exhaustibility and fixity of natural resources in the face of growing population constitute a case for greater abstention.

It is just possible that these two forces exactly cancel out. This will happen with a Cobb–Douglas aggregate production function, or if technical progress augments natural resources fast enough to allow balanced growth. Here, and only here, the Golden Rule results emerge unscathed. In general, the introduction of technical progress and natural resources will render them useless.

V:2 *The Keynes–Ramsey Rule (KRR)*

In the KRR, assumption B1 is retained, but B2 and B3 are generalized. q and z are non-stationary. Since z is now a time path, not a number, it cannot be a maximand. Some other objective function is needed.

The central concept for the KRR is *intertemporal efficiency*. This is an extension to dynamics of Paretian efficiency rules. The dynamic analog of the production-composition rule (MRS = MRT) is that the correct balance be struck between consumption and investment. Consumption yields utility at once. Investment yields consumption, and utility, at a later date. Paretian intertemporal efficiency requires that MRIS (the marginal rate of *intertemporal* substitution) equal MRIT (the marginal rate of *intertemporal* transformation), in every relevant dynamic trade-off.

To see this, assume:

(i) a one-good economy, with two dates, j and $j + 1$. Call the good 'jam';
(ii) the good is sufficiently divisible;
(iii) the non-satiation axiom holds;
(iv) corner solutions and externalities are ruled out.

In this context, MRIS will be $(\partial U/\partial C_j)/(\partial U/\partial C_{j+1})$, and the corresponding MRIT is $1 + \phi'_{j+1}$, where ϕ'_{j+1} is the marginal product of 'jam-capital', at date $j + 1$, defined in units of jam.

For intertemporal efficiency we require

$$\frac{\dfrac{\partial U}{\partial C_j} - \dfrac{\partial U}{\partial C_{j+1}}}{\dfrac{\partial U}{\partial C_{j+1}}} = \phi'_{j+1}. \tag{9.41}$$

Now (9.41) states that the marginal product of capital should equal the proportionate decline in the marginal utility of consumption (MU). Note that (9.41) is an incomplete rule: it cannot by itself single out a particular path for consumption or capital, over a period. None the less, (9.41), and its continuous time version, constitute the Keynes–Ramsey Rule.

Now the left-hand side of (9.41) must be positive, given that q is increasing in k. There are two possible reasons why $\partial U/\partial C_j > \partial U/\partial C_{j+1}$. First, C_{j+1} may be *larger* than C_j. If there is diminishing marginal utility of consumption, this will be enough to imply $\partial U/\partial C_j > \partial U/\partial C_{j+1}$. Second, there may be *impatience*. This would place a premium on earlier consumption. This would imply that

$$\frac{\partial U_j}{\partial C_{j+1}} < \frac{\partial U_{j+1}}{\partial C_{j+1}}.$$

These two arguments may be combined and illustrated. Denote:

$\alpha =$ (minus) the elasticity of undiscounted marginal utility, to consumption per head;
$\beta =$ the rate of time discounting for utility.

Hence, MU at date $j = bz_j^{-\alpha} = $ (MU at date 0)$e^{\beta j}$ where b is some positive constant, e the base the natural logarithms, z_j is consumption per head at date j and MU is the marginal utility (viewed at the stipulated date) of consumption per head at date j.

Applying (9.41) to continuous time, we may infer that, in the limit as $j + 1 \to j$,

$$\beta + \alpha \hat{z} = \phi'_j. \tag{9.42}$$

(9.42) states that the marginal product of capital should equal the sum of: (i) the rate of time—discounting for utility, β; and (ii) the elasticity of marginal utility of z to z itself, multiplied by the growth rate of z. This result may be explained thus. From assumption B1 of the GR, which is retained for the KRR, q is increasing and concave in k. So the optimum k (k^*) is increasing in each of α, β, and $\hat{z}$. This suggests that a society may be justified in having a low value of k, and hence a high marginal product of capital, in three cases: if β, the time-preference rate, is high; if there are sharply diminishing returns in utility to consumption per head, so that α is high; and if consumption per head is rising rapidly (so that $\hat{z}$ is large).

There are some serious difficulties, however, with the rigorous demonstration of these points. Any analysis of optimum savings must consider these concepts, and stipulate assumptions about them:

(*a*) the horizon, and consumption or capital requirements at the horizon;
(*b*) the elasticity of substitution between utilities at different dates;
(*c*) the date-weights for utility;
(*d*) the elasticity of utility at date t to z at date t;
(*e*) the number of goods;
(*f*) the degree of foresight;
(*g*) population growth;
(*h*) technical progress;
(*i*) the number and type of factors of production other than labour;
(*j*) initial endowments.

The simplest model makes the following assumptions about these:

(*a*) ∞;
(*b*) ∞; this implies that the total social welfare function to be maximized is additively separable in social utility for each date;
(*c*) positive, declining exponentially over time;
(*d*) constant, defined as $1 - \alpha; \alpha > 0$;
(*e*) only one good, which may be consumed or invested;
(*f*) perfect foresight;
(*g*) n, an exogenous parameter. In Ramsey's original treatment, $n = 0$, so that total consumption, and consumption per head, always moved together;
(*h*) an exogenous parameter, μ, and exclusively labour-augmenting;
(*i*) no natural resources appear as arguments of the production function: capital is the only factor other than labour;
(*j*) initial endowments, specified at date 0, as k_0 and $k_0^\square$ (here, $k^\square \equiv$ capital per human efficiency unit. The ratio of k to $k^\square$ is the Harrod-neutral, labour-augmenting technology parameter, which grows at a speed of λ).

Expressing the production function in *per-human-efficiency-unit* terms, rather than per caput terms, we have

$$q^\square = \psi(k^\square), \psi' > 0 > \psi'' \tag{9.43}$$

and

$$z^\square = \psi(k^\square) - nk^\square - \dot{k}^\square \left.\vphantom{\begin{matrix}a\\b\end{matrix}}\right\} \tag{9.44}$$

equivalently

$$\dot{k}^\square = \psi(k^\square) - nk^\square - z^\square.$$

(9.44) is an equation giving the composition of output: output equals consumption plus investment, of which the latter may be decomposed into investment needed to keep $k^\square$ stationary, and increases in $k^\square$. It is illustrated in Figure 9.8. The curve *OBE* is the steady state solution, showing all $z^\square, k^\square$ pairs for which $k^\square$ is stationary.

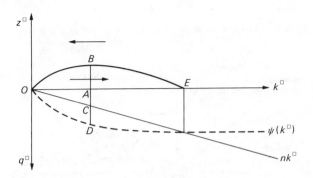

FIG. 9.8. Output and consumption per human efficiency unit.

At B, $z^\square$ is maximized. The vertical distances AB and CD are equal. Each depicts consumption per human efficiency unit, at its maximum permanent level. $K^\square$ will fall whenever $z^\square$ exceeds its value given by *OBE*, and rise whenever $z^\square$ is less than this. At $E, nk^\square$ exhausts output, so that consumption will be zero if $k^\square$ is stationary.

In addition, we have the (local efficiency) KRR equations in the model:

$$\psi' = \beta + \alpha[\dot{z}^\square + \mu] \left.\vphantom{\begin{matrix}a\\b\end{matrix}}\right\}$$

or

$$\dot{z}^\square = -\mu + \frac{1}{\alpha}[\psi' - \beta] \tag{9.45}$$

(9.45) is shown in Figure 9.9:

at G, $\psi' = \beta + \alpha\mu$, so that $\dot{z}^\square = 0$;

at H, $\psi' > \beta + \alpha\mu$, so that $z^\square$ will be rising;

at J, $\psi' < \beta + \alpha\mu$, so that $z^\square$ will be falling.

If the KRR for local efficiency is obeyed, then there is only one value of ψ', and only one value for $k^\square$, at which consumption per human efficiency unit is stationary. These are shown by points G and $G^\lozenge$ respectively. A larger marginal product of capital—i.e., a lower $k^\square$—will imply a rising level of consumption per human efficiency unit; a lower value, the reverse. The vertical line above $G^\lozenge$ is the stationarity boundary for the KRR. Combining these figures, we have Figure 9.10.

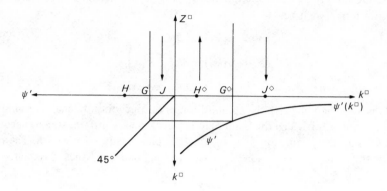

FIG. 9.9. The Keynes–Ramsey Rule equation for local efficiency.

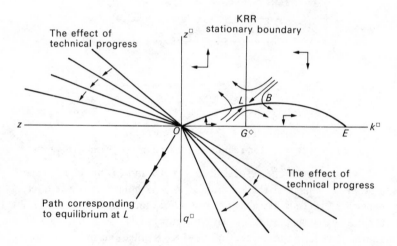

FIG. 9.10. The GR and KRR compared.

There are three types of terminal solution for $z^{\square}$ and $k^{\square}$. One is at L. A second is the vertical axis above the origin; but since this entails the disappearance of capital, it may be ruled out. The third is the horizontal axis between $G^{\diamond}$ and E, and since this entails that consumption vanish, it too may be ruled out. L is the only acceptable terminal solution. L may be very elusive. If the KRR is obeyed at all times and $k_0^{\square} \neq G^{\diamond}$, L must be approached along one of only two paths, one of which is (approximately) from the south-west, the other approximately from the north-east.

There is a major qualification to be made at this point. If the KRR stationarity line crosses the $k^{\square}$ stationarity path OBE to the right of the GR point B, point L ceases to be an optimum. When L is to the right of B, the rate of interest (or marginal product of capital) is less than the growth rate $(\mu + n)$ in steady state. The problem here is that the present value function grows faster than it is discounted.

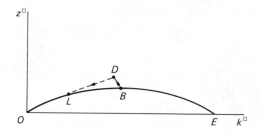

FIG. 9.11. The path from GR to KRR values of $k^\square$.

It will therefore always pay to defer consumption, even at $t = \infty$. If this nonsensical result is to be avoided, the KRR must be overridden. The true optimum capital per human efficiency unit is the lower of the two levels implied by the KRR and the CR. If B is to the left of L, B is the optimum; if to the right, L. The reason why L is to be preferred to B when L is to the left of B is as follows. Suppose one starts at B and, just for a short while, disobeys the KRR by increasing $z^\square$ slightly (e.g. to D in Figure 9.11). A path BZL may be plotted. For a time, $z^\square$ will exceed its GR value. Then, as time passes, and $k^\square$ falls, $z^\square$ tends to fall back, eventually to levels lower than the GR value at B. But the initial jump in $z^\square$ will have been worth the subsequent sacrifice, given the values of α, β, and μ. The higher any of these are, the greater the premium on early consumption.

Summary of Notation in Chapter 9

A	the average product of capital
A_G	the average gross product of capital
A_N	the average net product of capital
B	balanced growth rate
BG	balanced growth
C	autonomous expenditure
I	investment
K_t	the capital stock at date t
k_t	the capital–labour ratio at date t
N_t	the labour force at date t
n	the proportionate growth of population
P_s	vector for goods prices at date s
Q_t	output at date t
q_t	the average product of labour
R	the rate of interest
S	the duration of a working career
s	the marginal propensity to save out of profits
s_w	the marginal propensity to save out of wages
SGM	Standard Growth Model
T	the retirement date
V	the current nominal value of capital

$\bar{\bar{w}}$ subsistence wage

$\mathbf{X}_s$ the vector for activity levels N at date s

z consumption per head

δ the depreciation rate

θ_K the elasticity of Q to K

θ_N the elasticity of Q to N

λ the rate of investment to profits

μ the rate of Harrod-neutral technical progress

π the profit rate

References

(1) Akerlof, G. A., 'The Market For Lemons: Qualitative Uncertainty and the Market Mechanism', *QJE*, 84 (1970), 488–500.

(2) Akerlof, G. A., 'The Economics of Tagging as Applied to the Optimal Income Tax, Welfare Programs and Manpower Planning', *AER*, 68 (1978), 8–19.

(3) Allen, R. G. D., *Mathematical Economics* (London, Macmillan, 1960).

(4) Anderson, G. J., 'A New Approach to the Empirical Investigation of Investment Expenditures', *EJ*, 91 (1981), 88–102.

(5) Ando, A. and F. Modigliani, 'The "Life Cycle" Hypothesis of Saving: Aggregate Implications and Tests', *AER*, 53 (1963), 55–84.

(6) Arrow, K. J., 'The Economic Implications of Learning by Doing', *Re Stud*, 39 (1962), 155–73.

(7) Arrow, K. J., 'The Role of Securities in the Optimal Allocation of Risk Bearing', *Re Stud*, 31 (1964), 91–6.

(8) Arrow, K. J., 'The Firm in General Equilibrium Theory' in R. Marris and A. Wood (eds), *The Corporate Economy* (London, Macmillan, 1971).

(9) Arrow, K. J., *Essays in the Theory of Risk Bearing* (Amsterdam, North Holland, 1974).

(10) Arrow, K. J., H. B. Chenery, B. S. Minhas, and R. M. Solow, 'Capital Labour Substitution and Economic Efficiency', *Re Stat*, 43 (1961), 225–35.

(11) Arrow, K. and F. H. Hahn, *General Competitive Analysis* (San Francisco, Holden Day, 1971).

(12) Atkinson, A. B., 'The Time Scale of Economic Models; How Long is the Long Run?', *Re Stud*, 36 (1969), 133–52.

(13) Atkinson, A. B., 'How Progressive Should Income Tax Be?' in E. S. Phelps (ed.), *Economic Justice* (Harmondsworth, Middlesex, Penguin Books, 1973).

(14) Atkinson, A. B. and J. S. Flemming, 'Unemployment, Social Security and Incentives', *Midland Bank Review* (Autumn 1978), 6–16.

(15) Atkinson, A. B. and Stiglitz, J. E., *Lectures on Public Economics* (London, McGraw-Hill (UK), 1980).

(16) Azariadis, C., 'Implicit Contracts and Underemployment Equilibria', *JPE*, 83 (1975), 1183–202.

(17) Azariadis, C., 'On the Incidence of Unemployment', *Re Stud*, 43 (1976), 115–26.

(18) Bacharach, M. O. L., *Economics and the Theory of Games* (London, Macmillan, 1976).

(19) Bacon, R. and W. A. Eltis, *Britain's Economic Problem: Too Few Producers* (London, Macmillan, 1976).

(20) *The Ball Committee Report on Policy Optimization*, Cmnd. 7148 (London, HMSO, 1978).

(21) Barro, R. J., 'Inflationary Finance and the Welfare Cost of Inflation', *JPE*, 80 (1972), 978–1001.

(22) Barro, R. J., 'Are Government Bonds Net Wealth?' *JPE*, 82 (1974), 1095–117.

(23) Barro, R. J. 'Integral Constraints and Aggregation in an Inventory Model of Money Demand', *J. Fin.*, 31 (1976), 77–88.

(24) Barro, R. J., 'Rational Expectations and the Role of Monetary Policy', *JME*, 1 (1976), 1–32.

(25) Barro, R. J. and H. I. Grossman, 'A General Disequilibrium Model of Income and Employment', *AER*, 61 (1971), 82–93.

(26) Barro, R. J. and H. I. Grossman, 'Suppressed Inflation and the Supply Multiplier', *Re Stud*, 41 (1974), 87–104.

(27) Barro, R. J. and H. I. Grossman, *Money, Employment and Inflation* (Cambridge, Cambridge University Press, 1976).

(28) Barro, R. J. and A. M. Santomero, 'Household Money Holdings and the Demand Deposit Rate', *JMCB*, 4 (1972), 397–413.

(29) Barry, B., *The Liberal Theory of Justice* (Oxford, Oxford University Press, 1973).

(30) Basevi, G., 'The United States Tariff Structure: Estimates of Effective Rates of Protection of United States Industries and Industrial Labour', *Re Stat*, 48 (1966), 147–60.

(31) Baumol, W. J., 'The Transactions Demand for Cash: An Inventory Theoretic Approach', *QJE*, 66 (1952), 545–56.

(32) Baumol, W. J., *Business Behaviour, Value, and Growth* (New York, Macmillan, 1959).

(33) Becker, G. S., 'An Economic Analysis of Fertility', in *Demographic and Economic Change in Developed Countries* (NBER, Princeton, Princeton University Press, 1960).

(34) Becker, G. S., 'A Theory of the Allocation of Time', *EJ*, 75 (1965), 493–517.

(35) Beenstock, M., *The Foreign Exchanges* (London, Macmillan, 1978).

(36) Beenstock, M., *A Neoclassical Analysis of Macroeconomic Policy* (Cambridge, Cambridge University Press, 1980).

(37) Begg, D. K. H., 'Rational Expectations and the Non-Neutrality of Systematic Monetary Policy', *Re Stud*, 47 (1980), 293–303.

(38) Benassy, J. P., 'Neo-Keynesian Disequilibrium Theory in a Monetary Economy', *Re Stud*, 42 (1975), 503–23.

(39) Benjamin, D. K. and L. A. Kochin, 'Searching for an Explanation of Unemployment in Interwar Britain', *JPE*, 83 (1979), 441–78.

(40) Birati, A. and A. Cukierman, 'The Redistributive Effects of Inflation and the Introduction of a Real Tax System in the US Bond Market', *J. Pub. Ec.*, 12 (1979), 125–39.

(41) Blinder, A. S. and R. M. Solow, 'Analytical Foundations of Fiscal Policy', in A. S. Blinder *et al.*, *The Economics of Public Finance* (Washington, Brookings Institution, 1974).

(42) Bliss, C. J., *Capital Theory and the Distribution of Income* (Oxford, North Holland, 1975).

(43) Borch, K., 'A Note on Uncertainty and Indifference Curves', *Re Stud.*, 36 (1969), 1–4.

(44) Branson, W. H., 'Asset Markets and Relative Prices in Exchange Rate Determination' (University of Stockholm, Institute for Economic Studies, No. 66 (1976)).

(45) Break, G. F., 'The Incidence and Economic Effects of Taxation', in A. S. Blinder *et al.*, *The Economics of Public Finance* (Washington, Brookings Institution, 1974), 119–237.

(46) Brechling, F., *Investment and Employment Decisions* (Manchester, Manchester University Press, 1975).

(47) Brown, A. J., *The Great Inflation, 1939–1951* (Oxford, Oxford University Press, 1955).

(48) Brown, C. and J. Medoff, 'Trade Unions in the Production Process', *JPE*, 86 (1978), 355–8.

(49) Brown, J. A. C. and A. S. Deaton, 'Models of Consumer Behavior: A Survey', *EJ*, 82 (1972), 1145–236.

(50) Buiter, W. H., ' "Crowding Out" and the Effectiveness of Fiscal Policy', *J. Pub. Ec.*, 7 (1977), 309–28.

(51) Burk, A., 'Real Income, Expenditure Proportionality, and Frisch's "New Methods of Measuring Marginal Utility" ', *Re Stud*, 4 (1936), 33–52.

(52) Cagan, P., 'The Monetary Dynamics of Hyper Inflation', in M. Friedman (ed.), *Studies in the Quantity Theory of Money* (Chicago, University of Chicago Press, 1956).

(53) Cairncross, Sir A. (ed.), *Britain's Economic Prospects Reconsidered* (London, Allen & Unwin, 1971).

(54) Calvo, G. A. and S. Wellisz, 'Supervision, Loss of Control, and the Optimum Size of the Firm', *JPE*, 85 (1978), 943–52.

(55) Champernowne, D. G., 'Unemployment, Basic and Monetary: The Classical Analysis and the Keynesian', *Re Stud*, 3 (1935-6), 201–16.

(56) Champernowne, D. G., *The Distribution of Income* (Cambridge, Cambridge University Press, 1973).

(57) Christ, C. F., 'A Simple Macroeconomic Model with a Government Budget Restraint', *JPE*, 76 (1968), 53–67.

(58) Clark, C., 'Wages and Profits', *OEP*, 30 (1978), 388–408.

(59) Clark, J. M., 'Business Acceleration and the Law of Demand: A Technical Factor in Economic Cycles', *JPE*, 25 (1917), 217–35.

(60) Clower, R. W., 'The Keynesian Counter-Revolution: A Theoretical Appraisal', in R. W. Clower (ed.), *Monetary Theory* (New York, Pengun Books, 1970).

(61) Clower, R. A., 'Is There an Optimal Money Supply?' in M. D. Intriligator (ed.), *Frontiers of Quantitative Economics* (London, North Holland, 1971).

(62) Coase, R., 'The Nature of the Firm', *Eca*, 4 (1937), 386–405, reprinted in G. J. Stigler and K. E. Boulding (eds), *Readings in Price Theory* (Homewood Ill., Irwin, 1952).

(63) Cobb, C. W. and P. H. Douglas, 'A Theory of Production', *AER*, Supplement (1928), 139–65.

(64) Cohen, K. J. and F. S. Hammer, 'Linear Programming Models for Optimal Bank Dynamic Balance Sheet Management', in G. P. Szegö and K. Shell (eds), *Mathematical Methods in Investment and Finance* (London, North Holland, 1972).

(65) Corden, W. M., *Trade Policy and Economic Welfare* (Oxford, Oxford University Press, 1974).

(66) Corden, W. M., 'Keynes and the Others: Wage and Price Rigidities in Macroeconomic Models', *OEP*, 30 (1078), 159–80.

(67) Corden, W. M., 'Taxation, Real Wage Rigidity, and Employment', *EJ*, 91 (1981), 309–29.

(68) Courakis, A. S., 'Monetary Policy: Old Wisdom Behind a New Facade', *Eca*, 40 (1973), 73–86.

(69) Courakis, A. S., 'Monetary Targets: Conceptual Antecedents and Recent Policies in the US, UK and West Germany', in A. S. Courakis (ed.), *Inflation, Depression and Economic Policy in the West* (London, Mansell: and Oxford, Alexandrine Press, 1981).

(70) Cragg, J. S., 'Some Statistical Models for Limited Dependent Variables with Applications to the Demand for Durable Goods', *E'metrica*, 39 (1971), 829–44.

(71) Craven, J., *The Distribution of the Product* (London, Allen & Unwin, 1979).

(72) Cubbin, J. S. and K. Foley, 'The Extent of Benefit Induced Unemployment in Great Britain: Some New Evidence', *OEP*, 29 (1977), 128–40.

(73) Currie, D., 'Macroeconomic Policy and the Government Financing Requirement: A Survey of Recent Developments', in M. J. Artis and R. Nobay (eds),

Studies in Contemporary Economic Analysis, Vol. 1 (London, Croom-Helm, 1978).

(74) Cyert, R. and J. March, *Behavioural Theory of the Firm* (Englewood Cliffs, Prentice-Hall, 1963).

(75) Darby, M. R., 'The Allocation of Tansitory Income among Consumers' Assets', *AER*, 62 (1972), 928-41.

(76) Dasgupta, P. and G. Heal, *Economic Theory and Exhaustible Resources* (Welwyn, Herts., James Nisbet, and Cambridge, Cambridge University Press, 1980).

(77) Davidson, P., *Money and the Real World* (New York, Wiley, 1978).

(78) Davidson, J. E. H., D. F. Hendry, *et al.*, 'Econometric Modelling of the Aggregate Time Series Relationship Between Consumers' Expenditure and Income in the UK', *EJ*, 88 (1978), 661-92.

(79) Deaton, A. S., 'Involuntary Saving Through Unanticipated Inflation', *AER*, 67 (1977), 899-910.

(80) Deaton, A. and J. Muellbauer, *Economics and Consumer Behaviour* (Cambridge, Cambridge University Press, 1980).

(81) Desai, M., *Marxian Economics* (Oxford, Basil Blackwell, 1979).

(82) Diamond, P. A., 'Mobility Costs, Frictional Unemployment and Efficiency', *JPE*, 89 (1981), 798-812.

(83) Diamond, P. A. and J. A. Mirrlees, 'Optimal Taxation and Public Production; I: Production Efficiency; and II: Tax Rules', *AER*, 61 (1971), 8-27 and 261-78.

(84) Dimsdale, N. H., 'British Monetary Policy and the Exchange Rate 1920-1938', in W. A. Eltis and P. J. N. Sinclair (eds), *The Money Supply and the Exchange Rate* (Oxford, Oxford University Press, 1981).

(85) Dixit, A. K., 'On the Optimum Structure of Commodity Taxes', *AER*, 60 (1970), 295-301.

(86) Dixit, A. K., *The Theory of Equilibrium Growth* (Oxford, Oxford University Press, 1976).

(87) Dixit, A. K., 'The Accumulation of Capital Theory', *OEP*, 29 (1977), 1-29.

(88) Dixit, A. K., 'The Balance of Trade in a Model of Temporary Equilibrium with Rationing', *Re Stud*, 45 (1978), 393-404.

(89) Dixit, A. K. and V. Norman, *Theory of International Trade* (Cambridge, Cambridge University Press, 1980).

(90) Domar, E. D., 'Expansion and Employment', *AER*, 37 (1947), 34-55.

(91) Dornbusch, R., 'Devaluation, Money, and Non Traded Goods', *AER*, 62 (1973), 871-80.

(92) Dornbusch, R., 'Expectations and Exchange Rate Dynamics', *JPE*, 84 (1976), 1161-76.

(93) Dow, J. C. R., *Management of the British Economy, 1945-1960* (Cambridge, Cambridge University Press, 1964).

(94) Drèze, J. H., 'Some Theory of Labour Management and Particpation', *E'metrica*, 44 (1976), 1125-39.

(95) Duesenberry, J. S., *Income, Saving, and the Theory of Consumer Behaviour* (Cambridge, Mass., Harvard University Press, 1949).

(96) Eckstein, O. and J. A. Girola, 'Long Term Properties of the Price Wage Mechanism in the United States: 1891-1977', *Re Stat*, 60 (1978), 323-33.

(97) Edgeworth, F. Y., 'The Mathematical Theory of Banking', *JRSS*, 51 (1888), 113-27.

(98) Eltis, W. A. and P. J. N. Sinclair, *The Money Supply and the Exchange Rate* (Oxford, Oxford University Press, 1981).

(99) Eppen, G. D. and E. F. Fama, 'Solutions for Cash Balance and Simple

Dynamic Portfolio Problems', *Journal of Business of the University of Chicago*, 41 (1968), 94–112.

(100) Eppen, G. D. and E. F. Fama, 'Cash Balance and Simple Dynamic Portfolio Problems with Proportional Costs', *Int. Ec. Review*, 10 (1969), 119–33.

(101) Evans, M. K., 'A Study of Industry Investment Decisions', *Re Stat*, 49 (1967), 151–64.

(102) Fama, E. F., 'Efficient Capital Markets: A Review of Theory and Empirical Work', *J. Fin* (P & P), 25 (1970), 383–417.

(103) Feige, E. L. and D. K. Pearce, 'The Casual Causal Relationship between Money and Income: Some Caveats for Time Series Analysis', *Re Stat*, 61 (1979), 521–48.

(104) Feldstein, M. S., 'Mean Variance Analysis in the Theory of Liquidity Preference and Portfolio Selection', *Re Stud*, 36 (1969), 5–12.

(105) Feldstein, M. S., 'Social Security, Induced Retirement and Aggregate Capital Accumulation', *JPE*, 82 (1974), 905–26.

(106) Feldstein, M. S., 'The Welfare Cost of Permanent Inflation and Optimal Short Run Economic Policy', *JPE*, 87 (1979), 749–68.

(107) Feldstein, M. and L. Summers, 'Is the Rate of Profit Falling?' *BPEA*, 1 (1977), 211–28.

(108) Ferber, R., 'Consumer Economics, A Survey', *J. Ec. Litt*, 11 (1973), 1303–42.

(109) Fisher, I., 'A Statistical Relation between Unemployment and Price Changes', *International Labour Review*, 13 (1926), 785–92, reprinted in *JPE*, 81 (1973), 408–502.

(110) Fisher, I., *The Theory of Interest* (New York, Augustus M. Kelly, 1965— reprint of the 1930 edition).

(111) Fischer, S. and A. Modigliani, 'The Real Effects and Costs of Inflation', *Weltwirtschaftliches Archiv* (1978), 810–33.

(112) Flemming, J. S., 'The Consumption Function when Capital Markets are Imperfect: The Permanent Income Hypothesis Reconsidered', *OEP*, 25 (1973), 160–72.

(113) Flemming, J. S., *Inflation* (Oxford, Oxford University Press, 1976).

(114) Flemming, J. S., 'Aspects of Optimal Unemployment Insurance: Search, Leisure, Savings and Capital Market Imperfections', *J. Pub. Ec.*, 10 (1978), 403–25.

(115) Flemming, J. S., L. D. D. Price, and S. A. Byers, 'The Cost of Capital, Finance and Investment', *BEQR*, 16 (1976), 193–202.

(116) Frenkel, J. A. and H. G. Johnson (eds), *The Monetary Approach to the Balance of Payments* (London, George Allen & Unwin, 1976).

(117) Frey, B. S. and F. A. Schneider, 'A Politico-Economic Model of the United Kingdom', *EJ*, 88 (1978), 243–53.

(118) Friedman, B. M., 'Crowding Out or Crowding In?: Economic Consequences of Financing Company Deficits', *BPEA*, 3 (1978), 593–654.

(119) Friedman, B. M., 'Optimal Expectations and the Extreme Information Assumptions of "Rational Expectations" Macromodels', *JME*, 5 (1979), 23–41.

(120) Friedman, M., *Essays in Positive Economics*, Part III: 'Monetary Theory and Policy' (London, University of Chicago Press, 1953).

(121) Friedman, M., *A Theory of the Consumption Function* (Princeton, Princeton University Press, 1957).

(122) Friedman, M., 'The Demand for Money—Some Theoretical and Empirical Results', *JPE*, 67 (1959), 327–51.

(123) Friedman, M., 'The Role of Monetary Policy', *AER*, 58 (1968), 1–17.

(124) Friedman, M., 'The Optimum Quantity of Money', in M. Friedman, *The Optimum Quantity of Money and Other Essays* (London, Macmillan, 1969), Ch. 1.

(125) Friedman, M., 'The Quantity Theory of Money: A Restatement', in R. W. Clower (ed.), *Monetary Theory: Selected Readings* (New York, Penguin Books, 1970).

(126) Friedman, M., 'Government Revenue from Inflation', *JPE*, 79 (1971), 846–56.

(127) Friedman, M. and D. Meiselman, 'The Relative Stability of Monetary Velocity and the Investment Multiplier in the United States, 1897–1958', in Commission on Monetary Credit, *Stabilization Policies* (Englewood Cliffs, Prentice-Hall, 1963).

(128) Friedman, M. and J. Schwartz, *A Monetary History of the United States, 1867–1960* (Princeton, Princeton University Press, 1963).

(129) Furubotn, E. G., 'The Long Run Analysis of a Labour Managed Firm: An Alternative Interpretation', *AER*, 66 (1976), 104–23.

(130) Georgescu-Roegen, N., 'Some Properties of a Generalized Leontief Model', in T. C. Koopmans (ed.), *Activity Analysis of Production and Allocation* (London, Cowles Commission for Research in Economics, 1951).

(131) Girgis, N. M., 'Optimal Cash Balance Problems', *Management Science*, 15 (1968), 130–40.

(132) Glyn, A. and R. Sutcliffe, *British Capitalism, Workers, and the Profit Squeeze* (London, Penguin Books, 1972).

(133) Goldthorpe, J. H. and F. Hirsch (eds), *The Political Economy of Inflation* (London, Martin Robertson, 1978).

(134) Goodhart, C. A. E., D. H. Gowland, and D. Williams, 'Money, Income and Causality: The UK Experience', *AER*, 66 (1976), 417–23.

(135) Goodwin, R. M., 'The Non-Linear Accelerator and the Persistence of Business Cycles', *E'metrica*, 19 (1951), 1–17.

(136) Gordon, R. J., 'Recent Developments in the Theory of Inflation and Unemployment', *JME*, 2 (1976), 185–219.

(137) Gould, J. P., 'Adjustment Costs in the Theory of Investment of the Firm', *Re Stud*, 35 (1968), 47–55.

(138) Grossman, S. J., 'An Introduction to the Theory of Rational Expectations under Asymmetric Information', *Re Stud*, 48 (1981), 541–59.

(139) Grossman, S. J. and J. E. Stiglitz, 'Stockholder Unanimity in Making Production and Financial Decisions', *QJE*, 94 (1980), 543–66.

(140) Grubel, H. G., *Forward Exchange, Speculation and the International Flow of Capital* (Stanford, Stanford University Press, 1968).

(141) Hahn, F. H., 'Professor Friedman's Views on Money', *Eca*, 38 (1971), 61–80.

(142) Hahn, F. H., 'The Monetary Approach to the Balance of Payments', *J. Int. Ec.*, 7 (1977), 231–49.

(143) Hahn, F. H., 'On Non-Walrasian Equilibria', *Re Stud*, 45 (1978), 1–17.

(144) Hall, R. E., 'Stochastic Implications of the Lifecycle–Permanent Income Hypothesis: Theory and Evidence', *JPE*, 86 (1977), 971–87.

(145) Hammond, P. and P. Dasgupta, 'Fully Progressive Taxation', University of Essex Economics Discussion Papers, No. 113 (June 1978), forthcoming in *J. Pub. Ec.*

(146) Hanoch, G. and M. Honig, 'The Labour Supply Curve under Income Maintenance Programs', *J. Pub. Ec.*, 9 (1978), 1–16.

(147) Harrod, R. F., *Towards a Dynamic Economics* (London, Macmillan, 1948).

(148) Harrod, R. F., *Economic Essays* London, Macmillan, 1952), Essays 12 and 14.

(149) Harrod, R. F., 'Domar and Dynamic Economics', *EJ*, 69 (1959), 451–64.

(150) Harrod, R. F., 'Comment (to J. de Graaff)', *EJ*, 70 (1960), 851.

(151) Harrod, R. F., 'Themes in Dynamic Theory', *EJ*, 73 (1963), 401–21.

(152) Harrod, R. F., 'Imperfect Competition, Aggregate Demand, and Inflation', *EJ*, 81 (1972), 392–401.

(153) Hart, O. D., 'On the Optimality of Equilibrium when Markets are Incomplete', *JET*, 11–12 (1975), 418–43.

(154) Hawtrey, R. G., *Currency and Credit* (London, Longmans Green, 1950).

(155) Hay, D. A. and D. J. Morris, *Industrial Economics: Theory and Evidence* (Oxford, Oxford University Press, 1979).

(156) Heckscher, E., 'The Effect of Foreign Trade on the Distribution of Income', *Ekonomisk Tidskrift*, 21 (1919), 497–512, reprinted in AEA, *Readings in the Theory of Economic Trade* (Philadelphia, Blakiston, 1949).

(157) Heffernan, S. A., M.Phil (1980) and D.Phil (1981) dissertations, Oxford University.

(158) Henry, S. G. B., M. C. Sawyer, and P. C. Smith, 'Models of Inflation in the United Kingdom: An Evaluation', *NIER*, No. 77 (August 1976), 60–71.

(159) Hess, A. C., 'A Comparison of Automobile Demand Equations', *E'metrica*, 45 (1977), 683–702.

(160) Hester, D. D. and J. L. Pierce, 'Cross Section Analysis and Bank Dynamics', *JPE*, 76 (1968), 755–76.

(161) Hewson, J. and E. Sakakibara, 'The Euro-dollar Deposit Multiplier: A Portfolio Approach', *IMF Staff Papers*, 21 (1974), 307–28.

(162) Hicks, J. R., *Value and Capital* (Oxford, Oxford University Press, 1946).

(163) Hicks, J. R., *A Contribution to the Theory of the Trade Cycle* (Oxford, Oxford University Press, 1950).

(164) Hicks, J. R., 'A Suggestion for Simplifying the Theory of Money', (1935), ch. 4 in J. R. Hicks, *Critical Essays in Monetary Theory* (Oxford, Oxford University Press, 1967).

(165) Hicks, J. R., 'The Pure Theory of Portfolio Selection', ch. 6 in J. R. Hicks, *Critical Essays in Monetary Theory* (Oxford, Oxford University Press, 1967).

(166) Hicks, J. R., 'Mr Keynes and the Classics', in J. R. Hicks, *Critical Essays in Monetary Theory* (Oxford, Oxford University Press, 1967).

(167) Hotelling, H., 'The Economics of Exhaustible Resource', *JPE*, 39 (1931), 137–75.

(168) Hume, D., 'Of the Balance of Trade', in D. Hume, *Essays: Moral, Political and Literary*, Vol. I (London, Longmans Green, 1898), reprinted in R. N. Cooper (ed.), *International Finance* (Harmondsworth, Middlesex, Penguin Books, 1969).

(169) Intriligator, M. D., *Mathematical Optimization and Economic Theory* (Englewood Cliffs, Prentice-Hall, 1971).

(170) Johansen, L., 'The Report of the Committee on Policy Optimization—UK', *Journal of Economic Dynamics and Control*, 1 (1979), 101–9.

(171) Johnson, H. G., *Further Essays in Monetary Economics* (London, George Allen & Unwin, 1972), ch. 4.

(172) Jorgenson, D. W. and Hall, R. E., 'Tax Policy and Investment Behaviour', *AER*, 53 (1967), 247–59.

(173) Jorgenson, D. W. and C. D. Siebert, 'A Comparison of Alternative Theories of Corporate Investment Behaviour', *AER*, 58 (1968), 681–712.

(174) Jorgenson, D. W. and J. A. Stephenson, 'Investment Behaviour in US Manufacturing', *E'metrica*, 35 (1967), 169–220.

(175) Jorgenson, D. W. and J. A. Stephenson, 'Issues in the Development of the Neoclassical Theory of Investment Behaviour', *Re Stat*, 51 (1969), 346–53.

(176) Juster, F. T. and P. Wachtel, 'Anticipatory and Objective Models of Durable Goods Demand', *AER*, 62 P & P, (1972), 564–79.

(177) Kahn, R. F., 'The Relation of Home Investment to Unemployment', *EJ*, 41 (1931), 173–98.

(178) Kaldor, N., 'Wage Subsidies as a Remedy for Unemployment', *JPE*, 44 (1936), 721–42.

(179) Kaldor, N., 'Alternative Theories of Distribution', *Re Stud*, 23 (1955-6), 83-100.

(180) Kalecki, M., 'The Principle of Increasing Risk', *Eca*, 4 (1937), 440-7.

(181) Kemp, M., *The Pure Theory of International Trade and Investment* (Englewood Cliffs, Prentice-Hall, 1969).

(182) Keynes, J. M., *The General Theory of Employment, Interest and Money*, (Cambridge: Macmillan and Cambridge University Press, Royal Economic Society Edition, 1973: first published, 1936).

(183) Keynes, J. M., 'The General Theory of Employment', *QJE*, 51 (1937), 209-23, reprinted in R. Clower (ed.), *Monetary Theory* (Baltimore, Maryland, Penguin Books, 1969).

(184) King, M. A., 'The United Kingdom Profits Crisis: Myth of Reality?' *EJ*, 85 (1975), 33-54.

(185) Knight, F. H., *Risk, Uncertainty and Profit* (New York, A. M. Kelley, 1964 (first published, 1921)).

(186) Kuska, E. A., 'The Post-Devaluation Time Profile of Reserves and Prices under Neoclassical Assumptions', *Eca*, 44 (1977), 289-92.

(187) Kuznets, S., 'Proportion of Capital Formation to National Product', *AER*, 42 (1952), 507-26.

(188) Laidler, D., 'The Rate of Interest and the Demand for Money: Some Empirical Evidence', *JPE*, 74 (1966), 545-55.

(189) Laidler, D., *The Demand for Money*, second edition (London, Harper and Row, 1977).

(190) Lancaster, K., 'A New Approach to Consumer Theory', *JPE*, 74 (1966), 132-57.

(191) Layard, P. R. G. and S. J. Nickell, 'The Case for Subsidizing Extra Jobs', *EJ*, 90 (1980), 51-73.

(192) Lewis, W. A., 'Economic Development with Unlimited Supplies of Labour', *Manchester School*, 22 (1954), 139-91.

(193) Lintner, J., 'The Valuations of Risk Assets and the Selection of Risky Investments in Stock Portfolio and Capital Budgets', *Re Stat*, 47 (1965), 18-37.

(194) Lipsey, R. G., 'The Relation between Unemployment and the Rate of Change of Money Wage Rates in the UK, 1862-1957: A Further Analysis', *Eca*, 27 (1960), 1-41.

(195) Lucas, R. E., 'Adjustment Costs and the Theory of Supply', *JPE*, 75 (1967), 321-34.

(196) Lucas, R. E., 'Expectations and the Neutrality of Money', *JET*, 4 (1972), 103-4.

(197) Lucas, R. E., 'Some International Evidence on Output–Inflation Tradeoffs', *AER*, 63 (1973), 326-34.

(198) Lucas, R. E., 'Econometric Policy Evaluation: A Critique', *JME* (1976), Supplement #1.

(199) Lucas, R. E. and E. C. Prescott, 'Investment under Uncertainty', *E'metrica*, 39 (1971), 659-81.

(200) Lucas, R. E. and L. Rapping, 'Real Wages, Employment and Inflation', *JPE*, 77 (1969), 721-54.

(201) MacDougall, G. A. D., 'The Benefits and Costs of Private Investment from Abroad: A Theoretical Approach', in J. Bhagwati (ed.), *International Trade* (Harmondsworth, Middlesex, Penguin Books, 1969).

(202) McCloskey, D. N., 'Did Victorian Britain Fail?', *Economic History Review*, 23 (1970), 446-59.

(203) Maki, D. and Z. A. Spindler, 'The Effect of Unemployment Compensation on the Rate of Unemployment in Great Britain', *OEP*, 27 (1975), 440-54.

(204) Malinvaud, E., *The Theory of Unemployment Reconsidered* (Oxford, Basil Blackwell, 1977).

(205) Malinvaud, E., *Profitability and Unemployment* (Cambridge, Cambridge University Press, 1980).

(206) Marris, R., *The Economic Theory of Managerial Capitalism* (London, Macmillan, 1964).

(207) Marshall, A., *Principles of Economics* (London, 1890).

(208) Marx, K., *Capital*, 1867.

(209) Matthews, R. C. O., 'Why Has Britain Had Full Employment Since the War?' *EJ*, 78 (1968), 555–69.

(210) Matthews, R. C. O., 'Postwar Business Cycles in the United Kingdom', in M. Bronfenbrenner (ed.), *Is the Business Cycle Obsolete?* (New York, John Wiley & Sons, 1969).

(211) Mayer, T., *Permanent Income, Wealth, and Consumption* (Berkeley, University of California Press, 1972).

(212) Meade, J. E., 'The Theory of Labour Managed Firms and of Profit Sharing', *EJ*, 82 (1972), 402–28.

(213) Miller, M. H. and D. Orr, 'A Model of the Demand for Money by Firms', *QJE*, 80 (1966), 413–35.

(214) Miller, M. H. and D. Orr. 'The Demand for Money by Firms: Extension and Analytic Results', *J. Fin.*, 23 (1968), 735–59.

(215) Minhas, B. S., 'The Homohypallagic Production Function, Factor Intensity Reversals and the Heckscher–Ohlin Theorem', *JPE*, 70 (1962), 138–56, reprinted in J. Bhagwati (ed.), *International Trade* (Harmondsowrth, Middlesex, Penguin Books, 1969).

(216) Mirrlees, J. A., 'The Dynamic Non-Substitution Theorem', *Re Stud*, 36 (1969), 67–76.

(217) Mirrlees, J. A., 'An Exploration in the Theory of Optimum Income Taxation', *Re Stud*, 38 (1971), 175–208.

(218) Mirrlees, J. A., 'The Optimal Structure of Incentives and Authority within an Organization', *BJE*, 7 (1976), 105–31.

(219) Mishkin, F. S., 'Does Anticipated Monetary Policy Matter? An Econometric Investigation', *JPE*, 90 (1982), 22–51.

(220) Modigliani, F. and R. Brumberg, 'Utility Analysis and the Consumption Function: An Interpretation of Cross-Section Data', in K. Kurihara, ed., *Post-Keynesian Economics* (New Brunswick, N.J., Rutgers University Press, 1954).

(221) Modigliani, F. and M. H. Miller, 'Cost of Capital, Corporation Finance, and the Theory of Investment', *AER*, 48 (1958), 261–97.

(222) Monti, M., 'Deposit, Credit, and Interest Rate Determination Under Alternative Bank Objective Functions', in G. P. Szegü and K. Shell (eds), *Mathematical Methods in Investment and Finance* (London, North Holland, 1972).

(223) Morishima, M., *Marx's Economics* (Cambridge, Cambridge University Press, 1973).

(224) Morishima, M. and M. Saito, 'A Dynamic Analysis of the American Economy 1900–1952' in M. Morishima, *et al, The Working of Econometric Models* (Cambridge, Cambridge Unviersity Press, 1972).

(225) Mortensen, D. T., 'A Theory of Wage and Employment Dynamics', in E. S. Phelps (ed.), *Microeconomic Foundations of Employment and Inflation Theory* (New York, Norton, 1970).

(226) Muellbauer, J. and R. Portes, 'Macroeconomic Models with Quantity Rationing', *EJ*, 88 (1978), 788–821.

(227) Mussa, M., 'The Two Sector Model in Terms of its Dual', *J. Int. Ec.*, 9 (1979), 514–26.

(228) Muth, J. F., 'Rational Expectations and the Theory of Price Movements', *E'metrica*, 29 (1961), 315–35.

(229) Nagatani, K., *Macroeconomic Dynamics* (Cambridge, Cambridge University Press, 1981).

(230) Neary, J. P., 'Dynamic Stability and the Theory of Factor Market Distortions', *AER*, 68 (1978), 671–82.

(231) Neary, J. P., 'Non-Traded Goods and the Balance of Trade in a Neo-Keynesian Temporary Equilibrium', *QJE*, 95 (1980), 403–29.

(232) Neary, J. P., 'On the Short Run Effects of Technological Progress', *OEP*, 33 (1981), 224–33.

(233) Neary, J. P. and K. W. S. Roberts, 'The Theory of Household Behaviour under Rationing', *European Economic Review*, 13 (1980), 25–42.

(234) Neave, E., 'The Stochastic Cash Balance Problem with Fixed Costs for Increases and Decreases', *Management Science*, 6 (1970), 472–90.

(235) Negishi, T., 'Monopolistic Competition and General Equlibrium', *Re Stud*, 28 (1960–61), 196–201.

(236) Negishi, T., *Microeconomic Foundations of Keynesian Macroeconomics* (Amsterdam, North Holland, 1979).

(237) Neumann, J. von, 'A Model of General Economic Equilibrium', *Re Stud*, 13 (1945–46), 1–9.

(238) Neumann, J. von and Morgenstern, O., *Theory of Games and Economic Behaviour* (Princeton, Princeton University Press, 1947).

(239) Nickell, S. J., *The Investment Decisions of Firms* (Cambridge, Cambridge University Press, 1978).

(240) Nickell, S. J., 'The Effect of Unemployment and Related Benefits on the Duration of Unemployment', *EJ*, 89 (1979), 34–49.

(241) Niehans, J., *The Theory of Money* (Baltimore, Johns Hopkins University Press, 1978).

(242) Nordhaus, W. D., 'The Political Business Cycle', *Re Stud*, 42 (1975), 169–90.

(243) Ohlin, B., *Interregional and International Trade* (Cambridge, Mass., Harvard University Press, 1933).

(244) Oppenheimer, P. M., 'Non-Traded Goods and the Balance of Payments: A Historical Note', *J. Ec. Litt.* 12 (1974), 882–8.

(245) Orr, D., *Cash Management and the Demand for Money* (New York, Praeger Publishers, 1970).

(246) Pareto, V., *Manuel d'economie Politique*, 2 vols. (Lausanne, F. Rouge, 1896–7).

(247) Patinkin, D., *Money, Interest and Prices*, 2nd edition (New York, Harper & Row, 1965).

(248) Pearce, I. F., 'The Problem of the Balance of Payments', *International Economic Review*, 2 (1961), 1–28.

(249) Penrose, E., *The Theory of the Growth of the Firm* (Oxford, Oxford University Press, 1959).

(250) Perry, G. L., 'Slowing the Wage Price Spiral: The Macroeconomic View', *BPEA*, 2 (1978), 259–99.

(251) Phelps, E. S., 'The Golden Rule of Accumulation', *AER*, 51 (1961), 638–43.

(252) Phelps, E. S., 'Money Wage Dynamics and the Labour Market Equilibrium', in E. S. Phelps *et al.*, *Microeconomic Foundations of Employment and Inflation Theory* (New York, W. W. Norton & Co. Ltd., 1970).

(253) Phelps, E. S., 'Wage Taxation for Economic Justice', in E. S. Phelps (ed.), *Economic Justice* (Harmondsworth, Middlesex, Penguin Books, 1973).

(254) Phelps, E. S. and J. B. Taylor, 'Stabilizing Powers of Monetary Policy under Rational Expectations', *JPE*, 85 (1977), 163–90.

(255) Phillips, A. W., 'Stabilization Policies in a Closed Economy', *EJ*, 64 (1954), 290–323.

(256) Phillips, A. W., 'The Relation between Unemployment and the Rate of Change of Money Wage Rates in the UK: 1861–1957', *Eca*, 25 (1958), 283–318.

(257) Poole, W., 'Optimal Choice of Monetary Policy Instruments in a Simple Stochastic Macro Model', *QJE*, 84 (1970), 197–216.

(258) Radcliffe Report, *The Committee on the Working of the Monetary System* Cmnd. 827 (London, HMSO, 1959).

(259) Ramsey, F. P., 'A Contribution to the Theory of Taxation', *EJ*, 37 (1927), 47–61.

(260) Ramsey, F. P., 'A Mathematical Theory of Saving', *EJ*, 38 (1928), 543–59.

(261) Rawls, J., *A Theory of Justice* (Cambridge, Mass., Harvard University Press, 1971).

(262) Reddaway, W. B., *Effects of UK Direct Investment Overseas, Final Report* (Cambridge, Cambridge University Press, 1968).

(263) Ricardo, D., *On the Principles of Political Economy and Taxation*, third edition (London, 1821): in Vol. I of P. Sraffa (ed.), *The Works and Correspondence of David Ricardo* (London, Cambridge University Press, 1951).

(264) Robinson, J., 'Equilibrium Growth Models', *AER*, 51 (1961), 360–9.

(265) Ross, S., 'The Economic Theory of Agency: The Principal's Problem', *AER*, 64 (1974), 122–36.

(266) Salter, W. E. G., 'Internal and External Balance: The Role of Price and Expenditure Effects', *Economic Record*, 35 (1959), 226–38.

(267) Samuelson, P. A., 'Interactions between the Multiplier Analysis and the Principle of Acceleration', *Re Stat*, 21 (1939), 75–8.

(268) Samuelson, P. A., *Foundations of Economic Analysis* (Cambridge, Mass., Harvard University Press, 1947).

(269) Samuelson, P. A., 'Abstract of a Theorem Concerning Substitutability in Open Economy Leontief Models', in T. C. Koopmans (ed.), *Activity Analysis of Production and Allocation* (London, Cowles Commission for Research in Economics, 1951).

(270) Samuelson, P. A., 'The Pure Theory of Public Expenditure', *Re Stat*, 36 (1954), 387–9. 'Diagrammatic Exposition of a Theory of Public Expenditure', *Re Stat*, 37 (1959), 350–6.

(271) Samuelson, P. A., 'Wages and Prices: A Modern Dissection of Marxian Economic Models', *AER*, 47 (1957), 884–912.

(272) Samuelson, P. A., 'A New Theorem on Non Substitution', in *Money, Growth and Methodology*, published in honour of Johan Åkerman, Vol. 20 (Lund, Sweden, Lund Social Science Studies, 1961).

(273) Samuelson, P. A., 'Proof that Properly Anticipated Prices Fluctuate Randomly', *Industrial Management Review*, 6 (1965), 41–9.

(274) Samuelson, P. A., *Economics*, 6th edition (New York, McGraw-Hill, 1970).

(275) Samuelson, P. A. and R. M. Solow, 'Analytical Aspects of Anti-Inflation Policy', *AER*, 50 (P & P) (1960), 177–94.

(276) Santomero, A. M., 'A Model of the Demand for Money by Households', *J. Fin.*, 29 (1974), 89–102.

(277) Sargan, J. P., 'A Model of Wage Price Inflation', *Re Stud*, 47 (1980), 97–112.

(278) Sargan, J. P., 'The Consumer Price Equation in the Post War British Economy: An Exercise in Equation Specification Testing', *Re Stud*, 47 (1980), 113–35.

(279) Sargent, T. J., 'Observations on Improper Methods of Simulating and Teaching Friedman's Time-Series Consumption Model', *Int. Ec. Review*, 18 (1977), 445–62.

(280) Sargent, T. J., *Macroeconomic Theory* (New York, Academic Press, 1979).

(281) Sargent, T. J. and N. Wallace, 'Rational Expectations and the Dynamics of Hyperinflation', *Int. Ec. Review*, 14 (1973), 328–50.
(282) Sargent, T. J. and N. Wallace, ' "Rational" Expectations, the Optimal Monetary Instrument, and the Optimal Money Supply Rule', *JPE*, 83 (1975), 241–77.
(283) Schramm, R., 'The Influence of Relative Prices, Production Conditions and Adjustment Costs on Investment Behaviour', *Re Stud*, 37 (1970), 361–76.
(284) Schumpeter, J. A., *Business Cycles* (London, McGraw-Hill, 1939).
(285) Scitovsky, T., *The Joyless Economy* (New York, Oxford University Press, 1976).
(286) Seade, J. K., 'On the Shape of Optimal Tax Schedules', *J. Pub. Ec.*, 7 (1977), 203–36.
(287) Seidman, L. S., 'Tax Based Incomes Policies', *BPEA*, 2 (1978), 301–36.
(288) Seidman, L. S., 'The Role of a Tax-Based Incomes Policy', *AER*, 69 (P & P, 1979), 203–6.
(289) Sen, A. K., *Growth Economics* (Harmondsworth, Middlesex, Penguin, 1970).
(290) Sen, A. K., *On Economic Inequality* (Oxford, Oxford University Press, 1973).
(291) Shackle, G. L. S., *Uncertainty in Economics and Other Reflections* (Cambridge, Cambridge University Press, 1955).
(292) Sharpe, W., *Portfolio Theory and Capital Markets* (New York, McGraw-Hill, 1970).
(293) Shavell, S., 'Risk Sharing and Incentives in the Principal and Agent Relationship', *BJE*, 10 (1979), 55–73.
(294) Shiller, R. J., 'Rational Expectations and the Dynamic Structure of Macroeconomic Models: A Critical Review', *JME*, 4 (1978), 1–44.
(295) Shull, B., 'Commercial Banks as Multiple Product Price Discriminating Firms', in D. Carson (ed.), *Banking and Monetary Studies* (Homewood, Ill., Irwin, 1963).
(296) Shupp, F., 'Control Theory and Stabilization Policy: A Review of the Report of the Committee on Policy Optimization', *Journal of Economic Dynamics and Control*, 1 (1979), 111–16.
(297) Simon, H. A., 'Theories of Decision Making in Economics', *AER*, 49 (1959), 253–83.
(298) Sims, C. A., 'Money, Income and Causality', *AER*, 62 (1972), 540–52.
(299) Sims, C. A., 'Macroeconomics and Reality', *E'metrica*, 48 (1980), 1–48.
(300) Sinclair, P. J. N., 'Unions, Closed Shops, Technology, and Factor Shares', *Greek Economic Review*, 2 (1980), 207–19.
(301) Sinclair, P. J. N., 'When Will Technical Progress Destroy Jobs?' *OEP*, 31 (1981), 1–18.
(302) Slater, M., 'The Managerial Limitation to the Growth of Firms', *EJ*, 90 (1980), 520–8.
(303) Slitor, R. E., 'Implementation and Design of Tax-Based Incomes Policies', *AER*, 69 (P & P, 1979), 212–15.
(304) Solow, R. M., 'A Contribution to the Theory of Economic Growth', *QJE*, 70 (1956), 65–94.
(305) Solow, R. M., 'Distribution in the Long and Short Run', in Marchal, J. and B. Ducros (eds), *The Distribution of National Income* (London, Macmillan, 1968).
(306) Solow, R. M., 'Some Implications of Alternative Criteria from the Firm', in R. Marris and A. Wood (eds), *The Corporate Economy* (London, Macmillan, 1971), pp. 318–42.
(307) Spence, M., 'Job Market Signaling', *QJE*, 87 (1973), 355–74.
(308) Sraffa, P., *The Production of Commodities by Means of Commodities:*

Prelude to a Critique of Economic Theory (Cambridge, Cambridge University Press, 1960).

(309) Stern, N. H., 'On the Specification of Models of Optimum Income Taxation', *J. Pub. Ec.*, 6 (1976), 123–62.

(310) Stiglitz, J. E., 'A Re-Examination of the Modigliani–Miller Theorem', *AER*, 59 (1969), 784–93.

(311) Stiglitz, J. E., 'Portfolio Allocation with Many Risky Assets', in G. P. Szegö and K. Shell (eds), *Mathematical Methods in Investment and Finance* (London, North Holland, 1972).

(312) Stiglitz, J. E., 'On the Irrelevance of Corporate Financial Policy', *AER*, 64 (1974), 851–66.

(313) Stoneman, P. A., 'A Simple Diagrammatic Apparatus for the Investigation of a Macroeconomic Model of Temporary Equilibria', *Eca*, 46 (1979), 61–6.

(314) Swan, T. W., 'Economic Growth and Capital Accumulation', *The Economic Record*, 32 (1956), 334–61.

(315) Szegö, G. P. and K. Shell (eds), *Mathematical Methods in Investment and Finance* (New York, American Elsevier, 1972).

(316) Teigen, R. L., 'Demand and Supply Functions for Money in the U.S.: Some Structural Estimates', *E'metrica*, 32 (1964), 476–509.

(317) Tinbergen, J., 'An Economic Policy for 1936', in J. Tinbergen, *Business Cycles in the United Kingdom, 1870–1914* (Amsterdam, North Holland, 1951).

(318) Tobin, J., 'Liquidity Preference and Monetary Policy', *Re Stat*, 21 (1947), 124–31.

(319) Tobin, J., 'A Dynamic Aggregative Model', *JPE*, 63 (1955), 103–15.

(320) Tobin, J., 'Liquidity Preference as Behaviour Towards Risk', *Re Stud*, 25 (1957–58), 65–86.

(321) Tobin, J., 'A General Equilibrium Approach to Monetary Theory', *JMCB*, 1 (1969), 15–29.

(322) Tobin, J., 'Money and Income: Post Hoc Ergo Propter Hoc?' *QJE*, 84 (1970), 301–29.

(323) Tobin, J. and H. S. Houthakker, 'The Effects of Rationing on Demand Elasticities', *Re Stud*. 18 (1950–51), 140–53.

(324) Tsiang, S. C., 'The Role of Money in Trade Balance Stability: Synthesis of the Elasticity and Absorption Approaches', *AER*, 51 (1961), 912–36.

(325) Tsiang, S. C., 'The Monetary Theoretic Foundation of the Modern Monetary Approach to the Balance of Payments', *OEP*, 29 (1977), 319–38.

(326) Turnovsky, S. J., *Macroeconomic Analysis and Stabilization Policy* (Cambridge, Cambridge University Press, 1977).

(327) Varian, H. R., *Microeconomic Analysis* (New York, W. W. Norton & Company, 1978).

(328) Vial, J. P., 'A Continuous Time Model for the Cash Balance Problem', in Szegö, G. P. and K. Shell (eds), *Mathematical Methods in Investment and Finance* (New York, American Elsevier, 1972), 244–91.

(329) Wan, H. Y., *Economic Growth* (New York, Harcourt Brace Jovanovich, 1971).

(330) Weiss, L., 'The Role for Active Monetary Policy in a Rational Expectations Model', *JPE*, 88 (1980), 221–33.

(331) Whalen, E. L., 'A Rationalization of the Precautionary Demand for Cash', *QJE*, 80 (1966), 314–24.

(332) White, B. B., 'Empirical Tests of the Life-Cycle Hypothesis', *AER*, 68 (1978), 547–60.

(333) Williams, D., C. A. E. Goodhart, D. H. Gowland, 'Money, Income and Causality: The UK Experience', *AER*, 66 (1976), 417–23.

(334) Williamson, J., 'Profit, Growth, and Sales Maximization', *Eca*, 33 (1966), 1–16.

(335) Winter, S. G., 'Satisficing, Selection, and the Innovating Remnant', *QJE*, 85 (1971), 237–61.

(336) Wolff, E. N., 'The Distributional Effects of the 1969–1975 Inflation on Holdings of Household Wealth in the US', *Review of Income and Wealth*, 25 (1979), 195–207.

(337) Yarrow, G., 'Management Utility Maximization under Uncertainty', *Eca*, 40 (1973), 155–73.

SUPPLEMENTARY REFERENCES

(338) Andrews, M. and S. J. Nickell, 'Unemployment in the United Kingdom since the War', *Re Stud*, 49 (1982), 731–59.

(339) Begg, D. K. H., *The Rational Expectations Revolution in Macroeconomics* (Oxford, Philip Allan, 1982).

(340) Begg, D. K. H., 'The Economics of Floating Exchange Rates: the Lessons of the 170s and the Research Programme for the 80s', *London Business School Econometric Forecasting Unit Discussion Paper 105*, 1983.

(341) Bilson, J. F. O., 'The Rational Expectations Approach to the Consumption Function: a Multi-country Study', *European Economic Review*, 13 (1980), 273–99.

(342) Brown, C., G. Curtis, and A. Kohen, 'The Effect of the Minimum Wage on Employment and Unemployment', *J. Ec. Litt.* 20 (1982), 487–528.

(343) Buiter, W. H., 'The Superiority of Contingent Rules over Fixed Rules in Models with Rational Expectations', *EJ*, 91 (1981), 647–70.

(344) Buiter, W. H. and M. Miller, 'Real Exchange Rate Overshooting and the Output Cost of Bringing Down Inflation', *European Economic Review*, 18 (1982), 85–123.

(345) Diamond, P. A., 'Aggregate Demand Management in Search Equilibrium', *JPE*, 90 (1982), 881–94.

(346) Dixit, A. K. and A. Woodland, 'The Relationship Between Factor Endowments and Commodity Trade', *J. Int. Ec.*, 13 (1982), 201–14.

(347) Dunne, J. P. and R. P. Smith, 'The Allocative Efficiency of Government Expenditure', *European Economic Review*, 20 (1983), 381–94.

(348) Fama, E. F., 'Banking in the Theory of Finance', *JME*, 6 (1980), 39–57.

(349) Feldstein, M. S., 'Inflation, Tax Rules and Investment: some Econometric Evidence', *E'metrica*, 50 (1982), 825–62.

(350) Feldstein, M. S., 'Government Deficits and Aggregate Demand', *JME*, 9 (1982), 1–20.

(351) Frenkel, J. A., 'The Collapse of Purchasing Power Parities During the 1970s', *European Economic Review*, 16 (1981), 145–65.

(352) Grossman, S. J. and O. D. Hart, 'An Analysis of the Principal-Agent Problem, *E'metrica*, 51 (1983), 7–45.

(353) Hart, O. D., 'Optimal Labour Contracts Under Asymmetric Information: an Introduction', *Re Stud*, 50 (1983), 3–35.

(354) Hoffman, D. L. and D. E. Schlagenhauf, 'An Econometric Investigation of the Monetary Neutrality and Rationality Propositions from an International Perspective', *Re Stat*, 64 (1982), 562–71.

(355) Jovanovic, B., 'Inflation and Welfare in the Steady State', *JPE*, 90 (1982), 561–77.

(356) Kydland, F. E. and E. C. Prescott, 'Time to Build and Aggregate Fluctuations', *E'metrica*, 50 (1982), 1345–70.

(357) Loewenstein, M. A., 'Worker Heterogeneity, Hours Restrictions and Temporary Layoffs', *E'metrica*, 51 (1983), 69–78.

(358) Muellbauer, J., 'Surprises in the Consumption Function', *EJ Conference Papers Supplement* (1983), 34–50.

(359) Nickell, S. J., 'The Determinants of Equilibrium Unemployment in Britain', *EJ*, 92 (1982), 555–75.

(360) Pesaran, M. H., 'A Critique of Proposed Tests of the Natural Rate–Rational Expectations Hypothesis', *EJ*, 92 (1982), 529–54.

(361) Ramanathan, K., *Introduction to the Theory of Economic Growth*, Lecture Notes in Economics and Mathematical Systems, 205 (Berlin, Springer-Verlag, 1982).

(362) Rotemberg, J. J., 'Monopolistic Price Adjustment and Aggregate Output', *Re Stud*, 49 (1982), 517–31.

(363) Tobin, J., 'Money and Economic Growth', *E'metrica*, 33 (1965), 671–84.

(364) van des Heuvel, P., *The Stability of a Macoreconomic System with Quantity Restraints*, Lecture Notes in Economics and Mathematical Systems, 211 (Berlin, Springer-Verlag, 1983).

Abbreviations used in References

AEA	The American Economic Association
AER	*American Economic Review*
BEQR	*Bank of England Quarterly Review*
BJE	*Bell Journal of Economics*
BPEA	*Brookings Papers on Economic Activity*
Eca	*Economica*
E'metrica	*Econometrica*
EJ	*Economic Journal*
IMF	International Monetary Fund
Int. Ec. Review	*International Economic Review*
J. Ec. Litt	*Journal of Economic Literature*
JET	*Journal of Economic Theory*
J. Fin.	*Journal of Finance*
J. Int. Ec.	*Journal of International Economics*
JMCB	*Journal of Money, Credit, and Banking*
JME	*Journal of Monetary Economics*
JPE	*Journal of Political Economy*
J. Pub. Ec.	*Journal of Public Economics*
JRSS	*Journal of the Royal Statistical Society*
NBER	National Bureau of Economic Research
OEP	*Oxford Economic Papers*
QJE	*Quarterly Journal of Economics*
Re Stat	*Review of Economics and Statistics*
Re Stud	*Review of Economic Studies*

Author Index

General Index